T0304317

Microsimulation Modelling for Policy Analysis
Challenges and Innovations

Modern policy problems require analysts to capture the inter-actions between policy and the complexities of economic and social life, as well as between policies of different types. Increasingly, microsimulation is employed to analyse these problems. This book brings together examples of microsimulation model-ling that are at the frontiers of developments in the field, either because they extend the range of techniques available to modellers, or because they demonstrate new applications for established methods. It represents the state of the art, with chapters on the use of microsimulation for comparative policy research and for challenging conventional assumptions, com-bining microsimulation with other types of economic models and the much-neglected subjects of model alignment and validation. Data and case studies are taken from regions includ-ing Asia-Pacific, Europe and North America.

LAVINIA MITTON was a Junior Research Officer at the Micro-simulation Unit, Department of Applied Economics, Univer-sity of Cambridge. She is now a research student at the London School of Economics.

HOLLY SUTHERLAND is a Senior Research Officer in the Department of Applied Economics, University of Cambridge and Director of the Microsimulation Unit.

MELVYN WEEKS is a Senior Research Officer at the Depart-ment of Applied Economics, University of Cambridge. He has previously lectured in Economics and Statistics at the University of York.

University of Cambridge
Department of Applied Economics

Occasional papers 65

**Microsimulation Modelling for Policy Analysis
Challenges and Innovations**

DAE Occasional papers

Earlier titles in this series and in the DAE Papers in Industrial
Relations and Labour series may be obtained from:
The Publications Secretary, Department of Applied Economics,
Sidgwick Avenue, Cambridge CB3 9DE

Microsimulation Modelling for Policy Analysis
Challenges and Innovations

EDITED BY
LAVINIA MITTON,
HOLLY SUTHERLAND
AND
MELVYN WEEKS

CAMBRIDGE
UNIVERSITY PRESS

University Printing House, Cambridge CB2 8BS, United Kingdom

Cambridge University Press is part of the University of Cambridge.

It furthers the University's mission by disseminating knowledge in the pursuit of education, learning and research at the highest international levels of excellence.

www.cambridge.org
Information on this title: www.cambridge.org/9780521790062

© Department of Applied Economics, University of Cambridge 2000

First published 2000

A catalogue record for this publication is available from the British Library

ISBN 978-0-521-79006-2 Hardback

Contents

Figures

Tables

Contributors

ROLF AABERGE, *Senior Research Fellow at the Research Department, Statistics Norway*

CAROLE BONNET, *Economic researcher at the French Ministry of Labour and Social Affairs*

STEVE CALDWELL, *Professor at the Institute of Public Affairs and Department of Sociology, Cornell University*

GRANT CAMERON, *Chief, Personal Income Tax Division, Tax Policy Branch, Department of Finance, Ottawa*

DENIS CHÉNARD, *Head Model Analyst for the DYNACAN project in the Department of Human Resource Development, Ottawa*

UGO COLOMBINO, *Professor of Microeconomics at the University of Turin*

ANDRÉ DECOSTER, *Professor at the Catholic University of Louvain, Centre for Economic Studies and the Kortrijk Campus*

ALAN DUNCAN, *Reader in Economics at the University of Nottingham*

ROSS EZZEDDIN, *Policy analyst with the Privy Council Office of the Government of Canada in Ottawa*

RUTH HANCOCK, *Senior Research Fellow, Nuffield Community Care Studies Unit, University of Leicester*

ANN HARDING, *Professor of Applied Economics and Social Policy and inaugural Director of the National Centre for Social and Economic Modelling at the University of Canberra*

GEORGIA KAPLANOGLOU, *Currrently works in the Economic Research Department of the Bank of Greece, Athens, and has recently completed a PhD at the University of Cambridge*

RONAN MAHIEU, *Economic researcher at the French Institute of Statistics (INSEE)*

RICHARD MORRISON, *Senior Methodologist, DYNACAN project, Department of Human Resource Development, Ottawa*

CATHAL O'DONOGHUE, *Research Associate with the Microsimulation Unit, Department of Applied Economics, University of Cambridge*

RICHARD PERCIVAL, *Senior Research Fellow, National Centre for Social and Economic Modelling University of Canberra*

KATHERINE RAKE, *Lecturer in Social Policy at the London School of Economics*

STEINAR STRØM, *Professor in Economics, University of Oslo*

HOLLY SUTHERLAND, *Director of the Microsimulation Unit in the Department of Applied Economics at the University of Cambridge*

NEIL SWAN, *Was project manager at the Spatial Modelling Centre in Kiruna, Sweden from 1997–1998*

FRANCESCA UTILI, *Currently working at the Department of Development and Cohesion Policies, Ministry of Treasury, Italy*

GUY VAN CAMP, *Researcher at the Centre for Economic Studies, Catholic University of Louvain*

AGNES WALKER, *Senior Research Fellow, National Centre for Social and Economic Modelling, University of Canberra*

MELVYN WEEKS, *Senior Research Officer at the Department of Applied Economics, University of Cambridge*

TOM WENNEMO, *Works in the Research Department of Statistics Norway*

Foreword

In August 1998, the Microsimulation Unit of the Department of Applied Economics held a conference in Cambridge that attracted an impressive array of papers, many of which are presented in this volume. Microsimulation is the logical approach for the practical study of policy design, and it is particularly fitting that the conference was held in Cambridge. The Faculty of Economics and Politics has a strong tradition in the theory of public finance, going back to Pigou before the war, and pursued from the 1960s by James Meade (our first Cambridge Nobel Laureate in Economics), Jim Mirrlees (who was recently awarded the Nobel Prize for his work on optimal taxation), Tony Atkinson and Mervyn King. They did much to develop the theory of optimal taxation and the issues that must be confronted in the design of tax systems.

On the applied side, the first Director of the Department of Applied Economics, Sir Richard Stone (also a Nobel Laureate) was developing the statistical and quantitative techniques to test economic theory and quantify the impacts of economic policy decisions. Theory without measurement in economics is just mathematics or philosophy, measurement without theory is anecdote, but the combination of theory and measurement was the hallmark of Stone's vision for the Department. Stone's growth model of the British economy was one of the earlier simulation models that captured some of the micro-detail of the economy, and which served as a framework to organise a substantial research endeavour into consumer demand, industry-level employment determination and company behaviour.

The rapid development of the ambition and power of microsimulation techniques owes much to the development of computers, and it is instructive, looking back at Stone's early papers, to see the subtle change in the meaning of the word. When he referred to computors he meant teams of hard-working operatives hand-cranking calculating machines. It was only later that the Cambridge mainframe computer (Titan, one of the first time-shared computers anywhere) allowed him to develop his input–output simulations, first for the Cambridge Growth Project model, and later for developing Social Accounting Matrices.

One of the direct consequences of the post World War II interest in public finance in Cambridge was the setting up of the Meade Committee 1975 by the Institute for Fiscal Studies with a brief to take a fundamental look at the UK tax structure. Since then, sophisticated microsimulation models have been developed at the London School of Economics under the guidance of Tony Atkinson, and transferred with the Microsimulation Unit to Cambridge. The Unit has not only developed its UK model but has now extended its brief to the whole of the European Union.

In parallel with the rise in computing power, the improvement in the quality and quantity of cross-section and time-series data provided the raw materials to which to apply the growing power of modern technology. When my colleagues and I analysed the Hungarian household budget survey data from the period before and after the tax reforms of 1988, we had to place the three linked waves of 12,000 households each with their 600 observations in the Manchester supercomputer for analysis. Now, the data can be manipulated on a PC, making it sufficiently accessible for research students to be able to use it as a resource for comparative research on different countries.

This improvement in speed and portability is critical in making microsimulation models accessible to policy-makers. This is essential if such techniques are to be genuinely useful in policy-making. As it becomes easier to develop compact and user-friendly models to predict who would gain, who would lose, and by how much as a result of a policy change, and make these available to the press and the media, perhaps policy-making will become both more rational and more democratic. One of the striking features of the conference was the combination of and interaction between academe and government. The book reflects this constructive dialogue in that roughly half the contributions come from outside the university sector.

The conference was boldly titled 'Microsimulation in the New Millennium' and the title was well chosen – not just because of its timing, but also because of the step change in the power and range of techniques that has taken place over the last decade of the old millennium. These techniques allow theory and measurement to achieve their full potential in informing decision-making and equip social scientists with laboratories for policy experiments. It will be interesting to see how much progress is made in the next decade; I am confident that Cambridge will continue to play its role in developing and applying the theory, the econometrics and the models to further this progress.

David M. Newbery
Department of Applied Economics
University of Cambridge
5 October 1999

Acknowledgements

The chapters on this book are a selection chosen from papers that were presented at a workshop entitled 'Microsimulation in the New Millennium: Challenges and Innovations' which was held in Cambridge in August 1998. We are grateful to the Department of Applied Economics at the University of Cambridge, and in particular the Department's Director, David Newbery, for supporting the workshop.

As a measure of the extent of interest in microsimulation as a technique for policy analysis, the workshop was attended by some 100 people, drawn from universities, research institutes, private sector bodies, government departments and international organisations from around the world. As well as participants from most countries of the European Union, the workshop involved people from Australia, Brazil, Canada, Hungary, New Zealand, South Africa, Slovenia and the US. We are very grateful to all the authors of the papers, discussants and session chairs for making the meeting a productive, stimulating and enjoyable occasion. As well as the contributors to this volume, we should like to thank Phil Agulnik, Leif Andreassen, Emanuele Baldacci, Dave Boutwood, Pierre Concialdi, Neela Dayal, Richard Eason, Ingemar Eriksson, Carlos Farinha Rodrigues, François Gardes, Thesia Garner, Michel Grignon, Anthony King, Horacio Levy, Bertrand Lhommeau, Magda Mercader Prats, Joachim Merz, Julian McCrae, Georg Mueller, Ronald Naylor, Jan Nelissen, Sophie Pennec, Tamás Rudas, Peter Smedley, Amedeo Spadaro, Christophe Starzec, Peter Szivós, István Tóth, Gert Wagner, Paul Williamson and Michael Wolfson.

Finally, special thanks are due to Heather Henchie and Ann Newton who organised the workshop and the editing of this volume with care, patience and skill.

Lavinia Mitton, Holly Sutherland and Melvyn Weeks
October 1999

1 Introduction

Lavinia Mitton, Holly Sutherland and Melvyn Weeks

Microsimulation models use micro-data on persons (or households, or firms or other micro-units) and simulate the effect of changes in policy (or other changes) on each of these units. Differences before and after the change can be analysed at the micro-level or aggregated to show the overall effect of the change. It is the dependence on individual information from the micro-data at every stage of the analysis that distinguishes microsimulation models from other sorts of economic, statistical or descriptive models.

Modern policy problems require analysts to capture the interactions between policy and the complexities of economic and social life, as well as between policies of different types. Microsimulation is increasingly a technique that is employed to analyse these problems. At the same time, developments in computing power and analytical techniques allow a greater sophistication in the view of the world that microsimulation models can attempt to portray, and hence in the range of questions that they may address. This book brings together examples of microsimulation modelling that are at the frontiers of developments in the field, either because they are extending the range of techniques available to modellers, or because they demonstrate new applications for established methods.

The problem of determining the impact of a proposed change in policy has been succinctly summarised by Heckman and Smith (1995, p. 87) as being:

the fundamental evaluation problem that arises from the impossibility of observing what would happen to a given person in both the state where he or she receives a treatment (or participates in a program) and the state where he or she does not. If a person could be observed in both states, the impact of the treatment on that person could be calculated by comparing his or her outcomes in the two states, and the evaluation problem would be solved.

In principle, the effect of a policy change can be isolated by the comparison of 'before' and 'after' observations, or comparison of two groups that

1

are considered identical except that one group has received the treatment. However, despite the use of a range of statistical techniques, the difficulty of creating *ceteris paribus* conditions may result in selection bias, distorting the true impact of the treatment. Often we do not observe all the significant characteristics that need to be controlled for. Furthermore, we may wish to use models to inform the design of new types of policy or to predict their impact in changed social or economic conditions. In these situations, microsimulation models can provide a consistent and structured framework in which to explore a range of 'what if' questions about the outcomes of policy reforms.

Traditionally, microsimulation models are divided into two types: *static* and *dynamic*. Microsimulation is essentially a set of methods for the generation of missing information, and the distinction between static and dynamic depends on the particular method that is used. Most critical is the method for *ageing* the micro-units (Harding, 1996; Merz, 1991). Static models typically use a combination of re-weighting of micro-units and indexation of money amounts to update cross-sectional micro-data to the required point in time. Some static models may use no ageing at all, and may operate in terms of the time at which the underlying data were collected. Dynamic ageing, on the other hand, changes the characteristics of the micro-units in response to accumulated experience or the passage of time. At the most basic level, units are older by a year in each year of the updating. As the unit gets older, combinations of stochastic and deterministic methods are used to predict changes in status. In models of persons, the changes in status typically include labour force participation, co-habitation and parenthood. At each stage, incomes are estimated, based on current status and circumstances and past history. Dynamic models generate long-term or lifetime data describing each micro-unit. They may operate in a time warp, abstracting from real changes such as economic growth, or they may either predict the future or fill in missing information about the past (see Harding, 1990). Dynamic ageing is sensitive to assumptions about macro conditions (such as unemployment) and dynamic models may be used to explore the effects of incorporating alternative assumptions about the future, or alternative representations of the past.

In principle, static or dynamic models may be augmented by introducing behavioural response, which allows the calculation of second-order effects due to changes in, for example, labour supply or fertility, following a policy change. For dynamic models, incorporating behavioural response means altering the nature of the transition probabilities that are used to age the micro-units. In practice, this is rarely done.

The way in which behaviour change is estimated is clearly an important issue. The principal drawback of behavioural models derived from cross-sectional data is one of interpretation. Given that cross-sectional models lack an explicit time dimension, it is not possible to examine the time profile of the impact of a particular policy change. Further, it is not possible to differentiate between the two major problems in predicting individual behaviour – namely heterogeneity and time dependence (see Heckman, 1981). The increasing availability of panel data provides us with prospects for improvement on two fronts: first, the opportunity to estimate econometric models of behavioural response that incorporate 'dynamics'; and second, better-founded estimation of transition probabilities that are used to age the sample in a dynamic microsimulation model.[1]

The choice of whether to use a static or dynamic microsimulation model, and whether to include behavioural modelling, depends in principle on the policy question to be addressed and also on the quality and suitability of available data. (In practice, it also depends on the institutional context and the speed with which an answer to the question is necessary. These issues are considered below.)

Static microsimulation is generally used when only cross-sectional information is needed to answer a policy question. For example, in this volume, Kaplanoglou models the distributional effect of a change in tax rates. Dynamic methods are used when a set of repeated cross-sections is needed, as when modelling the effects of pension reform (see Bonnet and Mahieu in this volume), or when long-range future prediction is required for a current sample, such as in Hancock's paper exploring the financing of long-term care. In either case, whether behavioural responses to the policy changes are modelled depends on a number of factors. In some circumstances we may want to know the first-round effects (for example, if we are concerned about the perception of the fairness of the reform) or we may want to know both the first-round effects and the full effects because we believe behaviour will take some time to change. In addition, whether we model changes in behaviour depends on the availability of suitable data for the estimation of behaviour, and whether we believe that our estimation is sufficiently reliable to make the exercise worthwhile. However, in cases where the proposed policy is designed to alter behaviour – such as the provision of subsidised child-care, considered by Duncan and Weeks in this volume – then an estimate of the revenue cost using only a deterministic set of rules will, in general, generate a misleading estimate of the overall impact.

On the other hand, the introduction of a behavioural component will also introduce an additional element of uncertainty, generated by the parameter estimates. All microsimulation model results are subject to some degree of error. The great strength of microsimulation based on micro-data is that the full range of variation in circumstances is captured.

However, many of the processes that are part of building any microsimulation model – updating and uprating, imputing missing values and re-weighting, as well as estimation – involve some degree of aggregation and approximation. The effect of sampling error on the reliability of a range of static model outputs has been calculated by Pudney and Sutherland (1994). The same authors have estimated the additional error due to a labour supply response model (Pudney and Sutherland, 1996).[2] It is often a question of judgement as to whether the bias introduced by failing to capture important effects (such as behaviour change, or differences between small groups) is outweighed by additional uncertainty due to imperfect estimation procedures or underlying data. The calculation of confidence intervals around model results that account for *all* sources of error remains a major challenge.

In dynamic microsimulation modelling, the simulation of a realistic ageing of the population depends on the existence of reliable transition probabilities. Since these probabilities are estimates, they naturally introduce an additional element of uncertainty. Given the nature of these models, any error in one component is likely to be compounded with repeated use during the ageing process. Devising methods to assess the extent of error in dynamic model outputs, particularly those that cannot be subjected to direct or 'collateral' comparison with independent information, is currently 'an art rather than a science' (see Caldwell and Morrison in this volume).

The categorisations 'static', 'dynamic' and 'behavioural' are useful from the model-builder's perspective because the nature of the work involved, and the physical resources required to carry out these three types of modelling are quite different. For these reasons the sections in this book follow traditional divisions: the first section includes papers that use static methods innovatively; the second focuses on developments in dynamic model building and the third on modelling behaviour change. This introduction considers the papers in each section in turn and concludes with some reflections on the process of model building.

1.1 New directions for microsimulation

Part One of this volume contains chapters on what would traditionally be termed static models. However, it is increasingly the case that microsimulation models do not fall conveniently into the established categories of static and dynamic models, either with or without behavioural change. Indeed, some of the contributors to this volume would challenge the taxonomy that we have set out above. Thus, many of the chapters in Part One incorporate an innovative dimension that makes the choice of ageing method less relevant as a classification criterion. For example, the pensions model described by Rake could be defined as static in that it employs a single cross-section for its data source and uses static ageing. But it also contains elements in common with dynamic models in relation to the methods used to simulate lifetime earnings and pension contributions of the sample individuals that were not recorded in the original survey data.

The aim of Rake's chapter is to illustrate how microsimulation can be used when conducting cross-country comparative social policy research. In the field of social policy, cross-national comparisons are frequently limited to the descriptive: the researcher can become overwhelmed by the variation between national policies. Microsimulation can strip away some of the underlying national variations in order to improve our understanding of the link between policy and outcome. Thus, Rake is able to show the effect of the British, French and German pensions systems in 'exaggerating, replicating or mitigating the earnings differential between women and men'.

Another innovation in microsimulation is the linking of micro-models to macro-models of various kinds. The paper by Cameron and Ezzeddin describes a preliminary exercise to link two established models together in order to incorporate some macroeconomic second order effects. The models are a static microsimulation model and a regional input–output model for Canada. The linked models simulate both the direct and indirect effects on micro-level economic well-being of various tax/transfer and social policy alternatives in the Canadian Provinces. They can also be used to assess the distributional effects on households of changes to the economic climate and the industrial base. Although its preliminary nature means that some of the links are crude (the adjustments to micro-level earnings are proportional, for example), this paper demonstrates the potential for integrating personal and industrial sector models.

The models described in Part One are not used simply to measure the effects of actual or prospective policy reforms – the original motivation for the development of static microsimulation models. Policy simulations are also used as analytical devices to understand the operation of existing systems (as in Rake's paper) and the sensitivity of results to conventional assumptions. For example, Kaplanoglou uses microsimulation methods to discover that the apparent mild progressivity of the Greek indirect tax system is due solely to taxes on private transport: if car taxes are treated as road use charges rather than pure taxes, the regressive parts of the system are left to dominate the overall pattern. Some of the apparent progressivity arises from the lower rates of car ownership among less well off groups. Based on her results from simulating a uniform VAT as an alternative to the immensely complex Greek indirect tax structure,

Kaplanoglou is able to make a strong argument for simplifying Greek indirect taxes.

Decoster and Van Camp also use microsimulation to explore the sensitivity of results to conventional assumptions, at the same time as providing a distributional analysis of the 1988 Belgian tax reform. They consider the issue of the unit of analysis and the effect of the choice between fiscal unit and household on conclusions about the distributional characteristics of the tax system. Using a statistical matching procedure, a link is made between an administrative fiscal data set and the household budget survey for Belgium. This allows personal tax liabilities to be imputed for each fiscal unit within each household in the survey, and hence for the implications of either unit of analysis to be explored. One finding is that the redistributive power of the tax system was reduced by the reform, and that this conclusion is *not* sensitive to the choice of unit. However, for both the pre-reform and post-reform tax systems, the choice of the unit of analysis *does* affect conclusions about the redistributive effect of the systems themselves. In both cases, use of the fiscal unit leads to *higher* parameters of the tax system than if the household is used.

Taking the issue of sensitivity of results in another direction, the paper by O'Donoghue *et al.*, focuses on the comparability of model results across countries. Using a prototype of the EUROMOD model, a static tax–benefit model for the whole European Union, it addresses the question of the sensitivity of European model results to the way in which incomes are measured across household types and across countries. It shows that the country composition of quantiles of the European income distribution can be sensitive to the choice of equivalence scale, adjustments for apparent differences in the quality of micro-data, and exchange rates. It implies that the evaluation of policy at the European level requires careful interpretation in the light of the assumptions that have been chosen.

Finally, the paper by Walker *et al.*, extends the use of static microsimulation into a new policy area: the growth in expenditure on the Australian Pharmaceutical Benefits Scheme (PBS) which subsidises the cost of medicines. The model uses static ageing techniques and detailed information on a range of types of prescribed medicines. The paper illustrates the potential of the model by analysing the likely outcomes for the present scheme in 2020 under three scenarios: an ageing population; a continued upward trend in medicine costs; and a general improvement in Australians' health leading to lower usage of prescribed medicines. The analysis finds that increases in drug prices are likely to have the greatest impact on the cost of the PBS, and population ageing the least impact, but suggest that improvements in Australians' health have the potential to limit cost increases significantly.

1.2 Dynamic modelling

The development of microsimulation models can challenge the results achieved through other methods. Two of the papers in Part Two – by Caldwell and Morrison, and by Bonnet and Mahieu – confront other types of model that are traditionally used to analyse policy issues related to pensions. Bonnet and Mahieu contrast the use of dynamic microsimulation with that of Computable General Equilibrium 'overlapping generations' models. Their dynamic model is able to study the transfers within generations as well as between them. Caldwell and Morrison confront the dynamic model, DYNACAN, with results from the Canadian actuarial model of pensions in a more direct way: it is expected to produce results that are consistent with the more traditional actuarial approach.

Population ageing and slower rates of economic growth raise many questions about the future of intergenerational public transfers in countries such as France with generous pay-as-you-go public pension systems. Bonnet and Mahieu describe their dynamic microsimulation model, *Destinie*, and use it to explore the implications of six alternative economic, demographic and policy scenarios. Since they are concerned to compare the microsimulation approach with overlapping generations models, their focus is mainly on the differential effects on successive generations. However, they also examine effects by gender and income level within cohorts.

As Caldwell and Morrison point out in their paper, validation is a vital part of integrating the use of microsimulation models into the policy development process. They present a range of types of validation and reconciliation for two dynamic models sharing a common basic structure (DYNACAN for Canada and CORSIM for the US). They note the lack of literature or theory on which to base a validation exercise, but are nonetheless optimistic, maintaining that validation is 'not a problem to be avoided, but an asset to be exploited'. It can be seen as an opportunity for improving understanding of the modelling process itself.

Hancock uses dynamic microsimulation to simulate the contributions that older people will make towards the cost of care in a residential home, should they need it. She simulates what older people in a relatively high-risk group might pay towards care costs, both now and in 15 years' time. She explores a range of charging options including the use of housing wealth. Of particular interest to prospective builders of dynamic microsimulation models is Hancock's 'progress through small steps' approach. Most dynamic model construction projects involve teams of people, a long-term and large-scale resource commitment (by social science standards) and the associated costs of management and co-ordination. In contrast,

Hancock single-handedly focuses on the new and particular issues raised by her research questions, leaving aside for later development aspects of the model that are not central to them.

At a practical level, building microsimulation models is all about detail, on the one hand, and finding ways of representing complex processes in a tractable form, on the other. Chénard's paper describes the solution found to one particular problem faced by the Canadian dynamic model, DYNACAN. It does so in a way that graphically illustrates to the non-practitioner the process of constructing a dynamic microsimulation model, at the same time as documenting, for the fellow-modeller, a neat solution to a difficult problem. The problem is migration. While migration itself affects a whole family, keeping the model consistent with external totals ('alignment') must be done on an individual basis. The technique developed in the paper is based on the *pageant* principle ('many are called but few get chosen'). It allows alignment on an individual basis at the same time as transition on a family basis, and is in principle applicable to problems other than migration.

1.3 Modelling behavioural response

Three papers include some behavioural response modelling. The chapter by Swan examines the distortionary effects on migratory behaviour of unemployment benefit in Sweden. The model *Sverige* is in the early stages of development as a dynamic microsimulation model. The design is fairly standard, but with two important innovations. The first is that the underlying data include information on the location in Sweden of every person in the sample to within 100 square metres. Thus there is enormous potential to explore the spatial aspects of policy. In this chapter, a logistic regression approach is used to estimate separately the effects on migration of changes in unemployment and changes in unemployment benefits. The results show that there is a significant – but small – effect of benefit levels on migration. However, the effect is purely monetary in the sense that unemployment itself does not appear to have a significant effect.

The second innovative feature that is planned is the ability to choose between alternative labour market functions in the model. The standard treatment is to use 'natural rate of unemployment' theory to achieve alignment during simulation. Using other theories would give rise to different results for changes in regional and national unemployment rates following migration. In the case considered by Swan, the small predicted migration effect would give rise to – at most – small changes in unemployment under any theoretical assumption. However, the general prospects for users of being able to choose their preferred theoretical framework, is a significant step. Indeed, the laying bare of underlying theoretical assumptions is an innovation in this context.

The two remaining chapters both focus on the problems of modelling labour supply responses. Unlike the majority of models of labour supply, the study by Aaberge *et al.*, considers the *joint* labour supply of household members. A second innovation is the incorporation of demand constraints. Otherwise unconstrained choices are adjusted by the likelihood of obtaining jobs with given hours and wages combinations. Previous studies (see van Soest, 1994) have noted the empirical tendency of labour supply models to overestimate predicted part-time employment. This is due, in part, to the focus on the supply-side characteristics of individuals, thereby ignoring the influence of the fixed costs of employment on the availability of part-time employment.

Using Italian survey data, the authors simulate the impact of a number of tax reforms including the introduction of a flatter profile of tax rates and a negative income tax regime. The reforms involve incentives for some people to work less and others to work more, such that the more productive decide to work longer hours. However, if the quantity constraints on hours choice are removed, an increase in the participation rates for individuals in the poorest income deciles is predicted. This result provides further evidence that models of labour supply that ignore demand-side factors will on average over-predict participation rates for lower income groups whose opportunity set consists mainly of home production and difficult-to-find part-time jobs.

The problem of the tendency to over-predict part-time working in discrete choice models of labour supply is also addressed in the chapter by Duncan and Weeks. They recognise that a discrepancy between observed and predicted choice is not a problem if the analyst is simply interested in predicting aggregate frequencies. However, if the estimation model is linked to a microsimulation model in order to predict the costs of, for example, the introduction of subsidised child-care, then the within-sample forecasts of the underlying choice model need to be accurate.

The chapter assesses the performance of a number of transition estimators, including the maximum probability rule estimator and estimators based upon calibration. Using both a Monte Carlo study and labour market data from a household survey, substantial differences in performance between the alternative estimators are found. Significantly better properties are exhibited by those based on calibration, where the baseline model is adjusted to remove discrepancies between observed and predicted outcomes.

1.4 Investing in microsimulation models

Several of the chapters in this volume refer to their models as being proto-types, 'preliminary' or work in progress. In practice, most microsimulation models are – as far as their builders are concerned – major enterprises requiring many person-years of expertise, attention to detail and stamina. As investment in research capacity, they can all be considered to be work in progress in some sense or another. They may develop one step at a time, as resources permit (in this volume, see Hancock). Or they may be set up as large-scale enterprises with multiple goals and a relatively long time horizon (in this volume, see Caldwell and Morrison, and Chénard (DYNACAN); Swan (*Sverige*); O'Donoghue *et al.*, (EUROMOD)).[3] It is also the case that some models may never be distinct objects with identifiable histories. They may be a collection of procedures and tech-niques that are assembled, re-assembled or discarded in the search for methodological improvement (in this volume see Aaberge *et al.*; Duncan and Weeks). Some model builders consider themselves to be answerable to a set of 'users' or 'clients' (see Caldwell and Morrison in this volume, and also Immervoll *et al.*, 1999). This can constrain the model development process. It can also provide a valuable focus and discipline. For others, there are no distinctions or separations between model builder, model user or user of the model's output.

These differences are related to the range of types of institutions in which microsimulation model construction and analysis takes place (see Sutherland, 1998). This volume combines chapters reporting on modelling efforts in government departments with modelling developments that are carried out in academic environments. The institutional differences can be important in understanding the motivation for the project and the con-straints under which it operates. For example, modelling by government departments is often initiated by policy-makers' needs to find answers to specific questions. These may be regular or multiple needs, encouraging investment within government in the development of durable and flexible models. The incentives in the academic world for this investment are less obvious, although the EUROMOD project shows that it is possible. It is also quite clear that innovation in technique is not the preserve of acade-mic modellers: in some countries, many of the most exciting projects are carried out by government analysts. At the same time, academics do have the freedom to look beyond the analytical needs of current policy agendas, both in the direction of technical virtuosity and in order to model inde-pendent, alternative or dissident policy ideas.

Thus there is not only a role for microsimulation modelling in each type of institution, but also a set of good reasons to encourage and maintain a lively – and international – dialogue between them. This volume, and the workshop on which it is based, represent part of that dialogue. It is one of a series of such international volumes, including Orcutt, Merz and Quinke (eds) (1986), Harding (ed.) (1996), and Gupta and Kaipur (forthcoming).[4] Given the analytical challenges posed by modern policy development, and the innovative directions in which microsimulation is moving, hopefully it will not be the last!

Notes

1 It is important to be clear that the terms 'static' and 'dynamic' have different meanings in the vernacular of econometrics from those used here in relation to microsimulation models.
2 See also the Appendix to Aaberge *et al.,* in this volume.
3 It is notable that two of the newer models – DYNACAN and *Sverige* have taken the short cut of inheriting the model structure of a more mature model (CORSIM).
4 There are many other collections of papers that are not focused solely on microsimulation or which have a less international scope. Brunner and Petersen (eds) (1990) consider simulation models in general. For models for North America, see Lewis and Michel (eds) (1990) and Citro and Hanushek (eds) (1991), and for the UK, see Hancock and Sutherland (eds) (1992).

Part One

New directions for microsimulation

2   The unit of analysis in microsimulation models for personal income taxes: fiscal unit or household?

André Decoster and Guy Van Camp

2.1 Introduction

Microsimulation models have now become very popular, as much for the design and evaluation of policy measures, as for the empirical implementation of theoretical research. A wide variety of models have been constructed, focusing on a well-defined set of policy instruments: personal income taxes, indirect taxes, benefits, or social security contributions. For an overview of existing static models in Europe, we refer to Sutherland (1995). Behind the many differences between these models, the core and structure of most of them is of course very similar: simulation and evaluation of a change in policy parameters at the *individual or household level*. But up to now relatively little attention has been paid to this last characteristic: the definition of the unit of observation.

In this paper we start from a double observation. On the one hand, a considerable number of microsimulation models, certainly those that deal with personal income taxes, are based on administrative data.[1] They run on databases which use the *fiscal unit* as the basic unit of observation. The definition of this fiscal unit follows from tax law definitions and may diverge considerably from the sociological concept of a *household*. Moreover, in most cases these fiscal databases suffer from a lack of representation of the whole population because people with income below a certain threshold drop out of the income tax system. On the other hand, both from a theoretical point of view and from the perspective of the policy-maker who asks for an evaluation, most people agree that the sociological household is the basic unit. In this chapter we build a bridge between the two approaches and investigate how sensitive the results of a personal income tax model are with respect to the definition of the unit of observation. The practical relevance of this test should not be underestimated. In the US, for example, there has been extensive research and debate about the effects of the tax reforms in the 1980s on progressivity and redistribution with, not unexpectedly, conflicting empirical evidence. Bishop *et al.,* (1997) explicitly point to the difference in the recipient unit of the tax files of the TCMP database and the family unit of the CPS data as part of the explanation.[2] Also, Wagstaff and Van Doorselaer (1997) state that they are hampered by the fact that they can rely only on tax record data to compare the performance of different OECD tax systems.

The major obstacle to providing evidence on this question is the absence of a personal income tax model that runs on a representative household survey. There are at least two explanations for the lack of such a model in Belgium. First, the only operational personal income tax model (SIRe) has been built within the Ministry of Finance. It has thus naturally been based on an administrative file (IPCAL) of tax forms returned by people liable to pay income tax in Belgium. Second, a more substantial reason is that the existing household surveys in Belgium (*viz.*, the Panel Study of Belgian Households (PSBH) and the household budget survey) do not contain the gross income information on which tax calculations can be based.

To answer our question, we have complemented the budget survey with gross income information, taken from the fiscal data, by means of a *statistical match*. To make this possible, we first had to split the households in the budget survey into fiscal units. We then looked for the most similar fiscal unit in the administrative file, and transferred its gross income information, needed to calculate tax liabilities, to its budget survey counterpart.[3]

The approach adopted here is an empirical one. We study the results of the Belgian microsimulation model for personal income taxes, SIRe, which runs on an administrative file, after its output has been transferred into another database, the Belgian household budget survey. The specific simulated results used in our exercise are those that reflect the policy changes which have occurred in personal income tax legislation between 1988 and 1993. Therefore, as a by-product of the core question, we can also provide some tentative policy conclusions about the distributional effects of this reform.

In section 2.2 we describe the data. The different steps in the matching procedure are explained in section 2.3. In section 2.4 we present the empirical results. We first give a brief overview of the policy changes in personal income tax in the 1980s and then compare the distributional effect of these reforms, analysed using the administrative data and the household budget survey. There is also a short discussion of the outcome of the distributional analysis itself. Section 2.5 concludes.

2.2 The two data sets

The fiscal data set IPCAL and the personal income tax model SIRe

Every year, the tax administration draws a random sample from an administrative tax file, called IPCAL. IPCAL consists of the tax forms that are submitted by persons who are liable to pay income tax in Belgium. The sample we used, which we will call the *fiscal data set*, consists of tax forms returned in 1994.[4] The administrative nature of these data shows up clearly in the basic version of the personal income tax model, SIRe, that is based on it. In fact, the basic version of SIRe reproduces the calculation of the tax administration of a given year. The advantage of this approach lies in the degree of accuracy of the model. The calculated tax liabilities are nearly exact. A drawback of this is some loss in flexibility in defining reforms. Furthermore, the model does not contain estimates of behavioural responses to changes in personal income taxes. In direct tax–benefit models this is rather the rule than the exception, however.

The administrative origin of the database also implies that administrative units of observation are used. In principle, such a fiscal unit is an individual, since each Belgian citizen who receives a sufficient amount of income is liable to pay income taxes and thus has to complete a tax form. However, if a person is legally married, they submit a tax form jointly with their spouse.[5] Therefore, the final tax liabilities, produced by the model, are calculated on the basis of income that is received by either one or two people.

Despite the fact that the tax liability for each of these units is nearly exact and the fact that the sum of all tax liabilities is a good approximation of the total revenue, the underlying database is not representative for the Belgian population as a whole. For some people it is obvious that the administrative calculation of tax liability will show that they are not liable to pay income tax. These people do not have to complete a tax form. Hence, the 10,343 units in our sample are a representative sample, but only for the population of fiscal units that have filed taxable income including those for whom it was not immediately clear whether they had to pay taxes or not.[6]

The household budget survey of 1987–88

The household budget survey has been designed as a representative sample of all households living in Belgium. A *household* is defined as all people living under the same roof, using the same accommodation and deciding commonly on their expenditures. The sample consists of 3,235 households who registered expenditures during the period of May 1987–May 1988.[7]

Besides the very detailed expenditures at the household level, the budget survey also contains information on common income sources, such as labour income and most social security benefits. These income sources are reported for each member of the household individually while, for example, income from property and savings is reported at the household level. All income information in the budget survey is net of taxes. In addition, the survey also contains a large number of variables that characterise both the household and its members. Counted over all households, 812 different expenditure codes, 234 different revenue codes and 285 characteristics were registered. Especially when it comes to the evaluation of reforms, the informational richness of the budget survey offers an advantage over IPCAL.

But the budget survey also has one major disadvantage. The sample consists of 3,235 households.[8] However, because of the lengthy registration period, these 3,235 households only make up 11% of the original sample. Despite the fact that weights have been constructed to compensate for the attrition bias, this low response rate casts doubt on the representativity of the simulated results (see Verma and Gabilondo, 1993, p. 99).

To provide a better overview of the aforementioned differences and similarities between the fiscal data set and the household budget survey, we give a summary in Table 2.1.

2.3 The matching procedure

Table 2.1 clearly reveals the two basic problems to be solved: the difference between households and fiscal units (row 2), and the lack of gross income information and hence tax liabilities in the budget survey (rows 7 and 8). Since we will tackle the second one by a statistical match between the two data sets, the solution of the first problem is logically prior to it. To express the nominal variables of the budget survey at a level comparable to the one of the final data set we have inflated the variables in the budget survey by a factor of 1.404. This captures the nominal growth of national income in the National Accounts between 1987–88 and 1993. The use of a uniform growth rate implies that we do not take into account any change in the income distribution between 1987–88 and 1993.

Disentangling households into fiscal units

Many non-married but income-earning people live under the same roof, take joint decisions about most of their expenditures and therefore make up one household. But since they are not married they are treated as separate fiscal units. It is impossible to construct IPCAL-households on the basis of

Table 2.1. *IPCAL and the budget survey compared*

		IPCAL	Budget survey
1	Date	1994	1987–88
2	Unit of observation	fiscal unit	household
3	Population covered	all fiscal units that file taxable income	all households living in Belgium
4	Population size	4,109,965	3,867,506
5	Sample size	10,343	3,235
6	Representativity	yes	yes
7	Income	gross (taxable) income	n.a.
8	and	tax liabilities (from SIRe)	n.a.
9	tax information	income net of taxes	income net of taxes
10	Characteristics	limited number of characteristics	extended set of characteristics

Source: Decoster *et al.* (1998), p. 6.

the information in the fiscal data set. Hence we can only proceed by disentangling the households, observed in the budget survey, into fiscal units.

To do this, one needs to know two things: the income position of each household member and information on the family ties that exist between the different household members. Since information on family ties is most carefully registered in the survey for the reference individual (the person who registers the expenditures and who was interviewed on other subjects), we started to check whether the reference individual was part of a fiscal couple. This involves checking whether the individual is married and still lives together with his/her partner. After that, the family ties between the reference individual and the other members of the household were investigated.

Having done this, we were left with fiscal units containing couples or individuals, and other people potentially dependent on either this couple or the individual. For those potentially dependent, it was necessary to check then the size of their income. If their income was sufficiently high, they were split off again as a separate fiscal unit. To check this income condition, we had to construct an income variable for each member of the household. An assumption was required here, however, since not all the income observations in the budget survey were registered for a specific member of the household. For example, income from property appeared as household income. When such household income was observed, it was attributed to the household member that already had the highest amount of individually registered income.

According to these rules, the 3,235 households in the budget survey could be separated into 3,444 fiscal units. We call this manipulated budget survey *the fiscal unit budget survey (FUBS)* (the original is *the household budget survey, HBS*). Since the households in the original budget survey were weighted to be representative for the household population, we also assigned the weight of household *x* to each fiscal unit belonging to household *x*. At the population level, the increase in the number of households (from sociological to fiscal ones) was only 5.7%. This is much less than we had expected before we carried out the split and it might indicate that multi-earner households (more than two income earners) are under-represented in the household budget survey.

We still face the problem that the IPCAL data and the FUBS cover different populations. Since fiscal units do not enter the fiscal data set if it is obvious that they will not have to pay income taxes, IPCAL only contains a subset of the fiscal units that appear within FUBS. We therefore checked for each unit of FUBS whether it was liable to pay income taxes, by applying the administrative rules. After this operation, the number of units in the fiscal unit budget survey dropped from 3,444 to 3,217. We denote this truncated fiscal unit budget survey by *TFUBS*. The corresponding truncated household budget survey is indicated by *THBS*.

Selection of the matching variables and specification of the distance function

In the TFUBS data set the empty cells in Table 2.1 are still empty. But since both data sets contain information on common variables (net income figures in row 9 and other characteristics in row 10) we can apply statistical matching techniques to supplement the TFUBS-data set with the missing information. For this, we have chosen the direct approach of minimising a distance function to define the fiscal unit in IPCAL which most resembles the fiscal unit of TFUBS.

Altogether, we identified 28 common variables which could be used to identify similar fiscal units in IPCAL and TFUBS (such as labour income for each member of the fiscal household, pensions, unemployment benefits, income from property, age, number of dependent children, gifts and other deductible expenses, etc.). In principle we therefore minimise for each fiscal household *j* in TFUBS the distance function in equation (2.1) by calculating for each fiscal unit *k* of the fiscal data set:

$$D_{jk} = \sum_{i \in M} w_i \left| \frac{x_{ij}^{BS} - x_{ik}^{FD}}{Std(x_{ij}^{BS})} \right| \tag{2.1}$$

where $M=$ the subset of the n common variables used in the matching procedure

$x_{ij}^{BS} =$ the value of common variable i for fiscal unit j in the Truncated Fiscal Unit Budget Survey (TFUBS)

$x_{ik}^{FD} =$ the value of common variable i for fiscal unit k in the fiscal data set IPCAL

$w_i =$ the weight of common variable i in the total distance

$Std(x_i^{BS}) =$ the standard deviation of common variable i in TFUBS.

The objective is to minimise the distance function given in equation (2.1). Yet, this does not imply that the best match corresponds to a distance measure D_{jk} that equals zero. After all, one also has to choose the number of matching variables and the probability of exact matches can easily be increased by decreasing the number of matching variables. Take the case where we only use one single matching variable, e.g. labour income. The probability of finding exact matches will be very high, but one might seriously doubt whether we impute the right tax liabilities. This illustrates that the distance measure alone is not necessarily a good indicator of the success of the matching procedure. The crucial point in matching is the correlation between the common variables and the missing ones (e.g. tax liabilities). In Decoster et al., (1998) we describe in detail how a stepwise regression has been used to identify the 14 most important variables to explain tax liability.

Next to the variable selection itself, the regression also provided the weights w_i in the distance function. Both the 14 selected common variables and their weights are tabulated in decreasing order of their weight, in Table 2.2.

Table 2.2. *The 14 variables used in the distance function and their weight*

Variable	Weight	Variable	Weight
1 Highest labour income	37.73	8 Highest health insurance benefit	0.64
2 Self-employed income	34.62	9 Fiscal couple (yes or no)	0.47
3 Highest pension	16.26	10 Highest unemployment benefit	0.45
4 Lowest labour income	5.40	11 Mortgage capital repayments	0.15
5 Property income (house)	2.08	12 Received maintenance allowance	0.06
6 Dependent children	1.33	13 Mortgage interest	0.05
7 Lowest pension	0.73	14 Gifts to charity	0.03

Source: Own calculations; Decoster et al. (1998), Table A7.2, column match 14.

2.4 Empirical results for the personal income tax reform in Belgium between 1988 and 1993

We have used the IPCAL, the TFUBS and the HBS data sets to simulate changes in personal income tax in Belgium between 1988 and 1993. In Decoster *et al.,* (1998) we describe in detail which measures have been taken into account in the simulations, and which have been omitted. Since the lion's share of the simulated measures were included in the tax reform act of 1988, we start with a short overview of this reform.

The reform of personal income taxes in 1988

Belgium did not stand aloof from the reforms in personal income taxes that swept through the western countries in the second half of the eighties. An important reform of the personal income tax was agreed in 1988. TRA88, as we shall call it, became effective for the declaration year 1990, when taxpayers had to declare their income earned in 1989. The three basic components of the reform were

- a thorough *restructuring of the tax rates* (broader and hence fewer brackets, lower marginal rates)
- *separate taxation* of the main income earned by spouses (labour income, unemployment benefits, pensions, etc.)
- the *transformation of tax reductions into exemptions* (e.g. for children) and of *deductions of taxable income into tax reductions* (e.g. expenditures for life insurance contracts or capital redemptions due to mortgage loans).

Table 2.3 shows that the brackets have been widened, resulting in a reduction from 14 to 7 brackets. Marginal rates for high incomes (above 1,574,000 Belgian francs) have been reduced, while for the other old brackets the new rate is something like an average of the old rates. Until 1989, there also existed a 'maximal mean tariff'. Tax liability could not exceed 66.3% of global taxable income. In the post-reform column of Table 2.3 we give the brackets and rates as they applied in the declaration year 1990.[9]

It is clear that the new rate structure might have considerable redistributive effects. Although there seems to have been a general feeling that the higher income ranges gained relatively more from the new rate structure, it is very difficult to test this conjecture without the use of a microsimulation model.

The second major element of TRA88 was the *separate taxation of professional income* and the creation of the 'wedding fraction' for spouses that make up a fiscal couple. Although in principle Belgian personal income

Table 2.3. *Rate structure before and after the reform of 1988*

Tax bracket (in BEF)		Marginal tax rate for the part of taxable income ≥ L and ≤ U	
lower bound (L)	upper bound (U)	before reform	after reform (1990)
0	– 120,000	300 BEF	25.0%
120,001	– 209,500	24.0%	25.0%
209,501	– 230,000	27.7%	25.0%
230,001	– 262,000	27.7%	30.0%
262,001	– 305,000	35.8%	30.0%
305,001	– 314,000	35.8%	40.0%
314,001	– 419,000	39.4%	40.0%
419,001	– 435,000	43.6%	40.0%
435,001	– 524,500	43.6%	45.0%
524,501	– 787,000	45.0%	45.0%
787,001	– 1,000,000	46.6%	45.0%
1,000,001	– 1,049,000	46.6%	50.0%
1,049,001	– 1,500,000	51.6%	50.0%
1,500,001	– 1,574,000	51.6%	52.5%
1,574,001	– 2,099,000	56.5%	52.5%
2,099,001	– 2,200,000	61.9%	52.5%
2,200,001	– 3,148,000	61.9%	55.0%
3,148,001	– 4,197,000	67.8%	55.0%
4,197,001	– 14,685,085	70.8%	55.0%
14,685,686	–	66.3%	55.0%

Source: Own calculations; Decoster *et al.* (1998), Table A3.1.

tax is a global tax on all income together, in practice one distinguishes four broad categories of income: income from property, income from capital, income from various sources, and professional income. By the term 'professional income' one denotes a broad class of income sources that are more or less related to some kind of professional activity. Examples of these revenues are wages and salaries paid to employees, salaries paid to managers, profits from agricultural or trading activities, and replacement incomes such as unemployment benefits and retirement pensions. To determine the net amount of income, an individual is allowed to deduct costs incurred in carrying out these professional activities, such as transportation costs. It is necessary to provide receipts that 'prove' that these expenditures have been made. If the individual does not provide this kind of information the tax administration automatically applies a scheme of fixed deductions that depend on the size of the professional income.

Until the declaration year 1989, professional revenues were added together with the other general taxable revenues and the progressive tax scheme applied to it to determine the taxes to be paid by the couple. Only below rather low ceilings was there some form of separate taxation for both spouses. This could result in a large difference between the amount of taxes paid by a married couple and by a couple living together while not being married. Especially when both spouses earned income, these differences could become significant. The implementation of fully separate taxation of professional revenues was intended to solve this problem. It was complemented by a system which corrects for very unequal division of professional income between both partners. When one of the spouses has earned less than 30% of the sum of professional incomes for both partners, this partner is deemed to have earned 30% while the professional income of the other spouse is reduced by the deemed increase. This 'redistribution' is limited to a ceiling, which in the declaration year 1990 amounted to 270,000 Belgian francs (BEF). In the case where they both earn more than the maximum amount of the 'wedding fraction', the married couple still has a slight disadvantage in comparison with the non-married couple. This is because the exemption levels for single persons are higher than those for spouses.

The third component of the reform had to do with the complex system of deductions, tax credits and exemptions. A detailed list of all changes in this field of personal income tax is beyond the scope of this text, and we only mention the most important ones. Before the reform of 1988, family size was taken into account through a tax credit. Although this credit was calculated as a percentage of tax liability, it was bounded by floor and ceiling amounts which were so close to each other that in practice the tax credit was a fixed amount. The reform of 1988 replaced these credits with a system of *exemption levels*. These exemption levels depend on family structure, such as being married or not and the number of dependent children. We give the most important exemption levels in Table 2.4. They are applied at the bottom of the tax schedule which implies, for example, that with an exemption of 165,000 BEF and an income of 300,000 BEF, 65,000 BEF of the residual taxable income of 135,000 BEF is taxed at 25% and 70,000 BEF at 30% (see Table 2.3).

The reform of 1988 also substituted tax reductions for deductions. Contributions to life insurance contracts, capital redemptions due to mortgage loans, expenses on assets distributed by employers and payments to group insurance contracts were no longer deducted from professional incomes, and contributions to private pension funds were no longer deducted from general income. Instead, all these expenses resulted in a reduction in tax liability.

Table 2.4. *Exemption levels after the tax reform of 1988 (Belgian francs)*

Married or not	
Single	165,000
married person	130,000
Number of dependent children	
1 child	35,000
2 children	90,000
3 children	202,000
4 children	327,000
each child above the fourth	125,000
Special exemptions	
other dependants	35,000
spouse or others with handicap	35,000
widow(er) with care of children	35,000
lone parent	35,000
spouse with low income:	
in year of marriage	35,000
in year of death	90,000

Source: Decoster *et al.* (1998), Table 12.

Sensitivity of the distributional evaluation to the choice of unit of analysis

Unlike other countries (for the US, e.g., see the extensive survey of analyses of TRA86 in Auerbach and Slemrod, 1997), there has been no profound analysis of the distributional effects of the Belgian tax reform act of 1988. A detailed discussion of these effects is given in Decoster *et al.,* (1998). Here we focus on sensitivity to the choice of unit of analysis. Therefore, we present the distributional analysis by means of *aggregate* measures. These measures summarise the effects of the reform throughout the different income groups into one number (for an overview of a wide range of measures, see Lambert, 1993).

The measurement can go two ways. One can measure the deviation of the tax system from proportionality. This is what is done by, for example, the Kakwani index of *liability progression* (see Kakwani, 1977). In TRA86 in the US, one of the objectives of tax reform was to be distributionally neutral, which was explicitly defined as 'equal percentage reductions in tax liabilities at all income levels' (see McLure and Zodrow, 1987). This boils down to an unchanged liability progression. The other possibility for a definition of distributional neutrality in a tax reform is an 'equal percentage change in after-tax income at all income levels'. In that case, the measurement of the progressivity or distributional characteristics of a tax system focuses on the change in the inequality of after-tax income. Measures which gauge this redistributive effect or *residual progressivity* of the tax system were proposed by Musgrave and Thin (1948) and Reynolds and Smolensky (1977). In Appendix 2.1 we give the expressions for both measures in terms of the Lorenz and concentration curves of income before and after tax. The link between the two concepts is provided by the average tax rate. A very progressive system can have a minor redistributive impact if the average tax rate is very low. The distinction between the two components of the redistributive power of a tax system has attracted considerable attention in the literature (e.g. Formby *et al.*, 1990 for a summary of the discussion and the possibility of a welfare interpretation of both approaches).

A final remark concerns the pre-tax income we have used in the calculations. For IPCAL and TFUBS, we used the pre-tax income of the fiscal unit as the income concept to construct the Lorenz and concentration curves. In the budget survey, households report their 'disposable income' directly. This variable differs from the concept we use at the fiscal unit level, but we presume that it gives a better indication of the welfare level of the households. Hence, for THBS and for HBS, we have constructed pre-tax income as the sum of this disposable income concept and the personal income tax liabilities which were obtained by the matching process. It was impossible to use this construction in IPCAL and TFUBS since 'disposable income' is defined at the household level, while IPCAL and TFUBS give observations only at the fiscal unit level.

The results are given in Table 2.5, where the notation between brackets for the different measures refers to the notation used in Appendix 2.1. Given the aim of this chapter, we focus on the horizontal reading of the table by comparing the figures for the four different columns. The vertical structure of the table reveals the effects of the reform itself. The first panel gives the information about the pre-reform situation, the middle panel about the post-reform situation, and the bottom panel gives the percentage difference between the two.

Let us begin at the bottom left of the table. There is a good chance that a government official who asks the administration for an evaluation of a tax reform proposal will be given the figure of 2.8%. The researcher of the Ministry of Finance will explain that percentage changes in tax burdens have been calculated at different income levels on a representative sample of the tax compliance file. These results indicate that the reform of personal income taxes in 1998 was a very slightly progressive one. In fact, statistical

Table 2.5. *Sensitivity of the distributional analysis of TRA88 to the choice of unit of analysis*

	IPCAL	TFUBS	THBS	HBS
Unit of observation	Fiscal unit	Fiscal unit	Household	Household
Data set	Fiscal data	Truncated budget survey	Truncated budget survey	Full budget survey
Number of observations	10,343	3,217	3,134	3,235
Population size	4,109,965	3,746,799	3,654,248	3,876,508
Before tax reform of 1988				
(1) Mean tax rate (*t*)	0.264	0.309	0.234	0.230
(2) Gini pre-tax (G_X)	0.367	0.368	0.313	0.331
(3) Gini post-tax (G_{X-T})	0.298	0.285	0.267	0.283
(4) Redistributive effect (Π^{RS})	0.073	0.085	0.056	0.058
(5) Liability progression (Π^K)	0.202	0.189	0.183	0.193
After tax reform of 1988				
(6) Mean tax rate (*t*)	0.244	0.284	0.215	0.211
(7) Gini pre-tax (G_X)	0.367	0.368	0.313	0.331
(8) Gini post-tax (G_{X-T})	0.304	0.294	0.272	0.288
(9) Redistributive effect (Π^{RS})	0.067	0.077	0.051	0.052
(10) Liability progression (Π^K)	0.208	0.194	0.185	0.195
Effect of the reform				
(11) % change in redistributive effect	−7.5	−9.2	−9.3	−9.4
(12) % change in *t*/(1 − *t*)	−10.1	−11.4	−10.4	−10.3
(13) % change in liability progression	2.8	2.5	1.2	1.1

Source: Own calculations.

tests might even indicate that the change in the liability progression from 0.202 to 0.208 is not statistically different from zero.[10]

But does this imply that the redistributive power of the personal tax system did not change? Not at all, as the change in the Reynolds–Smolensky index indicates. Scaling down all the tax liabilities of a progressive system erodes the redistributive effect. The big drop in the average tax rate (from 26.4% to 24.4%) leads to a reduction of the Reynolds–Smolensky index of 7.5%. On the other hand, the residual progression of Belgian personal income tax remains high, when compared to other countries. For the US and Canada in 1985, Silber (1994) reports figures of 0.038 and 0.034 respectively, and from the figures in Kakwani (1980) we derive a residual progression of 0.035 for Australia in 1972, 0.024 for Canada in 1970, 0.043 for the UK in 1967 and 0.025 for the US in 1970. Again, it is the tax level which offers the explanation. The liability progression underlying this residual progression is not much lower, but average tax rates are.[11]

We now come to our basic point of interest: Is the above conclusion about the effects of the tax reform sensitive to the definition of the unit of observation? Looking at the bottom three lines of Table 2.5, the answer to this question is definitely: No. The choice of fiscal units or households did not influence the perception of the tax *reform*. Nor did it matter whether we omitted or included the households that did not pay taxes. In all cases, a considerable drop in the redistributive effect emerged. This drop was always due to the lower level of taxes. The liability progression, on the other hand, remained approximately unchanged.

Despite the stability of the measurement of the distributional effect of the reform, one observes important differences in the characteristics of the tax system itself over the different columns. The average tax rate drops considerably from column (2) to column (3). A further drop in the tax rate occurs if we add the households that are not liable to pay income taxes. Both in column (3) and in column (4) the redistributive effect is much lower than before the fiscal units were joined into households and the non-taxpaying population was added. The drop in the redistributive effect of joining fiscal units into households (column (2) to column (3)) comes both from the lower tax rate and the smaller degree of liability progression. Adding the non-taxpaying subpopulation (column (3) to column (4)) further lowers the tax rate, but liability progression increases. This leads to a slight increase in the redistributive effect, when compared to column (3). Yet it is still much lower than when measured on the fiscal data set.

Hence, if one compares the first and last columns of Table 2.5, one is tempted to say that the fiscal data lead to higher estimates of the parameters of the tax system (such as the tax rate, the redistributive effect and the liability progression) than if they are calculated at the household level. But one should be cautious about these conclusions, since more elements than the unit of observation alone differ between the first column and the last. As explained above, we also used a different income concept for the first two and the last two columns. To isolate any differences due to differences in the income concept of the columns of Table 2.5, we re-calculated these columns of figures using pre-tax income as measured in the fiscal data. The results are reported in Table 2.A2.1 of Appendix 2.2. It turns out that our conclusion about the robustness of the tax reform measurement with respect to the unit of analysis is unaffected. But, at the level of the tax system, the overestimation of the parameters seems to be caused by the difference in the income concept underlying the columns of Table 2.5.

To sum up, we are led to two main conclusions. Our measurement of the distributional effects of the tax reform does not depend on the unit of analysis that is used. The latter conclusion emerged despite the fact that there is empirical evidence for the overestimation of the parameters of the tax system when measured on a fiscal data set with fiscal units instead of measuring it on a household survey. The overestimation can be traced back to differences in the after-tax income of IPCAL and disposable income in the budget survey.

Equivalence scales once again

In the introduction (section 2.1) we referred to the conflicting evidence on the distributional effects of the TRA86 tax reform in the US. Among other possible explanations, Bishop et al., (1997) suggest that the adjustment for family size might be responsible for some of the divergent results. This should not come as a surprise. It is well known that the measurement of inequality and redistribution is sensitive to the use of equivalence scales and their specification (see Coulter et al., 1992; Jenkins and Cowell, 1994). We have therefore repeated the analysis of Table 2.5, having corrected the income figures with the OECD equivalence scale.[12] After all, this can be seen as one of the additional advantages of the statistical match. The budget survey contains more detailed information on the age of the household members than IPCAL does.[13] We could therefore use more precise equivalent income figures after the match had been executed.

The results after correction with the equivalence scale are presented in Table 2.6. Evidently, the use of equivalent incomes adds another possible dimension of comparison. Yet, we first concentrate on our basic question: Is the evaluation of the reform sensitive to the definition of the unit? Table 2.6 has exactly the same format as Table 2.5. Hence, to answer the question, we look at the different columns of the bottom panel in Table 2.6. Our basic

Table 2.6. *Sensitivity of the distributional analysis of TRA88 to the choice of unit of analysis after correction with an equivalence scale*

Unit of observation Data set	IPCAL Fiscal units Fiscal data	TFUBS Fiscal units Truncated budget survey	THBS Households Truncated budget survey	HBS Households Full budget survey
Before tax reform of 1988				
(1) Mean tax rate (t)	0.254	0.296	0.228	0.222
(2) Gini pre-tax (G_Y)	0.326	0.341	0.281	0.289
(3) Gini post-tax (G_{X-T})	0.261	0.271	0.236	0.240
(4) Redistributive effect (Π^{RS})	0.071	0.077	0.056	0.060
(5) Liability progression (Π^K)	0.208	0.183	0.190	0.210
After tax reform of 1988				
(6) Mean tax rate (t)	0.239	0.276	0.212	0.206
(7) Gini pre-tax (G_X)	0.326	0.341	0.281	0.289
(8) Gini post-tax (G_{X-T})	0.259	0.271	0.236	0.240
(9) Redistributive effect (Π^{RS})	0.072	0.076	0.055	0.059
(10) Liability progression (Π^K)	0.230	0.199	0.205	0.225
Effect of the reform				
(11) % change in redistributive effect	1.5	-1.4	-1.4	-2.4
(12) % change in $t/(1-t)$	-7.9	-9.6	-8.9	-8.9
(13) % change in liability progression	10.2	9.1	8.2	7.1

Source: Own calculations.

conclusion remains the same if different units of observation are considered *within* the HBS. The last three columns of Table 2.6, that contain the results for TFUBS, THBS and HBS, all indicate a small reduction in the residual progression (between 1.4% and 2.4%). This reduction follows from a considerable increase in liability progression which is counterbalanced by a larger decrease in the tax rate. However, when IPCAL data are used, the increase in liability progression exceeds the considerable drop in the tax rate. This leads to a small increase in residual progression.

Also robust is the conclusion that, in the tax system both before and after the reform, the IPCAL analysis overestimates the parameters of the tax system when compared to the analysis in terms of households. Again, the overestimation of the tax rate and hence of the residual progression has to do with the different income concepts in IPCAL and the HBS.[14]

Of course, all the above should not divert attention from the important differences between the figures in Table 2.5 and Table 2.6. To highlight this effect, we have replicated the two last columns of Tables 2.5 and 2.6 in Table 2.7. We have added a column which gives the ratio between the value of the statistic with and without correction with an equivalence scale. This leads to some useful insights.

It is not surprising that the use of an equivalence scale has a big impact on the description of the tax system both before and after the reform. Using the figures in the last column of Tables 2.5 and 2.6, we observe that the correction for family size, increases liability progression and decreases the tax rate in terms of equivalent income.[15] For the tax system before the reform, this results in a redistributive effect which is almost unaffected by the use of equivalence scales (0.058 compared to 0.060).

But the effect of the equivalence scale has itself been affected by the reform. The stability of the redistributive effect with and without equivalence scales, observed before the reform, has disappeared after the reform. The reason is that the reform has considerably strengthened the impact of the use of an equivalence scale on the measure of liability progression. After the reform, the correction for family size boosts up the Kakwani index by as much as 15%. This differential impact of equivalence scales before and after the reform also shows up in the bottom panel. The observed erosion of the redistributive effect of the tax system due to TRA88 is much smaller after correction with equivalence scales. This is due both to the smaller drop in the tax rate when a correction is used, and to the increase in liability progression which is much bigger when equivalence scales are used.

Since our equivalence scales only take into account differences in family size, their changing influence before and after the reform indicates that the reform has been family size-related. It is obvious that the translation of tax

Table 2.7. *Comparison of the distributional analysis of TRA88 with and without correction with an equivalence scale (e.s.) (results for households in the full HBS)*

	Without e.s.	With e.s.	Index
	col (4) Table 2.5	col (4) Table 2.6	with/without
Before tax reform of 1988			
(1) Mean tax rate (t)	0.230	0.222	96.605
(2) Gini pre-tax (G_X)	0.331	0.289	87.266
(3) Gini post-tax (G_{X-T})	0.283	0.240	84.787
(4) Redistributive effect (Π^{RS})	0.058	0.060	104.168
(5) Liability progression (Π^K)	0.193	0.210	108.923
After tax reform of 1988			
(6) Mean tax rate (t)	0.211	0.206	97.804
(7) Gini pre-tax (G_X)	0.331	0.289	87.266
(8) Gini post-tax (G_{X-T})	0.288	0.240	83.408
(9) Redistributive effect (Π^{RS})	0.052	0.059	112.244
(10) Liability progression (Π^K)	0.195	0.225	115.438
Effect of the reform			
(11) % change in redistributive effect	−9.4	−2.4	25.168
(12) % change in $t/(1-t)$	−10.3	−8.9	85.530
(13) % change in liability progression	1.1	7.1	663.873

Source: Own calculations.

credits into exemptions is family size-related since both are explicitly designed to take into account family size. But there could also have been another, implicit, family size-related effect. Married couples benefited more from the reform than did singles or cohabitating pairs because their professional income was treated separately after the reform, while other people had already been treated in this way before the reform. Since family size and being married are positively correlated, larger families might have benefited more from the reform than did smaller ones.

Next to the specific insights about the evaluated reform itself, our results illustrate again the importance of equivalence scales for the evaluation of reforms. The importance of these equivalence scales also underlines the relevance of the matching exercise as such. After all, the information necessary for the calculation of an equivalence scale, and hence for the construction of an appropriate welfare measure, is more readily available in a budget survey than in an administrative data set. Therefore, it seems advisable not to work with the latter but to transfer the necessary information from the administrative data into the survey.

2.5 Conclusion

There is a wide variety of data sets on which microsimulation models for personal income taxes can be based. A recurrent example is the difference between an administrative database such as a tax compliance file, and a household budget survey. As a consequence, the question arises whether the evaluation of a tax reform is sensitive to this heterogeneity of the data sets underlying the microsimulation model, and more specifically to the unit of observation. This has been the basic question of this paper.

We tried to answer this question empirically by simulating a major reform of the Belgian personal income tax system, which was introduced in 1988. The most obvious way to simulate this reform was to use the administrative data file, IPCAL. This is current practice in the evaluation of personal income tax reform, since normally administrative data do not require many data manipulations. They also contain sufficiently detailed information for the calculated tax figures to be fairly accurate, or even exact, estimates of the taxes one really pays. But administrative data have the disadvantage that they are measured for fiscal units, which are typical administrative constructs, and therefore less relevant from a sociological point of view. For welfare analysis, the household definition which is used in surveys seems to be more appropriate. Furthermore, surveys have the advantage over administrative data in containing much more background information about the observed units. They are also intended to be representative of the population as a whole, while administrative data generally only cover those that are obliged to complete a tax form. Surveys, on the other hand, have the disadvantage that they contain less information than do administrative data for calculating tax figures.

To see whether the use of such different data sets would have an influence on perceptions of the tax reform, we first simulated the tax reform with the administrative data. Next, we established a link between the administrative fiscal data set and the household budget survey such that the simulated tax figures could be transferred into the household budget survey. This not only allowed us to study the differences between an evaluation at the level of the fiscal unit and at the level of the household, but also to see the effect of using either the complete population or only the subset of those that were obliged to return a tax form.

To establish the link between both data sets we first disentangled the households of the budget survey into fiscal units. We then exploited the common information in both data sets to connect each unit in the budget survey with its most similar counterpart in the fiscal data set. In this way we could impute for each household in the budget survey its personal income tax liabilities. This allowed us to estimate the distributional effects of the tax reform both at the level of the fiscal unit and at the level of the sociological household. The empirical results pointed towards the following conclusions.

(1) The reform of the Belgian personal income tax in 1988 *eroded the redistributive power* (or residual progression) of the tax system. This was due only to the considerable drop in the average tax rate, not to a decrease in the liability progression. The latter even increased.

(2) With unadjusted incomes, and at the level of the *reform*, this conclusion is *robust with respect to the definition of the unit of observation* (fiscal unit or household), and is not affected by the inclusion or exclusion of the non-tax-filing units.

(3) Yet, this insensitivity to the unit of analysis, or to the data set used, is only apparent when considering the effect of reform. For either the pre- or post-reform tax system, fiscal data which exclude the non-tax-paying units *lead to higher estimates of the parameters of the tax system,* as compared to calculations at the household level.

(4) This conclusion seems to depend on the *difference in income definitions* underlying the fiscal data and the household budget survey. This difference produces an average tax rate in the fiscal data set that is considerably higher than the one obtained from the household budget survey. In turn, this higher tax rate in the fiscal data set leads to a larger redistributive effect compared with that measured using the household data.

(5) Conclusion (2) is largely unchanged after a correction for family size is introduced by means of an equivalence scale. But the perception of the distributional effects of the reform (i.e., conclusion (1)) is substantially affected by the correction for family size. The erosion of the redistributive power of the personal income tax system is much smaller when calculated on the basis of equivalised income. This is mainly due to a *liability progression which is greater after correction with an equivalence scale*. The impact of the introduction of equivalence scales is different in the tax system before and after the reform. This indicates that the reform was related to family size.

Appendix 2.1 The measurement of liability progression and redistributive effect

Our use of the Kakwani index of liability progression and of the Reynolds–Smolensky index of residual progression relies heavily on the exposition in Lambert (1993, ch. 7). Nonetheless, the essentials for present purposes will be recapitulated here.

If the main objective of the evaluation of a tax reform is to give empirical content to the redistributive effects of different tax systems before and after the reform, a formal expression of the concept of redistribution is required. Redistribution is defined here as the shift of income which occurs in the post-tax distribution from high to low incomes. Hence, it can be measured by comparing the pre-tax Lorenz curve with the post-tax concentration curve. Our measure of redistributive effect is therefore defined as:

$$\Pi^{RS} = 2 \int_0^1 \left[L_{X-T}(p) - L_X(p) \right] dp \qquad (2.\text{A}1)$$

where the superscript of Π^{RS} refers to Reynolds and Smolensky (1977) who applied this measure to the US tax system, and

$$L_X(p) = \int_0^y \frac{x f(x) dx}{\mu} \qquad 0 \leq p \leq 1 \text{ and } p = F(y) \qquad (2.\text{A}2)$$

$$L_{X-T}(p) = \int_0^y \frac{(x - t(x)) f(x) dx}{\mu (1 - t)} \qquad 0 \leq p \leq 1 \text{ and } p = F(y) \qquad (2.\text{A}3)$$

are, respectively, the Lorenz curve of pre-tax income (x) and the concentration curve with respect to pre-tax income of after-tax income ($x - t(x)$), where:

p = the population share of the pre-tax distribution
$f(x)$ = the density function of x
$F(x)$ = the distribution function of x
μ = mean income (pre tax)
$t(x)$ = the tax liability corresponding with taxable income x
t = the average tax rate.

Defining areas by:

$$G_X = 1 - 2 \int_0^1 L_X(p) dp \qquad (2.\text{A}4)$$

$$C_{X-T} = 1 - 2 \int_0^1 L_{X-T}(p)dp \qquad (2.A5)$$

it is easily seen that the measure of redistribution, Π^{RS}, can be rewritten as

$$\Pi^{RS} = G_X - C_{X-T} \qquad (2.A6)$$

where G_X is of course the Gini coefficient of pre-tax income and C_{X-T} is the area between the diagonal and the concentration curve of post-tax income with respect to pre-tax income. The difference between the Lorenz curve of post-tax income and the concentration curve of post-tax income is important, if there is re-ranking. Only in the absence of re-ranking does C_{X-T} equal the Gini coefficient of the post-tax income distribution, and can Π^{RS} be interpreted as the reduction of the Gini coefficient.

The redistribution, if any, is obtained because the tax system is not proportional. It should not surprise us therefore that interesting relationships between measures of redistribution like Π^{RS}, and measures of *disproportionality* of the tax system, have been proved. The latter try to give an aggregate measure of the difference between the share in total income and the share in total taxes, for given fractions of the population. One of these measures was proposed by Kakwani (1977), and is based on the formal definition of proportionality as the coincidence of the pre-tax income Lorenz curve $L_X(p)$ and the concentration curve of tax liabilities, $L_T(p)$. Disproportionality, also called liability progression, is then measured as the difference between both curves:

$$\Pi^K = 2 \int_0^1 [L_X(p) - L_T(p)]dp = C_T - G_X \qquad (2.A7)$$

and can be used to measure the progressivity or regressivity of a tax structure, where progressivity is defined as an average tax rate which increases with pre-tax income. Theorem 6.1 in Lambert (1993) states that progressivity, defined as a departure from proportionality, and the redistributive effect defined as equalising post-tax incomes, are but two sides of the same coin. Hence, Π^{RS} and Π^K are closely related:

$$\Pi^{RS} = \frac{t}{1-t} \Pi^K \qquad (2.A8)$$

Note, however, that the amount of income equalisation which is obtained not only depends on the liability progression, but also on the average level of taxation, denoted by $t/(1-t)$, which is the tax rate as a percentage of income after tax.

We are interested in the change of the redistributive properties of the personal income tax system, induced by the reform of 1988. Denoting the pre-reform situation with a subscript 0 and the post-reform situation with 1, we calculated:

$$\Delta\Pi^{RS} = \Pi_1^{RS} - \Pi_0^{RS} \tag{2.A9}$$

This difference in redistributive effect can of course easily be decomposed into a term which captures the change in the liability progression, and a term which measures the change in the average tax level. Denoting the tax rate on net income $(t/(1-t))$ as τ, and expressing the differences into percentage changes, we have:

$$\frac{\Delta\Pi^{RS}}{\Pi_0^{RS}} = \frac{\Delta\tau}{\tau_0} + \frac{\Delta\Pi^K}{\Pi_0^K} + \left(\frac{\Delta\tau}{\tau_0}\right)\cdot\left(\frac{\Delta\Pi^K}{\Pi_0^K}\right) \tag{2.A10}$$

| percentage change in redistribution | = | percentage change in tax rate | + | percentage change in liability progression | + | residual term |

The left-hand side, and the first two terms at the right-hand side of equation (2.A10) appear in the bottom three lines of Table 2.5.

Appendix 2.2 Sensitivity of the distributional analysis with a uniform income concept

Table 2.A2.1. *Sensitivity of the distributional analysis of TRA88 to the choice of unit of analysis with a uniform income concept*

	IPCAL	TFUBS	THBS	HBS
Unit of observation	Fiscal units	Fiscal units	Household	Household
Data set	Fiscal data	Truncated budget survey	Truncated budget survey	Full budget survey
Number of observations	10,343	3,217	3,134	3,235
Population size	4,109,965	3,746,799	3,654,248	3,876,508
Before tax reform of 1988				
(1) Mean tax rate (t)	0.264	0.309	0.309	0.304
(2) Gini pre-tax (G_X)	0.367	0.368	0.362	0.375
(3) Gini post-tax (G_{X-T})	0.298	0.285	0.280	0.290
(4) Redistributive effect (Π^{RS})	0.073	0.085	0.085	0.088
(5) Liability progression (Π^{K})	0.202	0.189	0.189	0.202
After tax reform of 1988				
(6) Mean tax rate (t)	0.244	0.284	0.284	0.279
(7) Gini pre-tax (G_X)	0.367	0.368	0.362	0.375
(8) Gini post-tax (G_{X-T})	0.304	0.294	0.288	0.298
(9) Redistributive effect (Π^{RS})	0.067	0.077	0.077	0.080
(10) Liability progression (Π^{K})	0.208	0.194	0.195	0.207
Effect of the reform				
(11) % change in redistributive effect	−7.5	−9.2	−8.7	−8.7
(12) % change in $t/(1-t)$	−10.1	−11.4	−11.4	−11.3
(13) % change in liability progression	2.8	2.5	3.0	2.7

Source: Own calculations.

Table 2.A2.2. *Sensitivity of the distributional analysis of TRA88 to the choice of unit of analysis with a uniform income concept and after correction with an equivalence scale*

	IPCAL	TFUBS	THBS	HBS
Unit of observation	Fiscal units	Fiscal units	Household	Household
Data set	Fiscal data	Truncated budget survey	Truncated budget survey	Full budget survey
Before tax reform of 1988				
(1) Mean tax rate (t)	0.254	0.296	0.296	0.287
(2) Gini pre-tax (G_X)	0.326	0.341	0.342	0.346
(3) Gini post-tax (G_{X-T})	0.261	0.271	0.274	0.274
(4) Redistributive effect (Π^{RS})	0.071	0.077	0.075	0.079
(5) Liability progression (Π^K)	0.208	0.183	0.178	0.197
After tax reform of 1988				
(6) Mean tax rate (t)	0.239	0.276	0.275	0.267
(7) Gini pre-tax (G_X)	0.326	0.341	0.342	0.346
(8) Gini post-tax (G_{X-T})	0.259	0.271	0.274	0.275
(9) Redistributive effect (Π^{RS})	0.072	0.076	0.074	0.078
(10) Liability progression (Π^K)	0.230	0.199	0.195	0.213
Effect of the reform				
(11) % change in redistributive effect	1.5	−1.4	−1.3	−2.1
(12) % change in $t/(1-t)$	−7.9	−9.6	−9.7	−9.6
(13) % change in liability progression	10.2	9.1	9.3	8.2

Source: Own calculations.

Notes

This research has been supported by the DWTC (contracts DB/01/032 and PE/VA/07) and by the Fund for Scientific Research-Flanders (contract FWO G.0327.97). The PE-contract implied joint research with the Research Department of the Ministry of Finance. The expertise of the authors of the personal income tax model, Christian Valenduc and Isabel Standaert of the Ministry of Finance, was therefore of inestimable importance for our empirical work and is gratefully acknowledged. We should also like to thank Erik Schokkaert for his comments on an earlier version of this chapter. Of course, all opinions expressed in this chapter and all remaining errors are ours.

1 For an overview, see Wagstaff and Van Doorselaer (1997), Table 2, pp. 13–14.
2 TCMP stands for the Taxpayer Compliance Measurement Program, a database which is comparable to the IPCAL-database used in our study; CPS stands for the Current Population Survey.
3 In principle, we might have followed at least two other directions. First, we could have tried to reconstruct from the net incomes in the household survey, the gross or taxable counterparts and then use SIRe to calculate tax liabilities. But lack of information makes this option a blind alley or at least a very hypothetical one, since many *ad hoc* assumptions would have to be made. The second possibility was even more infeasible: to have reconstructed IPCAL households from the fiscal units, and in addition correct the fiscal data set for its lack of representativity.
4 This implies that the reported income figures are expressed in 1993 prices.
5 Both the definition of the fiscal unit, and the condition of being part of it when married, are only crude sketches of the real conditions. See Standaard Belasting-Almanak (1996), pp.7–15 for more detail.
6 The size of this population is 4,109,965 fiscal units.
7 A new survey had been completed in 1996, but the data of 1987–1988 were the most recent available to us.
8 This sample represents a population of 3,867,506 households.
9 Until 1993 these brackets only changed because they were adjusted for inflation.
10 Statistical tests for the shifts in Lorenz and concentration curves, and for the changes in the related indices of measurement of tax incidence and progressivity, have been developed recently. See Bishop, Chow and Formby (1994) and Davidson and Duclos (1997). We have not applied these tests in this chapter. But in Decoster *et al.* (2000) we show, in a slightly different analysis, that the change in liability progression is indeed statistically different from zero.
11 The liability progression for the US, reported in Silber (1994) is 0.176, while the average tax rate is 0.178. The residual progression figures we derived from Kakwani (1980) are based on liability progressions of 0.189 for Australia, 0.169 for Canada, 0.254 for the UK and 0.156 for the US. The tax rates for these countries are respectively 0.157, 0.123, 0.145 and 0.137. Another numerical estimate of the liability progression for the US is found in Formby *et al.*, (1989) who give an estimate of 0.201 for 1976.

12 The scale gives a weight of 1 to the first adult, 0.7 to all other adults and 0.5 to children. One is considered a child up to the age of 13.

13 The most appropriate translation of the OECD scale would require one to take into account the age-barrier of 13 to separate children from adults. Since no information on the children's age is available in IPCAL, we have limited ourselves to the variable 'child in charge' to construct the OECD scale for the IPCAL observations. The same construction was used at the fiscal unit level in the fiscal unit budget survey. But at the household level we were able to take into account the age information that is available in the budget survey.

14 To underpin the latter conclusions we recalculated Table 2.6 with the uniform income concept. The results are reported in Table 2.A2.2 of Appendix 2.2.

15 The average tax rate is defined here as the ratio of the sum of all equivalised tax liabilities over the sum of all equivalised taxable incomes. Although the average tax rate for a single household is unaffected by the equivalence scale (the scale cancels out in numerator and denominator), the average tax rate for the whole population is affected by the use of an equivalence scale.

3 Assessing the direct and indirect effects of social policy: integrating input–output and tax microsimulation models at Statistics Canada

Grant Cameron and Ross Ezzeddin[1]

3.1 Introduction

Direct fiscal relations between individuals and governments work in both directions – individuals pay income and commodity taxes to governments, while governments provide transfers to individuals, almost exclusively in the context of social programmes. In Canada, the provincial and federal governments effectively share responsibilities in these policy areas. Budgetary constraints, political changes, and the uneasy federal–provincial partnership have prompted several major policy initiatives in recent years. When assessing the impacts of actual and proposed tax and transfer policies there are two inter-related issues: *What will be the full impact of the policy?* and, *What will be the distributional impact, i.e. who will be affected and to what extent?*

In measuring the impact of a policy change, it is important to both specify and differentiate between the direct and indirect effects that constitute the total effect. In making this distinction, it is helpful to think of a circular flow of economic activity. Take an across-the-board income tax cut, for example. The immediate impact is that disposable (i.e. after-tax or net) income will increase for all income recipients, leading to increased consumer demand. This consumption shock will stimulate a response from the business sector of the economy: production will increase to meet the new demands. These impacts on disposable income, consumer demand, and the gross output of the business sector are the *direct effects* of the tax cut. However, the impact is not complete, as the increase in the output of the business sector will cause aggregate labour incomes to rise. This additional income will affect the tax liabilities of those individuals to whom it accrues; their disposable incomes and consumption will rise, prompting a business sector response, and so on. The process will repeat itself until the successive income changes approach zero. The income, consumption, and production changes induced by the *direct effect* of the tax cut are the *indirect effects*. The sum of the direct and indirect effects is the *total effect* of the policy.

The second issue is the distributional effects of a policy change. Policymakers are likely to be concerned about the impacts on the disposable income of families by income class, family type, and province. Similarly, the impact on gross output and labour income by industry and by province may also be an important consideration. In Canada, the regional impacts of any federal or provincial policy initiative are crucial considerations in the policy process; there is substantial interest in measuring the regional impacts of federal policies and the potential spillover effects of provincial initiatives. Will they be significant? Canada's ten provinces and two, soon to be three, territories vary greatly in size, economic base, and economic strength, while the provincial governments are major players in the realms of income tax and transfers to persons. In any assessment of policy incidence, the more detail available the better, whether about households or the business sector of the economy. As previous studies have shown, the indirect effects of policy changes – while smaller than the direct effects – are still significant and may have a much different pattern of incidence from that of the direct effects.

Microsimulation and input–output models

Two of the modelling families that have been pre-eminent in the domain of static policy analysis are static microsimulation models and regional input–output models. Each modelling family has a development history at Statistics Canada and has its own strengths and explanatory power.

A major application of microsimulation modelling in the social sciences has been to evaluate the impacts of changes to tax and transfer policies at the level of the individual or household. These models typically consist of a database of individual, or household, observations and a series of tax and transfer simulators. The tax and transfer simulators replicate the rules and regulations of government programmes that involve financial transactions with persons: for example, personal income taxes, commodity taxes, unemployment insurance benefits, and social assistance. These simulators contain a multitude of parameters, such as tax rates, that can be modified by the user to simulate a policy change. The database is a population sample constructed from either survey or administrative sources, or both, and contains sufficient economic, geographic, and demographic information to assess the policy questions at hand. The database and simulators are usually set to a common base year to facilitate the analysis of the changes triggered by counterfactual policy scenarios. Such models can predict the initial impacts on disposable income of these tax and transfer policy changes at a highly disaggregated level.

A simulation is initiated by user-specified changes to the parameters that underpin the tax and transfer simulators. Each individual is subsequently passed through the simulators and the results are compared to the baseline values on the database. Winners and losers can be determined at the individual level, as can the magnitude of their change in disposable income. The wealth of demographic and economic information stored on the database makes feasible virtually any type of detailed analysis of the policy impacts. However, the explanatory power of microsimulation models generally ends with the determination of changes to disposable income. They do not simulate the response of the production side of the economy and further economic activity thereby generated.

Input–output (I–O) accounts are a standard component of the System of National Accounts; several nations construct these accounts on a regional as well as a national basis. Regional input–output accounts contain a wealth of information with respect to inter-regional trade flows of goods and services, inter-industry linkages, the production process, and final demands – in other words, the inherent linkages of the domestic economy. The accounting framework is a set of tables or matrices that track the outputs of each industry, the inputs to the production of each industry, the final demand for commodities, and the inter-regional trade of commodities.

Multiregional input–output models – constructed to simulate the impact of a demand shock on the business sector of the domestic economy – can be specified through a series of linear transformations of the regional input–output accounts. I–O models are quantity-adjusting models that tend to be based on several key assumptions: fixed prices, the absence of any supply constraints, fixed technology, fixed capital, fixed trade flows and fixed leakage coefficients.[2] Because of these assumptions, I–O models are strictly linear in nature and are generally viewed as more effective in impact analysis for relatively modest shocks – for very large shocks, the assumptions of fixed prices, technology, and capital, and of unlimited resources may be unrealistic. Input–output models specify a new equilibrium in response to a shock without describing the path by which this equilibrium is reached or the time required (Poole, 1993).

The input–output properties of linearity mean that the proportion of demand for commodity x in region a met by industry y in region b is constant, as are the proportions of specific intermediate and primary inputs used in the production of commodity x by industry y in region b. There are no constraints with regard to the supply of inputs or the transportation of goods – it is assumed that all demands can be met. For example, in a Canadian context, a fixed percentage of the demand for passenger automobiles in Alberta will be met by the automotive industry in Ontario. In turn, the proportions of steel, glass, prefabricated parts, paint, etc. used in the production of passenger automobiles by the automotive industry in Ontario are fixed as are the industry and geographic sources of these intermediate inputs. It is thus possible to predict, on a regional basis, which domestic industries will alter production in order to meet changes in demand. These supplying industries will in turn purchase goods and services as inputs from other industries, who will in turn purchase inputs and so on. This process will be repeated until all inputs have been identified in the full chain of the production process (see again Poole, 1993). The end result is the total impact of the demand shock on industrial production.

The strength of the regional input–output modelling approach lies in its ability to calculate the regional impact of a demand shock in considerable detail. The input–output framework does not facilitate the detailed calculation of further economic impacts – in other words, the indirect effects – that are driven by the input–output model outcomes. However, the calculation of changes to labour income that result from a demand shock provides an indication as to what these effects may be. A conventional regional I–O model cannot translate these changes to household-level gross income changes and subsequently to disposable income, consumption, and production changes. There is no household database, no allocation mechanism for wages and salaries, no tax-transfer simulators, and no consumption functions in regional input–output models.

A prototype integrated social and economic accounting model

We propose to marry Statistics Canada's Social Policy Simulation Database and Model and Regional Input–Output Model to create the Integrated Social and Economic Accounting Model (ISEAM). The SPSD/M and Regional I–O Model are not modified, but merely linked together to form a closed system. The value added in the creation of ISEAM will be the ability to estimate both the direct and indirect effects of policy changes while preserving and capitalising on the detailed analytical framework of its constituent models.

In the ISEAM prototype, changes in consumption demand calculated on the SPSD/M – the results of a change in tax and transfer policy – are passed to the Regional Input–Output Model. Changes in wages and salaries from the resulting demand shock in the Regional Input–Output Model are passed back to the household database on the SPSD/M. In this way, ISEAM can measure the full impact of a policy change. Changes in tax and transfer policy can be translated in sequence to changes in disposable income, consumer demand, industrial production, wages and salaries (and therefore total income), and back to disposable income, and so on, until successive changes become inconsequential. This mechanism is in the tradition of comparative statics analysis, as there is no time dimension over which this sequence of events occurs. The approach assumes that the final results reflect a new equilibrium condition. Details regarding the behavioural assumptions, or lack thereof, which drive this system to its new equilibrium will be described below.

The SPSD/M component of the model allows for micro-level analysis of the incidence of any policy change. Provincial impacts, impacts by income group, and impacts broken down by a host of demographic characteristics, can all be assessed. It is possible to compare the incidence and magnitudes of the direct and indirect effects. Any number of economic variables can still be tracked at the household and individual levels.

Assessing the prototype

The development of the ISEAM prototype raises some questions regarding the general performance of such a framework. Will the integrated model actually work? Will the model converge? Will the results make sense? A second set of questions is concerned with the anticipated value added of ISEAM. How large will indirect effects not addressed by the SPSD/M and the regional I–O model prove to be? What will be the incidence of these indirect effects? Will policies propagated by a provincial government have significant inter-regional impacts? In order to answer these questions we run three counterfactual policy experiments through ISEAM and make assessments of their impacts.

The results of these experiments are being assessed in order to judge the prospects for the future development of ISEAM as a policy analysis tool. The two linkage mechanisms between the models in the prototype are fairly simplistic; the usefulness and effectiveness of the prototype is an obvious prerequisite for any further work in this regard. Attempts to model the individual behavioural responses inherent in consumption and labour market decisions are a possible next step. Alternatively, the imputation of non-cash benefits such as the value of public health care and education to individuals could be performed. A more fully developed ISEAM could also serve as the basic core for efforts to model policy impacts on social and economic phenomena not captured directly by the traditional economic measures inherent in the SPSD/M and the regional I–O model.[3]

3.2 Model specifics

The difficulty in integrating the microsimulation and input–output models lies in the difference in the conceptual definition of what is meant by 'persons' and how their economic activity is measured. Perhaps more surprising are the differences, stemming from measurement error, in regional wages and salaries by industry – a concept which is equivalent in both worlds. In this section, the substantial differences in concepts and measurement are examined in the light of finding the most appropriate method of integrating the models in this prototype study. In addition, some pertinent details of each model are discussed.

Definition of persons

The input–output model is constructed on input–output tables – one of the constituent components of the Canadian System of National Accounts (CSNA). These accounts comply, for the most part, with the sectoring defined internationally for all systems of national accounts. Thus, all spending in the economy is allocated to one of the following four sectors: businesses, governments, persons and unincorporated business, and foreigners. The personal sector of the CSNA is made up of more than individuals in their family context; it also comprises non-profit organisations, universities, some insurance activities, and cultural organisations. These bodies do not exist as part of a microsimulation database of individuals whose origins typically lie in household surveys of income and labour force participation.

Concept and measurement of personal incomes and expenditures

The personal expenditures of households within the CSNA personal sector include some imputed items. The substantial imputed expenditures, namely imputed rent on owner-occupied dwellings and imputed expenditures on banking services, exist to balance the ledger on the income side in the estimates of Gross Domestic Product.[4] It is self-evident that these imputed items cannot be captured in family expenditure surveys. In addition, business-related expenditures for some unincorporated personal service providers are a component of spending in the CSNA personal sector. For instance, the wage bill and other operating expenses of nannies are considered personal expenditures in the context of the input–output tables. Household survey-based expenditure data will, correctly, not contain these wages in their estimates.

The conceptual differences in personal income are more problematic – especially in the components of income other than wages and salaries. For example, personal investment income in the CSNA includes interest income earned on trusteed pension plans and life insurance plans. Persons responding to an income survey questionnaire will be unaware of these forms of revenue as they reside in a general investment fund. The imputed rental income accrued to owner-occupied dwellers is another major component of CSNA income which goes missing in income surveys. The definition of personal sector net income differs substantially in the case of farmers, where the change in the value of gains in inventories alters the value of farming net income. Finally, the income of other personal sector bodies which reside in the CSNA definition of the personal sector (i.e. charities, universities, etc.) present additional problems for integration.

Unfortunately, conceptual differences are not the end of the story when comparing incomes between income surveys and the CSNA. The difference in the measurements of the wage bill in some industries is remarkably large. For example, wage and salary estimates in the agriculture industry, as measured by surveys of employment, can differ in some provinces by more than 30% when compared with wage estimates from either the population census or income surveys. Differences in the wage bill between business and household surveys are equally large for other industries such as finance and real estate or wholesale trade.

Static tax microsimulation: the social policy database and model

The SPSD/M is a mature technology with a ten-year history of development at Statistics Canada (STC). The latest version of the database component, the SPSD, has been constructed using 1992 survey and administrative sources and consists of a range of social and demographic characteristics, income sources, expenditure patterns, and savings levels on a sample of over 100,000 individuals. The individual-level data have been constructed both to represent accurately the population of each Canadian province[5] and to allow analyses at the individual, census family, and household levels. This feature of the SPSD is essential to the success of the ISEAM simulations since the individual incomes are combined at the household level to provide the link to household expenditures and savings.

The core of the SPSD is an augmented version of Statistics Canada's household income survey – the Survey of Consumer Finances (SCF). The SCF, which surveys over 100,000 Canadians annually, collects income by type – earned and otherwise. For respondents who earn income, the industry in which the majority of the income was earned is recorded.[6] This classification is critical to the wage and salary linkage between the Regional I–O model and the SPSD in ISEAM; it enables the allocation of changes to wages and salaries by industry and province to individuals on the SPSD. In addition, the SPSD has been corrected for the known under-reporting of social assistance (i.e., welfare), unemployment insurance benefits, and Canada Pension payments, and the under-sampling of extremely high-income earners that occurs on the SCF. These imputations provide the SPSD with a more robust estimation of the distribution of economic well-being in Canada.[7]

The source of SPSD expenditure and savings levels is the Canadian Survey of Family Expenditures (FAMEX). This expenditure survey, which is typically conducted on about 12,000 Canadian households, collects information on over 1,000 separate expenditure items and sources of savings. The quality of these estimates is enhanced through the collection of income sources thus providing an explicit income/consumption identity for each household record.

The set of SPSD household records is created by imputing, via common income and other pertinent socio-demographic variables, the expenditures of each of the 12,000 FAMEX households[8] to one or more of the 40,000+ 'corrected' SCF households. The expenditure detail on each FAMEX record has been aggregated to 40 personal expenditure categories that are conceptually equivalent to the 40 personal expenditure categories found in the Canadian Input–Output Tables, providing the crucial consumption linkage in the ISEAM system. Although the SPSD does not impute expenditures to individual household members, it does maintain the sources of incomes, earned and otherwise, on an individual basis.

The model component (SPSM) consists of a series of computer algorithms that simulates the financial transactions between governments and individuals in Canada. All income taxes, transfers, and commodity taxes are covered at the federal and provincial levels; however, local government taxes, the bulk of which are property taxes, are beyond the scope of this model. The model parameters are derived from the rules and regulations of the various tax regimes and transfer programmes. The policy instruments can be altered through a vast array of model variables that the user is able to adjust. Note that the SPSD/M does not incorporate any constraints on government budgets – an increase in government expenditures does not trigger a tax increase, for example. Although the most recent version of the database is founded on 1992 data, the tax-transfer parameters of the SPSM have unique values up to the current year. *Via* the parameters, a suite of growth factors, and alternative weight files, current policy changes can be assessed on a database which conforms to the general current year population. However, for the purposes of this analysis, all the scenarios have been assessed against a base year of 1992 as the most accurate representation of the population's characteristics is always found for the year for which the database is constructed.

The model has been designed to adjust the expenditure and savings levels of the household observations to changes in the *modelled* incomes brought on by varying the tax/transfer parameters. The mechanism by which this is achieved is quite simple – a change in disposable income will precipitate an equal change to each expenditure and savings category in percentage terms. The assumption here is that the average propensity to consume is equal to the marginal propensity to consume in each household. Therefore, if, through a change in taxation, a household receives $1000 additional income to spend or save, the pattern of disposal of the additional income is the same as the initial pattern. Although many would argue that this is a significant model shortcoming, this link does provide the means by which changes to incomes can affect changes in expenditures.

The SPSM assumes no behavioural response with respect to the labour market, and the existing stock of employed individuals therefore bear the effect of the input–output impacts in ISEAM. Thus, if aggregate demand is stimulated, the simulated effect on wages and salaries can be interpreted as either a change in hours worked per employed individual at a constant wage rate or a proportional increase/decrease to wage rates holding the amount of hours worked fixed. The current structure of the SPSD/M makes no allowance for individuals to adjust their supply of labour should their average wage rates change, nor is there a mechanism to alter the proportion of unemployed individuals on the database as labour demands change. For simplicity, this prototype complies to these assumptions.

The regional input–output model

The input–output model is derived *via* the linear transformation of the provincial input–output tables. The central idea behind the regional I–O model is to express the gross output in each industry, in each province, as a linear function of the demand for goods and services from within the province, from other provinces in Canada, and from other countries. As the wages and salaries component is an explicit factor of production to industry gross output, one can determine the impact on industry-specific wages and salaries arising from changes to final demand. The standard I–O model assumptions apply – fixed prices, the absence of any supply constraints, fixed technology, fixed capital, fixed trade flows and fixed leakage coefficients.

Through these relationships, the implications of changes to consumer demand in, for example, clothing can reveal the changes to industrial output not only from the clothing industry, but also from all 'upstream' industries whose outputs are intermediate inputs for the clothing industry. The regional dimension of the model relates the impacts of demand changes in one region to the industry output in all parts of Canada and to the foreign sector. The demand for clothing in Newfoundland could be satisfied from the production of clothing in Quebec; the demand for textiles necessary to produce the clothing in Quebec may be met in Ontario. *Via* the regional model, all industry production associated with a specific regional demand may be identified.

By way of further explanation, consider the following steps that are implicit in the estimation, by the regional I–O model, of wages and salaries derived from a final demand shock:

1. How much of the demand will be met in Canada and how much from foreign sources (i.e. the propensity to import goods and services from abroad)?
2. Which provinces will meet the portion of demand derived in 1 (i.e. the propensity to import goods and services from other regions of Canada)?
3. Which industries in each province will meet the portion of demand derived in 2 (i.e. the market shares of goods and services by various industries in each province and territory found in the regional output matrices)?
4. What inputs will be required to attain the production in 3 (i.e. the mix of factors of production necessary to produce a given industry's output in each province and territory found in the regional input matrices)? From this, what will be the necessary *wage bill*?
5. Return to 1 for these secondary demand requirements: How much of the demand for inputs in 4 will be met within each province, from other regions of Canada, and abroad? Which industries will respond within Canada? What inputs will be required? What will the wage bill be? And so on.

The regional model used here is based on 1990 regional input–output tables – the most recent published by Statistics Canada. The model is specified to determine the wages and salaries for 12 industries in 13 specific regions (10 provinces, 2 territories, and government installations abroad) based on a vector of regional final demands. As previously indicated, the final demands from sources other than the personal sector are held fixed. This version of the I–O model does not include the public sector – as a result, wages and salaries in the SPSD/M industry 'Public Administration' are held constant. As the SPSD/M does not have observations on individuals residing in the territories or abroad, the demands in these areas were held constant during the simulations. The commodity detail underlying the model specification was carried out at the finest detail available – 627 commodities in all.

Model integration

The way in which the I–O model and the SPSD/M are linked, or inte-grated, in this prototype will greatly affect the magnitude and distribu-tional characteristics of the resulting simulations. Generally, there are two conventional methods of overcoming conceptual and empirical differences that exist between the microsimulation and input–output frameworks. In the first method, the microsimulation database and the input–output system must be brought into conceptual alignment before an iterative, or 'closed', solution can be found. In the second approach, no adjustment to either data set is performed; rather, the wages and salaries and the per-sonal expenditure variables are adjusted in both data sets, in each itera-tion, until the adjustment factors converge.

In the first approach, the micro-level adjustments involve imputing the missing income and expenditures to individual observations and then systematically adjusting the weights of the micro-level observations to meet the personal income/expenditure aggregates. This method of concep-tual alignment can be extremely time-consuming and runs the risk of per-turbing the linkages between the micro-level income and expenditure variables on which the database was initially constructed. Given these shortcomings, this method was discarded.

The second method, which was adopted here, is to pass rates of change of the wages and salaries and the personal expenditure variables between the two models rather than aggressively adjust the input–output or microsimulation data for conceptual differences. In this way, the models are linked *via* the personal income/personal expenditure–savings identity which resides in each household of the microsimulation database and implicitly in the specification of the regional I–O impact equation. In this version of ISEAM, only the wage and salary component of personal income is iteratively modified with changes in personal expenditures. This decision was taken in light of the large conceptual, and empirical, differences in the other types of earned income which were highlighted above.

Each of the four ISEAM test scenarios below begins with a change in policy parameters which leads to a change in modelled family disposable income. As will be described in detail below, a feature of the SPSD/M is the existence of a disposable income and expenditure identity for each household on the database. Therefore, modelled changes to disposable income – whether they result from changes in tax/transfer policy, the demand for wage earners, or lump sum receipts – are converted to new levels of savings and expenditures. These disposable income/expenditure levels are the *direct* household effects of the policy changes. As the expenditures are categorised in the SPSD/M at the same level of detail that is found in the input–output tables, it is a straightforward process to pass the percentage change in total family spending, by expenditure category and province, to the regional I–O model.

Applying these rates of change to the personal expenditures in the regional model specification is the first phase of estimating the *indirect* effects of the policy change. The regional I–O model in ISEAM then estimates the wages and salaries by industry and by province as a function of personal expenditure. The resulting percentage changes in the wage bill are applied to each employed individual on the microsimulation database on the basis of province of residence and industry of work. This adjustment to earned income leads to further changes in family spending and savings levels which provide a new adjustment factor to personal expenditures in the input–output system. The process of adjusting the personal incomes and expenditures in each model continues until the *differences* in the rates of change for the wages, over subsequent iterations, are nil. Subtracting the final income change estimates from the *direct* estimates of the policy changes gives the *indirect* effects. Figure 3.1 shows the flow of control in this framework.

The 'solution' generated by ISEAM is partial-equilibrium in nature, since there is no behavioural response on the part of persons or businesses to changes in the prices of the goods they buy; there is no mechanism by which the international balance of trade is maintained. To expand on this second point, a critical assumption of the input–output system is fixed propensities to import and import levels in the system are thus implicitly adjusted with the changes in expenditure levels in the personal and business sectors created in the model simulations. As Figure 3.1 indicates, the system holds all sources of demands fixed outside the personal expenditures – one of which is exports. Therefore, the total effects estimated by ISEAM are a function of a new implicit balance of trade.

There is little current evidence in the Canadian experience to hold fixed the import–export relationship throughout the iterative process by adjusting export demands accordingly. Canada has a relatively small economy with respect to its major trading partners and, therefore, increases to the disposable incomes of Canadians do not have a major impact on the aggregate demands of foreign sector economies. As Canada is a price-taker for most of its merchandise trade, the level of Canadian exports is determined by a combination of changes in the relative prices of traded goods combined with changes to aggregate demand of the foreign sector.

This method of passing rates of change between the constituent model components seems appropriate given the prototypical nature of this study. Should the experiments below reveal that the indirect effects on individuals

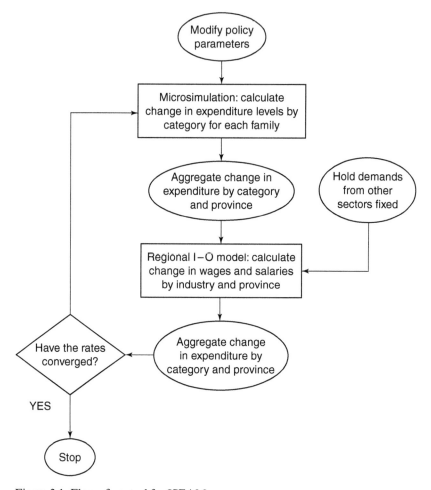

Figure 3.1 Flow of control for ISEAM

arising from policy changes are, indeed, significant to their economic well-being, then a more rigorous effort to link the two modelling families could be pursued.

3.3 Previous work in this area and model limitations

There is a long and robust history of modelling efforts aimed at incorporating the effects of household incomes and spending into an input–output framework. Typically, these efforts have involved adding columns and rows to the coefficient matrix in an attempt to treat household activity as another industry. Thus, household consumption is treated as purchases necessary to provide household 'sales', i.e. incomes, to other industries. A good overview of this modelling strategy is found in Batey and Weeks (1989). These authors describe a series of models that attempt to endogenise the activity of households into the impact matrix with successive disaggregations of the household sector. One specification allows for new workers to the region to demand different wage rates and have household consumption patterns that are different from individuals already employed in the region. A final specification allows for adjustments to the labour supply and the explicit modelling of a redistributive effect associated with an unemployment benefit.

An alternative approach to this form of household endogenisation can be found in Batey and Madden (1981). In this paper, the authors articulate the impact matrix such that simulated economic impacts can be constrained by demographic variables. Through this common framework, economic forecasts can be made consistent with demographic constraints and *vice versa*. Yet another variation can be found in the Social Accounting Matrix (SAM) framework discussed by Stone (1978). In the SAM, the household sector is disaggregated into seven income classes, thereby allowing for a measure of heterogeneity in consumption patterns. However, there is no direct linkage between the individual household sub-groupings and the labour income data – disaggregated by industry – contained in the SAM.

The first two of these approaches are more sophisticated than ISEAM in their handling of labour response to economic shocks. Nevertheless, none of the three modelling frameworks fully exploits the underlying heterogeneity of micro-level household data in terms of individual consumption patterns.

The instances where input–output and microsimulation models have been integrated are much rarer. However, ISEAM is not the first model to link a household microsimulation model to a regional input–output model to create a closed system of economic activity. The Social Welfare Research Institute of Boston College, funded largely by the United States Department of Health and Human Services, developed the Multi-Regional Policy Impact Simulation Model (MRPIS) in the 1980s (SWRI, 1985).[9]

As is the case with ISEAM, a typical MRPIS simulation is based on a counterfactual policy scenario. MRPIS contains four modules that constitute a circular flow of economic activity: two sectors – a household sector and a business sector – and two markets – a product market and a labour market.[10] The product market transforms changes in household disposable incomes into industry-specific consumption demands that are met by the business sector. The labour market allocates demand for workers by the business sector to individuals in the household sector of the model, thus closing the model. There are 51 regions – the 50 states and the District of Columbia – and 124 industries, each producing one commodity. In some of the MRPIS routines, families are divided into 20 gross income vingtiles on a national basis. Despite the fact that ISEAM was originally conceived without any knowledge of MRPIS, the two models are superficially very similar. There are some important differences in both the quality of the data sets and the nature of the linkage mechanisms between the two models. The ISEAM prototype appears to have a stronger basic data foundation in the SPSD/M and the provincial I–O accounts, while MRPIS incorporates extensive behavioural response modelling into the linkage mechanisms between the microsimulation and input–output worlds. MRPIS passes changes in corporate profits that accrue to households – in the form of changes in dividend distributions – from the business sector to the household sector (SWRI, 1988). In effect, both labour income and investment income accruing to households close the model.

3.4 Assessing the direct and indirect effects of different policy options

The dynamics of ISEAM are now analysed through three different policy experiments. The test scenarios are based on actual or proposed policy initiatives, but we have exaggerated the changes in many cases in order to have larger direct and indirect impacts that are more useful in assessing the efficacy of ISEAM. Each scenario assumes no constraints on government budgets – they do not act as a stabilising mechanism. Additional revenues or spending reductions do not result in any additional government spending and conversely, revenue declines do not prompt spending cuts.

In each case, the micro-level results are presented on a Census family basis[11] using the families' average disposable income[12] in 1992 Canadian dollars as a metric. The winners and losers presented below are Census families who have gained, or lost, at least $75 in disposable income as a result of an experiment. The terms direct and indirect winner/loser refer to the incidences of the direct and indirect effects. Of course, a Census family could be a winner/loser in both the direct and indirect portions of the table, since they could gain from an initial tax cut and then gain again *via* the increase in wages and salaries, for example. Examining their consequences for five separate income categories assesses the distributional aspects of the effects. The number of Census families within each category is, roughly, equal. Finally, some Canadian provinces are grouped together in the presentation of the regional analysis. For the purposes of this paper, Newfoundland, Prince Edward Island, Nova Scotia, and New Brunswick

Table 3.1. *Summary of direct and indirect effects for each scenario*

	50% Reduction in social assistance in Ontario	Reduction in the Ontario tax fraction	Reduction in the Newfoundland tax fraction
(a) Total impact in millions of $1992			
Direct effects (within province)	−2,962	4,775	136.5
Indirect effects (within province)	−639	870	23.2
Indirect effects (other provinces)	−95	131	11.1
Total effect	−3,696	5,776	170.8
(b) Percentage of total effect			
Direct effects (within province)	80.1	82.7	79.9
Indirect effects (within province)	17.3	15.1	13.6
Indirect effects (other provinces)	2.6	2.3	6.5
Total effect	100.0	100.0	100.0

constitute the Maritime Provinces, while Manitoba, Saskatchewan and Alberta make up the Prairie Provinces.

General findings

In each of the scenarios, ISEAM converged relatively quickly – after 5 iterations. The prototype version of ISEAM runs across two computing platforms. The SPSD/M component was performed on a Pentium 233 running Windows NT 4.1 while the regional I–O calculations are performed using a matrix package running on a DEC Alpha 4100. The total elapsed time of a simulation was roughly ten minutes. As illustrated in Table 3.1, the relative size of the indirect effects was fairly stable, ranging from 17.3% to 20.1% of the total effects. In comparing the results of experiments 2 and 3 – the equivalent tax cuts in Ontario and Newfoundland – it is clear that the proportions of in-province and out-of-province indirect effects may well vary dramatically, depending on the province where the policy change occurs. Interestingly, the out-of-province indirect effects may be larger in relative terms in Newfoundland, but they are insignificant in absolute terms.

Social assistance is halved in Ontario

The Canadian income security system consists of multiple programmes financed and administered by the provincial and federal governments. In

Table 3.2. *Halved social assistance in Ontario*

Census Family Income $000	<15	15–25	25–40	40–60	60+	All
(a) Average change in Census family income, $1992						
Direct effects (Ont.)	−1,261	−1,335	−758	−381	−115	−669
Indirect effects						
Maritimes	−1	−2	−6	−11	−18	−7
Quebec	−2	−6	−12	−24	−42	−17
Ontario	−14	−43	−91	−155	−313	−144
Prairies	−1	−5	−9	−18	−33	−13
BC	−1	−3	−5	−9	−17	−8
All	−5	−18	−38	−72	−158	−62
(b) Percentage of Census families who lose $75 or more						
Direct effects (Ont.)	43.0	31.1	17.9	9.7	3.2	17.9
Indirect effects						
Maritimes	0.0	0.0	0.0	0.1	1.6	0.3
Quebec	0.1	0.0	0.2	4.3	17.3	4.2
Ontario	4.6	26.6	48.6	64.3	81.5	50.2
Prairies	0.0	0.0	0.0	0.3	8.8	1.9
BC	0.0	0.0	0.0	0.0	1.0	0.2
All	1.9	9.2	17.0	26.5	41.8	20.1

the context of the SPSD/M, 'social assistance' refers to the welfare systems run by the provincial governments, sometimes in partnership with local authorities. Welfare is funded by the provinces and the federal government – in the past costs were shared equally by both levels of government under the Canada Assistance Plan. Recently, this funding scheme has been replaced by a block grant, the Canada Health and Social Transfer, through which the provinces receive federal funding for welfare, health care, and post-secondary education. Welfare is the ultimate social safety net for individuals with insufficient income to satisfy basic needs and who do not qualify for other specialised income-security programmes such as worker's compensation, unemployment insurance, disability pensions, and the guaranteed income supplement for senior citizens. The monthly cash benefit generally depends on family size and there are other non-cash benefits, many of them related to health care. The exact details of the system vary from province to province, although the intergovernmental transfer arrangements have always specified some minimum standards.

The first scenario simulates the impact of a 50% decline in social assistance income in Ontario from its 1992 level of $5.9 billion – the 50%

Table 3.3. *Reduction in Ontario's tax fraction*

Census Family Income $000	<15	15–25	25–40	40–60	60+	All
(a) Average change in Census family income, $1992						
Direct effects (Ont.)	19	137	454	1,007	2,721	1,079
Indirect effects						
Maritimes	1	3	8	15	24	9
Quebec	2	9	17	33	58	23
Ontario	22	55	122	210	419	197
Prairies	2	6	13	24	46	18
BC	1	4	7	13	24	10
All	7	24	52	98	212	84
(b) Percentage of Census families who gain $75 or more						
Direct effects (Ont.)	10.9	52.2	84.0	98.2	99.6	75.5
Indirect effects						
Maritimes	0.0	0.0	0.1	0.2	3.4	0.6
Quebec	0.1	0.1	2.0	11.1	31.2	8.5
Ontario	10.4	27.1	50.9	67.9	85.3	54.2
Prairies	0.0	0.0	0.3	2.5	22.5	5.1
BC	0.0	0.0	0.0	0.0	3.7	0.8
All	2.9	9.7	18.8	30.2	49.1	23.3

decline is applied to all individuals who received social assistance income in 1992. Ontario is Canada's most populous and industrialised province – it had a population of 10.1 million in 1991 out of a national total of 27.3 million, while its provincial gross domestic product constituted just over 40% of the Canadian total.

In the deficit-fighting climate of the mid to late 1990s in Canada, there has been a move to target the significant expenses of welfare programmes. The government of the province of Ontario lowered its monthly welfare rates – then the highest in Canada – unilaterally by roughly 20% in 1996. Scenario 1 was designed to parallel the actual cuts, but at a much higher rate. Tables 3.1 and 3.2, show the results of this experiment.

All social assistance recipients lose exactly one half of their social assistance income as if welfare rates have been cut in two. The direct effect of this change is a province-wide decline in disposable income of $3.0 billion. As one might expect, disposable incomes drop the most for those families with less than $25,000 of total income. Over one third of these families lose at least $75 – the average loss is around $1,300 per year. Families with between $15,001 and $25,000 in income lose the most, although the percentage of

Table 3.4. *Reduction in Newfoundland's tax fraction*

Census Family Income $000	<15	15–25	25–40	40–60	60+	All
(a) Average change in Census family income, $1992						
Direct effects (Nfld)	12	124	433	913	2,173	658
Indirect effects						
Newfoundland	12	34	81	179	303	112
Other Maritime Prov.	0	1	3	5	7	3
Quebec/Ontario	0	0	1	1	3	1
Prairies	0	0	0	0	1	0
BC	0	0	0	0	0	0
All	0	1	2	4	6	3
(b) Percentage of Census families who gain $75 or more						
Direct effects (Nfld)	7.2	44.2	92.0	99.0	99.4	66.8
Indirect effects						
Newfoundland	4.6	16.2	39.0	67.4	83.6	40.0
Other Maritime Prov.	0.0	0.0	0.0	0.0	0.2	0.0
Quebec/Ontario	0.0	0.0	0.0	0.0	0.0	0.0
Prairies	0.0	0.0	0.0	0.0	0.0	0.0
BC	0.0	0.0	0.0	0.0	0.0	0.0
All	0.1	0.3	0.7	1.2	1.1	0.7

direct losers is highest amongst the lowest income group. As disposable incomes increase beyond $25,000 per year, the number of losing families and average losses decline significantly.

The indirect effects on disposable incomes of the policy change are $734 million dollars – roughly 20% of the total impact – $95 million of which are felt outside Ontario. Slightly more than half of these inter-regional spillovers manifest themselves in the neighbouring province of Quebec. The pattern of incidence of the indirect effects is the exact opposite of the direct effects and the impact is more diffuse. Families with over $60,000 of income in Ontario lose an average of $313 – 81.5% of these families lose at least $75. The percentage of losers and average loss decline as family income falls. Despite the relatively small size of the indirect effects outside Ontario, 9.6% of all families earning more that $60,000 lose at least $75.

Clearly, the indirect effects of the social assistance reduction fall most heavily on families with higher incomes. At first glance, this is not surprising because the policy change precipitates a negative demand shock that results in a reduction in wages and salaries when output declines. The impacts on wages and salaries in our model are proportional to wages earned – we apply a percentage change to workers in a given industry in a given region. For this reason, one would expect the average changes in disposable income from the indirect effects to be larger as family incomes increase, *ceteris paribus*. However, if one examines the pattern of *percentage changes* in family disposable income that results from the indirect effects, families with higher incomes lose more, although the differences are less pronounced. One explanation may be that as family incomes increase, the likelihood that at least one member of the family is a wage earner increases.

The total effects of the social assistance cut are a decline in disposable income of $3.7 billion, 25% higher than the direct impact. Within Ontario, the pattern of incidence of the total effects parallels that of the direct effects, although the pattern of the indirect effects mitigates the disparities somewhat. With the exception of the highest income group, the average direct effect per family is of significantly greater magnitude than the average indirect effect.

Tax cut in Ontario

Provincial governments have significant spending responsibilities and significant powers of income and commodity taxation. In 1992, the provinces received just over one quarter of all income taxes remitted in Canada. Except for the province of Quebec, federal and provincial income taxes are collected by one agency, Revenue Canada, and only one tax return is filed. The starting point for the calculation of an individual's provincial income tax payable is a fixed percentage of federal tax payable – this percentage is known as the provincial tax fraction. Under this structure, the provincial governments implicitly adopt the federal income tax base – the federal tax brackets, definitions, deductions, and tax credits are all built into the calculation of federal tax payable. The provinces do apply their own tax credits and surtaxes, but generally speaking, provincial income tax is a 'tax on tax' proposition with a single 'tax on tax' rate per province (except Quebec).

Since 1996, the provincial tax fraction in Ontario has been reduced in stages from 58% to 40.5% of federal tax payable. The third scenario simulates the effect of a one-time cut in the Ontario income tax fraction from 58% to the current 40.5%. Tables 3.1 and 3.3 contain the results of this experiment.

The direct impact on disposable income is an increase of $4.8 billion. In a progressive tax system, those with higher family incomes will benefit more from an across the board cut – families in the top income class receive an average of $2,721 in additional income, while families with incomes below $25,000 receive less than $100 on average. Only 10.9% of the poorest families benefit by more than $75 while the percentage of direct winners reaches 99.6% at the top end.

The indirect effects are $1 billion, roughly 17.3% of the total effects of the tax cut. Of these indirect effects, $131 million or 13% are felt outside the province with neighbouring Quebec leading the way with $71 million. Again, and for the same reasons outlined above, the indirect effects also accrue disproportionately to those with higher incomes, although the disparity across income groups is not nearly as great as is the case with the direct effects. The percentage of indirect winners in Ontario ranges from 10.4% of low income families to 85.3% of families in the top income group. The incidence of the out-of-province indirect effects is identical, the average benefit per family is only $17, but 19.6% of families earning more than $60,000 per year gain by at least $75.

The total impact of the tax cut is a national increase in disposable income of $5.8 billion – 20.9% higher than the direct impact. The patterns of incidence of the direct and indirect effects across income groups within Ontario are identical: as incomes rise, the average increase in family disposable income per family rises. In absolute magnitude, the indirect effects are much smaller, except for families in the lowest income group. The disparity in the incidence of the direct benefits of the tax cut across income classes is thus enhanced by the indirect effects.

An analogous tax cut in Newfoundland

Newfoundland is a much smaller province – with a population of roughly 568,000 in 1991 – than Ontario with a much more open economy with respect to the rest of Canada and the world. The province has a limited manufacturing base, and thus the level of imports from the rest of Canada and the world is considerable. This scenario simulates a tax cut analogous to that simulated for Ontario. The provincial tax fraction is lowered from its 1992 level of 64.5% to 45%. Of major interest is the regional pattern of the indirect effects of the cut – one would expect larger regional spillovers than those resulting from the Ontario tax cut owing to Newfoundland's higher dependency on inter-provincial imports to satisfy consumer demand. The results of this parallel experiment can be found in Tables 3.1 and 3.4.

The direct impact on disposable income is an increase of $137 million. As is the case with the Ontario tax cut, families with higher incomes benefit to a greater extent – the average gain roughly parallels the figures for Ontario. Only 7.2% of the poorest families benefit by more than $75, while 99.4% of the top income group are direct winners.

The indirect effects on disposable income are $34 million, roughly 20% of the total. Of these indirect effects, $13 million or 38% occur outside the province. The incidence of these indirect effects across income groups is consistent with that observed in the previous experiments – the higher family income, the greater the increase in disposable income. Amongst Newfoundland families with incomes greater than $60,000, 83.6% experience an increase in disposable income of greater than $75. Though the out-of-province indirect effects are a high percentage of all indirect effects, owing to the small size of Newfoundland, they hardly register on the radar screen. The average impact is $1 per family and no family outside Newfoundland is an indirect winner.

There appears to be a kind of a paradox involved in the size of the out-of-province indirect effects resulting from provincial tax and transfer policies. Smaller provinces tend to have higher propensities to import goods and services from the rest of Canada and abroad; thus one would expect larger out-of-province indirect effects as a higher proportion of consumption demand is satisfied out-of-province. However, the absolute impact of such effects will be minimal given the relative size of these provinces.

The total impact of the tax cut is an increase in disposable income of $171 million, roughly 25% higher than the direct impact. As with the Ontario tax cut, the incidence of the indirect and direct effects is identical across income groups within Newfoundland. The relationship between the size of the direct and indirect effects is very similar to that observed in the second experiment.

3.5 Conclusions

It is clear from the results of the three experiments that ISEAM, in general, is a stable modelling environment. Although each of the direct effects expressed in the three experiments concentrated on very different groups of individuals on the SPSD/M, the ratio of total to direct effect remained stable at around 1.25. The total effect was arrived at after five model iterations in all three cases. This rate of convergence was more rapid than was anticipated and, from a systems perspective, implies a runtime of about 10 minutes from the initial direct shock to the full model solution. The speed by which the total effects were simulated eliminates computing time as a restriction for future experimentation.

There are two distinct areas that remain to be explored within the context of this model prototype. The first area of interest is a sensitivity analysis which would examine the stability of the ratio of total to direct effects as a function of the magnitude of the direct effects. The experiments studied here were all quite large in terms of their dollar values. Would smaller policy changes reveal the same relative amount of indirect activity? As the input–output system is linear one would, *a priori*, anticipate a constant ratio between the total and direct effects. However, given the non-linearities found within the tax/transfer system, it is unclear whether this assumption would hold over a variety of policy alternatives.

The second area of additional analysis would investigate the location of the indirect effects as a function of the size of provincial economies. As the results indicate, the out-of-province effects, in relative terms, were much greater when income tax levels were cut in Newfoundland when compared to the analogous cut in Ontario. Since all but one of the provincial economies lie between Ontario and Newfoundland in terms of economic strength, it would be interesting to apply the same cut to all provinces and analyse who would benefit from the indirect effects.

In addition, there is a value added potential to ISEAM that goes beyond analysing the changes to economic well-being of individuals with changes in tax and transfer policy. An articulated version of ISEAM could be seen to bring together the measurement of the total effects of social policy changes with the estimation of non-cash transfers accruing to individuals as a result of publicly funded health care and education.[13] Through this framework, a more complete analysis to social policy change could be assessed. Consider the case of the new Canada Health and Social Transfer (CHST) – a block grant made by the Canadian government to all provinces to partially fund welfare, health care, and post-secondary education expenditures made by the provincial governments. A significant change in CHST levels and subsequent provincial expenditures in all three areas would have a direct monetary impact on welfare recipients, indirect economic effects in the form of changed earned income, and consequences to the level of non-cash benefits to individuals benefiting from these public programmes. Future versions of ISEAM would be able to shed light on the well-being of households relating to changes in this monolithic transfer scheme.

Notes

1 The opinions expressed are those of the authors.
2 Leakages refer to demand satisfied outside of current domestic production by the business sector – by imports, inventory withdrawals, or the government, for example.
3 For a thorough discussion of these possibilities see Ertl (1998).
4 See Adler and Wolfson (1988) for a full description of the conceptual differences.

5 Unfortunately, the SPSD/M does not carry information on individuals in the two Canadian territories (the Northwest Territories, the Yukon Territory) nor on Canadians living abroad. However, the economic activity of these regions is well under 0.5% of the total Canadian personal expenditure.

6 The industry-level detail which appears on the SPSD is as follows: Never Worked, Agriculture, Other Primary, Manufacturing, Non-durables, Manufacturing, Durables, Construction, Transportation & Communication, Wholesale Trade, Retail Trade, Finance Insurance and Real Estate, Community Services, Personal Services, Business & Misc. Services, Public Administration, and Worked >5 Years Ago.

7 See Bordt *et al.,* (1990).

8 Households are defined as individuals, related or otherwise, who share a place of residence with a common entrance. For example, three unrelated adults sharing an apartment or single dwelling constitute a household. A duplex dwelling, however, would be two households, following the conventions of the SPSD. In this case, it is unlikely that incomes would be pooled across separate residences to share the burden of household expenditures.

9 The original plans called for five levels of MRPIS to be built, with each successive level of the model being a more complex and realistic simulation of economic activity. The final two levels were to be 'full-response' models incorporating flexible prices, capacity constraints, labour migration, endogenous investment in physical and human capital, and changes in monetary policy. This initial plan of action is cited in the references as SWRI (1981). Owing to changes in government priorities, diminished funding, increasingly challenging data requirements, and the limits of the computer technology of the time, the development of MRPIS did not continue beyond MRPIS Level 3.0 (hereafter referred to as MRPIS), a quantity-adjusting partial response model calibrated to a base year of 1985.

10 See SWRI (1992).

11 A Census family consists of both a husband and wife, or a parent with one or more children (adopted and stepchildren under 21) who have never married, living together in the same dwelling. For example, a married couple with young children or an elderly female living with her never-married daughter would constitute Census families. Students sharing an apartment would not.

12 Disposable income is defined in the SPSD/M as total income minus total federal and provincial income taxes. It therefore represents the amount of income an individual or family has available for spending (e.g. shelter, food, or savings).

13 See Cameron and Wolfson (1994).

4 A microsimulation analysis of the distribution of the indirect tax burden among Greek households

Georgia Kaplanoglou

4.1 Introduction

Considering that the decline in the role of the state in the economy is less pronounced than the rhetoric suggests, at least to judge by the rising share of tax revenue in GDP in the majority of OECD countries (including the US), the study of the distributional aspects of tax systems remains as important as ever. Greece, in particular, witnessed a substantial rise in the level of taxation during recent years, with the tax/GDP ratio rapidly rising from less than 30% to converge to the European Union (EU) average of over 40% in the period of fifteen years since the beginning of the 1980s. This can partly be explained in terms of the international empirical evidence on the positive relationship between growth and urbanisation on one hand, and the demands for revenue on the other (Tanzi, 1987; Burgess and Stern, 1993), the increased budgetary demands resulting from EU membership, the preferences of the newly elected socialist government in favour of income redistribution, and the establishment of a minimal welfare state.

The main feature of the Greek tax system is its heavy reliance on indirect taxes as the primary source of revenue, with indirect taxes representing around 70% of total tax revenue throughout the 1980s and early 1990s, and the relative shares of direct and indirect taxes in total tax revenue being exactly the reverse of the EU averages of 70% and 30% respectively. Furthermore, the dependence of Greek governments on tax revenue is unlikely to decline in the future, given the need for budgetary discipline imposed by the Maastricht criteria, the difficulty in drastically curtailing public expenditure as growing shares represent structurally immovable amortisation payments of an increasing public debt, and the severe costs of alternative options for revenue raising (i.e. deficit or debt financing) in terms of inflation and crowding out of private investment. At the same time, the aspiration of even the conservative Greek governments to reverse the indirect/direct tax balance has not been realised, probably because of the lack of ability and/or political will to curb extensive income tax evasion.

Although, given the above, the potential redistributive role of indirect taxation is apparent, and cannot be reversed at low cost by other parts of the revenue or expenditure sides of the government budget, there has been a surprising lack of any systematic attempt to assess its effects. The most relevant past studies which attempt to allocate taxes by income groups in Greece (Karageorgas, 1973; Provopoulos, 1979) refer to the 1960s and 1970s respectively and although valuable at the time, become increasingly out of date, especially as the structure of indirect taxation in Greece has since undergone major changes. These include, as a result of Greece's accession to the EC in 1981 and the subsequent introduction of Value Added Tax (VAT) in 1987, the abolition of import tariffs and the partial harmonisation of excises.

This paper attempts to assess the redistributive role of the Greek indirect tax system using the relatively recent methodology of microsimulation modelling. The latter simulates actual or potential public policy alternatives by incorporating them into detailed micro-data sets representative of the national population, and provides improved information for the evaluation of such alternatives.[1] The present research applies the static microsimulation approach to indirect taxation (of the sort used, for example, in Redmond *et al.*, 1996; Davies *et al.*, 1987; Baker *et al.*, 1990 and Decoster *et al.*, 1996) to a new micro-data set, the Greek 1987/8 Household Expenditure Survey (HES), and to model a far more complex indirect tax structure involving several cascaded taxes imposed on different tax bases and at different rates. It attempts to answer questions such as 'Who pays indirect taxes in Greece?' and 'Does the imposition of indirect taxes have an equalising effect on the income distribution in comparison to a uniform equal-yield indirect tax structure?'

Section 4.2 deals with some methodological issues, while section 4.3 explains the structure of the Greek indirect tax system and the mechanics of its incorporation into the HES database. Section 4.4 presents the distribution of the indirect tax burden among Greek households on the basis of welfare level and other status characteristics. Section 4.5 assesses the effects of the actual indirect tax system on income inequality against an equal-yield uniform indirect tax structure. Section 4.6 summarises the main findings and concludes.

4.2 Methodological choices

Any microsimulation analysis of taxation requires choices on certain methodological issues. The choices made here are defended on grounds of both theoretical guidance and practical considerations regarding data quality.

One such issue regards the degree of indirect tax shifting, that is the degree that an indirect tax change is passed on to consumer prices. In this case it is assumed to be 100% and is equivalent to constant producer prices. This assumption is adopted in the vast majority of similar studies and it can be defended both theoretically and, in the Greek case, empirically. Standard microeconomic theory suggests that in a partial equilibrium setting, although the shifting of indirect taxes will always be between 0% and 100% under perfectly competitive markets, which effectively assumes constant returns to scale, it can be on either side of 100% under alternative market structures, so that full tax shifting is a reasonable intermediate assumption and not a polar case (see, Lockwood, 1988; Stern, 1987). In a general equilibrium setting, the estimation of the degree of tax shifting involves the solution of an analytically tractable competitive general equilibrium model, which presents further complications (see Dilnot et al., 1990; Shoven and Whalley, 1984). Furthermore, empirical studies in Greece (Karageorgas, 1973; Karageorgas and Pakos, 1988; Georgakopoulos, 1991) suggest that the degree of indirect tax shifting is near to and even exceeds 100%.

Next, the evaluation of the distributional effects of indirect taxation is conditional upon a ranking of individuals in terms of welfare levels and, thus, relies on the choice of a basis of comparison of individuals, which itself involves several methodological issues. The first is *who* is to be compared? A choice must be made over the unit of analysis, that is the unit for which the calculation of welfare, indirect tax payments and so forth takes place. In this case, the only plausible unit is the household (as opposed to the family or the individual), since information on individual expenditure, but not individual consumption, is available in the HES. On the other hand, attributing indirect tax payments to members who actually carried out the purchases lacks any plausibility. Moreover, even the notion of individual consumption is in some cases meaningless, for example, in the case of *public goods* like heating, television or shelter.

The second choice refers to *what* is being compared, that is, the choice of a welfare indicator, since welfare itself cannot be directly observed. The HES data provide information on several concepts of household income and household consumption. Theoretical arguments, mainly based on the permanent income hypothesis and the closely related theory of life-cycle consumption smoothing developed by Friedman (1957) and Modigliani and Brumberg (1954), suggest that consumption is a better approximation of 'life-cycle' or 'permanent' income, since current income may reflect different phases of the life-cycle earning profiles of individuals or be subject to short-term fluctuations which do not reflect changes in the underlying welfare levels. The use of consumption may itself be suspect, considering the absence of perfect capital markets on which the permanent income hypothesis depends and that current (and expected) future tastes and needs may vary (see Blundell and Preston, 1994 and 1995). None of the above limitations, however, offers reasons to prefer income. The above theoretical considerations coupled with the practical limitation that income is severely under-reported in the HES, lead to the adoption of household consumption as a welfare indicator.[2]

A further complication arises from the fact that the HES records current expenditure rather than current consumption and the two notions may substantially differ in the case of consumer durables, such as home repairs, cars and refrigerators. Expenditure on durable items is thus excluded from the definition of consumption expenditure owing to its highly stochastic nature. Furthermore, household expenditure on non-durables was adjusted to mid April 1987 prices in order to neutralise the effects of inflation (17% at the time).

Finally, differences in household size and composition have to be accounted for with the use of an equivalence scale, that is, some concept of 'the relative income yielding the same utility level under different family size and composition' (Pashardes, 1988, p. 1). The theoretical debate about the construction of equivalence scales has not yet been resolved, despite the importance of doing so in view of the sensitivity of inequality and poverty calculations to the choice of equivalence scale. The empirical literature suggests that differences in measured inequality first decrease and then increase in a systematic way as the elasticity of the equivalence scale to family size increases. In this case, the sensitivity of household ranking (as measured by the Spearman rank correlation coefficient) with respect to the choice of equivalence scale has been examined. The main conclusion is that the use of equivalence scale indeed matters in comparison to the benchmark case of not adjusting for household size and composition; the choice, however, between the rather generous OECD scale and the more refined McClements scale did not seem to have very strong implications, since the Spearman rank correlation coefficient attained values of over 0.97 for the whole sample and also within each quintile of the expenditure distribution. Consequently, the OECD equivalence scale was used for the analysis.

To sum up, in what follows, households are ranked by equivalent expenditure on non-durables for the assessment of the distributional effects of indirect taxes, while the calculation of inequality measures is derived by assigning equivalent household expenditure to each equivalent member. It should be noted that the use of equivalent expenditure implicitly assumes that all household resources are pooled and then shared out *equally* among household members. This is fairly standard in the vast majority of studies on tax incidence, inequality and poverty, but does not fully correspond to reality and, in fact, better understanding of the within household distribution might significantly alter policy responses to inequality, labour supply problems etc (see Jenkins, 1991 and 1994; Sutherland, 1996a). In the case of indirect taxes, the limitation is not as crucial.

4.3 Modelling the Greek indirect tax system

The importance of indirect taxes as the main source of government revenue has deep historical roots in the era of the Ottoman occupation beginning in the sixteenth century, which the process of economic development hardly affected. The immensely complicated structure of the Greek indirect tax system by the time of Greece's accession to the EC in 1981, involving 82 main taxes and several less important ones, was the historical product of an accumulation of a large number of indirect taxes imposed mainly with cash targets in mind. The simplifications in the indirect tax structure which had to be introduced as a result of EC membership (mainly the replacement of a large number of cumulative taxes by VAT and the abolition of import tariffs) improved the efficiency of revenue raising in less distortionary ways and are, thus, to be judged favourably. However, they hardly had any impact on the direct–indirect tax revenue balance and thus on the importance of indirect taxes for households' budgets.

This analysis examines the distributional impact of the majority of indirect taxes, which altogether yield over 85% of indirect tax revenue. Details are presented in Table 4.1. These mainly include the VAT,[3] several excise duties (on tobacco, alcohol and malt, petroleum products,[4] passenger vehicles), transport dues, the regulatory tax,[5] the business turnover tax on insurance companies, the consolidated special consumption taxes[6] and stamp duties on insurance and rent. Analysis of the remaining indirect taxes (yielding altogether 15% of total indirect tax revenue) is not considered cost-effective, either because these taxes are levied at different and complex rates and have very low yields (e.g. import taxes, see Table 4.1) or because their allocation at a household level on the basis of the HES data does not make much sense. For example, the extent to which the tax on the transfer of capital and the special banking tax (levied on the gross income of banks) falls on final consumers is not clear, and furthermore, the final consumers are likely to be firms rather than individuals. Similarly, some other taxes (e.g. the stamp duties on wages and salaries) have the nature of an income tax rather than an indirect tax.

Table 4.1. *Sources of indirect tax revenue and their inclusion in this analysis*

Sources of indirect tax revenue (in billion drachmae)	1985	1986	1987	1988	Included in the analysis?
Revenue from Customs Offices	102.1 (14.4)	120.8 (12.7)	44.5 (3.9)	52.8 (4.3)	no
Import taxes and dues	6.0 (0.8)	0.1 (0.1)	0.1 (0.0)	0.0 (0.0)	partly
Special contributions on imported goods	1.1 (0.2)	1.5 (0.2)	1.8 (0.2)	1.9 (0.2)	partly
Consumption taxes on imported goods	94.9 (13.4)	118.4 (12.4)	42.2 (3.7)	50.2 (4.0)	partly
Other import taxes (export dues)	0.0 (0.0)	0.0 (0.0)	0.0 (0.0)	0.0 (0.0)	no
Consumption taxes	303.9 (42.9)	461.9 (48.4)	324.7 (28.6)	337.9 (27.2)	
Business turnover tax	85.7 (12.1)	109.7 (11.5)	32.2 (2.8)	8.3 (0.7)	partly
Tobacco tax	49.8 (7.0)	62.3 (6.5)	48.0 (4.2)	73.6 (5.9)	yes
Tax on alcohol and alcohol drinks	5.7 (0.8)	6.5 (0.7)	6.6 (0.6)	8.3 (0.7)	yes
Entertainment and luxury taxes	35.9 (5.1)	4.0 (0.4)	1.3 (0.1)	0.1 (0.1)	partly
Transport dues	23.1 (3.3)	24.9 (2.6)	26.0 (2.3)	28.0 (2.3)	yes
Other consumption taxes	136.0 (19.2)	254.5 (26.7)	210.6 (18.5)	218.9 (17.6)	partly
Transaction taxes	285.6 (40.3)	352.4 (36.9)	748.1 (65.8)	827.7 (66.7)	
Transfer of capital	17.6 (2.5)	24.8 (2.6)	26.2 (2.3)	37.5 (3.0)	no
Stamp	184.0 (26.0)	229.7 (24.1)	104.6 (9.2)	63.4 (5.1)	partly
Consolidated special consumption taxes	11.7 (1.5)	20.1 (2.1)	21.4 (1.9)	27.2 (2.2)	yes
Regulatory tax	72.3 (10.2)	77.7 (8.1)	63.8 (5.6)	48.2 (3.9)	yes
Value Added Tax	—	—	498.8 (43.9)	599.0 (48.3)	yes
Special banking tax	—	—	33.4 (2.9)	52.3 (4.2)	partly
Other transaction taxes	0.0 (0.0)	0.0 (0.0)	0.0 (0.0)	0.0 (0.0)	no
Back taxes and arrears due	9.6 (1.4)	10.6 (1.1)	10.7 (0.9)	12.9 (1.0)	no
Supplements, fines etc.	—	4.8 (0.5)	4.7 (0.4)	5.2 (0.4)	no
Taxes in favour of third parties	3.8 (0.5)	3.6 (0.4)	3.5 (0.3)	4.0 (0.3)	no
Other indirect taxes	3.5 (0.5)	0.0 (0.0)	0.0 (0.0)	0.0 (0.0)	no
Total indirect taxes	708.5	954.1	1,136.1	1,240.5	
% of indirect taxes to be analysed			82.6%	87.6%	

Note: Numbers in parentheses refer to shares in total indirect tax revenue.
Source: NSSG (1992).

The full tax shifting assumption is equivalent to the assumption of constant producer prices and allows the calculation of the tax paid per unit of product T, and the tax rate as a percentage of the retail price τ, as follows:

$$T=p-q \text{ and } \tau=\frac{T}{p}=\frac{p-q}{p} \tag{4.1}$$

where p is the retail price and q is the producer price. Multiplying throughout by purchased quantity (x) we get:

$$Tx=px-qx \qquad \tau=\frac{Tx}{px}=\frac{px-qx}{px} \tag{4.2}$$

where Tx is total tax paid on the commodity, px is total expenditure on the commodity and qx is pre-tax expenditure. The information we have is px (i.e. total expenditure) and τ, which can be imputed on the basis of the tax legislation, which gives information on the rates, the order and the basis on which different taxes are levied. In particular, indirect tax payments are calculated as $Tx=px\tau$.

In the case where only VAT is levied, for example bread, $p=(1+t)q$, where t is the VAT rate and p and q as before. Consequently:

$$\tau=\frac{p-q}{p}=\frac{(1+t)q-q}{(1+t)q}=\frac{t}{t+1} \tag{4.3}$$

In all other cases, where taxes are cascaded, matters get considerably more complicated. A presentation of the relevant calculations for the complete set of HES commodities is neither possible nor necessary here (for details, see Kaplanoglou, 1999). Here, we give two indicative examples, those of spirits and cars. Spirits are subject to a flat rate excise duty charged on the alcohol content, an *ad valorem* duty of 58% charged on the production or import price, and the top VAT rate of 36% charged on the production price augmented by all other taxes. The flat rate excise was charged at 150 drachmae (dr.) per kg of pure alcohol. A typical 75cl bottle of whisky of 40% volume contains 30cl of pure alcohol which, given that the specific gravity of alcohol is equal to 0.79433, corresponds to 0.24 kg of alcohol. The consumption tax paid is therefore $0.24*150\cong 36$ dr. Considering the above, the retail price p is derived from the producer or import price q on the basis of

$$(q+q*a+f)\,(1+t)=p \tag{4.4}$$

where q and p as before, a is the rate of *ad valorem* tax, f is the flat rate excise duty and t is the VAT rate.

From (4.4),

$$q=\frac{p-f(1+t)}{(1+a)(1+t)} \tag{4.5}$$

Replacing (4.5) into (4.1) gives

$$\tau=\frac{p-\dfrac{p-f(1+t)}{(1+a)(1+t)}}{p}\ \text{ or }\ \tau=\frac{a+t+at}{(1+a)(1+t)}-\frac{f}{p(1+a)} \tag{4.6}$$

A representative price of a bottle of whisky (75cl, 40%) for 1988 is 1538 dr. (National Statistical Service of Greece, Department of Price Indices) and (4.6) gives $\tau\approx55\%$.

Cars are another interesting case. They are subject to a special consumption tax, $C(ccm)$, calculated as a function of the cubic centimetres of the car's engine, VAT of 6%, a special lump sum due, $L(ccm)$, also calculated as a function of the cubic centimetres of the car's engine, and a due for issuing a circulation licence, which is a fixed monetary amount, d. The relationship between the producer (or import) and consumer price is given by

$$p=q(1+C(ccm))(1+t)+L(ccm)+d$$

$$q=\frac{p-L(ccm)-d}{(1+C(ccm))(1+t)}$$

So that the formula for the calculation of the tax is

$$\tau=\frac{p-q}{p}=\frac{p-\dfrac{p-L(ccm)-d}{(1+C(ccm))(1+t)}}{p}$$

Furthermore, the $C(ccm)$ is a complicated function of the cubic centimetres of the car's engine, as follows: (*i*) for engines of up to 1,200 ccm, 23 dr. per ccm, (*ii*) for engines of 1,201–1,800 cm, 28 dr. per ccm, and (*iii*) for engines over 1,801 ccm, 40 dr. per ccm. The total tax calculated by the above method cannot exceed a total of 100,000 dr. This tax is, however, increased by 0.4% for every 1,000 dr. of the car's taxable price, after deducting from the latter the amount of 25,000 dr. $L(ccm)$ is a simpler function of the cubic centimetres of the car's engine, as follows: (*i*) for engines of up to 1,200 ccm, 100 dr. per ccm, (*ii*) for engines of 1,201–1,800 ccm, 100 dr. for the first 1,200 ccm and 200 dr. for each additional ccm, and (*iii*) for engines over 1,801 ccm, 150 dr. for the first 1,200 ccm and 300 dr. for each additional ccm. Finally, d is 2,000 drachmae.

Information on the cubic centimetres of the car is not available in the HES, but it can be deduced from the amount of transport dues paid, information on which is available. The latter is a function of the car's horse power from which the cubic centimetres can be derived on the basis of a given formula.

Table 4.2. *Indirect tax burden by expenditure group, 1988*

Households grouped by equivalent non-durable expenditure (OECD scale)	Average percentage of tax in total expenditure[a]
Poorest 10%	9.36
11%–20%	10.69
21%–30%	11.27
31%–40%	11.62
41%–50%	11.88
51%–60%	12.04
61%–70%	12.86
71%–80%	12.75
81%–90%	12.70
Richest 10%	12.81
All groups	11.80

Note:
[a] Expenditure includes own production, etc. I assume no taxes are paid on non-bought commodities.
Source: Kaplanoglou (1999).

The tax component of the retail price has been calculated for all 293 commodity groups recorded in the 1987/8 HES following the above procedure.[7] Consequently, the tax paid by each household can be calculated for any desirable level of commodity aggregation and its distribution can be analysed in detail.

4.4 The distribution of the indirect tax burden among Greek households

The average proportion of total household expenditure absorbed by indirect taxes is approximately 11.8%. As far as the distribution of the indirect tax burden is concerned, the data in Table 4.2 suggest at first sight a modest degree of progressivity by expenditure groups. The average indirect tax burden rises progressively from the first decile (9.4%) to the seventh decile (12.9%) and then stabilises at a slightly lower level (around 12.75%). Although the total indirect tax burden generally increases with expenditure, indicating that the whole indirect tax system is slightly progressive, the breakdown of this burden into taxes corresponding to different commodity groups (e.g., food, tobacco, housing, etc.) suggests that the observed pattern is the result of averaging out some clearly progressive and other clearly regressive taxes, rather than the result of adding up taxes with similar progressivity characteristics.

This is apparent in Figure 4.1, in which taxes have been ranked in order of regressivity. A negative slope indicates a regressive tax, as the respective tax payments represent a declining share of expenditure across deciles. In this sense, tobacco tax is the most regressive and taxes on transport and 'other goods and services' the most progressive. Among the regressive taxes one can identify taxes on food, which are important although levied at quite low rates, as a result of the large budget share of food.[8] Tobacco taxes, as stated before, are even more regressive than food taxes. In contrast with food, although recorded tobacco expenditure has a very small average budget share (2.6%), less than one tenth of the food budget share (32%), it is subject to such high taxation that tobacco taxes account for almost the same proportion of total expenditure as food taxes. In fact, households belonging to the lowest half of the expenditure distribution pay on average a higher proportion of their expenditure to taxes on cigarettes alone than on all food items together. Taxes on housing (that is, rent, water and drainage, electricity etc.), heating oil, telecommunications and medical expenditure) are also regressive.

On the side of more progressive taxes, one can place taxes on clothing and footwear, household goods (durable and non-durable), personal care, education, recreation and transport. Taxes on transport are particularly important both because they display a high degree of progressivity and also because they constitute a very large proportion of total indirect taxes (more than 30%). The latter is to be explained by the fact that, although the budget share of transport is not extraordinarily large (around 9%), the taxes on certain transport goods are among the highest (indirect taxes constitute on average 57% of the retail price of cars, 67.5% of that of petrol, and transport dues are also included here). The proportion of total household expenditure absorbed by taxes on transport rises steadily from 0.49% in the lowest decile to about ten times this value (4.24%) in the highest decile. In fact, it is mainly this category of taxes that outweighs the effects of the regressive taxes on food, housing, tobacco and so on, and renders the whole indirect tax system even slightly progressive (see Figure 4.1). The effect of the other progressive taxes cannot be compared in magnitude with transport taxes since these taxes are either less progressive (for example, taxes on household goods) or they have a much smaller tax base (for example, recreation or clothing).

However, there are two lines of argument which throw doubt on the assertion that indirect taxation is indeed progressive. The first one follows a recently growing literature (Walters, 1968; Dewees, 1979; Harrison *et al.,* 1986; Newbery, 1988; HMSO, 1993) on road taxation and efficient road pricing. The argument is that some part of road taxes (that is, car purchase taxes, annual transport dues, petrol taxes) should be viewed as road

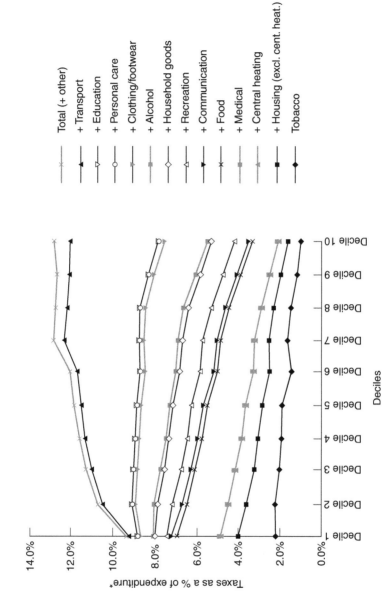

Figure 4.1 Cumulative indirect taxes by deciles of expenditure (taxes ranked by degree of regressivity)
Note: *Expenditure includes own production, etc. No taxes are assumed to be paid on non-bought commodities.
Sources: 1987/8 HES data (NSSG, 1994); own calculations.

Legend:
— Total (+ other)
— + Transport
— + Education
— + Personal care
— + Clothing/footwear
— + Alcohol
— + Household goods
— + Recreation
— + Communication
— + Food
— + Medical
— + Central heating
— + Housing (excl. cent. heat.)
— Tobacco

charges rather than pure taxes. The road network can be thought of as a good whose provision implies a certain social cost.

Individuals are the consumers who choose whether to 'consume' this good by using the road system. What is the most efficient way to ration and charge for road space? Modern public finance theory provides powerful principles for setting prices and taxes in terms of equating producer price with marginal cost and levying VAT on this base (for seminal work in the application of these principles to the case of roads, see Newbery, 1988 and 1996).

Applying the principles of marginal cost pricing to charging for roads might seem complicated, but there are examples for charging for other public utilities that suggest a constructive approach. The ideal is to charge at short-run marginal social cost and expand capacity until the average of these short-run prices is also equal to the long-run marginal cost. The short-run marginal social cost of using roads includes congestion and other environmental externalities, both of which are hard to measure. Present technology does not yet readily permit charging different amounts for different roads and at different times of the day, so simpler charging methods will have to do, at least until technology improves and has been demonstrated successfully. The practical methods for charging at present therefore involve just fuel and vehicle taxes. One logical way to set these charges is at the long-run marginal cost of supplying roads, plus a tax to cover any additional environmental costs. Newbery, 1995, found that the 1993 UK road taxes were roughly equal to the long-run marginal cost of providing roads, plus a generous estimate of the environmental costs.

Even though, as suggested above, efficient and equitable road pricing would demand much more careful planning of both the appropriate level and especially the structure of a system of input taxes, purchase taxes and licence fees, the relevant literature reveals a strong case for arguing that 'the revenues associated with road pricing should be regarded as a charge rather than a tax' (House of Commons, 1995). If Greek road taxes are set, as seems roughly to be true in other EU countries, at a level which meets the full cost of road provision, then they can be regarded as a means of charging (in the case of Greece, at an unknown level of efficiency) for the use of the highway network. Once road taxes are taken out of the picture, the indirect tax system becomes regressive (in fact, the lowest indirect tax burden is faced by the two highest deciles as shown in Table 4.3).

The other line of argument is related to the question of whether car ownership is linked to the overall progressivity of the indirect tax system. Eurostat statistics reveal that the number of passenger cars per 1,000 inhabitants in Greece is the lowest among all European Union countries (189 pass. cars/1,000 inhabitants in 1993: Drettakis, 1997). Thus, it is only

Table 4.3. *The effect of car taxes on the progressivity of the Greek indirect tax system*

Deciles of equivalent non-durable expenditure	Average percentage of total taxes in total expenditure[a] (1)	Average percentage of car taxes in total expenditure (2)	Average percentage of all taxes excluding car taxes in total expenditure (1) − (2)
Decile 1	9.36	0.45	8.91
Decile 2	10.69	1.42	9.27
Decile 3	11.27	2.02	9.25
Decile 4	11.62	2.44	9.18
Decile 5	11.88	2.68	9.20
Decile 6	12.04	3.04	9.01
Decile 7	12.86	3.68	9.18
Decile 8	12.75	3.58	9.17
Decile 9	12.70	3.87	8.83
Decile 10	12.81	4.29	8.52
All groups	11.80	2.75	9.05

Note:
[a] Expenditure includes own production, etc. I assume no taxes are paid on non-bought commodities.
Source: 1987/8 HES data (NSSG, 1994); own calculations.

a small proportion of the population which is paying high taxes on vehicles, their maintenance and circulation. Furthermore, car owners seem to be systematically wealthier than non-car owners; the null hypothesis that mean expenditure is higher for households with cars than for households without cars could not be rejected at the 0.01 significance level for four different expenditure measures (household and equivalent expenditure on all and on non-durable commodities).

Splitting the sample into car and non-car owners reverses the picture of mild progressivity, as shown in Figures 4.2 and 4.3, which are constructed in the same way as Figure 4.1. The indirect tax burden is distributed in approximately constant proportion to expenditure among the non-car owners, while taxes by commodity groups retain the regressivity/progressivity characteristics identified before.

Perhaps more surprisingly, in the car owners subsample, the taxes on transport now become strongly regressive, with the relevant indirect tax burden declining (though not uniformly) from 7.3% of total expenditure in the lowest decile to 5.7% of total expenditure in the highest one. In the absence of any influential progressivity component (since the progressive taxes on, e.g., clothing or recreation are not large enough to affect the whole picture) the total indirect tax system becomes regressive.

So, how does the picture of mild progressivity emerge when the two sub-samples are blended together? Figure 4.4 is informative. It shows, for each decile of the total household sample, the average proportion of expenditure absorbed by indirect taxes over all households belonging to the given decile (line A), over those households in the given decile which do not own a car (line B) and over the remaining households in the given decile, which own a car (line C). Thus, line A is a weighted average of lines B and C, the weights changing over deciles depending on the relative number of households present in each decile which own a car as compared to those households in the same decile which do not own a car.

Regarding the shape of line A, there are two effects working in opposite directions. On the one hand, the relative number of households with cars increases across deciles (recall that households with cars are on the whole wealthier). Thus, the weight of the higher indirect tax burden borne by those households on the indirect tax burden of the whole sample increases along deciles. This means that line A (indirect tax burden of the whole sample) will be dragged further and further towards line C (indirect tax burden of households which own a car) and thus it will become upward sloping, since households with cars face higher tax rates, making the whole indirect tax system appear progressive. On the other hand, line C is itself downward sloping (among households with cars indirect taxes were shown to be regressive) and this regressivity becomes more apparent in the indirect

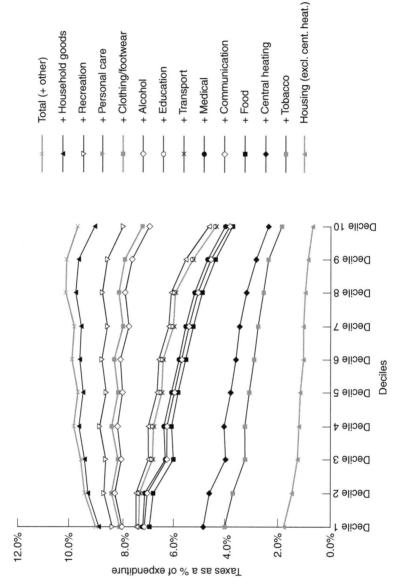

Figure 4.2 Tax incidence by deciles: households without cars (taxes ranked by degree of regressivity)
Sources: 1987/8 HES data (NSSG, 1994); own calculations.

Legend:
- ✕ Total (+ other)
- ▲ + Household goods
- △ + Recreation
- ✳ + Personal care
- ▪ + Clothing/footwear
- ◇ + Alcohol
- ○ + Education
- ✕ + Transport
- ● + Medical
- ◇ + Communication
- ■ + Food
- ◆ + Central heating
- ▪ + Tobacco
- ◂ Housing (excl. cent. heat.)

Y-axis: Taxes as a % of expenditure (0.0%, 2.0%, 4.0%, 6.0%, 8.0%, 10.0%, 12.0%)
X-axis: Deciles (Decile 1 through Decile 10)

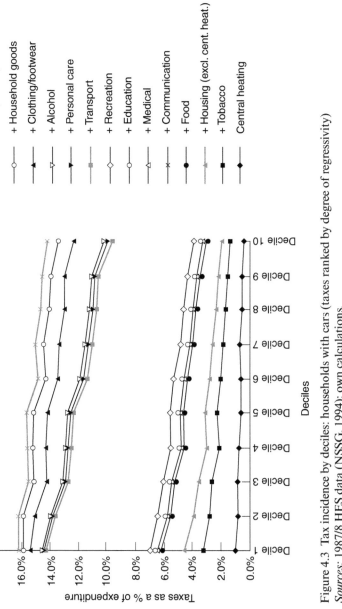

Figure 4.3 Tax incidence by deciles: households with cars (taxes ranked by degree of regressivity)
Sources: 1987/8 HES data (NSSG, 1994); own calculations.

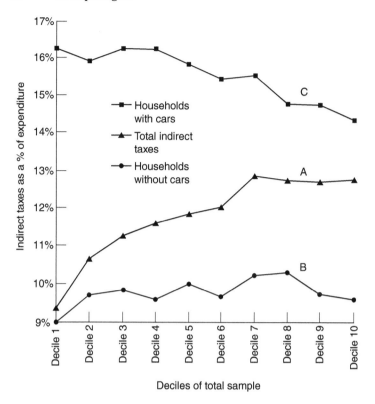

Figure 4.4 Differences in the indirect tax burden within each decile between households with and without cars
Sources: 1987/8 HES data (NSSG, 1994); own calculations.

tax burden of the whole sample as we move to the highest deciles, where more and more households own a car.

In fact, the distribution of the indirect tax burden across deciles (shape of line A) can be explained in terms of the above analysis. The former increases uniformly until the seventh decile, as the presence of households owning a car and facing indirect tax rates around 15.5% to 16% becomes increasingly pronounced as we move up the expenditure distribution.

More precisely, households belonging to the lowest half of the expenditure distribution in the sample of car owners, who face distinctly higher indirect tax rates than the households in the upper half of the same distribution, are dispersed among the first seven deciles of the expenditure distribution of all households in increased proportions as we move up the deciles. This explains the upward sloping part of line A. In the three highest deciles, although the proportion of households with cars increases further, these households (which comprise the upper half of the expenditure distribution of all households which own cars) face relatively lower indirect tax burdens in comparison to households owning a car present in the lowest seven deciles. The regressivity of the indirect tax system among households with cars starts biting and the overall result is a flattening out of the line of total indirect tax rates in the highest three expenditure deciles (see line A in Figure 4.4).[9]

An econometric analysis of the distribution of the indirect tax burden among Greek households reinforces the same result. Equations 4.1 and 4.2 of Table 4.4 present the results of estimating the regression of household indirect tax burden (defined as indirect taxes paid over total household expenditure) against expenditure and a range of demographic and socio-economic characteristics, according to Lee and Pashardes (1988). Equation 4.2 is different from 4.1 in that the effects of car taxes have been eliminated through subtracting the latter from the indirect tax burden.

To keep the analysis consistent with the previous sections, expenditure on non-durables per equivalent adult was used as a measure of household expenditure. Before proceeding to the discussion of the results, it should be noted that the equation estimates have been controlled for heteroscedasticity using a degrees of freedom corrected version of White's (1980) method (see MacKinnon and White, 1985). The equation was also tested in several ways for the presence of multicollinearity and influential outliers, none of which seemed to be a problem.

The elimination of car taxes changes the sign of the expenditure coefficient from statistically significantly positive to statistically significantly negative, suggesting that once car ownership is taken into account, the proportion of indirect taxes paid falls as household expenditure rises.

Equation 4.2 also presents the net effect of other household status variables on the level of the indirect tax burden. A brief analysis of these effects leads to several interesting conclusions (for a detailed analysis, see Kaplanoglou, 1999). The age of the head of the household has a negative effect on the indirect tax burden faced by the household. This reflects the lower incidence of smoking among older people and also the fact that older people consume rather than build up a stock of relatively highly taxed durable goods. The lower indirect tax payments by older households are also due to the smaller budgets of these households, taken up almost exclusively by necessities. The fact that older households are amongst the least well off is not accidental, considering the type of family structures prevailing in Greek society. The same family net that supports student or unemployed members of the family is also there to protect its elderly members. The cases where elderly people live on their own are bound to be

Table 4.4. The effects of household characteristics on the indirect tax burden, 1988: a regression analysis

	Equation 4.1		Equation 4.2	
Dependent Variable: TBURDEN[a] (Equation 4.1) **Dependent Variable: TBURDEN1[b] (Equation 4.2)**	*t*-ratios in parentheses (significant coefficients in bold)			
Intercept	**0.1405**	(29.31)	**0.1134**	(40.55)
Expenditure level:				
Non-durable expenditure per equiv.adult	**0.150E-6**	(5.78)	**-0.800E-7**	(5.18)
(Non-durable expenditure per equiv.adult)	**-2.814E-13**	(4.34)	**7.930E-14**	(2.03)
Age of head of household	**-0.808E-3**	(14.69)	**-0.444E-3**	(12.97)
Household composition:				
Number of adults (ref. hous.[c] one adult)	**0.0154**	(12.27)	**0.0056**	(8.15)
Number of adult females (ref.hous.: no female)	**-0.0120**	(6.91)	**-0.0037**	(3.65)
Dummy for head female (ref. hous.: male head)	**-0.0113**	(5.29)	-0.0020	(1.57)
One child in the household (ref.hous.:no children)	**-0.0042**	(2.39)	**-0.0034**	(3.18)
Two children in the household	-0.0003	(0.18)	**-0.0079**	(7.27)
Three or more children in the household	-0.0035	(1.22)	**-0.0082**	(4.26)
Number of retired people in the household (ref. hous.: no retired people)	**-0.0052**	(5.00)	**-0.0015**	(2.15)
Degree of Urbanisation: (ref. hous.: urban area)				
Rural area	**-0.0117**	(7.05)	**-0.0059**	(5.76)
Semi-urban area	**-0.0068**	(3.35)	-0.0015	(1.18)
Regional Location: (ref.hous.: E. Sterea and Islands)				
Peloponese and West Sterea	**-0.0100**	(5.17)	**-0.0028**	(2.17)
Crete	**-0.0080**	(3.33)	**-0.0047**	(2.75)
Macedonia	**0.0055**	(3.36)	**0.0070**	(7.30)

	TBURDEN[a]	TBURDEN1[b]
Thessalia	0.0040 (1.57)	0.0062 (4.13)
Islands of East Aegeon	−0.209E-4 (0.01)	0.0033 (1.74)
Ipiros	−0.0007 (0.24)	0.0039 (1.70)
Thraki	−0.0020 (0.65)	0.0077 (1.50)
Head's occupation: (ref.hous.:empl. in public sector)		
Self-employed (without employees)	−0.0089 (5.06)	−0.0028 (2.66)
Student	−0.0382 (8.36)	−0.0064 (1.89)
Employer (own business with employees)	0.0013 (0.39)	−0.0055 (1.95)
Employee in the private sector	0.0001 (0.05)	0.0008 (0.72)
Unemployed	0.0016 (0.27)	−0.0014 (0.51)
Level of education of head: (ref.hous.:no/basic ed.)		
High-school education (middle educ.)	0.0019 (1.19)	−0.0035 (3.76)
Higher education	−0.0026 (1.28)	−0.0091 (7.60)
Housing tenure: (ref.hous.: owner-occupier)		
Rent	0.0106 (6.7)	0.0127 (13.90)
Residual Sum of Squares	13.92	5.10
F-Statistic	63.02	39.71
R² (R² adjusted)	0.2085 (0.2051)	0.1404 (0.1368)

Notes:

[a] TBURDEN: total indirect taxes/total expenditure

[b] TBURDEN1: indirect taxes excluding car taxes/total expenditure

[c] Ref.hous.: reference household

Source: Kaplanoglou (1999), NSSG (1994).

cases where this family net for some reason does not exist, implying lower levels of welfare. Within a formal theoretical framework, the well known life cycle model (Modigliani and Brumberg, 1954) instead of taking place in official credit markets, takes place within informal 'family credit markets' (see also Porta and Saraceno, 1997). In the latter case, people in the middle period of their life lend resources to the young with some implicit contract to be taken care of in old age. These effects also account for the negative sign of the coefficient of the number of retired people present in the household.

Each additional adult adds to the proportion of expenditure paid as indirect taxes. However, if this additional adult is female, then the indirect tax burden is reduced (which is probably due to the lower incidence of smoking and drinking among women). A dummy for female head is negative, but not statistically significant.

The elimination of car taxes makes the effect of children on the indirect tax burden more transparent. Once car taxes are eliminated (see equation 4.2), this effect becomes stronger both in magnitude and in statistical significance (t-ratios) and is a positive function of the number of children. The reasons are easily understood: the more children present in the household, the more resources the household has to devote to food, education (both of which bear very low taxes) and also the more pressing the need for some means of private transport becomes. Once the latter effect is eliminated, the former dominates, driving down the overall tax burden.

Housing tenure also seems to have an effect, with households renting a house paying relatively more. This is reasonable, considering that there is a tax on rent. The geographic location of the household does not seem to be particularly important for the determination of its indirect tax burden. The occupation of the head of the household also does not seem to play any significant role in the differentiation of the indirect tax burden faced by different households. The coefficients for occupational groups are either not statistically significant or too small in magnitude to matter. The level of the indirect tax burden is negatively affected by the educational level of the household head, probably as a result of the lower incidence of smoking among educated people and the low tax rates on educational goods and services, likely to be more heavily consumed by this group.

To sum up, the modest degree of progressivity by expenditure groups of the indirect tax system in Greece suggested at the beginning is rather misleading. This progressivity is mainly due to the presence of high taxes on transport, borne by the wealthiest segments of the population. However, it has been suggested that car taxes should be considered as charges for using the road network, rather than pure taxes. Once these taxes are removed, the whole tax system displays mild regressivity features, since the other progressive taxes (e.g. on clothing) are not important enough to outweigh the effect of regressive taxes (e.g. on food, housing, tobacco, etc.). Even when car taxes are treated as pure taxes, it was shown that the reason why poorer households pay relatively less tax (at least until the seventh decile) is not the progressivity of the indirect tax system as such, but the fact that these households pay less tax on transport, precisely because they have fewer cars, on which high taxes are levied. Even among car owners, car taxes appear to be regressive, while indirect taxes among households without cars are roughly constant as a proportion of expenditure. This regressivity is eventually responsible for the non-sustainability of the mild progressivity features of the tax system towards the top of the expenditure distribution.

4.5 The effects of indirect taxation on the income distribution: a comparison with an equal-yield uniform tax

The evaluation of the effects of indirect taxation on income (or, in this case, expenditure) inequality demands the identification of the pre-tax and post-tax distribution. Furthermore, the comparison with a uniform equal-yield tax structure calls for the identification of a post-tax distribution corresponding to the uniform tax.

The post-tax distribution is the one which emerges after deducting indirect taxes paid from household expenditure, by analogy with the identification of disposable income as the after-tax income in the direct tax case. The identification of the pre-tax distribution is not straightforward. The relevant question is what the expenditure distribution would be in the absence of indirect taxation. This question has no direct answer. The general problem here is that it is hardly possible to make a satisfactory comparison of the actual situation where indirect taxes exist with a hypothetical situation of an economy without indirect taxes, since the parameters to be changed would be numerous (for example, consumer behaviour, the supply of goods and services by the state).

In so far as consumer behaviour is concerned, and in the absence of necessary data to simulate complicated behavioural responses, we can adopt the fairly simple assumption of constant expenditure, i.e. that households will spend the same amount on commodities under prices corresponding to different tax regimes and will only adjust the quantity bought so that the budget constraint is satisfied (this corresponds to a price elasticity of demand equal to -1). Under this assumption, the situation without taxes would correspond to the recorded expenditure patterns of households before indirect taxes are subtracted.

The additional complications arising from assuming that no indirect taxes are levied and the respective government revenue is foregone can be avoided by introducing the equal-yield uniform indirect tax structure. For a family of expenditure distributions corresponding to a system of uniform indirect taxation, the recorded inequality would be the same irrespective of the rate of this uniform tax (the rate of zero corresponds to no indirect taxes) for any mean-independent inequality measure. For such measures, the expenditure distribution as recorded in the HES, before indirect taxes are subtracted, is equivalent in terms of inequality (but not welfare) to a system of uniform indirect taxation, which is distributionally neutral (the uniform rate can be chosen so as to satisfy the equal-yield requirement).[10] One can therefore approximate the inequality displayed by the expenditure distribution under the assumption of no indirect taxes or uniform equal-yield indirect taxes with the inequality displayed by the expenditure distribution before indirect taxes are subtracted. It is precisely the expenditure distribution before indirect taxes are subtracted that will be called the uniform tax distribution. If this distribution is more unequal than the expenditure distribution that one gets after subtracting the indirect taxes actually paid, then one can deduce that the existing system is playing a positive redistributive role.[11]

It should be noted that the comparison made here is one of 'differential incidence analysis' (the term was introduced by Musgrave, 1959), in which the changes in the income distribution resulting from substituting one tax system with another are analysed and where both systems produce the same yield, and the level and composition of other parts of the budget are held constant. This methodology in conjunction with the crucial full tax shifting assumption allows the comparison of stable steady states, but neglects the possibility that changes in the indirect tax system might induce a change in the behaviour of the economy. This possibility has been much more widely appreciated in the macroeconomic literature (Blanchard and Fischer, 1993; Ordover and Phelps, 1979; Flemming, 1987).

The results appear in Figures 4.5 and 4.6 and suggest that the Greek indirect tax system has an equalising effect on the expenditure distribution, at least to judge by the dominance of the actual post-tax Lorenz curve over the uniform tax Lorenz curve.[12] Even though the two Lorenz curves in both figures are very close, they do not intersect. The robustness of this result is reinforced by the unanimous decrease in inequality according to all inequality measures employed (see Table 4.5). In spite of the fact that there is a clear move towards equality as the result of the imposition of the actual indirect tax system as compared to a distributionally neutral one, the change towards equality is very small in magnitude. This change is even smaller in the case where only non-durable expenditure and taxes on the latter are considered.

Having already established in the previous section the importance of car

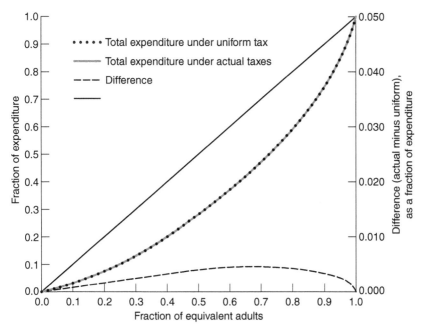

Figure 4.5 Lorenz curves for the distribution of total expenditure under the actual indirect tax system and under a uniform system
Note: The difference is measured on the right axis.

taxes on determining the progressivity features of the indirect tax system, it is worth investigating how the redistributive effects of the system alter if taxes on cars and their circulation[13] are taken out of the picture. The results appear in Figures 4.7 and 4.8 (constructed similarly to Figures 4.5 and 4.6) and reveal that the indirect tax system acts in an unambiguously adverse way as far as the equalisation of expenditure is concerned. The Lorenz curve under uniform taxes corresponds to a more equitable distribution than the one corresponding to the actual tax distribution. Again the two curves do not intersect, indicating an unambiguous ranking.

Even when total taxes and expenditure are considered, it is interesting to note that the replacement of the present complicated, and thus inefficient, indirect tax structure with a uniform equal-yield one, only marginally worsens the income distribution, as is apparent in Table 4.5 and Figure 4.5. Results are even less encouraging when car taxes are excluded from the analysis, see Figure 4.7. In reality, uniformity is a theoretical benchmark, rather than a desirable applicable alternative. The results, however, point to the potential for simplifying the present indirect tax structure.

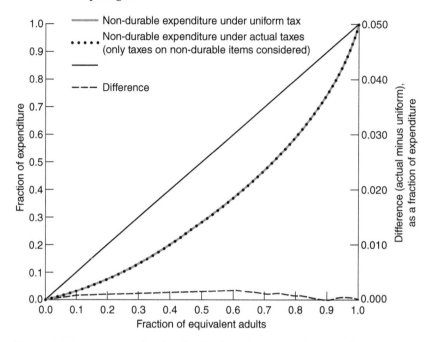

Figure 4.6 Lorenz curves for the distribution of non-durable expenditure under the actual indirect tax system and under a uniform system
Note: The difference is measured on the right axis.

4.6 Conclusions

This chapter has examined the redistributive aspects of indirect taxation in Greece after Greece's accession to the EU in 1981, using tax microsimulation methods. The results are important both for policy-makers and the general public, given the increased dependence of Greek governments on tax revenue collection as a principle means of complying with the EU macroeconomic directives and the amount of indirect tax collected.

From a methodological perspective, this research is innovative in that it has applied microsimulation techniques to a new data set and, furthermore, it has adjusted these techniques to simulate a far more complex tax structure, thus comprising an interesting modelling exercise.

The results reveal that the 'at first sight' apparent mild progressivity of the Greek indirect tax system is misleading and closer inspection unravels a much less favourable story. Taxes on private means of transport and their circulation are rendered responsible for the characterisation of the whole system as mildly progressive. However, there are theoretical arguments which would lead to their removal from the tax calculations on the grounds

Table 4.5. *Present system of indirect taxes vs a uniform system of indirect taxes: a comparison of inequality measures*

Inequality measure	Uniform ind.tax: all commodities	Actual ind.tax system: all commodities	Percentage reduction in inequality	Uniform ind.tax: non-dur comm.	Actual ind.tax system: non-dur comm.	Percentage reduction in inequality
Relative mean deviation (M)	0.464	0.454	2.2	0.439	0.437	0.5
Coefficient of variation (c_v)	0.681	0.667	2.1	0.642	0.641	0.2
Logarithmic variance (v)	0.385	0.369	4.2	0.345	0.338	2.0
Variance of logarithms (v_l)	0.354	0.340	4.0	0.319	0.313	1.9
Gini coefficient (G)	0.326	0.320	1.8	0.310	0.308	0.6
Atkinson ($\varepsilon=0.5$) $A_{0.5}$	0.086	0.083	3.5	0.078	0.077	1.3
Atkinson ($\varepsilon=1$) A_1	0.162	0.156	3.7	0.147	0.145	1.4
Atkinson ($\varepsilon=2$) A_2	0.300	0.290	3.3	0.276	0.271	1.8
Atkinson ($\varepsilon=5$) A_5	0.600	0.586	2.3	0.575	0.564	1.9
Theil index (T)	0.183	0.176	3.8	0.164	0.163	0.6
Theil index (N)	0.179	0.172	3.9	0.161	0.159	1.2
Robin Hood index (RHI)	0.232	0.227	2.2	0.220	0.218	0.9

Source: Kaplanoglou (1999); NSSG (1994).

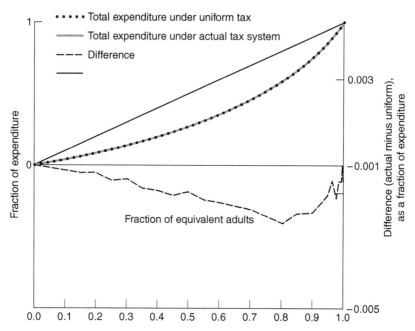

Figure 4.7 Lorenz curves for the distribution of total expenditure under the actual indirect tax system and under a uniform system (excluding car taxes)

that they consist of road user charges rather than pure taxes. This would leave the regressive parts of the tax system dominating the overall pattern.

Even if car taxes are considered pure taxes, it was shown that the fact that poorer households pay relatively less tax is not the outcome of an indirect tax system which is progressive overall, but is due to the fact that these households do not own a car and therefore are not liable to the high car taxes. Splitting the HES sample into car and non-car owners has shown that indirect taxes are regressive in both subsamples (even car taxes are regressive in the car owners' subsample) and it is only the mixing of the two subsamples that creates the picture of mild progressivity.

The importance of car taxes has also become apparent when evaluating the effects of the actual indirect tax system on the income distribution as compared to a uniform equal-yield one. When car taxes were included in the calculations, the after-tax Lorenz curve of the prevailing system clearly dominates the curve corresponding to the hypothetical distributionally-neutral one, and the decrease in a wide range of inequality measures was uniform. Exclusion of car taxes on theoretical grounds led to a complete reversal of results.

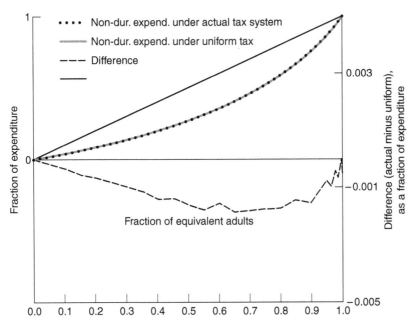

Figure 4.8 Lorenz curves for the distribution of non-durable expenditure under the actual indirect tax system and under a uniform system (excluding car taxes)

The government in fact has several policy instruments for redistributing resources, the indirect tax system being just one. Thus, it might well be the case that it is not concerned with the existence of a regressive indirect tax system, because it uses the latter as a revenue raising device, while it redistributes income through the expenditure side of the budget or through a progressive income tax schedule. Whether this is the case will be the object of a future research which will include all the parts of the existing tax and transfer system and prospects for potential restructuring of these parts. However, given that about two-thirds of total tax revenue come from commodity taxation, any adverse impact of indirect taxation cannot be overturned at low cost (for example, a strongly progressive income tax schedule might have adverse effects on labour supply). What this research has firmly established is that the fact that the replacement of the present complex indirect tax structure with a uniform equal-yield one only marginally worsens the income distribution is a strong argument for either simplifying the existing tax structure or retargeting the system so that the efficiency costs of its complexity are outbalanced by the equity gains of an improved redistributive role.[14]

Notes

I am deeply grateful to David Newbery for supervising this research, to Vassilis Rapanos and Manolis Drettakis for valuable discussions and suggestions and to Holly Sutherland and Lavinia Mitton for very helpful comments. Financial support from the British Economic and Social Research Council under Contract R00429514173 of the Postgraduate Research Studentships programme and from the Commission of the European Communities under Contract ERBFMBI-CT95–0291 of the Marie Curie Fellowship programme is gratefully acknowledged. The usual disclaimers apply.

1 For a useful review of microsimulation models in Europe, see Sutherland (1995).
2 Household consumption includes purchases, consumption of own production, imputed rent for owner-occupied accommodation and consumption of income in kind, all evaluated at market prices. Only purchases are assumed to bear indirect taxes.
3 VAT was levied at four rates: 3% for a limited range of commodities considered as merit goods (e.g. books, newspapers and theatres), 6% for necessities covering around 40% of the budget (e.g. foodstuffs, pharmaceutical products, heating oil etc.), 16% for a wide range of goods and services representing around 30% of the household budget (e.g. clothing, household durables and non-durables, telephone etc.) and a high rate of 36% imposed on luxury, semi-luxury or de-merit products (e.g. spirits, tobacco, cameras and photographic equipment, motor fuel and so on). Finally, several services were tax exempt, for example, the services of doctors and hospitals, education, water supply, legal services.
4 Excise duties were not uniform across all petroleum products. The government made an effort to place heavier taxes on products used by final consumers and lower ones on those mainly used by producers or intermediate consumers (primarily industrial users) in an attempt to minimise the deadweight loss incurred by the taxation of production inputs. Finally, it should be noted that the flat rate excise duty on petrol used in these studies is a weighted average for the period 1/1/87–31/10/88. The change in the petrol excises reflected the policy of 'stable retail prices' followed by Greek governments since the second oil crisis and during the 1980s, in an attempt to control the distortionary effects of the changes in the world price of oil on the domestic economy, which is highly dependent on oil imports.
5 The regulatory tax was imposed on imported products for a limited period (1984–1989) in order to prevent adverse shocks to the trade balance resulting from the abolition of a large number of taxes applying to imports. The abolition of any additional taxes on imports was imposed by the EC as part of the 'equal terms of competition' policies.
6 The consolidated special consumption tax was introduced in 1984 with the aim of replacing a large number of taxes on luxury products (e.g. alcohol, photographic cameras).
7 The collection of all the necessary information to complete such an analysis has been a particularly burdensome task. Although there have been several

attempts to describe the Greek indirect tax system, these attempts are far from giving a description of tax rates and tax bases detailed enough to be applied to the entire range of commodity groupings recorded in the HES. Furthermore, the legislation concerning different taxes is scattered in time and in legislative texts, and different indirect taxes are administered by different departments of the Ministry of Finance. Thus, the description of the indirect tax system inherent in the analysis is the outcome of the time-consuming process of gathering information from several pieces of legislation and from discussions with numerous employees from various departments of the Ministry of Finance and the State Chemical Laboratory.

8 In fact, taxes on food items are even more regressive taking into account the effects of the Common Agricultural Policy on the prices of agricultural products, which have not been incorporated here.

9 The indirect tax burden of households without cars also declines in the highest deciles and this reinforces the reversal of any progressivity features.

10 Note that one would still have to assume unit price elasticity.

11 This approach is also followed in other similar studies (see, for example, Decoster *et al.,* 1997; Yitzhaki, 1994). The same methodology is implicit in the estimation of the redistributive effect of indirect taxation by the Office for National Statistics in the UK, which is published yearly in *Economic Trends,* where income inequality before and after indirect taxes are subtracted is compared.

12 To be consistent with the previous analysis, the distribution of expenditure is derived by assigning the value of expenditure per equivalent adult (using the OECD scale) to each equivalent adult in the household.

13 Taxes on cars and their circulation include taxes on vehicles, spare parts, petrol, car insurance, transport dues etc.

14 For an analysis of the plausibility and desirability of such a policy option, see Kaplanoglou (1999).

5 Can we do better comparative research using microsimulation models? Lessons from the micro-analysis of pensions systems

Katherine Rake

5.1 The problem of comparative research

The opportunities afforded by cross-national comparison of social policy are numerous. In any one policy field, the international arena will demonstrate a broad spectrum of policy responses. This gives academics and policy-makers a concrete indication of the range of policy options available and opens up the possibility of learning policy lessons 'from abroad'. Looking comparatively across national welfare states also raises questions about the link between particular welfare state arrangements and welfare outcomes. What explains the low level of income inequality in welfare state A, or high levels of female poverty in welfare state B? How do welfare states with similar institutional structures produce different outcomes and, equally, how is it that similar outcomes can follow from quite distinct welfare state structures? Which features of the national welfare state are important in explaining a given outcome? Is a given outcome attributable to the welfare state or is it a result of national patterns of individual behaviour and broader socio-economic conditions? When conducting comparative research, it becomes quickly apparent that answering such questions is a complex process. Those searching for simple rules which link the level of spending and the effectiveness of the welfare state in targeting the most needy or which link the institutional form of particular benefit types (e.g. the use of social insurance) and the effectiveness and generosity of coverage of recipients will quickly be deceived.

The challenge in establishing links between welfare state provision and individual outcomes arises because such outcomes are a product both of the nature of welfare state provision and of the context in which that welfare state operates. Even for national studies, the impact of a particular policy change cannot be truly isolated when it is accompanied by changes in individual behaviour or the broader socio-economic context. Comparative, cross-national studies come with such problems built in: the national welfare state both shapes and responds to national patterns of labour market participation, fertility, nuptiality etc. Further, the national welfare state operates in a broader national socio-economic context, with national levels of employment, growth, inflation etc. also having a determining influence on welfare outcomes. Put simply, the problem of comparative research is one of too much variation. For comparability to be enhanced so that analysis of the distributive impact of the welfare state can take place, some of this variation needs to be eliminated.

One way of stripping out some real world complexity in order to see more clearly the distributive impact of policy is through microsimulation modelling (similar applications of microsimulation modelling in the national context are made by Johnson and Webb, 1993; Redmond et al., 1998; for cross-national applications see Atkinson et al., 1988; De Lathouwer, 1996). In this paper I present the Micro Analysis of Pension Systems (MAPS), a microsimulation model of the incomes of the older population in three welfare states (Britain, France and Germany) which I use to examine the impact of policy on the differentials between the incomes of women and men in old age. The model individuals used in MAPS are drawn from a representative sample of a cohort of older British individuals, with the survey providing rich information on lifetime labour market participation, marriages, number and timing of children. From this lifetime data, we can simulate pension and other benefit entitlements and tax liabilities of the individuals according to the three national policy regimes. By holding constant all factors bar the structure and mechanisms of the three national welfare states, we can make cross-national comparisons of the distributive impact of policy regimes with greater ease.[1]

Of course, this comparability is achieved at a cost. In holding all other factors constant, we ignore the impact of national-level differences in lifetime labour market participation on the distribution of income *and* the way in which policy, and other macro-level variables, shape national patterns of micro-level behaviour. Further, as with many microsimulation models, this simplifying exercise moves us beyond the bounds of reality and, in so doing, we lose claims to true national representativeness. However, as I hope to show below, what we gain is an understanding of the distinct distributive impact of three complex sets of policies, an understanding which would be difficult to grasp using real national-level data. What is more, this exercise has an advantage over a commonly used alternative in comparative research – the analysis of the impact of several national sets of policies on a set of hypothetical individuals or families (see, for example, Bradshaw et al., 1993; Bradshaw, 1995; Evans, 1996; Johnson and Rake, 1998). Such an exercise works on similar principles to MAPS – by using the same hypothetical cases, micro-level behaviour is held constant so that cross-national comparisons of the impact of policy can more easily be made. Whilst this method of comparison has its uses, and has the advantage of being relatively quick and easy to perform, limitations also arise because of the representativeness of the hypothetical cases chosen (Atkinson and Sutherland, 1983). The ability to perform any kind of analysis of the distributive impact of the national welfare state using only a few hypothetical cases is obviously limited – one cannot estimate the mean position from the outcomes of the hypothetical cases, with any more complex analysis ruled out. In contrast, the model individuals in MAPS are drawn from representative data (and are not simply a construct of the researcher) and embody a broad range of lifetime experiences with which we can conduct detailed analysis of the distribution.

The remainder of this paper uses MAPS to illustrate the application of microsimulation modelling to a particular field of comparative inquiry. In section 5.2, I offer a description of the structure of MAPS. The output of the model can be analysed in a great number of ways, but I here focus on two types of analysis that illustrate best the use of the model in comparative analysis: in Section 5.3 some specific features of the pension systems (the link between earnings and pension and the operation of pension credits) are examined and this is followed by an assessment of the impact of changing life-course scenarios on the distribution of simulated income under the three national regimes (section 5.4).

5.2 Simulating incomes in old age using MAPS

MAPS was built with the specific aim of exploring the impact of national welfare state structures on income in old age. As such, the model allows us to:

- examine how three sets of national policy differentiate between individuals with identical sets of labour market patterns. What rewards/costs do national welfare states attach to different types of life course? Are some national policies more effective at equalising gender differences in lifetime behaviour than others?
- analyse the effect of particular policy mechanisms on the distribution of income in old age, and on the difference between women's and men's income;
- alter life-course patterns of individuals in the base data to see the impact on each national distribution of income.

An overview of the structure of MAPS is given in Figure 5.1 which represents the process of microsimulation as a number of discrete units which,

STAGE 1: Simulation common to all three countries

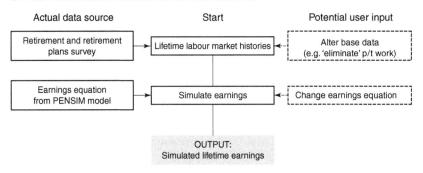

STAGE 2: Separate simulation for each country

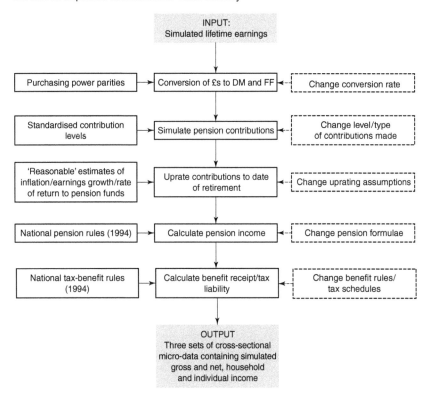

Figure 5.1 The structure of MAPS

once linked together as shown below, produces three micro-data sets containing information on simulated income arising from the British, French and German pension and tax–benefit systems (for all detailed descriptions of MAPS, see Rake, 1998). The figure illustrates both the data which underpin the simulation (the boxes on the left) and the actual processes undertaken in the microsimulation (the middle boxes), with the boxes on the right illustrating the ways in which the simulation process could be altered in order to conduct further model validation or to examine the effect of changing the assumptions built into MAPS.

As the figure shows, the first stage of the simulation was common to all three countries. The model individuals used in MAPS are drawn from a subsample of the 1988 British Retirement and Retirement Plans Survey (RRPS) which surveyed approximately 3,500 individuals aged 55 to 69 (or married to an individual in that age group) (OPCS, 1992). A subsample of individuals aged 65 or with a spouse aged over 65 were selected for use in MAPS and this left 1,718 model individuals (by selecting only those older than the statutory retirement age, the problem of having to simulate the remainder of the working life in order to calculate pension entitlement was avoided). The next stage – simulating earnings – is crucial to the simulation of income in old age as all national pension systems simulated here have some link to prior earnings. Earnings were based on the same regression equation used in PENSIM (Pudney, 1991; Hancock *et al.*, 1992),[2] and were simulated for the entire lifetime on the basis of the labour market histories recorded in RRPS. Data on lifetime earnings were then fed into Stage 2 of the model.

The first process in Stage 2 was to convert earnings which were recorded in pounds sterling into French francs and Deutschemarks using the purchasing power parities calculated by the OECD in 1994. The conversion factor for pounds into French francs was 10.33 and for pounds into Deutschemarks, 3.307 (OECD, 1994).[3] This conversion was necessary as some of the rules applied in the French and German simulations included absolute values (e.g. lower and upper earnings limits used by the social insurance systems). The next stage involved the simulation of contributions to different national pension schemes. A number of pension schemes were included in the simulation to reflect the diversity of pension provision in each country. For Britain, occupational and personal pensions were included alongside state provision in the form of the basic pension and the state earnings-related pension (SERPS). Data on patterns of membership of occupational/personal pensions were drawn from the RRPS. Characteristics of occupational pension schemes (whether or not contracted out; whether final salary or money purchase; contribution rates to money purchase schemes; accrual rates in final salary schemes etc.) were assigned using the Monte Carlo process on the basis of probabilities calculated from a cross-sectional survey of occupational schemes (Government Actuary Department, 1994). For France, basic regime (*Régime Générale*) and complementary regime (*Régimes Complémentaires*) pensions were simulated (with separate complementary regime pensions simulated for 'cadres' and 'non-cadres'). For basic regime pensions, contributions were simulated at the statutory level; for members of complementary regimes, some standardisation of contribution rates was necessary as actual contribution rates vary quite considerably between scheme members. For Germany, the social insurance pension (*Gesetzliche Rentenversicherung*) was the only pension scheme simulated, and contribution rates were simulated at the statutory level.

Where pension income was calculated according to previous earnings and/or according to the rate of return on a pension fund 'reasonable' estimates of the real rate of earnings growth and the real rate of return to a pension fund had to be made.[4] The rate of real earnings growth was set at 1.5% per annum with the real rate of return to a pension fund set at 3%. The next stage involved applying the rules concerning the calculation of pension income as they stood in 1994.[5] Finally, entitlement to other benefits (notably means-tested social assistance) was calculated for model individuals as was their individual or joint tax liability. The principal characteristics of the three national level simulations are summarised in Table 5.1.

As with all microsimulation models, MAPS has limitations which need to be fully examined. By drawing its model individuals from a British survey of older individuals, MAPS captures any behavioural responses made by this cohort to the prevailing British welfare system. These individuals are then suspended from real time and space, as they are passed through three different welfare systems as they stood in 1994. Being a static model, MAPS does not simulate behavioural responses – for example, MAPS individuals cannot re-enter the labour market in response to a low pension income resulting from one set of national rules. In consequence, even though the base data in MAPS are extracted from real British life-courses, the data generated by the simulation are illustrative of the functioning of the welfare regimes but do not perfectly represent either current or future cohorts of older individuals in any of the three countries. Although the data are not synthetic, the model individuals exist in hypothetical time and space in a simulation which operates as if their characteristics were universal across countries, with their life-courses occurring instantaneously under the pension and broader tax–benefit regimes according to 1994 legislation. As MAPS does not replicate either the current or the future distribution of income in Britain, France or Germany, any external validation of the results

Table 5.1. *Principal characteristics of the three national-level simulations*

Britain

Pension schemes included in simulation	National Insurance basic pension SERPS Final salary and money purchase occupational pensions Private pensions
Other sources of income	Earnings Income Support

Main assumptions	Standardised contribution rates and
	    rates of return for money purchase
	    occupational pensions and personal
	    pensions
	Standard levels of administrative
	    charges and annuity rates applied
	100% take up of income support

France

Pension schemes included in simulation	Basic regime pension (*Régime Générale*)
	Complementary regime pension
	    (*Régimes Complémentaires*) –
	        ARRCO for non-cadres
	        AGIRC for cadres

Other sources of income	Earnings Minimum pension (*Minimum vieillesse*) Social assistance to the unemployed

Main assumptions	All individuals in employment
	    contribute to basic and
	    complementary regime pension
	Standardised contribution rates for
	    complementary regime pensions
	'Cadres' corresponds to the Registrar
	    General's classification of social class I
	100% take up of minimum pension and
	    other forms of social assistance

Germany

Pension schemes included in simulation	Social insurance pension (*Gesetzliche Rentenversicherung*)
Other sources of income	Earnings Social assistance (*Sozialhilfe*)

Main assumptions	Index of average earnings of pension
	    scheme members (ARW) accurately
	    reflects the rise in earnings
	100% take up of social assistance

would be impossible to achieve. The simulation belies the complexity of the accumulation of pension rights in the real world – in reality, individuals acquire entitlements to a pension and other benefits over their lifetime with the real distribution of income in old age reflecting the accretion of rights from a number of systems. The desire to look at only one set of rules per country means that for this exercise such complexity was ruled out.

The output of MAPS also suffers similar drawbacks to those of real cross-sectional data. As a cross-section, MAPS is not suited for the analysis of income dynamics in the period of retirement. Further, some income components are missing from MAPS data. For all countries, I decided to omit investment income and housing costs and benefits, with the German occupational pension tier also absent.[6] The level of survivor's pension was an income component for which direct estimation could not be made, as the data set did not contain information about the labour market histories of deceased spouses, on which, in all three countries, survivor's entitlement was based. Whilst the simulation could have omitted the survivor's pension, this would have produced unrealistic results, especially for widows who are heavily dependent on such benefits. Instead, the first round of the MAPS simulation was used to calculate the mean pension income of all married men with a separate estimate made for all married women. A standardised level of widow's and widower's pension was then imputed to those who met national conditions of entitlement, with distinctions made only on the basis of the sex of the recipient. The use of mean entitlement will underestimate inequality amongst widows: widows of low-earning males with an earlier than average mortality and richer widows, who in France and Germany in particular benefit from the strong earnings link of their spouses' entitlements, will be under-represented in the simulated data.[7] In all other respects, simulated income was as complete as possible, and included means-tested social assistance benefits alongside pensions and earnings, although it was necessary to use some simplifying assumptions in the simulations. Inevitably, such practice runs the risk of introducing errors specific to the different national runs, meaning that the final national level results may be distorted in quite distinct ways. For this reason, we should be cautious about making direct cross-national comparisons of the absolute levels of income of individuals or groups of individuals. Even with such a restriction, there remains plenty of scope to analyse the fortunes of groups of individuals relative to other model individuals where simulated income is produced by the same national run.

5.3 Using microsimulation to analyse features of the pension system

This section examines the distributive impact of two distinct policy mechanisms – the strength of the link between lifetime earnings and pension income, and the operation of pension credits given for time spent caring for children or adult dependants. These are key features of the pension system which we would expect to have an important impact on gender differentials in old age. In both cases, the mechanisms will be examined for their impact on income received by the individual. A measure of income at the individual level is preferred over a household measure, for a number of reasons. Individual income gives us the best indication of the returns which accrue to the individual in old age from their participation in the labour market. An individual measure of income may be more appropriate where there is a frequent dissolution of households and consequent individualisation of the life-course. Lastly, although many argue that a measure of individual income overlooks the welfare an individual derives from being a member of a certain household, questions have long been raised about whether full income sharing actually occurs within all households (see, for example, Davies and Joshi, 1994; Sutherland, 1997). The choice of an individual measure of income constrained my other choices – taxation in France and Germany occurs at the level of the household and, although we know the level of taxation, we cannot know from where taxation will be paid (or the incidence of taxation). Although it would have been possible to simulate the distribution of the burden of taxation, it was decided for this exercise to look instead at individual gross income.

The strength of the link between lifetime earnings and pension income is easily measured using the MAPS simulation. As all three national pension systems are based on the same earnings equation and same life-histories, the differences that arise between lifetime earnings and pensions directly reflect how far the pension system exaggerates, replicates or mitigates gender inequalities in earnings. To get a measure of the impact of the pension system on gender inequalities, we need first to assess the differences in women's and men's lifetime average earnings which feed into the simulation in the three countries. There is, of course, no one measure of lifetime average earnings: any time out of the labour market will mean that there is a difference between earnings averaged over periods in the labour market and averaged over periods when the individual is 'of working age' and, theoretically at least, available to participate in the paid labour market. This difference is likely to be particularly pronounced for women who, on average, experience more prolonged periods out of the labour market. In recognition of this, Table 5.2 gives us two measures of earnings: earnings averaged over periods in the paid labour market and earnings averaged over a theoretical working life of 49 years. For convenience, the table gives the value of earnings in pounds sterling; given that the earnings in each country are based on the same equation, the relative difference between women and men will be the same in each country.

Table 5.2. *Women's and men's simulated lifetime earnings (£s per week)[a]*

Earnings	Averaged over periods with earnings	Averaged over 49 years
Men	£206.7	£153.8
Women	£115.4	£45.7
Women's earnings as % of men's	55.8%	29.7%

[a] Discounted at the rate of simulated real earnings growth (1.5% per annum).
Source: MAPS, author's analysis.

Pension policies are in a unique position in being able retrospectively to compensate for (or exaggerate) gender differentials in lifetime earnings. As the figures in Table 5.2 suggest, gender differentials in lifetime earnings are large – a pension system which closely translates lifetime earnings into income in old age is bound to lead to poorer outcomes for women. The table also indicates that where pension entitlements are based on previous earnings, the period over which earnings are averaged is key, and averaging over shorter periods favours women disproportionately. If we compare relative mean pension income to the relative mean earnings presented in Table 5.2, we can get some measure of the impact of national pension policies on gender differentials. Where women's mean pension income is worth less than 29.7% of men's, the pension system is exaggerating gender differentials, as the outcome is poorer than under either measure of average lifetime earnings. Where women's mean pension falls close to 29.7% of men's, the pension system is simply reproducing gender differentials in lifetime earnings. If women's relative mean pension income falls between the two measures of earnings (29.7%–55.8%), the pension system offers some 'forgiveness' for time spent out of the labour market. Lastly, if women's mean pension income is worth more than 55.8% of men's, gender differentials in lifetime earnings have been mitigated, with greater degrees of equalisation of outcomes occurring the closer that women's average pension income comes to being worth 100% of men's.

Table 5.3 looks at simulated mean pension for women relative to men for all the systems simulated in the three countries. It shows large cross-national variation in the relative returns to women and men in the pension system. Of all systems, the British basic pension is unique in mitigating the inequality in lifetime earnings – the pensions gap between women and men is smaller than the gap between either measure of women and men's earnings. This is explained by the fact that, once individuals qualify for the basic pension, it pays out a flat-rate benefit regardless of previous earnings (the

Table 5.3. *Women's mean weekly
pension as a percentage of men's*

Britain	
Basic pension	70.6
SERPS	37.2
Occupational/personal pension	15.8
Total pension income	42.5
France	
Basic regime	30.6
Complementary regime	25.9
Total pension income	28.5
Germany	
Social insurance pension	29.2
Total pension income	29.2

Source: MAPS, author's analysis.

basic pension does not completely equalise gender differentials as the qualification criterion of having contributory years for nine-tenths of the working life remains more difficult for women to meet). The state earnings-related pension scheme (SERPS) offers some quite limited 'forgiveness' for periods spent out of the labour force: for all women, SERPS income is some 7.5% closer to men's SERPS income than earnings averaged over the life-course. This 'forgiveness' is explained by the operation of Home Responsibility Protection and by the existence of an upper and lower earnings limit which squashes the distribution of SERPS income relative to earnings. Averaged over all women, occupational and private pensions are worth a mere 15.8% of men's income from that source. The occupational/personal pension sector exaggerates gender inequality in earnings because of the gendered pattern of membership of these schemes. The patterns of membership of British occupational pension schemes is drawn from that recorded in the RRPS – over the lifetime of this cohort, only 23.2% of women had ever been members of an occupational or private pension scheme compared to 65.6% of men. (Contemporary cross-sectional data suggests that this position may improve somewhat for future cohorts of retirees, although gender differentials remain marked: of all full-time members of pension schemes, 37% are women, with 38% of female employees, compared to 56% of male, covered by occupational provision (OPCS, 1996, Table 8.2)). Given the very different distributive impact of different parts of the pension system, it is not surprising that the equalising influence of the basic pension is watered down when looking at the system as a whole – the average woman receives total pension income worth 42.5% of the average man, a smaller differential than that offered by lifetime earnings averaged over 49 years, but still some way off the differential in earnings averaged over periods of work.

As a whole, the French pension system comes close to simply reproducing gender differentials in lifetime earnings. There is, however, a slight difference between the impact of the different tiers of the pension system – the operation of credits and a ceiling and floor on pension income in the basic regime means that some very slight forgiveness is offered for periods out of the labour market. This contrasts with the complementary regime which exaggerates slightly the already highly unequal distribution of lifetime earnings. The poor return for women can be explained by restrictions on access to the privileged complementary schemes which serve the 'cadres' only, and by the high degree of earnings-relatedness of the scheme. Nevertheless, the complementary regime distinguishes itself from occupational pensions in Britain by being more inclusive, and therefore offering a significantly better return on average for all women.

Lastly, the German social insurance pension replicates closely gender differentials in lifetime earnings, although there appears to be some very slight 'forgiveness' for time spent out of the labour market. This shows that despite the operation of pension credits the German system operates a strong principle of equivalence between lifetime earnings and pension income, with the pension system operating as an extension of the differential rewards offered by the labour market (Clasen, 1997).

Looking at the magnitude of gender differentials in pension income is only one part of the story – women may be doing relatively well not because of their own high pension incomes, but because men are doing particularly poorly under a given pension system. To get some measure of this, Table 5.4 compares mean weekly pension to mean weekly earnings (with earnings averaged over periods in work), which offers a measure of the replacement rate that the pension affords.[8]

Looking cross-nationally, our attention is immediately drawn to the different value of pensions relative to earnings in each country. Relative pension income for men in France appears particularly high, with a very marked differential between the replacement rate which women and men receive. In contrast, the overall returns for men and women in the German scheme are low. This doubtless reflects on the inclusion of only one pension scheme in the German simulation and/or on errors specific to the German run of the simulation. It also draws our attention to the need for caution when comparing across pension schemes, and to the difficulties in ensuring that we compare like with like when the national mix of pensions

Table 5.4. *Mean weekly pension as a percentage of mean weekly earnings*

	Men	Women
Britain		
Basic pension	25.8	32.7
SERPS	13.6	9.0
Occupational/personal pension	24.5	7.0
Total pension income	63.9	48.7
France		
Basic regime	54.0	29.6
Complementary regime	42.3	19.6
Total pension income	96.3	49.1
Germany		
Social insurance pension	59.9	31.4
Total pension income	59.9	31.4

Source: MAPS, author's analysis.

is so different. There are good arguments for looking both at the pension scheme as a whole and for the performance of its component parts. However, different measures and a focus on different parts of the system inevitably produce different rankings of countries which, in turn, rule out simple conclusions about the relative performance of different national systems. For example, the relative position of German men (and to a lesser degree women) is very different if we compare it to the state sector in Britain (summing the basic pension and SERPS men's pension income is worth 39.4% of mean weekly income, and women's 41.7%) or to the basic regime in France.

Looking across schemes, we can see that the relatively low level of gender differentials produced by the British basic pension is, indeed, partly explained by the poor performance of the British pension for men (even if we sum the basic pension and SERPS, British men's replacement rate is lower than that of either the French basic regime pension or the social insurance pension, with the relatively strong position for British men overall explained by the addition of occupational/private pension income). The table also neatly demonstrates how caution should be exercised when judging the woman-friendliness of schemes: the German social insurance pension which offers little pro-female redistribution pays out a pension income relative to earnings which is only slightly less than that offered by the highly redistributive basic pension in Britain.

The second feature of the pension system to be examined using MAPS is that of pension credits. The systems of credit examined comprise:

> **Britain:** Home Responsibility Protection (HRP) is granted to those caring for children and in some instances dependent adults.[9] It affects entitlement to the basic pension and SERPS by crediting years into an individual's 'pension account'. For the basic pension the individual needs to have a minimum of 20 years of contributions, with HRP years acting as top-up years. For SERPS, final SERPS income is calculated as a fraction (20%) of earnings between the upper and lower earnings limit averaged over 49 years.[10] HRP reduces the number of years over which earnings are averaged.

> **France:** The credits simulated in the French system affect the calculation of the pension rate for the basic regime pension (the maximum pension rate being 50%, with final pension income based on the best 25 years of earnings up to the level of the social security ceiling). The pension rate is normally calculated according to the number of years of contributions that have been made (the full rate requires at least 40 years of contributions). The first type of credit ('baby gap' credit) is granted to mothers who have spent at least nine years out of the labour force caring for a child before its sixteenth birthday – such women are granted two years of contributions to their pension account. Manual workers who have raised three or more children receive a credit in the form of having their pension rate automatically set to the maximum 50% rate.

> **Germany:** For the German social insurance pension a maximum of three years of credits may be claimed per child. Unlike either British or French systems, these 'baby gap' credits add earnings to the individual's contribution record, and although the imputed earnings of 75% of average earnings seems to be a low value to attach to caring work, it may offer higher earnings than those carers would have been able to command in the labour market.[11]

MAPS is a valuable resource for analysing and quantifying the impact of credits. Without MAPS, it would be very difficult to estimate the impact of credits because of lack of suitable longitudinal data and/or because the credits have been introduced relatively recently, so that their impact has not fed through to the current generation of retirees.

Table 5.5. *The coverage of credits (all women)*

	Pension	Credit type	% of women receiving credit	Mean duration of credit (years)	Credit years as % of total years
Britain	Basic pension	HRP	77.5	13.8	39.5
	SERPS	HRP	77.5	13.8	39.5
France	Basic regime	Baby gap	57.6	4.4	17.0
	Basic regime	Manual workers	23.7	n/a	n/a
Germany	Social insurance pension	Baby gap	77.8	3.1	11

Source: MAPS, author's analysis.

The simulated coverage of women by the credit system in the three countries is presented in Table 5.5. Comparing the systems, we can see that credits affect a great number of women in each country. A full three-quarters of all women in the German and British simulations receive credits, while their more restrictive eligibility criteria of French 'baby gap' credits is reflected in its more limited coverage, while credits for manual workers cover less than a quarter of all women. In terms of the average number of years credited, the relative generosity of British HRP provision in terms of years is notable, with credited years contributing 39.5% of the total time women with credits spend within the National Insurance system. As the rules would suggest, the strict time limits operating on 'baby gap' credits in France and Germany mean that they are considerably less generous in terms of years covered – even so, these credited years make up a fair percentage of the total years that women spend within the pension system.

Table 5.6 offers some measures of the value of these credits for those women covered by credits. To isolate the impact of credits it was assumed, rather unrealistically, that no substitution of income would occur between the pension system and the rest of the benefit system. In reality, of course, the loss of credits and consequent loss of income would mean that many women receiving credits would source income from elsewhere, notably from means-tested benefits. However, in order to measure the impact of credits, they were assumed to operate in isolation from the rest of the benefit system. The first column presents the absolute monetary value of the credits. This was calculated by taking the difference between the average weekly pension with and without credits. The percentage change

Table 5.6. *The value of credits (mean for those women in receipt of credits)*

	Pension	Credit type	Absolute value of credits (£ per week)	% change in income if credits w'drawn	Credits as % of mean gross income
Britain	Basic pension	HRP	20.3	−45.2	18.3
	SERPS	HRP	3.5	−40.0	3.2
France	Basic regime	Baby gap	5.6	−27.7	3.8
	Basic regime	Manual workers	15.1	−50.0	10.3
Germany	Social insurance pension	Baby gap	7.5	−24.4	8.0

Source: MAPS, author's analysis.

in income following the withdrawal of the credit is given in the next column. The value of the credits relative to total gross individual income of the whole MAPS sample is given in the last column – this measure is necessary as, even if credits make a large contribution to the income of those in receipt of credits, these are amongst the poorest groups within the MAPS sample, and credits may not be deemed generous by any broader standard.

Looking firstly at HRP, the contribution of the credits to entitlement to the basic pension has the highest value cross-nationally of all measures. HRP coverage for SERPS appears less generous, reflecting the relatively small part that SERPS contributes to the income of the average older individual. The absolute value of HRP credits to SERPS is lowest of all credits examined here; even so, if HRP were to be withdrawn, there would be a large reduction in SERPS income for those women covered by credits.

In France, 'baby gap' credits are only marginally more generous than HRP coverage of SERPS, with the credit worth less than 4% of average gross income. In contrast, credits to manual workers are worth in absolute terms almost three times as much as those covering 'baby gaps'. Whether or not this is the conscious intent of French pension policy, the relative value of these two credits suggests that the perceived cost arising from having taken time out of the labour market to undertake caring duties is considerably lower than the perceived cost arising from the combination of having been a manual labourer and raised a large family. It is also interesting to note that, of MAPS individuals, marginally more men (25.0%) than women (23.7%) are eligible to receive this more generous credit, reflecting the predominance of men in the manual classes.

Lastly, although 'baby gap' credits in the German system are the least generous in terms of years covered, the absolute weekly value of the credit is £7.50,[12] or 8% of overall mean gross income, higher than the value of either HRP coverage of SERPS or the French 'baby gap' credits. While strict time limits on 'baby gap' credits constrain the value of the German crediting system in terms of years, their monetary value is ensured by the crediting of earnings into an individual's account. In this the German system contrasts with either British HRP coverage of SERPS or the French 'baby gap' credit. These latter credits only add years into the pension account so that the value of the credit depends crucially upon earnings in non-credited periods. The value of these credits is kept at a 'naturally' low level by the fact that those who have gained credits by undertaking unpaid caring labour frequently command low wages on their return to the labour market.

5.4 'Playing God':[13] altering the life-course of model individuals

A further type of analysis which can be conducted through microsimulation is the alteration of the underlying life-courses of model individuals in order to assess the impact of changing micro-level behaviour on the distribution of income. In the case of income in old age, where entitlements are accumulated over a long period, it is particularly difficult to make estimates of the impact of behavioural change on the final distribution of income without a simulation of the entire working life. In this instance, there are obvious advantages in having a microsimulation model which incorporates completed labour market histories which can be altered at will.

As the analysis above suggests, the degree to which gender differentials in lifetime earnings are reproduced depends crucially on the operation of the pension system, although when looked at as a whole none of the pension systems goes very far towards fully equalising gender differentials. In this section, we can look at this issue from the opposite perspective – what would happen to gender differentials in old age if women and men's lifetime labour market participation was itself made more similar? Put crudely, if women's labour market participation was made to look more like men's, would their incomes also come closer to men's?

To conduct these alterations in lifetime behaviour it is necessary first to identify the differences between the lifetime behaviour of male and female model individuals. Looking at MAPS data[14] differences arise because:

1. Women are active in the labour market for fewer years;
2. When women engage in the labour market they do so for fewer hours per week;

3. In part as a consequence of 2, in part from occupational segregation and in part from pure earnings discrimination, women are paid less than men for their labour market work.

The process of 'playing God' with the data therefore involved alterations to each of these differences in lifetime labour market participation. The original simulated data were compared to a total of four altered life-course scenarios, with changes applied to the whole data set although, as expected, they had most effect on women's outcomes. The scenarios are:

Scenario 1: The time spent out of the labour market following the birth of a child is halved. In order to limit the application of this change to those who were absent from the labour market following the birth of a child, only those who had some spell of work in the nine months previous to child birth and returned to work more than six months after having a child were affected. Of all women in the MAPS data, 31.7% were affected by this change. Of the remainder of MAPS women, 17.5% were childless, 11.6% had withdrawn permanently from the labour market by the time that they had their first child, 1% had never participated in the labour market and 10.1% had returned to work in less than six months of each birth or had never registered a break from the labour market. The remainder failed to register a gap because they were not in work in the nine months previous to childbirth. For those mothers affected by this alteration, the average time spent out of the labour market was reduced from 11.1 years to 5.4 years. The extended years of labour market participation changed relative earnings between women and men only slightly, with women's earnings averaged over 49 years increased from 29.7% to 31.6% of men's mean earnings.

Scenario 2: Women and men's pay is equalised. This involved assigning to women the wages normally assigned to men who registered the same occupation within the same industrial sector (where women registered part-time periods, they were assigned identical part-time wages as men in the same sector). The elimination of the earnings differential increased women's mean earnings (averaged over periods in work) from 55.8% to 81.9% of men's. The remaining 18% differential is a function of the gender segregation of the labour force (including women's greater propensity to undertake part-time work) which remains unchanged in this scenario. Using the hypothetical working life of 49 years, the increase in women's mean earnings is less dramatic, with a rise from 29.7% to 43.5% of men's mean earnings.

Table 5.7. *Women's mean gross individual income as a percentage of men's under three different life-course scenarios*

	Original data	Halved 'baby gap'	Equal pay	No part time work	All scenarios combined
Britain	52.1	53.0	61.1	60.0	67.9
France	39.9	43.5	51.2	46.1	60.7
Germany	39.3	41.8	51.8	48.1	61.7

Source: MAPS, author's analysis.

Scenario 3: Part-time working is eliminated. This involved imputing full-time earnings to those periods registered as part-time, with a separate equation maintained for male and female workers. This changed women's mean income less on average: women's earnings averaged over the actual working life were increased from 55.8% to 72.1% of men's, whilst earnings averaged over a hypothetical life course of 49 years rose from 29.7% to 37.4% of men's.

Scenario 4: Lastly, it was decided to run all three of the above scenarios simultaneously to see the combined effect on women and men's earnings and income in old age. Under this scenario, women's mean earnings when in work rose from 55.8% to 95.2% of men's, with earnings averaged over 49 years rising from 29.7% to 48.3%. The fact that, even with these dramatic changes in the life-course, earnings averaged over a whole working life did not reach 50% of men's earnings, reflects the enduring impact of women's shorter working lives.

The impact of these changes on the ratio between women and men's income in old age is given in Table 5.7. As this table demonstrates, the absolute and relative impact of these scenarios varies cross-nationally. Eliminating the earnings differential between women and men appears to have the largest effect overall in each country: in France and Germany, this change increases the relative fortunes of women by more than 10%; in Britain, the increase is somewhat less dramatic, but still the largest of any one scenario. The impact of this change is very closely followed by the impact of 'eliminating' part-time work; indeed in Britain, the effect of eliminating earnings differentials and doing away with part-time work is almost identical. In Britain the halving of time spent out of the labour market after child birth does not make a significant difference in women's average income. Halving the 'baby gap' does make a significant difference to women's average income in France and Germany; however, the impact of this change is considerably smaller than the changes in other scenarios. From a policy perspective, these finding have interesting implications. For pensions in Germany and France, the impact of a reduction in the 'baby gap' on pension income is equivalent to the extension of the period of pension credits for 'baby gap' years. For the average woman, at least, this does not appear to have a great effect on final pension income, suggesting that other policies, such as encouraging equal pay between women and men or loosening the link between earnings and final pension income may be better suited to addressing the pensions gap between women and men. It is also interesting to note from the table that, apart from the elimination of part-time work in the British simulation, none of these scenarios taken individually increases an average woman's income to much more than 50% of men's. Even when all scenarios are combined, women's income is raised to approximately 60% of men's in France and Germany, and just under 70% in Britain. Given the radical nature of the changes incorporated in the different scenarios, this is a rather surprising (and depressing!) finding, which would suggest that even more far-reaching changes would need to take place before the differential in women and men's incomes in old age was reduced.

Table 5.7 only gives an indication of the impact of the changing scenarios on the average woman. Figure 5.2 plots the change in gross income for each quintile of women under the alternative scenarios (with quintiles determined according to gross individual income of women), and reveals that the impact of these different scenarios is not evenly distributed between women. (Note that the different magnitude of impact of these changes means that the figures for the three countries are plotted on different scales.)

What is immediately striking about the figure is that the impact of changing life-course on the poorest quintile, Q1, is considerable in all three countries, especially France and Germany. In France, the conversion of part-time to full-time periods of work means that the poorest quintile more than double their income, while all scenarios combined cause an increase in income of 261.4%. For the poorest quintile in Germany, the impact is of a similar nature, but of a slightly lesser magnitude, with the halving of the 'baby gap' increasing the income of the poorest quintile of women by 30.5% compared to France's 71.0%. Even so, under the German simulation the elimination of part-time work almost doubles the income of the poorest quintile of women. For Britain, the impact of the changes on the poorest quintile is of a lesser magnitude, with halving the 'baby gap' having a notably small impact, but still the three scenarios combined cause a doubling of women's incomes in the lowest quintile.

(a) Britain

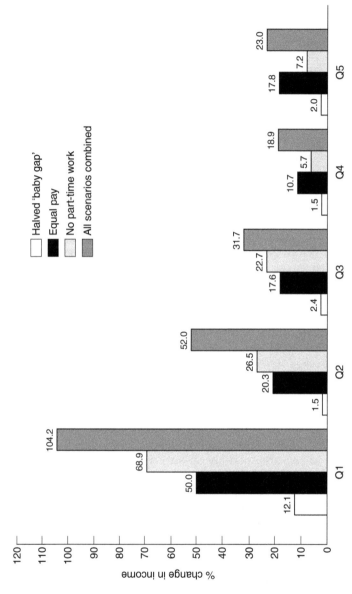

Figure 5.2 Change in women's income by income quintile following alterations to the life-course

(b) France

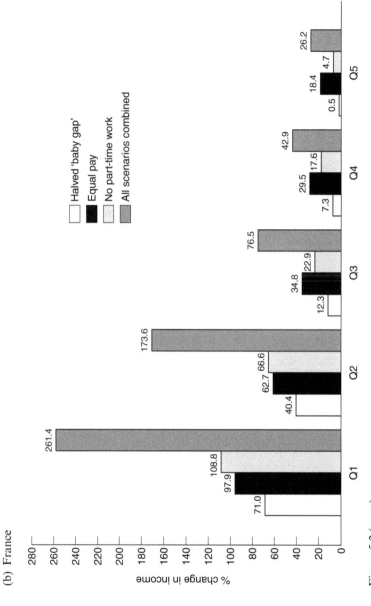

Figure 5.2 (*cont.*)

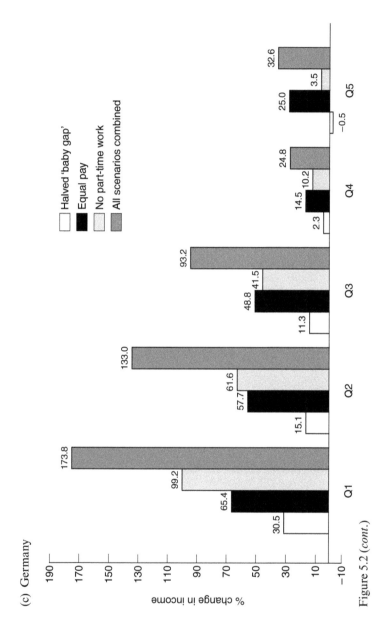

(c) Germany

Legend:
- Halved 'baby gap'
- Equal pay
- No part-time work
- All scenarios combined

Q1: 30.5, 65.4, 99.2, 173.8
Q2: 15.1, 57.7, 61.6, 133.0
Q3: 11.3, 48.8, 41.5, 93.2
Q4: 2.3, 14.5, 10.2, 24.8
Q5: -0.5, 25.0, 3.5, 32.6

% change in income

Figure 5.2 (*cont.*)

Across the remaining quintiles, the impact of changing life scenarios is less dramatic, with the relative importance of the changes shifting as we move up the quintiles. The richer MAPS women tend not to have worked part-time, to have remained childless or to have taken only a limited period of time out of the labour market following child birth. It is therefore not surprising that neither halving the 'baby gap' nor changing part-time to full-time periods has much effect on income on the richer quintiles. For the very richest quintile in each country it is, instead, the elimination of earnings differentials which causes the most important change in income. (Interestingly, for the richest quintile in Germany the reduction in time out following child birth actually reduces the income of the richest quintile of women which suggests that, even for this quintile, pension credits of 75% of average earnings may be of a greater value than the wages that those women would themselves command in the labour market.)

Across countries, changing life-course scenarios has an impact of a different magnitude, each affecting the relative income of women across the quintiles in a distinct way. This clearly demonstrates that, within existing policy regimes, no single prescription for a reduction in gender differentials in outcomes will hold true either across countries or for different women within the same country. For example, Figure 5.2 suggests that in France a policy of more generous 'baby gap' credits might have a significant impact on the poorest women whilst in Britain, its overall impact, in the context of already generous provision, would be limited. Better protection and credits for periods of part-time work would be needed if one wished to target the poorest women; for those further up the income quintiles, a reduction in earnings differentials or alternatively a weakening of the earnings–pension link might be more effective. Again, it would have been impossible to conduct such analysis on the basis of real data. In 'playing God' with the data, microsimulation modelling of the sort conducted by MAPS can be used to analyse the interaction of lifetime behaviour and income in old age. This type of modelling may be of use for policy-makers and academics in understanding how projected, or desired, changes in behaviour will affect income in old age, an event that takes place on a time horizon which is frequently beyond the reach of more traditional forms of analysis.

5.5 Conclusions

In this chapter I have set out to illustrate a number of uses which microsimulation might be put to when conducting comparative research. In terms of solving the problem of comparative research, we can use microsimulation to strip out some cross-national variation in order to make comparison more manageable. In so doing, we are, of course, creating a fiction but this fiction may be necessary for the kind of analysis of the distributive impact of policy conducted here. Microsimulation modelling appears to be a particularly useful tool when considering specific policy mechanisms adopted in different forms across countries (in a similar vein, see Atkinson *et al.*, 1988 for a comparison of the French and British tax system). MAPS allowed for the quantification of two important mechanisms of the pension systems in operation in Britain, France and Germany. By holding lifetime earnings and labour market histories of individuals constant, we clearly saw the effect of national pension systems in exaggerating, replicating or mitigating the earnings differential between women and men. With the exception of the British basic pension, and to a more limited extent SERPS, there was evidence that, despite pension credits, pensions strongly reward earnings and, possibly more importantly, time spent in the labour market. As such, with the exceptions mentioned, pensions rarely reflect women's relative earnings when they are in the labour market, with women bearing, in the majority of cases, the full cost of time spent out of the labour market. MAPS proved a useful tool in quantifying the impact of pension credits which lies beyond the reach of analysis of real data. Important cross-national differences were revealed in the impact of three national credit systems. The comparison demonstrated that the value of credits arose either from extensive coverage of years out of the labour market (HRP) or through the crediting of earnings into the individual's account ('baby gap' credits in Germany). As the analysis also revealed, very interesting differences in the relative value of credits may exist within one country – in France, the value of credits aimed at mothers was significantly less than credits which covered all manual workers. Finally, MAPS was used to 'play God' with the data and examine the effect of changes in micro-level behaviour on the distribution of income in order to assess more accurately what drives gender differentials in income in old age. Again, this highlighted the differential impact of changes both across countries and between rich and poor women. This exercise should, if nothing else, warn us against an over-optimistic assessment of the impact of current changes in women's labour market behaviour on their incomes in old age. The scenarios suggest that if the pension and wider tax–benefit systems are maintained in their present form, a narrowing of the differentials in women and men's income in old age will need a combination of far-reaching changes in lifetime labour market behaviour and in the structure of earnings.

As I hope the chapter has demonstrated, microsimulation modelling should take its place in the toolkit of the comparative social researcher. We nevertheless need to recognise the limits of microsimulation modelling in this context, notably the constraints on the representativeness of models and on the conclusions that can be drawn from such models. For this reason, I would suggest that microsimulation is a very useful supplement to (but not replacement of) traditional forms of analysis.

Notes

This research was undertaken as part of the ESRC SAGE Research Group which is investigating social policy in an ageing society (Grant No. M/565/28/1001). In building and analysing MAPS, I benefited enormously from the comments and advice of Tony Atkinson, Jane Falkingham, Ruth Hancock, and Holly Sutherland. I am also very grateful for the comments given by participants at the Cambridge Microsimulation Workshop and at the Welfare Policy Analysis Seminar at the LSE. All errors remain my own.

1 The approach adopted in MAPS is therefore distinct from that of EUROMOD. Apart from operating on a much larger scale than MAPS, the model individuals who constitute EUROMOD are drawn from national microdata. Differences in micro-level behaviour are therefore built directly into the model, allowing for a quite different set of questions to be answered (Sutherland, 1996).

2 Pudney's OLS regression on earnings used cross-sectional earnings data for 1988 (the regression was based on cross-sectional data as suitable panel data for that period were unavailable). These figures were adjusted by the growth in average earnings so that they more closely represented 1994 values. An additional process was used to deal with the large amount of unexplained variance in this regression model. If the values of the regression model alone had been fitted the true dispersion of earnings would have been greatly underestimated. One solution would have been to distribute the model's error term on a random basis year by year. There is, however, considerable evidence that there is a serial correlation of error which arises from individual characteristics which, though unobserved, remain constant over time (Atkinson et al., 1992; Lillard and Willis, 1978; Nickell, 1982). To reflect this reality, MAPS operates as follows. The error term is assumed to be normally distributed, and in year t is randomly assigned to MAPS individuals. In year $t+1$ an individual carries over a proportion of the error term attached to them in year t with the remainder being drawn from a newly generated random variable. This process is repeated for the whole of the individual's working life. The value of the correlation of earnings over time was set at 0.83 in line with Nickell's estimates (for more details see Rake, 1998).

3 As purchasing power parities are subject to considerable fluctuation across time, neighbouring years were checked to see if there were significant changes in the rate over time. The rates chosen proved to be typical of the rate in that period.

4 As discussed below, the model operates in hypothetical time. As a consequence,

past patterns of earnings growth/rate of return to a pension fund can only operate as a guide for setting these rates and, looking at past movements, the chosen rates chosen fall within 'reasonable' bounds. Alternative rates were used to test the model for sensitivity, and it was found that the French results were sensitive to a change in the rate of real earnings growth from 1.5% to 2% (Rake, 1998).

5 There are difficulties in capturing at any one point in time the rules which govern the pension system and the broader tax–benefit system. Looking at pensions as practised in 1994 would have meant simulating pensions which had been long since reformed. Instead, the simulation deals with pension rules which had been legislated for by 1994. This '1994 rule' was relaxed in the British case, where two additional pieces of legislation not fully in place in 1994 were considered of sufficient importance to include in the simulation – the equalisation of pension age (which will be phased in following the 1995 Pension Act) and the inclusion of SERPS in HRP coverage (the details of which are still to be fully decided). It should be noted that with pension legislation in particular, reforms are often phased in over a long period and may be subject to change in that period. As a result, the sets of pension and tax–benefit rules which make up the national regimes in MAPS are unlikely ever to see the light of day in the exact form simulated here.

6 This decision was taken because of lack of reliable and/or suitable data on which to base the simulation. For investment income, it is widely acknowledged that surveys capture poorly the real distribution of investment income (see for example Banks *et al.*, 1994). In a cross-national context, differences in coverage of different types of income and data collection techniques mean that any simulated investment income is unlikely to contain the same elements in each country (Atkinson *et al.*, 1995). Given what we do know about the distribution of investment income, we can assume that its omission will particularly affect the reliability of the MAPS estimates of income of those at the top of the income distribution, amongst whom, men and couples are disproportionately represented. As a result, the omission of investment income will most likely lead to the underestimation of income inequality overall, and the underestimation of the differences between women and men's incomes. The simulation of housing costs and benefits would also have been difficult within this cross-national context. Housing benefits in all three countries are set with some reference to local market rents, or at the exact level of rent paid. To simulate this across countries would not only have required enormously detailed information about regional rental markets, but would have necessitated the simulation of the geographical distribution of the population in the different countries. Given this complexity, the housing benefit element was omitted, leaving us with a measure of income that does not correspond exactly to either the before or after housing cost measure. However, given that housing benefit is omitted from the simulation, one of the drawbacks of using a before housing cost measure (the over-estimation of the income of the very poorest) is avoided. German occupational schemes were excluded from the simulation because, as far as I am aware, there is no national-level survey of the key features of the different occupational schemes in Germany of the kind provided by Government Actuary's

Department in Britain. The high degree of variation between schemes meant that it would be unwise to simulate such schemes in the absence of such information.

7 Sensitivity of results to an alternative imputation of survivor's pension based on median pension income was tested in the process of model building. The use of median income had a statistically significant impact on final income of widows in Britain and Germany (but not widowers who have some claim on a survivor's pension in Germany), but not on the income of the whole population. It would be possible to use other estimations of survivor's pension which incorporated inequality of survivors' entitlements – for example, the entitlements of different quintiles of MAPS individuals could be assessed and five rates of survivor's pension could then be randomly assigned to widows and widowers. Even with this more complex calculation, the problem of capturing differential mortality remains: the widows of low-earning men who have a shorter-than-average life expectancy would still be under-represented by such an exercise.

8 Replacement rates are most commonly calculated by comparing weekly earnings before retirement with weekly pension. This is a slightly different calculation, but similarly measures how far the pension replaces prior earnings.

9 Data limitations meant that HRP periods were only simulated when time was taken out of the labour market following the birth of a child.

10 The calculation of SERPS assumes that HRP has been fully incorporated (see note 5). The length of the working life is based on years in which the individual could be making National Insurance contributions – that is, between minimum school leaving age (16) and statutory retirement age. Currently, the difference in retirement age means that women's SERPS income is averaged over 44 years, but this will rise to 49 years as retirement ages are equalised. As noted earlier, MAPS uses the equalised pension age when simulating the British pension rules even though these have yet to be fully implemented.

11 Following the 1999 reforms, the value of these credits will rise to 100% of average earnings. A further credit is given to those caring for dependent adults and this is offered without time limit – again, data limitations meant that this credit had to be omitted from MAPS.

12 Converted back to DM the weekly value of the credit would be 24.7DM. Clasen estimates that the baby years credits are worth 30DM per month for each child (Clasen, 1997, p. 63). My estimate is high, although not implausible, given that the average number of children is 2.4 and that the simulation looks at the matured operation of the scheme.

13 I am borrowing the term 'playing God' from the creators of LIFEMOD (see Falkingham and Lessof, 1991 and 1992) who effectively played God on a much larger scale than I do in the following section.

14 As these individuals were drawn from a British sample, they incorporate British patterns of labour market behaviour including, for example, a higher propensity for women to have worked part-time than would have been the case for comparable cohorts of French or German individuals. If MAPS individuals had been drawn from either a French or German sample, the impact of eliminating part-time working would therefore have been less important.

6 Integrating output in EUROMOD: an assessment of the sensitivity of multi-country microsimulation results

Cathal O'Donoghue, Holly Sutherland and Francesca Utili

6.1 Introduction

As European countries integrate their economies more closely, there is a greater interest in comparisons of the operation of policies in different countries, in developing common objectives for national policy and in considering implementing complementary public policies. While microsimulation models are potentially valuable tools for the design and evaluation of policy, to date no Europe-wide model has been available. National tax–benefit microsimulation models have existed for many years to examine country-specific issues (for surveys, see Merz, 1991; Sutherland, 1995), but cross-country comparisons have been difficult for reasons of lack of comparability between the available data sets and assumptions built into the existing models (Callan and Sutherland, 1997).

The EUROMOD project is building an integrated tax–benefit model covering all 15 European Union countries, focused on social and integration policies and their implications for the economic resources of people who are at risk of social exclusion. The model is designed to examine:

- the impact of national policies within a consistent comparative framework
- the differential impact of coordinated European policy on individual Member States
- a Europe-wide perspective on social and economic integration policies that are implemented at national or regional level.[1]

The project is extending an established method in two respects. First, it seeks to overcome differences in modelling assumptions so that comparable analyses can be carried out at the national level. The second task is to be able to conduct policy analyses at the multi-country or European level. This requires the integration of national data sets to form a multi-country database and the integration of outputs so that European results can be obtained.

The main output from a tax–benefit model is a measure of disposable income at the household level. This is computed by making use of the information from a micro-database on the characteristics and pre-tax and transfer incomes of members of the household to simulate the elements of the tax and transfer system for each household. The output income measure is a combination of elements recorded in the database (such as earnings) and elements calculated by the model (such as child benefit or income tax). Changes in policy may be specified by the user of the model, and disposable incomes are re-calculated. Thus for each individual household we have a measure of change in income following the policy change. Once weighted up to the population level and aggregated, these changes can be translated into the national revenue cost of the change. Changes for all households in a representative sample can be analysed by any variables in the database. Typically, we are interested in the impact of policy across the income distribution. So measures of income by which to rank households are required.

Integration of model calculations and outputs involves two things. First, it requires that the income *change* variable is calculated in a comparable manner across countries. This means not only that the income concept should be as consistent as possible but also that the data on which the tax–benefit calculations rely should be comparable. Second, the variables that are used to *classify* the changes in income need to be comparable. We may group households by many criteria that are of interest in relation to public policy – such as housing tenure, household composition or the employment status of household members – and these criteria should be standardised or harmonised across countries if the cross-country results are to be meaningful. Grouping households by income level is a common output from a tax–benefit model and is necessary if we are to explore the impact of national or co-ordinated policy on the European income distribution. We therefore need a common measure of income across countries. It is this topic that forms the main focus of this paper.

In many respects, the income comparability issues that face EUROMOD are the same as those that face comparative studies of income distribution.[2] However, the solutions to problems may not always be the same because of the requirement of tax–benefit microsimulation models to measure income *change* as well as income *level*. Adjustments that improve the characteristics of the default income distribution in comparison with external standards may actually worsen the performance of the simulation model and the precision of estimates of income change (Sutherland, 1991). This paper draws heavily on the literature on comparability of income statistics across countries. It also attempts to highlight the issues that are of particular concern for policy simulation, and to suggest approaches that are appropriate for that task.

Section 6.2 outlines the main adjustments that may be necessary to improve comparability of output income measures from EUROMOD. Section 6.3 explains how the numerical illustrations of the effects of various adjustments have been calculated. Sections 6.4 to 6.10 examine each type of adjustment in detail. Section 6.11 summarises the results and the final section concludes with an agenda for further work.

6.2 Adjusting inputs and integrating outputs

There are a number of adjustments which may be necessary to achieve greater comparability.

- To ensure that national data sets are equally representative of their national household populations, the most serious non-response biases are corrected using *re-weighting*
- Incomes from different data sets may cover different time periods such as a week, month or year. Adjustment to a *common accounting period* may be a trivial exercise, or may need to take account of changes that take place within the accounting period (such as changes in employment status)
- Item non-response or under-reporting of incomes may require *adjustment to the income base*
- The original data sets were collected at different times. For comparative purposes the data must be adjusted to *a common point in time*
- A common currency unit is needed, so *exchange rates* must be chosen. Even when a common currency exists, we may wish to adopt exchange rates in EUROMOD that capture price differences (or other aspects affecting welfare) across countries
- Adjustments to account for the effect of *non-cash income* on the ranking of households may be needed if the prevalence and nature of free or subsidised services or the importance of owner occupation varies across countries
- Comparisons of the incomes of households of different types needs account to be taken of economies of scale and differences in household size and composition: *an equivalence scale* must be chosen[3]

In considering the need for each adjustment, we need to be aware of overlaps in their effect: the order of the adjustments is important. Here, we consider the adjustments in the order that seems logical. However, it is clear that a different order may be preferred if we have a concern for the comparability of a particular income source. Furthermore, we may have available independent control information that is compatible with some other ordering.

Some of these adjustments are likely to be necessary and common for all analyses using EUROMOD. For example, we are always likely to want to adjust for non-response bias in the original data source. However, other adjustments depend on the application of the model and on the interpretation we wish to put on the results. Choice of exchange rates, point-in-time adjustments, equivalence scales and treatment of non-cash income all come into this category. EUROMOD will offer the user choices in these adjustments and indeed, it is expected that applications of the model will include examining the effect of changes in assumptions about between-country differences, as well as changes in policy.

6.3 Method

Illustrations of the effect of the various assumptions are provided by applying them to the output from a prototype of EUROMOD, which we have named *Eur6*. This is based on micro-data from six countries: Belgium, France, Germany, Ireland, Italy and the UK. Subsamples of approximately 1,000 households have been drawn from each original survey.[4] In each of the six countries the following tax–benefit instruments are simulated in *Eur6*:

- social insurance contributions on wages (paid by employers or employees), on self-employment income and on other incomes
- income tax and other taxes on labour incomes
- family benefits: child benefits, housing benefits, out-of-work and in-work means-tested (social assistance) benefits.

Household disposable income is made up of these elements that are simulated for the 1994 financial year, plus employee and self-employment earnings, investment and other capital income, occupational and public pensions, unemployment benefits and other non-means-tested benefits taken from the database and updated to 1994.

Table 6.1 is an example of output from a 'default' run of the prototype model, in which no policy change is simulated. It shows the country composition of each decile of the six-country 'European' income distribution under prevailing policy in 1994. It also shows the mean of incomes in each decile using the same income measure that is used for ranking. This is the situation using the minimum and simplest integration methods. In the ranking of households the following applies:

- No differential weights are applied to adjust for sample bias: uniform weights are used to bring the national subsamples up to national population levels
- All incomes are assumed to apply to the whole of the year 1994

Table 6.1. *Country composition of the* Eur6 *income distribution using base assumptions*[a]

Decile	Mean income (ecu /year)[b]	Belgium	France	Germany	Ireland	Italy	UK	Total
1	4,233	0.4	18.7	19.3	2.3	28.8	30.5	100.0
2	6,525	2.7	19.6	30.7	1.1	18.6	27.3	100.0
3	8,075	3.3	24.0	35.0	1.0	16.7	20.1	100.0
4	9,628	4.2	23.9	30.3	1.0	20.0	20.5	100.0
5	11,233	4.1	29.6	29.9	0.9	17.9	17.6	100.0
6	12,910	4.2	25.0	32.8	0.7	19.5	17.8	100.0
7	14,777	5.4	22.1	30.7	0.7	19.4	21.7	100.0
8	17,360	6.4	20.1	34.0	0.9	14.2	24.4	100.0
9	21,337	6.5	18.6	35.0	0.8	12.1	27.1	100.0
10	38,299	4.7	19.1	36.2	0.6	15.7	23.6	100.0
Total	14,444	3.9	21.9	30.7	1.1	19.0	23.4	100.0

Notes:
[a] Assumptions: (1) uniform national weights; (2) no income base adjustment; (3) market exchange rate; (4) equivalence scale: square root of household size; (5) households counted once.
[b] Income definition is that used for ranking.
Source: Eur6.

- No allowance is made for under-reporting of incomes or differences in coverage in the national income bases
- All incomes are updated to 1994, but otherwise no adjustment is made for different timing
- Household disposable incomes in each country are converted to Ecu using the average market exchange rates for 1994
- No adjustment is made for non-cash incomes
- Household incomes are arbitrarily equivalised using the square root of household size.[5] Households are counted once (not weighted by the number of individuals)

Table 6.1 shows that households in Ireland, the UK and Italy tend to be disproportionately concentrated at the bottom of the *Eur6* income distribution, while Belgian, German and French households tend to be concentrated at the top.[6] The following seven sections (6.4–6.10) examine the possible effects of adjustments on the country composition of the 'European' distribution. In cases where suitable external information is readily available, we illustrate the effects by re-calculating the distributions shown in Table 6.1. The country composition is not the only dimension in

Table 6.2. *Country composition of the* Eur6 *income distribution: differential national weights*[a]

Decile	Mean income (ecu/year)[b]	Belgium	France	Germany	Ireland	Italy	UK
1	4,238	0.2	18.9	20.3	2.4	28.0	30.3
2	6,422	1.8	16.0	22.9	1.6	25.9	31.8
3	7,987	2.7	25.1	31.2	1.0	18.6	21.4
4	9,503	3.5	24.6	34.1	1.0	16.4	20.5
5	11,039	4.9	25.0	28.8	1.0	19.6	20.7
6	12,838	3.9	28.8	33.2	0.6	16.8	16.6
7	14,687	4.7	21.8	33.4	0.9	18.5	20.8
8	17,285	5.8	22.4	33.1	0.7	16.6	21.4
9	21,415	6.8	17.6	33.7	0.8	13.4	27.7
10	36,004	4.7	19.2	36.3	0.6	15.7	23.4
Total	14,145	3.9	21.9	30.7	1.1	19.0	23.4

Notes:
[a] Assumptions: (1) differential national weights; (2) no income base adjustment; (3) market exchange rate; (4) equivalence scale: square root of household size; (5) households counted once.
[b] Income definition is that used for ranking.
Source: Eur6.

which we believe the European distribution of income will be affected by alternative adjustment and integration factors. However, our choice of characterising model output in this way is in part due to the novel nature of these statistics. The relative position of countries is likely to be a high-profile aspect of EUROMOD output, so it is important to understand the sensitivity of these results to the assumptions that may be used.

6.4 Non-response bias

As the data sets used in our comparison are all based on voluntary sample surveys, the characteristics of the samples may not be representative of the household populations in each of the countries. For example, in the UK it is thought that there is an over-representation of households with children and an under-representation of single person households in the Family Expenditure Survey (Kelmsley *et al.*, 1980). To correct for this, grossing-up weights are usually applied. Thus household types which are under-represented will have higher weights.

Table 6.2 shows, in the same format as Table 6.1, the effect of using weights to adjust for non-response in the *Eur6* data sets. Here we can see that the impact is generally quite small at the extremes. In the centre of the distributions, Belgian and German households tend to move up the distribution, while UK and Irish households move down. Italian households tend to move from the centre to the extremes, whilst French households gradually shift upwards.

A potential source of lack of comparability arises from the type of non-response bias weights used. The UK data in *Eur6*, taken from the Family Expenditure Survey (FES), are grossed up to account for differential non-response by family type and age. However, there is also evidence to show that non-response to the FES is more likely among households recorded as belonging to ethnic minorities, and among those living in older local authority housing and young people sharing accommodation (Harris, 1998b). Thus the weights that are used do not correct directly for all aspects of differential response. They may – in an indirect fashion – either improve or worsen the representation of groups not controlled for. Thus, in general, there is no guarantee that all non-response bias has been dealt with, nor that the weights that have been used have not introduced new biases. Similar problems are likely to apply to the weights used to gross up the data sets for other countries and we cannot be sure that the extent of the adjustments is comparable across countries.

An issue that is related to the question of non-response bias is the coverage of the household population in the survey data set. Household surveys cover only people who live in households and ignore people living in institutions, such as the elderly, students, the military, prisoners and the homeless. Little is known about the economic circumstances of these groups in European countries or their differential importance across countries.[7] However, it is clear that EUROMOD should not attempt to include them in its frame of reference. It would be misleading to base the characteristics of the non-household population on the characteristics of people living in households. Furthermore, the social policy that EUROMOD aims to simulate is likely to apply in a very different way to those living in institutions. However, reconciliation of EUROMOD output with other sources should take account of the fact that part of the population is not represented in its database.

6.5 Accounting period adjustment

The accounting period adopted in the data sets can also be a source of comparability problems. In general, the longer the accounting period used, the lower the level of income inequality. Income measured over a year will smooth the weekly or monthly variations that these shorter accounting periods will capture. Three different accounting periods are used by the surveys that make up the *Eur6* database. In Belgium, Germany and Italy, respondents are asked about annual income (income received over a year in the past). In France, most of the income questions refer to a month. In Ireland and the UK, questions relating to some elements of income may refer to a period as short as a week.

Clearly, a minimum necessary adjustment is to bring all the income measures to the same period in arithmetic terms (*Eur6* uses annual income). These trivial transformations are all that is necessary in the case of people with no change in circumstance over the year. However, further adjustment to account for differences in the reference period of the data might be considered for people whose circumstances do change within the year. Since it is difficult to envisage the form of a single adjustment factor for this purpose, a more fruitful approach is either to attempt imputation of an annual income base from shorter periods or to impute a monthly or weekly base from information on a year.

6.6 Income under-reporting adjustment

Surveys may underestimate aggregate household income, even once survey non-response has been accounted for. If the degree of underestimation differs across countries, then it will bias any inferences made about the relative position of households in the different countries. External sources of information about household sector income are needed with which to validate the EUROMOD database. Clearly, a major requirement is that these external sources are themselves comparable across countries. National accounts household income is a potential source for comparison. Aggregate household disposable income in the *Eur6* database is shown in Table 6.3 as a percentage of national accounts household disposable income.[8] Although low, the ratios are similar to those found in other studies. What is noticeable is the difference between the UK with over 80% of national accounts disposable income and the continental countries with around 60%–70%.[9] Clearly, if national accounts data represent the true level of national household income then, without adjustment, UK households will tend to be higher up the European income distribution than if adjustments are made.

Table 6.4 shows the impact on the *Eur6* income distribution of using a simple multiplicative adjustment such that the aggregate income in each country matches that given by the national accounts figures in Table 6.3. The effect of this adjustment is to shift up the distribution the countries which have the biggest proportional shortfall between survey disposable income and national accounts. The UK, with the highest ratio of survey income to national accounts, shifts down the most, while Belgium shifts up the most.

Table 6.3. *Percentage of national accounts disposable income in* Eur6

Country	Percentage of national accounts (1)	Adjustment factor (2) = 1/(1)
Belgium	64.4	1.55
France	66.5	1.50
Germany	71.8	1.39
Ireland[a]	n/a	1.26
Italy	73.4	1.36
UK	80.7	1.24

Note:
[a] As household sector national accounts are not available for Ireland, we make an assumption about the percentage of household national income accounted for by the survey. We do this by comparing with the UK. Assuming the same proportion of national accounts represented as the UK, we find an adjustment factor of 1.24. Alternatively, assuming that the ratio of GDP per capita between countries is the same as the ratio of household disposable income per capita, we find an adjustment factor of 1.27. We arbitrarily assume a factor between the two of 1.26.
Source: Eur6 and OECD (1997).

Although this simple adjustment will maintain existing national distributional characteristics, it also assumes that all incomes are under-estimated to the same extent. This is most unlikely since, for example, a person reporting receipt of the maximum amount of a social assistance benefit cannot be *under*-reporting this income. Applying a uniform adjustment factor to all incomes will result in an *over*-estimation of incomes for households in receipt of such benefits. Studies described in Atkinson *et al.,* (1995) indicate that the degree of under-reporting varies by income source and that it is self-employment and investment income that tend to be particularly under-represented in survey data. The implications for cross-country comparisons may be serious, even if the degree of under-reporting of self-employment income is comparable, since the incidence of this source of income and the prevalence of self-employment itself varies across countries.

Lack of comparability between national accounts aggregates and the concepts that can be readily measured using household micro-data poses significant problems for the use of national accounts to validate or adjust

Table 6.4. *Country composition of the* Eur6 *income distribution: national accounts adjustment*[a]

Decile	Mean income (ecu /year)[b]	Belgium	France	Germany	Ireland	Italy	UK
1	5,480	0.1	14.5	14.1	2.6	23.9	44.8
2	8,452	0.4	12.6	23.3	1.7	26.6	35.4
3	10,811	2.1	18.4	32.0	1.3	20.1	26.1
4	12,889	2.6	22.3	34.1	1.0	18.0	22.0
5	15,136	4.5	24.5	30.2	1.0	20.3	19.6
6	17,575	3.9	26.9	33.2	0.8	16.7	18.4
7	20,159	3.8	27.1	32.2	0.5	18.8	17.6
8	23,526	5.8	24.4	34.6	0.8	15.6	18.8
9	29,037	8.2	23.0	34.5	0.6	14.6	19.0
10	49,377	7.7	25.4	38.7	0.4	15.0	12.8
Total	19,250	3.9	21.9	30.7	1.1	19.0	23.4

Notes:
[a] Assumptions: (1) differential national weights; (2) national accounts income base adjustment; (3) market exchange rate; (4) equivalence scale: square root of household size; (5) households counted once.
[b] Income definition is that used for ranking.
Source: Eur6.

the income base in the model. For example national accounts may include income from non-profit organisations in the personal sector accounts (Atkinson *et al.*, 1995). They include income from the non-household population, which is naturally not captured by household surveys. Furthermore, the reliability of some of the components of income in the household sector accounts – particularly self-employment income and investment income – is not thought to be good. For example, total interest payments may be known from institutional sources, but the share received by the household sector may in effect be determined by rules of thumb (see the discussion of Van der Laan, 1998). Thus we cannot regard national accounts information as necessarily being the 'true' level of income to which the survey base should be adjusted.

    Two further aspects deserve attention. First, the extent of under-reporting may vary by household type. There may be reasons why certain types of individual under-report income. A simple multiplicative factor will not capture these. Second, multiplicative adjustments do not deal with the fact that there may be zero-reporting of certain income types (when, in fact, some amount of income is received). An attractive solution is to re-weight households to account for differences between the numbers of income recipients in the survey and those who actually exist in the population. Typically, this information is available for benefit incomes from administrative statistics. However, adopting this approach in EUROMOD would need to be part of a general strategy for re-weighting that took account of the limited number of dimensions of adjustment that can usefully be accomplished simultaneously using grossing-up. EUROMOD has to depend on relatively small samples from survey sources and a large number of simultaneous adjustments would lead to some observations having very high weights. Model results would then be overly sensitive to simulations which affect these few households.

6.7 Common point-in-time adjustment

It is clear that EUROMOD will update the national data sets to a common point in time. This procedure will introduce a degree of error since typically only aggregate indices of income change are available and structural shifts in population characteristics and changes in the distribution of incomes are ignored. However, there is no reason to believe that updating procedures *necessarily* damage the degree of comparability across countries.

Even if data are collected for a common time, differences in living standards may be partly due to the fact that all countries are not necessarily in the same phase of the economic cycle. For example, there may be more or less unemployment or payment of bonuses. Figure 6.1 shows the growth rate of total household income (income before taxes and contributions) in the period 1984–94 in Italy and the UK. Although in general at similar growth levels, the peaks and troughs of the business cycle do not coincide in the two countries, with Italy appearing to operate with a time lag. In terms of total income, Italians would therefore appear to be poorer relative to the British if the countries were compared in 1990 than if they were compared during the following few years, because of higher growth rates in Italy, and yet relatively richer than in the previous years, because of higher growth rates in the UK during that period.

Furthermore, if the degree of national income inequality is itself related to national economic cycles, we should expect mis-matches in points in the cycle across countries to have additional effects on the country composition of the European distribution, owing to differences in within-country inequality, as well as those due to differences in mean incomes.

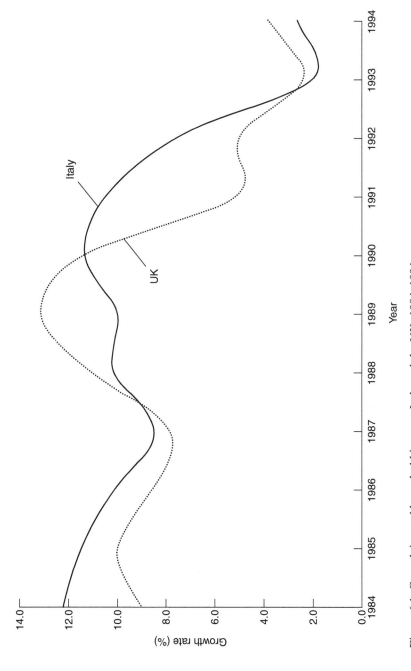

Figure 6.1 Growth in total household income: Italy and the UK, 1984–1994
Source: OECD National Accounts (1997).

Table 6.5. *National currency market and PPP exchange rates for ecu (1994 averages)*

Country	Market exchange rate	PPP exchange rate	Ratio
Belgium	39.7	40.1	1.010
France	6.58	7.12	1.082
Germany	1.92	2.23	1.161
Ireland	0.79	0.69	0.873
Italy	1,915.1	1,649	0.861
UK	0.78	0.69	0.885

Source: EUROSTAT (1997).

6.8 Exchange rate adjustment

Using nominal exchange rates to convert national components of EUROMOD output to a common currency does not account for different prices of goods and services in different countries. If goods cost relatively more in one country than in another, then its inhabitants will seem to be better off in money terms than they are in terms of actual living standards.

Studies which have compared living standards across countries such as Atkinson (1996) and Hagenaars *et al.*, (1994) have used purchasing power parity (PPP) exchange rates. Eurostat estimate PPPs for each of 29 consumption groups as well as for investment, government consumption, and trade (Eurostat, 1996). These are then aggregated using national expenditure weights to produce an average PPP measure for the whole country.

Table 6.5 shows that the ratio of PPP exchange rates to nominal exchange rates varies widely across the six countries considered. Belgium, France and Germany all have PPP exchange rates higher than their nominal exchange rates, whereas the other three countries have PPP exchange rates that are lower. The difference between the highest ratio and the lowest ratio is large: Italians who appear to have the same incomes as Germans on a nominal rate basis, would be 30% better off using PPP rates.

Table 6.6 describes the *Eur6* income distribution using purchasing power parity exchange rates rather than market exchange rates to convert national currencies into ecu. Germany, France and Belgium tend to shift down the distribution relative to the others as the result of having PPP rates that are higher than market rates. Germany has the largest positive differential and therefore moves down most, whereas Italy has the largest negative differential and moves up most.

Table 6.6. *Country composition of* Eur6 *income distribution: PPP exchange rate*[a]

Decile	Mean income (ecu /year)[b]	Belgium	France	Germany	Ireland	Italy	UK
1	5,663	0.2	18.0	28.5	2.2	16.0	35.3
2	8,599	1.2	14.2	29.7	1.5	19.3	34.1
3	10,612	2.2	20.8	38.3	0.9	19.6	18.2
4	12,605	3.2	23.5	32.8	1.0	15.5	23.9
5	14,828	4.3	24.7	33.0	1.0	17.4	19.4
6	17,113	4.1	28.1	33.9	0.9	15.6	17.5
7	19,757	4.9	27.2	26.5	0.8	19.3	21.3
8	23,188	5.7	22.2	28.5	0.7	22.6	20.4
9	28,511	7.1	19.8	23.8	1.0	22.4	25.9
10	47,961	6.1	20.8	31.7	0.8	21.9	18.6
Total	18,892	3.9	21.9	30.7	1.1	19.0	23.4

Notes:
[a] Assumptions: (1) differential national weights; (2) national accounts income base adjustment; (3) PPP exchange rate; (4) equivalence scale: square root of household size; (5) households counted once.
[b] Income definition is that used for ranking.
Source: Eur6.

However, PPP exchange rates based on the whole economy are not necessarily appropriate for comparing household sector incomes. Purchasing power parities based on household sector consumption weights may be more appropriate (Brungger, 1996). Furthermore, even within the household sector, consumption patterns can vary systematically with income. Poorer households tend to spend a larger share of their budgets on food and energy than do richer households. In principle, the derivation of appropriate exchange rates depends on the interpretation we wish to place on the model results. At one extreme, the *revenue* effect on national budgets of a policy change needs to be expressed in terms of unadjusted national currency (or the euro, using market exchange rates where necessary). At another extreme, when making welfare comparisons between households in different circumstances, we may wish to take account of price and consumption differences by income group, or by other characteristics such as region within countries. In this case, we can construct national exchange rates based on a weighted average for the various groups or we can apply a variety of exchange rates *within* a country, depending on each household's particular circumstance. In this latter case, the 'exchange rate' would begin to take on a similar role to the equivalence scale, which is the subject of the next section.

6.9 Equivalence scales

As with the choice of exchange rate, the choice of equivalence scale depends on the interpretation we wish to place on the model results. In our analysis so far we have made use of a simple but arbitrary scale which adjusts household incomes by the square root of household size. A commonly-used alternative is the OECD scale which distinguishes between children and additional adults.[10] The purpose of such scales is to allow the incomes of households of different sizes and composition to be compared. They can be placed within a general framework which provides a parametric approximation of equivalence scales (ES), based on a suggestion in Buhmann et al., (1988):

$$ES = S^e$$

where S is household size and e represents the equivalence elasticity and can take values between 0 and 1. The larger the value of e, the smaller the assumed economies of scale. Thus a value of $e = 1$, implies that there are no economies of scale and is the same as measuring income per capita. The extreme value of $e = 0$ ignores the size of the household and is equivalent to measuring income per household. When simply concerned with the aggregate revenue effect of a policy change, we typically use $e = 0$, or alternatively $e = 1$, but with each household weighted by the number of people in it.

Table 6.7 reports the mean equivalised disposable income (and also the rank) for each of the six countries using four values of e: 0.5 (the scale used in Tables 6.1, 6.2, 6.4 and 6.6); the OECD scale (approximately 0.7); 0 (per household); and 1 (per capita) with each household weighted by its size. The table also shows the mean household size for the samples for each country. The ranking of the countries can vary quite significantly with the choice of equivalence scale. For example, Germany, with a low average household size, moves from being ranked number 6 for unadjusted household income to 2 using the OECD scale. Ireland, with the highest average household size, moves in the opposite direction from rank 3 in terms of unadjusted household income to rank 6 when using the OECD scale. The ratio of average equivalent income with the lowest assumed economies of scale to that with the highest assumed economies of scale is greatest for countries with the smallest average household size. Weighting by the number of people, rather than the number of households, increases the relative importance of large households. The effect on mean income depends on the position of large households in the income distribution.

Table 6.7. *Mean equivalised disposable income (and rank of country) in Eur6 by equivalence scale elasticity (ecu per year)*

Definition of income (e)[a]	Belgium	France	Germany	Ireland	Italy	UK	Total
Household income (0)	37,238	29,634	25,890	30,457	34,468	26,662	29,011
	(1)	(4)	(6)	(3)	(2)	(5)	
Equivalent income : square root (0.5)	23,257	18,852	18,530	6,600	20,343	17,607	18,892
	(1)	(3)	(4)	(6)	(2)	(5)	
Equivalent income : OECD ($\approx$0.7)	18,663	15,573	16,020	12,419	15,674	14,605	15,611
	(1)	(4)	(2)	(6)	(3)	(5)	
Per capita income (1), weighted by household size	14,448	11,649	13,328	8,588	11,409	11,060	11,935
	(1)	(3)	(2)	(6)	(4)	(5)	
Average household size	2.58	2.54	1.94	3.55	3.02	2.41	2.41

Notes:
Incomes are adjusted in the same way as in Table 6.6.
[a] (e) is the equivalence elasticity (see text).
Source: Eur6.

Table 6.8. *Country composition of the* Eur6 *income distribution: per capita incomes*[a]

Decile	Mean income (ecu /year)[b]	Belgium	France	Germany	Ireland	Italy	UK
1	3,267	0.3	19.4	9.5	4.0	34.2	32.5
2	5,354	1.5	21.9	21.4	2.6	23.7	28.9
3	6,628	2.2	24.4	28.3	2.0	22.0	21.0
4	7,782	3.0	23.9	29.9	1.4	19.7	22.1
5	9,073	3.2	26.1	24.4	1.1	21.7	23.4
6	10,567	5.2	23.5	20.3	1.1	26.7	23.2
7	12,251	5.8	21.0	23.8	1.2	26.9	21.1
8	14,498	6.3	22.8	28.4	0.6	21.6	20.2
9	18,140	8.8	23.4	30.2	0.8	17.3	19.4
10	31,759	5.0	23.0	29.0	0.7	21.7	20.5
Total	11,935	4.1	22.9	24.5	1.6	23.6	23.3

Notes:
[a] Assumptions: (1) differential national weights; (2) national accounts income base adjustment; (3) PPP exchange rate; (4) equivalence scale: household size (per capita income); (5) households weighted by number of people.
[b] Income definition is that used for ranking.
Source: Eur6.

The country composition of the *Eur6* income distribution using per capita income weighted by the number of people is shown in Table 6.8 and can be compared with the effect of our previously defined $e = 0.5$ (each household counting once) in Table 6.6. The principal effect is to move countries with the most large households – Ireland and Italy – down the distribution. Not only does the per capita scale take no account of economies of scale within these households, but they also appear more frequently in the distribution.[11] The proportion of German households in the bottom *Eur6* decile falls from 29% in Table 6.6 (using the square root scale) to 10% in Table 6.8. In the same comparison, the proportion of Italians more than doubles. However, it is interesting to note that while the composition of the top half of the *Eur6* distribution is affected to some extent, the effect is much less dramatic. For example, the proportion of German households in the top 30% increases from 28% to 29% and the proportion of Italian households in the same group falls from 22% to 20%, comparing the assumptions used in Tables 6.6 and 6.8. Among the better off, household sizes vary less both across country and within country.

We have applied the same equivalence scale in each country. It is quite

Table 6.9. *Cash and non-cash social expenditure, 1992*

Country	Non-cash social expenditure (% of GDP)	Cash social expenditure (% of GDP)	Non-cash as a percentage of total social expenditure
Belgium	13.0	19.6	40
France	14.1	19.3	42
W. Germany	12.8	16.8	43
Ireland	11.5	14.7	43
Italy	11.9	17.9	40
UK	11.8	16.1	42

Source: OECD (1996).

possible that the appropriate scale is in fact different across countries. We can view the choice of equivalence scale to be quite analogous to the choice of exchange rate (see Section 6.8). Indeed, when we consider exchange rates that vary within countries together with equivalence scales that vary between countries, we can see that they have a common purpose within the EUROMOD framework.

6.10 Non-cash incomes

Non-cash benefits can have an important role to play in redistribution within countries and, if the size of these benefits is different across countries, then comparing relative living standards will not be the same as comparing relative cash incomes. Two households in similar circumstances, where one has access to free health care and the other does not, may have very different living standards. A similar problem arises in comparing the incomes of households whose rents are subsidised with those who receive cash housing benefits (Gardiner *et al.*, 1995). Table 6.9 shows that the proportion of non-cash to total (cash plus non-cash) social expenditures is in fact quite stable for the six countries that we consider, varying from 40% in Belgium and Italy to 43% in West Germany and Ireland. Thus we would not expect the ranking of countries by mean incomes to change much, if non-cash benefits were incorporated. However, Smeeding *et al.*, (1993) in studying the incidence of non-cash social expenditures (health, education and housing) in seven countries found that the amount of redistribution accomplished through these welfare services was different across countries. Inclusion of non-cash income does potentially have implications for the composition of countries in the EUROMOD income distribution as well as the ranking of households in within-country distributions.

As well as social expenditures, other sources of non-cash income may be considered when ranking households by income. For example, the value of owner occupation and own production both have a significant impact on income distributions in some countries in the European Union. However, it is not straightforward to extend the definition of income to include non-cash elements. On the one hand, valuation may be problematic. On the other hand, information about the incidence of income in kind is typically not available in micro-data sources. In either case, the impact on the income distribution may be very sensitive to the assumptions used in any imputation.

6.11 How sensitive are the results?

Choices made in the selection of adjustment factors can influence both relative mean incomes across countries and the distribution of income within countries. The interaction of these two effects determines the impact on the country composition of households in the European distribution.

The effect of adjustment factors which mainly affect relative mean incomes is generally transparent: if the mean income of a country shifts relative to the means of other countries, then all households from that country will shift within the *Eur6* income distribution in a corresponding manner. For example, the biggest impacts on the country composition in our illustrations arise from the income under-reporting adjustment and the purchasing power parity adjustments to exchange rates. These two adjustments, as implemented in the examples, work in opposite directions. Comparison of Tables 6.2 and 6.4 shows that countries with the greatest shortfall in national accounts income shift up the most when the adjustment factor is applied (Belgium, France and Germany). Households from these same countries shift down the distribution with the use of (higher) PPP exchange rates which reduce the relative value of their incomes (compare Table 6.4 with Table 6.6). Ireland, Italy and the UK, with lowered average exchange rates, move up the distribution. Comparison of Table 6.6 with Table 6.2, before either adjustment, shows that the combination has little overall effect on the position of Belgian and Irish households in the distribution. It shifts German households down the distribution, and to a lesser extent does the same to UK households. The opposite happens to French households, and more dramatically to Italian households, who are shifted up the distribution.

It is of particular interest to examine in more detail the effects of those shifts on the bottom of the distribution. Figure 6.2(a), taking as a baseline the choice of adjustment factors used in Table 6.2, shows the country composition of the lowest European decile relative to the average. The

(a) Baseline (Table 6.2) and national accounts adjustment (Table 6.4)

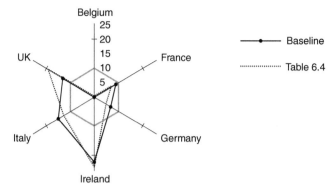

(b) Table 6.4 and PPP exchange rate adjustment (Table 6.6)

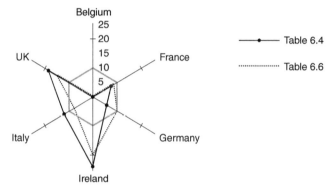

(c) Table 6.6 and income per capita, weighted per person (Table 6.8)

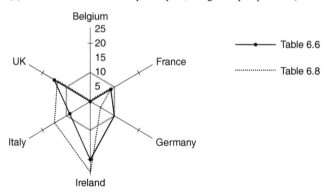

Figure 6.2 Percentages of country populations in the bottom decile of the *Eur6* distribution: cumulative effects of adjustments

numbers on the diagram represent the percentage of units (households or individuals) in each country in the lowest *Eur6* decile. A value of 10 in each country (indicated by the grey hexagon) represents the hypothetical situation of perfect cross-country equality where each *Eur6* decile contains 10% of the inhabitants of each country. For example, using the baseline (solid line), over 20% of Irish households are in the bottom decile, compared with Belgium at the other extreme which has less than 5% of its households in this low income group.

The dotted line in Figure 6.2(a) shows the composition of the bottom decile using the National Accounts income under-reporting adjustment (Table 6.4). As expected, this adjustment increases the proportion of the populations of UK and Ireland in the bottom decile, while the proportions of Italians, French and Germans are reduced. The cumulative effect of adding the PPP exchange rate adjustment is shown in Figure 6.2(b). The effects of the National Accounts adjustment (solid line) are substantially smoothed, if not reversed, when adjustment for purchasing power is added (dotted line).

Adjustment factors which mainly influence the within-country income distributions have a less predictable effect. They will not necessarily have a noticeable impact on the country composition *per se*, although they may alter the composition significantly in other respects. For example, the choice of differential non-response bias weights, has the smallest impact on the country composition of the *Eur6* distribution (compare Table 6.1 and Table 6.2). However, equivalence scales can have a major effect on both the within-country and between-country distributions. In the example we have focused on, the use of per capita income (weighted by persons) concentrates large households at the bottom of the *Eur6* distribution, compared with a scale that assumes some economies of scale. On the other hand, countries with small average household sizes make up a lower proportion of the aggregate population when household incomes are weighted by the number of people. The combined effect is to alter substantially the composition of the bottom of the *Eur6* distribution, leaving the top less affected. The changes are largest for those countries where the average household size differs most from the *Eur6* average. Figure 6.2(c) illustrates the cumulative effect on the bottom decile of using per capita income and weighting by the number of people (dotted line), compared with simply using the adjustment shown in Figure 6.2(b) and Table 6.6 (solid line). It shows strong movements in the opposite directions for Ireland and Italy, on the one hand, and Germany, on the other. The change in the UK is smaller, and is negligible in France and Belgium.

Interestingly, the cumulative effect of the three adjustments (dotted line in Figure 6.2(c)) produces a picture of the bottom *Eur6* decile that is most similar to the baseline case (solid line in Figure 6.2a). However, although the proportions of households that end up in the bottom *Eur6* decile are similar to those at the starting point, it should be clear that they are not necessarily the *same* households in each case.

6.12 Conclusions

All our results and much of our discussion has been in terms of the impact of assumptions on the way households are ranked to form the existing 'European' distribution. Also of concern is the measure of income that is used to determine 'gain' or 'loss' following a policy change, and these final comments focus on some of the issues that are involved.

Data quality

It is particularly important for policy simulation that the underlying data on income by source provide a good representation of reality in combination with the other characteristics necessary to simulate tax–benefit rules. The main problem associated with validating survey data in this respect is the lack of independent information that is comparable. Outside Nordic countries, where register data from administrative sources provide a rich source of control information, there is certainly very little multi-dimensional information (such as self-employment income by marital status) that is not itself drawn from survey sources.

A particular problem arises for policy simulation if survey incomes are adjusted to national accounts levels on an aggregate basis. In EUROMOD we discard the recorded amounts of elements of the tax–benefit system that we simulate. Thus, for example, social assistance payments will not be adjusted by the aggregate adjustment factor, but will be simulated using the appropriate adjusted income base (earnings, social insurance benefits and so on). The larger the income base, the smaller will be simulated entitlements to social assistance. Thus the more we correct for general under-reporting, the more we *reduce* our estimates of aggregate social assistance. The implications for this are two-fold. First, aggregate income adjustment may be inadvisable. Second, the strategy for adjustment that is adopted should be assessed in terms of its effect on the *simulated* components of income, as well as those drawn directly from the original data set.

There is some scope for moving beyond the use of national accounts data for external comparison in countries where administrative micro-data (eg., tax record data) or published tables (eg. counts of benefit recipients) are available in a suitable form. In these cases, validation and adjustment are essentially national processes, since the comparability of administrative statistics across countries raises quite different questions than does the comparability of survey data.

It is likely that EUROMOD will rely on a strategy of making under-reporting adjustments to particular income sources, combined with re-weighting to correct for non-response by recipients of certain sources of income. Comparability of aggregate income estimates as well as distributional information will remain an issue, and the solutions that are adopted will draw on work being done by the Canberra Group (see Harris, 1998a) and others. However, it is clear that adjustments to the income base and representativeness of survey data should be considered within a perspective that is cautious about our ability unambiguously to improve the quality of the original data.

Sensitivity in other dimensions

We have illustrated the effect of alternative adjustments and integration assumptions on the country composition of decile groups in the 'European' income distribution. Our choice of characterising model output in terms of country composition is in part due to the novel nature of these statistics. It is also the case that the country composition will underlie all the European results, since existing national policy will be the starting point for all the simulations. However, when we simulate the effects of policy changes, we shall find that other dimensions of composition will also be important. For example, the location of children, pensioners or the unemployed in the national distributions will influence the impact on the income distribution of reforms targeted on these groups. We should expect the adjustments we have considered which affect the within-country distributions to affect the location of these groups in the national distributions. Once we mix the national distributions in the European distribution, the location of the groups for each country will influence the distributional effect of policy changes considered at the European level. Thus a direction for further development will be a sensitivity analysis of the composition of the European distribution by characteristics of households that are of interest from a policy point of view.

Interpretation of results

In an effort to apply various definitions of income equivalence across countries, we have explored the effect of exchange rates and equivalence scales on the ranking of households from different countries. Whether the same adjustments should be applied to the measure of income change depends on the interpretation we wish to place on the results of the model. In evaluating the relative changes in *welfare* across countries, consideration needs to be given to the appropriate adjustments to cash income change. An example of the problem that the EUROMOD user faces, is how to compare a loss of £1 by a single pensioner living in local authority accommodation in London, with a loss of 10,000 lire by a couple with two children living and working on a farm in southern Italy. The intention is to offer a wide range of choice in these matters and to provide an assessment of the sensitivity of results to the choices that are made. This paper represents a first step in that process.

Notes

This paper was written as part of the EUROMOD project, financed by *Targeted Socio-Economic Research* programme of the European Commission (CT97–3060). Data from the Panel Study of Belgian Households have been supplied by the Universities of Liège (ULG) and Antwerp (ULA). Data from the French *Enquête sur le Budget des Familles* have been made available by the Institut Nationale de la statistique et des études économiques (INSEE). Data from the *German Socio-Economic Panel* have been made available by Deutches Institut für Wirtschaftforschung (DIW). Data for Ireland from the 1987 *Survey on Income Distribution, Poverty and the Usage of State Services* have been made available by the Economic and Social Research Institute (ESRI). Data from the Italian *Survey of Household Income and Wealth* have been made available by the Bank of Italy. Data from the UK *Family Expenditure Survey* are Crown Copyright. They have been made available by the Office for National Statistics (ONS) through the Data Archive and are used by permission. Neither the ONS nor the Data Archive bear any responsibility for the analysis or interpretation of the data reported here. The same disclaimer applies for ULG and ULA, INSEE, the DIW, the ESRI and the Bank of Italy for the Belgian, French, German, Irish and Italian data respectively. The EUROMOD project involves 35 individuals in 18 institutions from 15 countries. Thanks are due to the whole team, particularly Tony Atkinson and François Bourguignon, for their advice and helpful comments. We are also grateful to Thesia Garner and Lavinia Mitton for comments on an earlier version. The views that are expressed, as well as any remaining errors, are the sole responsibility of the authors.

1 For more information, see the report on the EUROMOD Preparatory Project (Sutherland (ed.) 1997).
2 See Atkinson *et al.*, (1995), Smeeding and Weinberg (1998), Harris (1998a).
3 This list is intended as a guide to the multiplicative or additive adjustments that may be made to simulated income. It is not a comprehensive list of all the aspects that must be considered in making national model outputs comparable and capable of being aggregated. Two additional factors, which are not addressed, stand out: the unit of analysis over which income is aggregated, and

the cash income definition itself. See Callan and Sutherland (1997) and Sutherland (ed.) (1997) for a general discussion of these issues.

4 The *Panel Study of Belgian Households* (1994), the French *Enquête sur le Budget des Familles* (1989), the *German Socio-Economic Panel* (1995), the Irish *Survey on Income Distribution, Poverty and the Usage of State Services* (1987), the Italian *Survey of Household Income and Wealth* (1993) and the UK *Family Expenditure Survey* (1991). These subsamples, although no replacement for the full samples, appear to be adequate for the purposes of the illustrations presented here. After standard grossing up procedures, we find that mean disposable incomes, taxes and benefits fit satisfactorily well with what is observed in the original full samples. For more information see Bourguignon *et al.*, (1998) and O'Donoghue (1998).

5 So if a one-person household has an income of 100 ecu they are assumed to be at the same point in the income distribution as a four-person household with an income of 200 ecu.

6 It is important to emphasise that the output from *Eur6* is based on small subsamples designed to be used for illustrative exercises. The results shown should not be treated as final estimates of the national or six-country income distributions.

7 Evans (1995) considers the size of these groups in the UK and France.

8 The national accounts figures are calculated from total national accounts household income less employer pension contributions, imputed rent, non-government current transfers and direct taxes taken from the OECD national accounts (OECD, 1997).

9 Interestingly, the UK Family Expenditure Survey has a lower overall response rate than is typical for income surveys in other countries (Harris, 1998a). This suggests that response rate itself is not necessarily a good indicator of general data quality or representativeness.

10 The OECD scale gives weight of 1 to the household head, 0.5 to each child (aged under 14) and 0.7 to other people in the household.

11 This is apparent when comparing the share of total *Eur6* population in Tables 6.6 and 6.8: for example, Irish households make up 1.1% of all households, but Irish individuals comprise 1.6% of all individuals.

7 The impact of demographic and other changes on expenditure on pharmaceutical benefits in 2020 in Australia

Agnes Walker, Richard Percival and Ann Harding

7.1 Why are health expenditures of concern?

Scope of paper

The main aim of this paper is to present a new microsimulation model of Australia's Pharmaceutical Benefits Scheme (PBS). This is done by reporting three illustrative policy-relevant simulations of what might happen by 2020 if the current scheme remained unchanged. The simulations concern the effects of population ageing, rising medicine costs and a generally healthier population by 2020.

The simulations were chosen to demonstrate the potential usefulness of the PBS model in examining the implications of existing trends for public expenditures (which need to be planned and budgeted for) and on distributional outcomes (which may also require policy attention).

Health generally

In Australia, expenditure on health services is shared between the public and private sectors, the public share in 1996–97 being about 69% of the total (AIHW, 1998, p. 164). The main areas of health expenditure are medical services and benefits, hospital and nursing home services and benefits, and pharmaceutical services and benefits. Together, these accounted for 77% of total recurrent expenditure in 1995–96 (AIHW, 1998, p. 167). Between 1975–76 and 1996–97, total health expenditure in Australia increased in real terms by an average of 3.5% a year (AIHW, 1998, p. 168). When expressed as a percentage of GDP, total expenditure on health increased from a little over 5% in 1970 to about 8.5% in 1996–97 (AIHW, 1998, p. 169).

While these figures appear to indicate that changes to health expenditure have been relatively stable and that their share of national resources has increased slowly, concerns about expenditure trends have been expressed for two reasons. First, the rate at which real health spending per person has been increasing appears to have accelerated in recent years (National Commission of Audit, 1996, p. 138). Second, some recent projections of health expenditure based on existing trends have shown health consuming much higher levels of GDP by the middle of the twenty-first century. Projected estimates of total health costs for Australia have ranged from 11% of GDP in the year 2051 (Clare and Tulpule, 1994, p. 36) to 17% in the year 2041 (National Commission of Audit, 1996, p. 138) and 19% in the year 2041 (Rothman, 1998, p. 15).

These growth estimates have been driven by projections of anticipated demographic change (principally, population ageing), of steadily increasing demand for health services, and of increases in costs as new and more expensive forms of health services are introduced and existing services are used more frequently (Podger, 1998, p. 7).

Pharmaceutical benefits in particular

Australia's Pharmaceutical Benefits Scheme was introduced by the federal government in 1948 to provide all Australians with reliable and affordable access to medicines. Medicines must first be approved for use in Australia and then be assessed as being cost effective in order to be listed on the scheme. The scheme covers Australian residents and eligible foreign visitors (unless they are treated in institutions, e.g., hospitals). Some 80% of prescribed drug sales are covered by the scheme and, on average, the government subsidises patients to the extent of 80% of PBS drug costs.

In the past few years the government has been concerned by PBS cost increases averaging over 14% a year – a rate considerably more rapid than that of the consumer price index. One response has been for the government to suggest that 'more of the costs must be borne by users of the Scheme' (Budget Papers, 1996b, p. 19). Accordingly, in recent budgets the level of contributions to be met by PBS patients has been increased and the list of drugs covered by the Pharmaceutical Benefits Scheme has been more tightly specified. This latter measure effectively reduced the number of drugs listed and eliminated the more expensive brands in cases where similar lower cost drugs were available. Currently around 80% of total government subsidies through the Pharmaceutical Benefits Scheme accrue to concessional patients – that is, those with specified Department of Social Security (DSS) cards[1] – and 20% to general patients.

Description of the Pharmaceutical Benefits Scheme

Under the Pharmaceutical Benefits Scheme the costs of some 1,700 medicines are subsidised. Since 1 January 1997:

- for *general* patients the maximum contribution for each PBS medicine is $20, the government paying for the rest
- for *concessional* patients an additional subsidy applies, so that their maximum contribution is only $3.20 per PBS medicine.

In essence, although some PBS medicines can cost over $100, patients are required to pay at most $20. If the full price of the drug is below $20 for general patients, or below $3.20 for concessional patients, then the patient pays the full price.

Families needing a lot of medicines in any one year are protected by the PBS safety net.[2] Since 1997, once a family has a record of spending beyond the safety net limit of $612.60 in a calendar year, general patients pay only $3.20 for each further PBS medicine within the same year. For concessional patients there is no cost once their families have a record of spending beyond the safety net limit of $166.40 in a calendar year. In this case, the government pays the full price of all further PBS medicines prescribed within the year. Each year, on 1 January, the safety net for each family is effectively reset to zero for administrative purposes.

If doctors do not prescribe the lowest price brand, patients may be required to pay an additional charge. However, this can be avoided by patients asking their doctor to prescribe the lowest price brand, or their pharmacist to substitute a less expensive brand. The policy settings of the Pharmaceutical Benefits Scheme for 1996–97, the base case for the simulations in this paper, are given in Table 7.1.

Table 7.1. *Policy settings of the Pharmaceutical Benefits Scheme for 1996–97: base case*

	From 1/7/1996 to 31/12/1996 $	From 1/1/1997 to 30/6/1997 $
Co-payment – Concessional		
Below safety net	2.70	3.20
Above safety net	0	0
Co-payment – General		
Below safety net	17.40	20.00
Above safety net	2.70	3.20
Safety net – Concessional	140.00	166.40
Safety net – General	600.00	612.60

Source: Unpublished information supplied by the Department of Health and Family Services.

7.2 Previous studies of the scheme compared with NATSEM's approach

Previous studies of the Pharmaceutical Benefits Scheme

Of the very few published studies in Australia that analyse expenditure on pharmaceuticals, nearly all estimate costs at one point in time. These have mostly been relatively simple distributional analyses of the benefits of pharmaceutical subsidies (for example, ABS, 1987, 1992; Harding, 1984; Percival and Schofield, 1995; Wilson, 1993). However, more recently a considerably more detailed analysis of pharmaceutical use and benefits has been undertaken by Schofield (1998). Apart from the health expenditure studies already mentioned, the study by Goss *et al.*, (1994) appears to be one of the few attempts to project health costs that includes expenditure on pharmaceuticals.

Most published studies have either subsumed the Pharmaceutical Benefits Scheme into total health expenditure or adopted a 'means-based' approach in their analyses.[3] While such an approach has the advantage of being simple and quick to develop, Schofield (1998) shows that it also has the disadvantage of greatly undervaluing the subsidies provided to low-income families – the main beneficiaries of the Pharmaceutical Benefits Scheme. As noted earlier, currently some 80% of PBS benefits go to those DSS cardholders who are users of prescribed medicines. Thus, to avoid significantly underestimating PBS benefits, it is essential to obtain accurate usage and cost estimates for a range of specific subgroups.

Schofield (1998) shows that an alternative method to the standard 'means-based' approach, which relies on person-based microsimulation techniques, is capable of providing considerably more accurate and detailed estimates.

NATSEM's approach

There are various alternative approaches that can be taken to projecting expenditures such as those of the Pharmaceutical Benefits Scheme. The simplest is to derive average per person expenditure amounts, typically by age and gender, and then to use similar age and gender population projections to estimate future total expenditure. More sophisticated variants of this approach can include adjustments for changes in, for example, mortality, the cost of drugs and the average use of drugs. Such approaches do not require a microsimulation model, particularly when the analysis is confined to estimating changes in aggregate expenditure.

A significantly more complex approach would be to use a dynamic microsimulation model such as NATSEM's DYNAMOD model (Antcliff *et al.*, 1996). If sufficient information were included in the modelling of health status and the usage of health services, a dynamic model would be able to analyse the impact on medical costs of changes such as increasing unemployment or more single person households. Particularly useful would be a dynamic microsimulation model that used survival functions to model life cycle changes (as described in Antcliff, 1993). When modelling the usage of health services, this would allow the number of years a person was away from death to be known. The value of this information has been established by Fuchs (1984), who argued that the number of years to a person's death is one of the best indicators of their level of health expenditure.

In this study an intermediate approach has been adopted, which uses a static microsimulation model, standard population projections and statistical ageing techniques.[4] While a static approach has limitations when projecting into the future, and does not consider the interrelationships that a dynamic model would, it allows trends to be analysed at a considerably greater level of detail than is common with a dynamic model.

As far as the authors are aware, no previous study has been undertaken to project the costs of pharmaceuticals using a microsimulation approach. The benefits of this approach comprise the more general benefits of microsimulation. These include the ability to change a greater variety of elements independently, and study budgetary and distributional effects in considerably greater detail.

The PBS Model is described briefly in Walker, Percival and Harding (1998) and at some length in Walker, Percival and Fischer (1998).

7.3 Scenarios

In this section selected simulations are reported to illustrate the capabilities of the PBS Model. In all simulations it is assumed that the 1996–97 policy settings of the Pharmaceutical Benefits Scheme remain unchanged over time.

Government and patient costs of the scheme in the base case (1996–97) and the projection year (2020) are compared under different scenarios. Also referred to are changes in other variables, such as the age and gender distribution of prescriptions and costs for concessional and general patients by 36 drug types, out-of-pocket expenditures by family type, and patient contributions as a proportion of family disposable income by income quintile.

This study was fortunate to have data at the level of 36 drug groupings (collected and made available for the first time in such detail) and to be able to match the groups with administrative prescription and cost data.

Using microsimulation techniques it was possible to simulate prescriptions and costs, individual by individual, or family by family. It was also possible to attach to each individual or family a much broader range of characteristics than is possible with conventional methods.

Selecting the scenarios

In selecting the scenarios, the aim was to focus on those factors that were most likely to have a major impact on PBS outcomes over the period 1996–97 to 2020. Nevertheless, the scenarios are only illustrative. Although based on past established or recently emerging trends, they do not represent predictions of what might actually happen.

Preliminary investigations suggested that the key factors likely to influence future PBS costs included an older but healthier population, a change in the ratio of concessional patients to general patients, an increase in the rate of prescription of PBS drugs, and an increase in the costs of PBS medicines. Currently available information on these factors suggests the following:

- Population ageing is likely to be important. The ABS (1996b) has projected that the proportion of people aged 65 years or over in the Australian population will rise from around 12% in 1995 to close to 17% by 2020. Discounting the possibility of a major disaster (such as war) or a return to 'post-war' levels of immigration, population ageing seems a near certainty. So population ageing was chosen as one of the factors to be simulated in the scenarios

- There could be a decline in the proportion of older people qualifying for the age pension (leading to fewer concessional PBS patients) as a result of recent policy initiatives such as the compulsory Superannuation Guarantee Charge. However, it has been estimated that the proportion of pension-age persons qualifying for the age pension (currently 82% if service pensions are included) is likely to be virtually unchanged by 2020, assuming that the current 'income testing' and 'flat rate' age-pension arrangements do not change (Rothman, 1997; unpublished information supplied by the Retirement Income Modelling (RIM) Task Force).[5] On this basis, it was assumed in the simulations that the qualifying rules for the age pension (and other DSS cards eligible under the Pharmaceutical Benefits Scheme) would remain unchanged over the study period

- The rate of increase in the price of PBS prescription drugs is likely to be important. The introduction of newer, more expensive drugs and the tendency of medical practitioners to prescribe these drugs rather than cheaper alternatives has had the effect of increasing the average price of PBS medicines. For this reason, future increases in the price of PBS drugs were chosen as a variable in the scenarios

- Increases in the number of scripts may not be as important as increases in their prices, since past trends suggest that such changes tend to be small compared with the rate of drug price increases. In the simulations, prescription increases arising from the ageing of the population were selected for analysis. However, other factors that may have led to additional increases in prescription numbers (e.g., if doctors tended to prescribe a higher number of medicines per patient visit) have not been considered

- Health risk factors are expected to be less important in future, in part because of government efforts to encourage people to adopt healthier lifestyles. If people responded to these efforts, the rate of increase in prescription numbers would be lower than otherwise. In this paper, the likely effects of healthier lifestyles on the Pharmaceutical Benefits Scheme will be illustrated by a lower prevalence of heart disease and related illnesses in 2020. Heart disease was chosen as an example because currently it is the major cause of death in Australia.

In summary, the factors selected for illustrative analyses are:

- population ageing
- PBS drug price rises
- a lower prevalence of heart disease arising from healthier lifestyles.

The factors studied in this paper have been structured into scenarios so that only one factor changes when moving from one scenario to the next. A key advantage of this approach is that it allows the various factors to be ranked in terms of their relative importance.

Projecting the elements of the scenarios to 2020

Projecting the PBS patient population
The bases for the population projections to 2020 were the ABS Series A projections (high fertility, low overseas migration and medium interstate migration) (see ABS, 1996b). These were considered by gender and five-year age groups.

However, these projections first needed to be scaled, since the input data to the PBS Model covered only residents in private dwellings (that is, they excluded those in institutions) and covered only persons who reported in the household expenditure survey that they had spent money on prescribed drugs.

For 2020, the scaling factors adopted were based on the shares of people living in private dwellings and of those living in institutions in Australia's total population, and the shares of those who had spent on prescribed drugs in Australia's total population. The scaling was carried out by:

(a) computing the proportion of 'drug spenders' among all Australians by age and gender;
(b) adjusting ABS population projections for 2020 (ABS, 1996b, Series A) so as to include only patients in private dwellings (that is those in institutions, such as hospitals, nursing homes and prisons were excluded). This was done by reducing the 2020 ABS projections by the base-year ratio of the population in private dwellings to the total resident population; and
(c) applying the proportion of 'drug spenders' among all Australians, as described in (a), to the 'institution adjusted' 2020 ABS projections, as described in (b).

Figure 7.1 shows the relationship between all Australians and spenders on prescribed drugs by age. It shows that spenders on prescribed medicines aged 50 years and over make up the highest proportion of the total population in their age group. The lowest proportion is for the 15–49 years age group, with children 0–14 years old falling in between. More importantly, for the purposes of this study, Figure 7.1 shows the target population for re-weighting the input data set to the PBS Model (that is, the population of spenders).

To re-weight the input data set to the PBS Model to match 2020 population targets, the utility CALMAR (calibration of margins) was used. CALMAR was developed by the French statistical agency, Institut National de la Statistique et des Études Économiques (INSEE), which kindly provided it to NATSEM. For details on CALMAR, see Deville et al., (1993) and Deville and Särndal (1992).

The usual way of re-weighting with CALMAR is at the individual level. However, by suitably rearranging the input data, re-weighting at a group level is also possible. For this study, re-weighting at the income unit (usually family) level seemed attractive, as this process could ensure that all members of a family had the same final weight. Experiments carried out for an earlier study (Walker 1997, appendix) showed that the family-linked option, with use of either the linear or the exponential optimisation method (of the four alternatives provided by CALMAR), was preferable for applications of this kind.

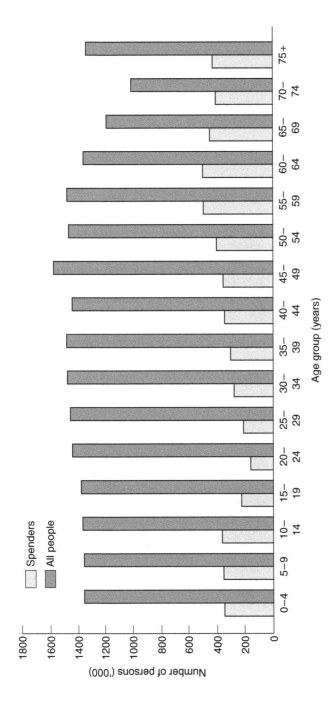

Figure 7.1 Spenders on prescribed drugs and all persons in private dwellings in 2020
Sources: for 'Spenders', the ABS 1993–94 Household Expenditure Survey; for 'All people', the ABS (1996b) Series A projections adjusted to exclude persons living in institutions.

Table 7.2. *PBS prescription numbers and expenditures (current prices)*

	1992–93	1993–94	1994–95	1995–96	1996–97
Number of scripts (millions)	n.a.[a]	115	119	125	124
Total cost ($m)	1,777	2,080	2,326	2,669	2,863
Change from previous year (%)		17	12	15	7
Cost to patient ($m)	360	396	445	478	530
Change from previous year (%)		10	12	7	11
Cost to government ($m)	1,417	1,685	1,882	2,191	2,333
Change from previous year (%)		19	12	16	6.5
Government share (%)	79.7	81.0	80.9	82.1	81.5

Note:
[a] Not available.
Sources: Department of Health and Family Services (1996a; 1997).

For this report re-weighting was carried out using the family-linked option combined with the exponential optimisation method.

Prescribed drug cost projections

Between 1992–93 and 1996–97, the cost to government of the Pharmaceutical Benefits Scheme increased by 15% a year and the total cost by 13% a year on average. Despite efforts to control increases in PBS public spending through higher co-payments and tighter control over drug eligibility, the government's share of total PBS expenditure had increased from 80% in 1992–93 to around 82% by 1995-96 (Table 7.2).

While budget estimates suggest that in the year to 1998–99 the cost to government of the Pharmaceutical Benefits Scheme is likely to increase by a relatively low 7% (Budget Papers, 1998a, pp. 4, 46), for the three years to 2001–02 they estimate the annual growth rate of the cost to government to be 12% a year on average (Budget Papers, 1998b). This is in line with a statement by Podger (1998) that, owing to people's expectations of further improvements in the standard of health care services, the upward pressures on health costs are likely to strengthen.

Overall, since the early 1990s, the total average cost of PBS subsidised medicines, after accounting for inflation, has shown a growth rate of around 10% a year.[6] The corresponding trend growth rate in the cost to government of PBS medicines would be higher, reflecting the much higher share of contributions by government than by patients.

In the input data to the PBS Model it is possible to change the total average cost (that is patient plus government costs divided by the total number of prescriptions) of each of the 36 drug types in line with the growth rates set for the scenarios. Through the simulations it is then possible to obtain estimates of the projected shares borne by government and by PBS patients.

Initially, the intention was to simulate the effects of a 'past trends continue' scenario, in which the government was assumed to be able to contain future total average cost (or price) increases to past levels. This would have required setting the growth in PBS drug prices to a rate close to 10% a year. However, it was found that over the 23-year study period such a growth rate would have led to extremely high cost increases.

In line with the 'illustrative' aims of this paper, it was assumed that the price of each of the 36 drug types (in 1996–97 dollars) would increase at a compound rate of 5% a year between 1996–97 and 2020.

Health status projections

There are two ways in which simulations of improved health status could be undertaken. The first would be to account for changes in age-specific health status as a result of increasing life expectancy. This could be undertaken as an adjustment to estimates of expected health expenditures to account for a decrease in mortality for different age and gender groups. The adjustment would take the form of an index, which would be derived from longitudinal data showing rapidly increasing health expenditure in the years just before death. As life expectancies increased and the proportion of each age and gender group which was approaching death fell, an adjustment would be made to account for the expected fall in health expenditures (Goss *et al.*, 1994, appendix 1).

The second way would be to account for expected changes in health status by simulating changes in the population due to reductions in the incidence and prevalence of specific diseases as a result of better health interventions and preventative strategies. This method would be more directly adaptable to projections based on a static microsimulation model. This is because it would allow the impact of reductions in particular diseases to be simulated and their effect on health costs to be estimated.

In this study, health expenditures were adjusted according to anticipated declines in deaths due to cardiovascular disease. For purposes of modelling the impact of such declines on PBS outlays, information about projected changes in morbidity – rather than mortality – would have been preferred. However, while there is an obvious relationship between mortality and incidence, incidence data for cardiovascular disease in Australia are very limited and were not available at the time the analyses reported in this paper were undertaken.

Accordingly, it was assumed that a reduction in mortality due to cardiovascular disease would be matched by a similar reduction in morbidity *and* drug usage. Implicit in this assumption is not only that declining mortality will correspond to declining morbidity,[7] but that it is as a result of improvements in health risk factors rather than earlier intervention or better treatment. In addition, no consideration was given to the possibility that an improvement in cardiovascular disease morbidity might be offset by subsequent increases in morbidity in other health areas (for example, cancers or dementia).

In Australia, cardiovascular disease has been identified by the federal government as one of five national health priority areas towards which resources and effort will be directed, with the goal of achieving improved outcomes (AIHW, 1997a, p. 2). The achievement of these outcomes is based on the expectation of continuing improvements in a range of specific health risk factors. For example, the Australian government has funded anti-smoking campaigns for many years and there is now evidence that such campaigns and other anti-smoking initiatives have resulted in a steady decline in smoking rates in Australia among most groups (AIHW, 1998, p. 143; Harding and Percival, 1997).

Between 1986 and 1994, deaths from cardiovascular disease declined in Australia by an average of 5.7% for men and 6.2% for women (AIHW, 1997b, p. 12). The targets that have been set by the government for the year 2000 approximately match this trend. However, when these targets were set it was stated that it was unlikely that all the health indicator targets would be met even over this short period as, for example, the decline in smoking may not continue and the proportion of overweight persons may continue to increase (AIHW, 1997a, p. 7). Accordingly, in studying the impact of a reduction in cardiovascular disease between 1996–97 and 2020, it was assumed that only 75% of the national health priority areas' target rate will be met over that period and that meeting the target will then become progressively harder. Thus, it was assumed that only 37.5% of the target rate will be met between 2001 and 2010, and 18.8% between 2011 and 2020. The resulting projected rate of decline in deaths is shown in Figure 7.2, with the same rate of reduction applied to both males and females.

It is quite possible, of course, that the projected rates of reduction may not be met, despite being based on fairly conservative assumptions. However, the purpose of this simulation is to estimate the effect on PBS outlays *if* such targets were met. As Table 7.3 shows, this scenario projects a fall of 28% in age standardised death rates from cardiovascular disease between 1997 and 2020.

Summary of the scenarios simulated

In summary, the scenarios studied were:

- Scenario 1 – *'unavoidable'* – which **aged** the **population** of 'users of prescribed drugs' to 2020 (based on ABS projections by gender and five year age groups);

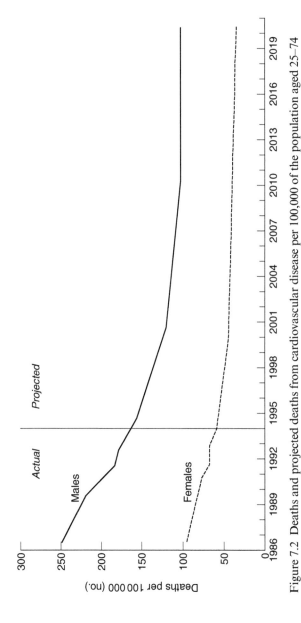

Figure 7.2 Deaths and projected deaths from cardiovascular disease per 100,000 of the population aged 25–74 years, Australia

Note: Standardised for age.

Data sources: AIHW (1997b, p. 12); authors' calculations.

Table 7.3. *Estimated change in deaths from cardiovascular disease per 100,000 of the population aged 25–74 years, Australia*

	1997 (no.)	2020 (no.)	Change (%)
Males	138	99	−28.0
Females	50	36	−28.0

Note: Standardised for age.
Sources: AIHW (1997b, p. 12); authors' calculations.

- Scenario 2 – *'higher cost'* – which combined ageing (as in scenario 1) with average **price rises** for the 36 drug categories at the rate of 5% a year in real terms;[8]
- Scenario 3 – *'lower cost'* – which combined scenarios 1 and 2 with a **healthier population** (illustrated by an assumed 28% decline over the period in the prevalence of heart and related diseases).

Note that all three scenarios are likely to be conservative. The main reason for this is that, since the early 1990s, PBS drug costs have tended to rise considerably more rapidly than the 5% yearly increases simulated. Indeed, as already noted, the 1998–99 budget allows for a 12% a year increase in the costs to government of the PBS over the three years to 2001–02. Another reason is that, to date, policies to reduce the mortality from heart disease have not been sufficiently successful to meet the set targets. This suggests that the targets simulated, although lower than those set by government, may still be over-optimistic.

Finally, the increases in the number of scripts have been under-estimated in the simulation. This is because, while this study allowed for prescription increases due to population ageing, it did not allow for the possibility that past trends toward a general increase in the usage of pharmaceuticals (both prescribed and non-prescribed) could continue in future.

7.4 Results

The illustrative simulations in this study relate to only those medications that attract a government subsidy under the Pharmaceutical Benefits Scheme. The high number of PBS prescriptions with a price below co-payment is thus not included in the results presented. Details of the 36 drug categories studied are in the Appendix Table 7A.1.

Table 7.4. *Total number of prescriptions: base case and scenarios*

	Year	Number of scripts (million)
Base case	1996–97	129.2
Scenario 1	2020	184.9
Scenario 2	2020	184.9
Scenario 3	2020	158.9

Source: PBS Model simulations.

Total prescription numbers

The differences in PBS subsidised prescription numbers between the base case and scenarios 1 and 2 arise from population changes between 1996–97 and 2020. The assumption underlying the simulations is that, within each age and gender cell, the pattern of usage across the 36 drug categories remains unchanged over time. Thus, reflecting the projected increase in the Australian population from 18 to 22 million between 1996–97 and 2020, as well as the fact that older people use more medication than younger people, the number of prescriptions attracting a government subsidy under the PBS will increase not only as the population grows, but also as it ages.

In scenario 3, there are additional changes to prescription numbers by drug type, arising from the assumption that prescribed medicine usage will be lower in line with the assumed reduction in people with heart and related diseases.

The numbers of prescriptions subsidised in the base case and in each of the scenarios are given in Table 7.4. The table shows that, under the assumptions adopted, PBS prescriptions attracting a government subsidy in the case of the first two scenarios increase from 129.2 million in 1996–97 to 184.9 million in 2020. This increase of 43% arises from changes in Australia's population only. With the same population structure, but with a lower prevalence of heart disease (scenario 3), the increase in prescriptions is limited to 23%.

Costs to patients and government

Results at the aggregate level

In all simulations the PBS co-payments and safety net thresholds were held at their 1996–97 levels. Thus, patient contributions per prescription did not change.

In scenarios 1 and 2, patient contributions will only change as a result of population ageing. Also, in scenario 3 patient contributions will be lower than for the other scenarios because of the assumption that people will use less medication as their health improves (Figure 7.3).

The cost to government of the Pharmaceutical Benefits Scheme in scenario 1 is estimated to increase from around $2.5 billion in 1996–97 to $3.5 billion by 2020 in constant 1996–97 dollars (Figure 7.4). This is a result of prescription number growth in line with increases in the size and the average age of Australia's population. Considerably greater increases are projected for scenario 2. This is because, with per unit patient contributions fixed, the cost of all growth in drug prices over the period will be borne by the government. Under this scenario the estimated cost to government in 2020 would be $12.5 billion (a change from around 0.5% of GDP in 1996–97 to 1.6% of GDP in 2020, assuming a 1% a year increase in productivity).[9]

While appearing large, the scenario 2 estimates are in fact quite conservative. First, the assumed 5% a year drug price rises are well below recent trends. Second, the estimates do not account for the prescription increases that would occur as a result of drugs moving, as their prices rise, from below co-payment in 1996–97 to above co-payment in 2020.

While theoretically the 5% a year price rises could be offset by similar increases in co-payments and safety net thresholds, such an option seemed unrealistic. This is mainly because already some 80% of prescriptions go to patients with concession cards (that is, to people receiving government support). Significant increases in PBS co-payment levels to such patients would imply corresponding increases in the income they received from government.

In addition, the trend in incomes of families over the period 1982 to 1993–94 shows virtually no increase in real terms (see Harding, 1997, p. 347). It may thus be difficult for future governments to increase patients' share of PBS costs to a significant extent. Indeed, as seen in Table 7.2, the recent trend has been for patient contributions as a proportion of total PBS costs to fall rather than increase. On that basis, no consideration was given to possible increases in PBS co-payments or safety net thresholds in these illustrative scenarios. Nor was an attempt made to assess the likely cost effects of 1996–97 below-co-payment drugs shifting into the above-co-payment group by 2020. While the model has an estimate of the number of below-co-payment drugs for 1996–97 by drug type, all that is known about their prices is that they were below co-payment (that is, $20 currently for general patients). It can also be safely assumed that very few, if any, drugs would have cost less than $3.20 in that year. In that case, the upward creeping of drug prices would be relevant to general patients only.

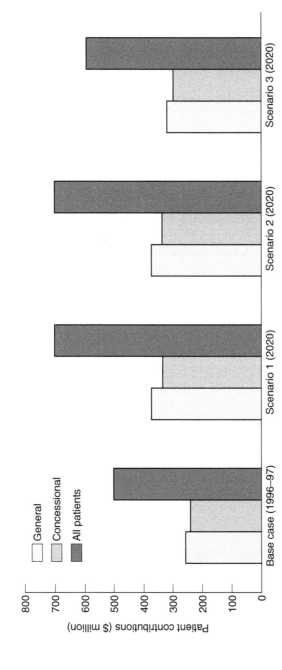

Figure 7.3 Patient contributions to PBS drug costs, base case and scenarios, 1996–97
Data source: PBS Model simulations.

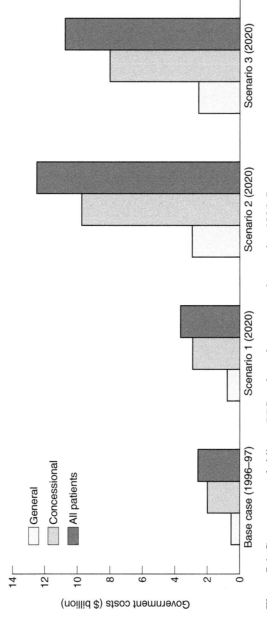

Figure 7.4 Government subsidies to PBS patients, base case and scenarios, 1996–7
Data source: PBS Model simulations.

Table 7.5. *Total costs to government, base case and scenarios (1996–97 prices)*

	Year	Government cost (\$ billion)
Base case	1996–97	2.5
Scenario 1	2020	3.6
Scenario 2	2020	12.5
Scenario 3	2020	10.6

Source: PBS Model simulations.

Table 7.5 shows that, as a result of population ageing alone, government expenditures on the Pharmaceutical Benefits Scheme would be \$1.1 billion higher (in 1996–97 prices) in 2020 than in the base case. This represents an increase of 44% over the period. To this would be added a further increase of \$8.9 billion due to higher drug prices (a three-and-a-half fold increase, or 247%). Such increases could, however, be limited to \$7 billion if fewer people suffered heart conditions (close to a three-fold increase, or 194% due to drug price rises). This represents a saving of \$1.9 billion on what would have occurred without the assumed improvements in Australians' health.

These results suggest that, of the variables studied, drug price rises are the most important in terms of their ability to influence future PBS-related government expenditures. Possible improvements in health are the next most important, especially if they could be extended beyond heart conditions. Population ageing, although having a significant impact, has been shown to be the least important.

As Podger (1998) noted, two of Australia's biggest uncapped programmes are Medicare and the Pharmaceutical Benefits Scheme. The model results provide a good illustration of the likely impact of the open-ended nature of the PBS – that is, an increase of at least 50% in the cost to government of the scheme, with much greater increases possible in the absence of policy initiatives.

Results by drug type, gender and age

The results reported above provided an indication of the likely impact of population ageing, higher drug prices and improved health on aggregate PBS characteristics. However, one of the advantages of microsimulation is the ability to 'unpack' the aggregate results so that outcomes can be analysed by drug type and by a range of socio-economic variables (such as age, gender and income).

Results concerning the ranking of government cost increases by the 36 medicine types, by gender and by broad age group are provided in Chapter 4 of Walker, Percival and Harding (1998). They show, for example, that the increases in the costs to government of the PBS would be concentrated around people aged 40 years or more. The highest increases would be for drugs associated with heart disease (serum lipid reducing agents, heart and blood pressure drugs and fluid/diuretic medications), such costs having been estimated to increase by over 60% under scenario 1.

Patient contributions as a proportion of income

Given the scenarios chosen for illustrating the capabilities of the PBS Model, spending on PBS medicines by families as a proportion of their disposable incomes is not expected to change much between the base case and scenario 1. This is because the levels of PBS co-payments, safety net thresholds and real (after inflation) disposable incomes were kept unchanged over the study period.

Since similar patterns would emerge for all the simulations considered, families' out-of-pocket expenditure on PBS medicines as a proportion of disposable income was analysed for the base case only. As noted earlier, this was the first time that socio-economic data could be linked to detailed PBS administrative data, and thus the first time that distributional analyses of patient spending on PBS drugs could be carried out. Results were reported in Walker, Percival and Harding (1998, Chapter 4). They showed, for example, that while, overall, around 2% of families' disposable incomes were spent 'out of pocket' on PBS drugs, this figure rose to 7% for general patients in the lowest disposable income quintile.

7.5 Summary and conclusions

This paper has described the use of a microsimulation model to shed new light on the distributional and other impacts of Australia's Pharmaceutical Benefits Scheme. Its main aim was to illustrate some of the potential uses of the model by examining projected PBS expenditures in 2020 under three illustrative scenarios. These covered population ageing, increases in PBS drug prices, and improvements in cardiovascular mortality and morbidity rates. In all scenarios the policy settings of the Pharmaceutical Benefits Scheme were held at their 1996–97 levels.

The simulations suggested that increases in government subsidies under the Pharmaceutical Benefits Scheme would benefit mainly Australians aged 40 or more; that population ageing was likely to have greatest impact on PBS drugs used for heart disease and related conditions; and that patients' contributions to the cost of subsidised PBS drugs made up a relatively small proportion of their disposable incomes (around 2% on average).

An unexpected but striking result was that, although per prescription medicine costs were projected to increase at only half the rates experienced in recent years, their impact on the extent of PBS subsidies was likely to be very large. While a *less than 50%* increase in government costs was projected from population *ageing*, a *five-fold* increase in subsidies occurred when *drug price rises* were also considered. This was reduced to a *four-fold* increase when likely *improvements* in the *health* of Australians were also accounted for.

Appendix 7.1 Classification of medications

The medication codes used in this paper and listed in Table 7A.1 are those of the Anatomical Therapeutic Chemical (ATC) classification index groupings (level 2). The medications belonging to each group are detailed in ABS (1996a, appendix B).

Table 7.A1.1. *Classification of medications*

ABS code	ATC code	Description
		1. Arthritis drugs
1	M01A	Anti-inflammatory and antirheumatic products, non-steroids
2	M01C	Specific antirheumatic agents
		2. Allergy drugs
3	R01A	Nasal decongestants for topical use
4	R06A	Antihistamines for systemic use
		3. Asthma medications
5	R03A	Adrenergics, inhalants
6	R03B	Other anti-asthmatics, inhalants
7	R03D	Other anti-asthmatics for systemic use
		4. Diabetes medications
8	A10A	Insulins
9	A10B	Oral blood glucose lowering drugs
		5. Heart and blood pressure drugs
10	C01A	Cardiac glycosides
11	C01B	Anti-arrhythmics
12	C01D	Vasodilators used in cardiac disease
13	C02A	Anti-adrenergic agents, centrally acting
14	C02C	Anti-adrenergic agents, peripherally acting
15	C02D	Arteriolar smooth muscle, agents acting on
16	C02E	Arteriolar smooth muscle, agents acting on[a]

Table 7.A1.1. (*cont.*)

ABS code	ATC code	Description
17	C07A	B-blocking agents, plain
18	C08	Calcium channel blockers
		6. Fluid/diuretic medications
19	C03A	Low-ceiling diuretics, thiazides
20	C03B	Low-ceiling diuretics, excl. thiazides
21	C03C	High-ceiling diuretics
22	C03D	Potassium-sparing agents
23	C03E	Diuretics and potassium sparing agents in combination
		7. Serum lipid reducing agents
24	B04A	Cholesterol and triglycerid reducers[a]
		8. Analgesic medications
25	N02A	Opiods
26	N02B	Other analgesics and antipyretics
		9. Psycholeptic medications
27	N05A	Antipsychotics
28	N05B	Anxiolytics
29	N05C	Hypnotics and sedatives
		10. Medications for anxiety/ depression/ nervous conditions
30	N06A	Antidepressants
		11. Other medications
31	0022	Vitamin and mineral supplements
32	0023	Cough/cold medications
33	0024	Skin ointments and creams
34	0025	Stomach medications (incl. antacids, drugs for treatment of peptic ulcer, flatulence)
35	0026	Laxatives
36	0027	Other medications (incl. antibiotics)[b]

Notes:
[a] The classification of Anatomical Therapeutic Chemicals has changed since 1995. C02E became C09A (ACE inhibitors) and B04A became C10A.
[b] In the case of national health survey data, ATC category 0027 includes drugs that could not be classified owing to a 'Don't know/can't remember' response.
Source: Anatomical Therapeutic Chemical Classification, World Health Organisation, 1994.

Notes

Work for this paper was carried out at the National Centre for Social and Economic Modelling (NATSEM). The authors are grateful for the advice and assistance of colleagues in preparing this paper. Acknowledgements, model description and additional simulation results are contained in other papers (referenced in the body of the text).

1 These cover the Pensioner Concession Card, the Commonwealth Seniors Health Card, the Health Benefit Card and the Health Care Card. For details, see the relevant Department of Social Security facts sheets.

2 A 'family' is defined as including a spouse (or *de facto* spouse), children under 16 years of age and full-time dependent students under 25 years of age.

3 A 'means-based' approach involves imputing the use and public cost of subsidised services by calculating the mean service use and cost for either the whole population or different subpopulations.

4 For a discussion of static microsimulation models and of projections obtained from them through use of statistical ageing techniques see Harding (ed.) (1996, pp. 2–6).

5 The RIM Task Force found that the Superannuation Guarantee Charge will not have a noticeable effect before 2016 and is unlikely to make a significant impact even after that date. RIM projections suggest that, without changes to the current rules of preservation (non-accessibility until retirement age), by 2020 about 84.6% of the population aged 65 years and over will qualify for the age pension. If preservation to age 65 became compulsory, then this ratio would be reduced to 83%.

6 Over the period 1992–93 to 1997–98, the inflation-adjusted trend growth rate was 9% a year when fitting an exponential trend line, and 11% a year when fitting a linear trend line.

7 Some support for this assumption is given in a report for one Australian State and on one measure (hospital admission with myocardial infarction). Between 1971 and 1982 there was an annual median fall in the incidence of myocardial infarction of 2% in males and 3% in females, most likely as a result of a reduction in the prevalence of risk factors (Martin *et al.*, 1989).

8 The 5% a year figure refers to compound growth rates. In the case of scenario 2, the same results would have been obtained if a 9% a year linear growth rate had been assumed.

9 These shares were calculated using projections of GDP reported in Clare and Tulpule (1994, p. 23). The projections were based on the assumption that productivity will grow at a rate of 1% a year on average. For a discussion on the considerable sensitivity of GDP projections to the assumed rate of productivity growth, see Walker (1998, Section 3.5).

Part Two

Dynamic modelling

8 Public pensions in a dynamic microanalytic framework: the case of France

Carole Bonnet and Ronan Mahieu

8.1 Introduction

Population ageing and slower economic growth rates raise many questions about the future of intergenerational public transfers. For some years now there have been growing concerns regarding the future net taxation payments and whether some generations would have to 'pay' more than others to satisfy the Social Security system liabilities.

Since the beginning of the 1990s, Generational Accounting has been developed to study these issues (Auerbach, Gokhale and Kotlikoff, 1994). This is because yearly public budgets and deficits cannot provide an adequate measure of long-run government liabilities and of fiscal policies consequences on the intergenerational distribution of the public debt. The studies of Auerbach *et al.* conclude that an intergenerational imbalance does exist in several countries.[1] If current policies were to be continued, future generations would have to face a fiscal burden much higher than current generations.

This paper does not aim to be exhaustive as regards transfers (education, health insurance, family allowances . . .) but rather focuses on public pensions in a more precise way. It does not adopt the same indicator of life cycle transfers as Auerbach *et al.* – which requires the choice of a discount rate – but a rather more neutral one: the rate of return. We thus compute rates of return for public pensions and point out the impact of long-run demographic and wage trends.

We use for this analysis the dynamic microsimulation model, *Destinie*, initially built by Blanchet (Blanchet and Chanut, 1998). A microsimulation model seems to be particularly appropriate for two major reasons. First of all, microsimulation models may provide multivariate distributions of any variables (by sex, year of birth, level of income). Secondly, pensions rules are quite complex and should be introduced as precisely as possible. The *Destinie* model was modified, compared to the

175

first version, with particular attention to its economic modules. We brought in several social benefits (old-age pensions, family allowances, health insurance, unemployment benefits) as well as various contributions and taxes, and we improved both the labour market and income modules. We computed pension benefits and contributions from 1945 (when the Social Security system was set up), and we simulated the socio-economic evolution of the population until 2040, relying on existing demographic and economic projections. From then until 2078, we extrapolated trends. Within this relatively long interval, we were able to compute the rate of return of public pensions for the generations born between 1920 and 1974.

Ageing is likely to have several important consequences that we do not consider in this paper. For instance, the increase in pensions transfers may be partly offset by a fall in public expenditure for education. In addition, the likely growth of contribution rates for pensions may affect the economic growth rate: it may discourage both labour supply and labour demand, and public investments may decrease to avoid a too large increase in global tax rates. These major issues will be ignored here.

Why a microsimulation instead of a computable general equilibrium approach?[2]

The use of a representative agent in macro-models may give accurate results concerning the evolution of average parameters; but analysing their dispersion requires disaggregate data. Microsimulation methods were first developed by Orcutt in the 1960s to tackle this very issue (Orcutt *et al.*, 1961). Microsimulation models (MSM) distinguish micro-units (individuals, households, etc) who experience randomly simulated social and economic events. The global population evolves along individual paths rather than through the projection of average parameters. Although they may require a lot of data, microsimulation methods (MSM) provide some major advantages:

- MSM enable us to model complex laws in detail: *Destinie* is particularly suitable for our study since computing pension benefits and simulating reforms requires information on the entire life of an individual (individual circumstances : number of contributing periods, retirement age; family circumstances: number of children).
- MSM take into account individual heterogeneities, which may have important consequences while analysing, for instance, an increase in the legal minimum retirement age. This requires

information not only on the average duration of occupations, but also on periods of non-participation and unemployment and their distribution throughout careers. MSM also enable us to assess the distributional impacts of public policies, between as well as within generations.

Of course, the populations may be divided into homogeneous subgroups in computable general equilibrium (CGE) models, in order to analyse these effects. But this approach raises several issues: first, adding up new discrete variables multiplies the number of subgroups in an exponential way (through the use of matrices), whereas MSM allow a much larger number of explanatory variables. Second, the division into subgroups may be criticised when considering continuous variables, because limiting the size of matrices involves a loss of information. And third, whatever the degree of disaggregation, CGE subgroups must be defined *ex ante*. MSM are more flexible since micro-units can be aggregated *ex post* according to any feature, thus avoiding any aggregation bias.

However, we should also mention some of the disadvantages of a microsimulation approach. First of all, large databases are needed or have to be simulated, and this involves huge investment in constructing and maintaining MSM. Second, the stochastic feature of the simulations means that we need to assess the variance induced in the results. Finally, if MSM make it possible to describe individuals' behaviour in detail, the assumptions often rely on microeconometric studies, whose results are not always conclusive.

8.2 Overview of the *Destinie* model

The database used by the model is derived from the 1991 Financial Assets Survey. The initial sample is composed of 15,000 households (about 37,000 individuals). The sample is representative of the French population at that time. Each person is described with demographic and economic information about age, income (social security benefits, wages, pensions, etc), relatives, position on the labour market. This population is then followed year by year from 1992 to 2040, and is modified by different kinds of events. Three main modules are passed through by each individual: the demographic module, the labour market module and the income module.

This paper does not aim at an exhaustive description of the entire model. We shall focus here on the main assumptions, and on the main changes that have occurred since the first version (Blanchet and Chanut, 1996).

The three main modules: demography, labour and income

The demographic submodule

This simulates jointly:

- simple demographic events like death, disability, birth, divorce, immigration and when children leave their parents' home
- complex events, like marriage. This requires a matching process.

School careers are not modelled. As soon as a person is born, we determine when he/she will leave school. This school-leaving age is one of the main variables of the model. It sums up the social class, the socioprofessional group and the qualification. The model links a person's school-leaving age with his/her father's and mother's school-leaving age, assuming a kind of 'social continuity'. This variable is computed in two stages. We first compute the cohort's average school-leaving age, and then model how the school-leaving age of each person belonging to the cohort deviates from it.

The average school-leaving age is computed for cohorts born between 1900 and 1970, relying on the 1997 Employment Survey. This age has not stopped rising since 1900. It rose from 15.5 for people born about 1900 to 19.8 for people born in 1970. It was then extended for the later cohorts to a top value of 24, using a logistic function.

The labour market submodule

Six economic occupations are distinguished. Two of them are working occupations: employed and unemployed. Four are non-working occupations: student, non-working (including, for instance, housewives), early retired and retired. The labour market module is organised in two stages. The first determines participation and the second determines whether a participating individual is employed or unemployed. Transition probabilities estimated on the basis of the 1991 Employment Survey determine whether an individual's economic activity changes. These probabilities are treated as first-order Markovian processes and depend on sex, age, school age, and, for women, on the number and the age of children. For each person whose schooling is over and who has not yet retired, the model randomly determines, given his/her transition probabilities, whether a person changes his/her labour force status. However, the retirement decision is not the result of a stochastic process: we assumed that people were mainly influenced by the strong incentives provided by the mandatory pensions scheme.

Estimating probabilities on a given year raises an important issue: we use cross-section estimators for longitudinal projections. We thus have to adjust the transition equation parameters to take into account the fact that 1991 belongs to a specific period and that the labour force participation rate of women has been rising since the early seventies. The parameters were therefore adjusted in order to benchmark the simulations to two different scenarios of unemployment: 10% (central scenario) or 6% in 2020.

The income submodule

Three different types of career may be chosen in the current version of *Destinie*: the first one is regular, rising and creates little mobility; the second one includes a randomised component creating a lot of mobility; the third one (the central scenario), estimated on mid-1980s data, leads to an intermediate mobility. These three types of career arise from the same wage equation but differ as regards the modelling of the residual. This earnings equation (equation 1) was estimated on the 1991 Financial Assets Survey, for each sex. The explained variable, the annual wage (w_{i90}), is related to the school leaving age (*School*) and the duration of the individual's past professional activities (*Dur*).

$$\ln(w_{i90}) = a + b(School_i) + c(Dur_{i90}) + d\left(\frac{Dur_{i90}^2}{100}\right) + r_{i90} \qquad (8.1)$$

For each year a person is employed, we calculate his/her wage, adding up the deterministic component derived from the earnings equation and a residual (Colin, Ralle, 1998). This residual is randomised (to create mobility) but is correlated with its past values. When a person is unemployed (early retired), he/she receives unemployment (early retirement) benefits. Once a person is retired, their pension benefit is indexed in line with price inflation. *Destinie* also simulates the survivors' pension and an old age minimum benefit.

Dynamic properties of Destinie

Evolution of the demographic structure

Population ageing might induce an increase in public expenditures during the following decades. Pension schemes will bear much of this pressure since their costs are highly dependent on the age structure of the population.

The old age dependency ratio, defined as the ratio between the population aged over 60 and the population aged between 20 and 59, will increase almost twofold between 1995 and 2040, mainly because of the growing share of the over 60s in the population. While there was one person aged over 60 for every three potential working people in 1995, the ratio is projected to be 1:2 in 2020 and 1:1.5 in 2040.

These changes to the demographic structure raise a double issue. On the one hand, the life expectancy growth increases the number of 'old' people (at least people who are entitled to pension benefits). On the other hand, the weight of the contributing population in the whole population continues to fall because of demographic (as well as economic) factors.

The evolution of wages

Given the regular raising of the school-leaving age, the wage equations induce an increase by about 1% per year in individual wages. Since we add a technological component (with an additional 1% increase each year), individual wages grow by 2% annually on average. The growth is slightly smaller at the end of the period. Nonetheless, the average growth rate of the aggregate wage bill continuously decreases from over 3% in the early 1990s to 1.5% in the 2030s. The decline in the working population accounts for this difference.

8.3 Overview of the French social security system

Mandatory public pensions represent about 50% of Social Security liabilities: the 1998 financial forecast for public pensions is about 1,050 billion French francs (FF) (12.5% of GDP), 71.5% of which are basic pensions. As a comparison, the 1998 forecast for public health care expenditure is about FF573 billion (7% of GDP).

All working people are assumed to fall under the *Régime Général* for pensions. This is a very rough approximation because a wide range of different systems exists, and because these systems provide quite different benefits. About 65% of working people (most wage earners in private firms) fall under the *Régime Général*, whereas civil servants, farmers or self-employed people have specific schemes.

Basic pensions

When considering French public pensions, we must keep in mind the existence of the Social Security wage ceiling, which draws an effective boundary between executives, and workers or employees. This wage ceiling currently amounts to FF14,090 (about £1,500) per month. When public pensions were first introduced there was only a basic pension. It still exists and is computed by considering that part of the wage under the ceiling. Wage earners pay a fixed rate on this amount to finance the system.

Computing the first basic pension is quite complex. We modelled it roughly in *Destinie* in the following way: for people born after 1948 (following the major reform of 1993) the formula may be simplified as:

$$R = \tau.w_{ref}.Min\left(1, \frac{d}{150}\right)$$

where d is the number of three-month periods worked, and w_{ref} is a reference wage.

When a person retires, their former nominal wages (truncated below the wage ceiling) are re-evaluated. The average of the 25 highest re-evaluated wages is then computed and is called the reference wage, w_{ref}. τ has a maximum value of 0.5 which is automatically reached when people retire at 65. Nonetheless, one can retire from 60 onwards. In this case, τ equals 0.5 only if the total number of contributing quarters is greater than 160. Otherwise it decreases by 0.0125 for each term missing to reach either the age of 65 or 160 contributing quarters. If a person retires at age a (in quarters) after d contributing quarters :

$$t = 0.5 - 0.0125 \ Max[0, \ Min(260 - a, \ 160 - d)]$$

We assume here that all working people retire as soon as they are entitled to the full rate of 50%: not before and not after.[3]

Once a person is retired, their pension is indexed in line with price inflation.

Complementary pensions

Beside this basic pension, two mandatory complementary systems exist for wage earners in private firms. We simplified them as follows: the ARRCO regime provides a complementary pension corresponding to the fraction of the wage under the ceiling, since the replacement rate reached through the basic pension is quite low – less than 50%. For executives – in the model *Destinie*, every person whose wage exceeds the ceiling – the AGIRC regime provides a pension corresponding to the fraction of the wage above the ceiling.

People may enjoy complementary pensions benefits before being entitled to the full rate of 50% for basic pensions: in that case, they get a downward adjustment to their pension. We have assumed in the model that nobody chooses to enjoy complementary benefits before being entitled to the full rate for the basic pension. Each year, people receive a number of points proportional to their contributions; the amount of their first pension equals:

$$R = N_p.v_p$$

where N_p is the total number of points they have accumulated since the beginning of their career and v_p is the current value of the point. This value roughly follows the consumption price index. Both ARRCO and AGIRC are pay-as-you-go schemes.

8.4 The simulation of contributions and benefits between 1945 and 2078

We study the generations born between 1920 and 1974. The microsimulation begins in 1992, using a sample from a survey carried on by the INSEE in 1991 (see section 8.2).

First step: reconstitution of career paths 1945–1991

The first step consists in simulating the career paths from 1945 – when Social Security was set up in France – to 1991. We use the available information on the individuals of the sample in 1991 (sex, age, wage, pension, etc.) and macroeconomic data (the average growth rate of wages over the period) to recreate career paths for the people questioned in the survey.

Of course, it was necessary to take into account people who died before 1991: they paid contributions and received benefits between 1945 and 1990. We used death rates by sex and age from 1945 to 1990 to recreate the real size of the generations for the period 1945–1990. Those death rates are assumed to be homogeneous within the population: in particular, we assumed that low-paid people did not die earlier on average – which is not actually the case. This approximation enabled us to compute not only the aggregate wage that each generation earned each year, but also the aggregate pension bill.

The knowledge of contribution rates for pensions from 1945 to 1990 then yields the contributions that each generation paid each year. We consider employers' contributions as a part of wages and also include them in our computations.

At the end of this first step, contributions and benefits for pensions are available for the generations born between 1920 and 1974 and the period 1945–1991.

Second step: simulating the evolution of the sample until 2040

The legislation about pensions in payment is assumed to remain unchanged. But our method differs from traditional generational accounting in the sense that the tax increases (necessary to finance pensions) are borne by all living generations.

The simulation of a person's career path then yields the year they retire and the amount of their first pension. We also obtain pensions benefits over the period 1992–2040 for our 55 generations.

We assume that the financial 'equilibrium' of Social Security is reached through changes in the employees' contribution rate for basic pensions:

$$\tau_{t+1} - \tau_t = \frac{P_t - C_t}{W_t}$$

where τ_t is the contribution rate of employees, P_t the sum of basic pensions, C_t the sum of contributions for basic pensions, and W_t the aggregate wage bill under the ceiling.

The basic assumption is also that employers' contribution rates remain unchanged, *except for complementary pensions*: variations in contribution rates are borne by employers at the rate of 60% of the total.

The end of the story: 2041–2078

At the end of the simulation, all people born before 1974 are either retired or dead (wage earners retire in the model at the latest at 65). People born before 1936 are dead, since nobody can live older than 104 in *Destinie*. Although the model cannot technically run after 2040, it is necessary to simulate the end of the story for people surviving at this date; otherwise the rates of return would be biased downwards for their generations.

Assuming that death rates remain constant beyond 2040 and are homogeneous within groups by sex and age, we apply these rates to the aggregate wage bill by sex and by generation. Pension contributions are zero since everybody is retired. At the end of this third step, we have information on contributions and pensions benefits for the period 1945–2078. Rates of return for all these generations can also be computed.

8.5 Long-run impact of demographic trends on the rate of return of pensions

The rate of return ρ may be defined as the value of the discount rate that makes the sum of financial flows B_t ($=$ benefits $-$ contributions) equal to zero. For a generation born in t_0 and whose last members die in $t_0 + T$, we may write:

$$\sum_{t=t_0}^{t_0+T} \frac{B_t}{(1+\rho)^t} = 0$$

This rate of return ρ may be compared with the rate of return and volatility of financial assets: stock markets should necessarily provide a higher rate of return than ρ to make a risk averse individual indifferent between contributing to a pay-as-you-go scheme and a funded one.

Which indicators for life cycle transfers?

There are a number of economic indicators that might be used to assess the effects of social transfers throughout the life cycle. First, as Auerbach *et al.* (1994) did to build generational accounts, one might compute the net discounted benefit. But the results are extremely sensitive both to changes in the growth rate of GDP and to the – quite arbitrary – choice of the discount rate. Besides, interpreting the results often appears to be difficult.

Second, one might assess the time taken to get contributions back. Although the results are easier to interpret than in the previous case, this method raises the same difficulties concerning the choice of the discount rate.

Computing the rate of return avoids choosing a discount rate. We thus decided to work with this indicator. Nonetheless, it provides no indication of the importance of the size of the transfers (it may yield the same value for a scheme with low contributions and low benefits and a scheme with high contributions and high benefits).

The central scenario

Conclusions about the existence and the amount of an intergenerational imbalance depend on the assumptions that are made, particularly as regards the breakdown of the various transfers (Accardo, 1998). For that reason, we did not model all public transfers but only pensions, which are financially the most important. Besides, the incidence of individual payments and benefits is much easier to establish for pensions than for education, for instance.

Figure 8.1 shows a sharp decrease in the rate of return of public pensions between generations 1920 and 1945, from over 9% to about 3.5%. This decline then almost stops for the 30 following years, despite a slight decrease after 1960.

The rate of return is very high for the generations born before the Second World War (over 4%). These generations are the first whose careers did not begin before the setting up of public pensions. Their whole career is also taken into account, and they get high pensions since they worked during the 30-year period of continuous economic growth (1945–1975). On the other hand, they did not have to contribute a great deal: the generations that came before (born before 1920) were not large, were mainly self-employed (especially farmers) and their careers began before 1945.

The next generations (the 'baby-boomers') have an average 3.4% rate of return. They mostly began to work after 1965 and have had pretty good careers, although they suffered a little from the slowdown of economic

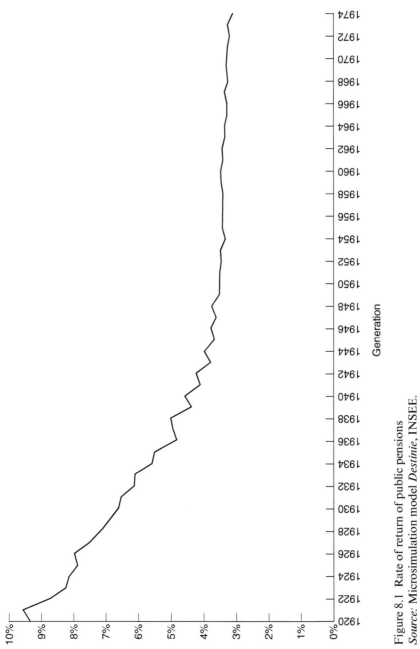

Figure 8.1 **Rate of return of public pensions**
Source: Microsimulation model *Destinie*, INSEE.

growth from the 1980s onwards. Nonetheless, the consequences of rising unemployment on pensions are relatively small because unemployment periods are considered as periods of contribution in the model to compute basic pensions (except that unemployment slows down the rise of wages and also induces a decrease in pensions). The smaller value of their rate of return mainly arises from the rise in contribution rates that is imposed progressively to finance the pensions of the generations born before 1945. In addition, the generations born after 1945 are the first to be affected by the 1993 reform, which slows down the growth of their pensions.

The generations born after 1965 must bear the financial burden of pensions paid to the large generations born before 1965 (the 'baby-boomers'). The big increase in the contribution rate (by about 15 points, see Figure 8.2) could induce a sharp decline in the rate of return. But the rate of return only decreases slightly since these generations benefit from a huge increase in life expectancy.

The rate of return is slightly higher for women than for men (see Figure 8.3): their higher life expectancy accounts for a large part of the difference; besides, both the basic and complementary schemes give women advantages that partly counteract non-participating periods devoted to bringing up children. Furthermore, the basic pension cannot be lower than a legal minimum for people entitled to the full rate. Since women get on average lower wages – and hence pay lower contributions – than men, even with the same skills, they can get larger benefits from this system. In 1994, 50% of women pensions are at the legal minimum.

Alternative scenarios

We now consider six alternative scenarios that might affect the rates of return of these 55 generations. These scenarios are based on the following assumptions:

1. **A 1-point increase in the growth rate of wages.** The yearly average growth rate of individual wages is increased by 1 point (to reach 3%) between 1992 and 2040.
2. **A decrease in unemployment.** The rate of unemployment sharply decreases after 1998 to reach a long-term value of 6% (instead of 10%). The 1998 rate of unemployment is about 12%.
3. **No decrease in death rates.** Death rates remain at their 1989 level. Life expectancy at birth in 2050 is now 73 for men (81 for women) instead of 82 (90).
4. **No reform of pensions.** The 1993 reform of basic pensions is assumed not to have existed: first, this reform increased the

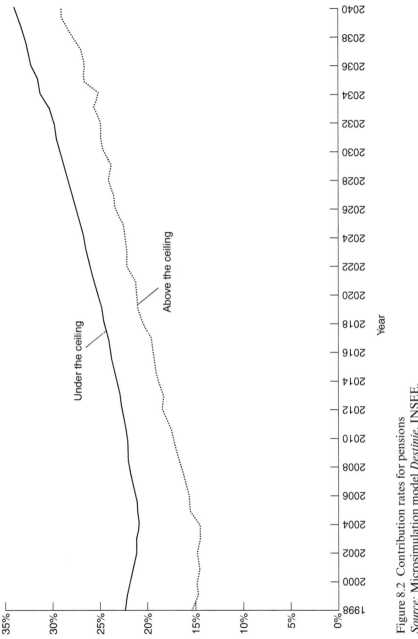

Figure 8.2 Contribution rates for pensions
Source: Microsimulation model *Destinie*, INSEE.

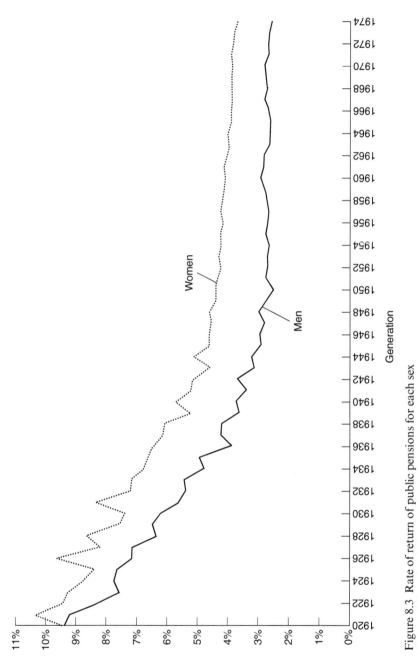

Figure 8.3 Rate of return of public pensions for each sex
Source: Microsimulation model *Destinie*, INSEE.

Table 8.1. *Average annual growth rates between 1998 and 2040 (%)*

Scenario	Central	1	2	3	4	5	6
Average gross wage	1.9	2.9	1.9	2.0	1.9	2.0	1.9
Average net wage	1.5	2.9	1.9	1.7	1.3	1.7	1.2
Aggregate basic pensions bill	2.9	3.3	1.9	2.9	3.5	2.5	3.7
Aggregate pensions bill	3.0	3.4	2.1	3.1	3.4	2.7	3.5

Note: In the central scenario, the number of retired people in 2040 should be twice the 1998 value and grows on average by 1.7% each year.
Source: Microsimulation model *Destinie*, INSEE.

number of years to be taken into account in computing the reference wage from 10 to 25; second, it raised the required number of contributing quarters for entitlement to the full rate from 150 to 160. But the legal minimum retirement age of 60 remained unchanged, and people are still entitled to the full rate if they retire at 65, whatever their number of contributing quarters.

5. **An increase in the retirement age.** The legal minimum retirement age is still 60 for people born before 1938, but is 61 for people born in 1939, 62 for people born in 1940, and 63 for the following generations. People born before 1938 are still entitled to the full rate (whatever their number of contributing periods) at 65, but this figure is 66 for the 1939 generation, 67 for the 1940 generation, and 68 for people born after 1941.

6. **An increase in the pensions index.** Basic pensions – that have been indexed by prices for the last ten years – are assumed to be indexed by the growth in the average net wage minus 0.5: if individual net wages grow on average by 2%, basic pensions are raised by 1.5%. But if the growth rate of wages is below 0.5%, basic pensions remain unchanged. Complementary scheme benefits remain strictly indexed to prices in this scenario. Note that this scenario has a double impact on the amount of pensions: pensions are raised each year by a higher figure and the amount of the first pension is increased since the former wages that are taken into account to compute the reference wage w_{ref} are re-evaluated following the pensions growth index.

For generations born between 1950 and 1959, the average retirement age is 62 years and 10 months in the central scenario and in scenarios 1, 2, 3 and 6. It falls to 62 years and 1 month in scenario 4 and increases to 66 years in scenario 5.

Table 8.2. *Increase in the global contribution rate for pensions from wages between 1998 and 2040 (in points)*

Scenario	Central	1	2	3	4	5	6
Under the ceiling	11.5	3.3	0.3	10.5	18.3	6.3	20.9
Above the ceiling	13.6	7.2	5.5	13.5	14.2	9.5	13.6

Source: Microsimulation model *Destinie*, INSEE.

Scenario 1 of course involves a relative decrease in the contribution rate (compared to the central scenario), which reaches 8 points in 2040 for wages under the ceiling (see Figure 8.5). In the long run, an increase of 1 point in the growth rate of wages should be followed by an increase of 1 point in the rate of return (see appendix to this chapter). For generations born in the early 1970s (see Figure 8.4), the increase exceeds 0.6 (their rate of return also grows to 4%).

The sharp decrease in the rate of unemployment (see Figure 8.5) in scenario 2 does not involve a large decrease in the contribution rate (which falls by only about 1 point). The effect on the rate of return is very low for people born before 1965 (see Figure 8.4). However, we observe a slight improvement for people born in the late 1960s and in the early 1970s. These generations may benefit more than those born before the decrease in contribution rates for pensions.

Scenario 3 involves a large decrease in the rate of return (see Figure 8.4), especially for the baby-boom generations, who get lower pensions (since they die earlier) without paying much lower contributions (since the generations born before are not so much affected by the stagnation in life expectancy). In this scenario, the rate of return for pensions would reach an asymptotical value of about 2.5%, which is consistent with the long-run assumption on the growth of wages. The quite high value of the rate of return for the youngest generations (about 3.3% in the central scenario) is also mainly a consequence of the expected decrease in death rates.

Scenario 4 has a low impact on the contribution rate above the wage ceiling, since the average retirement age only decreases slightly (9 months for people born between 1950 and 1959): the impact on the total amount of complementary pensions is hence small. But the reference wage for basic pensions (that now takes into account the 10 and not the 25 best years) increases considerably. This accounts for the 7 point surge in the contribution rate under the ceiling (see Figure 8.7). There is no significant impact for people born before the mid-30s since they were not affected by the 1993 reform. People born after the 1940 reform experience a fall of about 0.3 in their rate of return (see Figure 8.6).

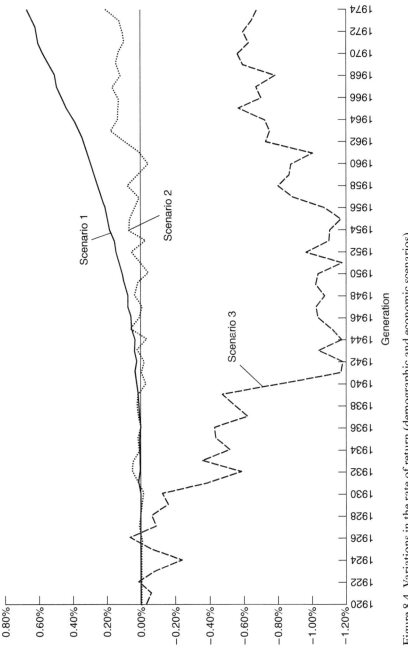

Figure 8.4 Variations in the rate of return (demographic and economic scenarios)

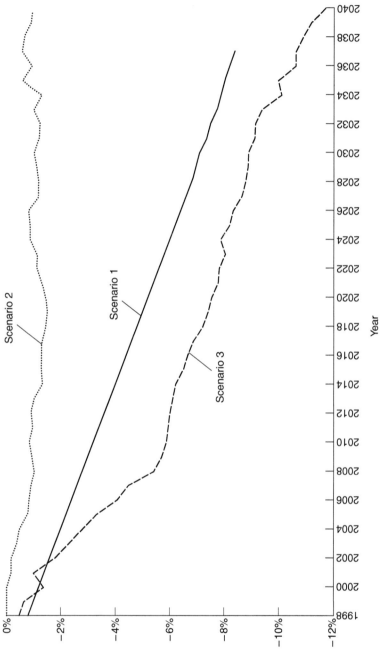

Figure 8.5 Variations in the contribution rate (demographic and economic scenarios)

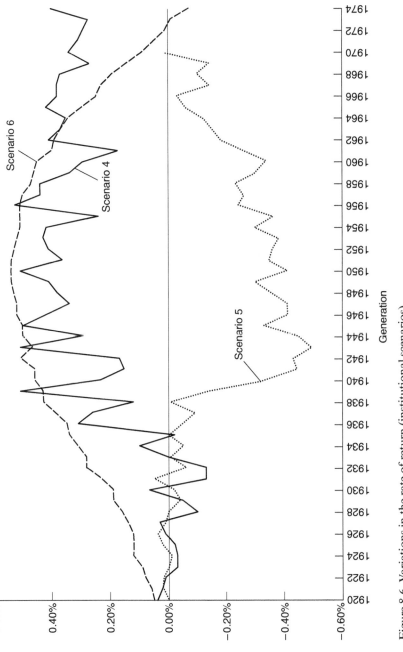

Figure 8.6 Variations in the rate of return (institutional scenarios)

Scenario 5 involves a larger change in the average retirement age: it increases by about 3 years. There is also a significant impact on the contribution rate above the ceiling, since people receive their complementary pensions benefits later (see Figure 8.7). There is a fall in the contribution rate under the ceiling of 5 points.

This scenario results in a substantial decrease in the rate of return for people born in the early 1940s: they pay roughly the same contributions as in the central scenario (the contribution rate has not yet decreased) but they lose several years of benefits (as compared to the generations born immediately before). For people born about 1970, the decrease in retirement life expectancy is roughly compensated by the decrease in the contribution rate, which explains why the change in the rate of return is roughly zero.

We now consider the impact of changes in the way pensions are raised each year. Scenario 6 shows a large increase in the contribution rate under the ceiling (see Figure 8.7): about 10 points in 2040. However, a theoretical analysis (see Appendix to this chapter) shows that in a steady-state world (i.e. where the demographic growth rate and the growth rate of wages do not change over time) such a measure has no impact on the rate of return.

Note that these conclusions might be strongly modified if we assume that the increase in contribution rates has a negative impact on wages (by discouraging labour supply and labour demand for instance). This is not the case here.

For the first generations (born before 1930) the impact of scenario 6 is quite low, since an important part of their pensions has already been paid in 1999. In 1999, generations born between 1935 and 1939 retire progressively. They get benefits from the reform without having to pay more to finance the increase in the financial burden. The net benefit of the reform keeps on growing with generations till the end of the 1950s: these generations face an increase in their contribution rates during their working time, but this loss is overshadowed by the increase in their pensions.

For generations born after 1960, the net benefit decreases sharply, falls quickly to zero and even becomes negative for the most recent generations: higher pensions are completely offset by lower net wages in the first part of their life. The generations born before enjoy higher pensions in this scenario, without having to pay higher contributions. The variation in the rate of return would also be zero if the model described a steady-state economy. Since this is not really the case – even in the long run – the very last generations considered here face a net loss.

Detailed analysis of scenario 6

We now compute the impact of this scenario on the future discounted income of each individual born between 1938 and 1942 or between 1958

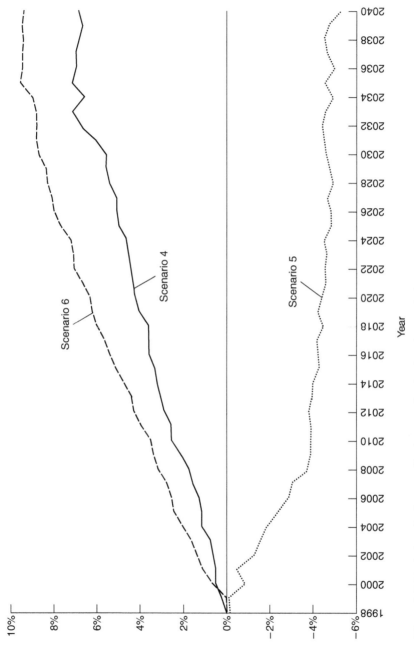

Figure 8.7 Variations in the contribution rate (institutional scenarios)

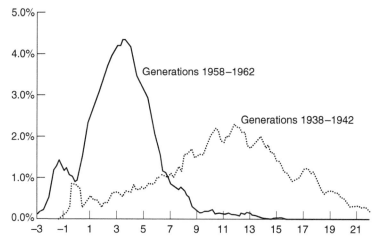

Figure 8.8 Distribution of the impact of scenario 6 on the future discounted income of people born about 1940 and 1960 (discount rate 3%)
Source: Microsimulation model *Destinie*, INSEE.

and 1962. We choose an arbitrary uniform discount rate of 3%. This assumption might be criticised since people with a lower life expectancy (for instance men, or low income people) should have a higher discount rate. Figure 8.8 confirms that the scenario has a very large impact for generations born about 1940 (whose future discounted income increases on average by over 11%), but that the impact is less for later generations: the future discounted income of people born about 1960 grows by about 3.5% on average. For a few people, scenario 6 results in a decrease in the future discounted income: these people die before retiring or at the very beginning of retirement (see Figure 8.8).

Next we consider separately low-income and high-income people born about 1960 in scenario 6: Figure 8.9a shows that the impact of this scenario is much larger for low-income people (with an average 4.8% increase in the bottom quartile of the income distribution) than for high-income people (with an average 2.4% increase in the top quartile). The basic pension clearly represents a much higher proportion of the total income of low-income pensioners than high-income pensioners. The scenario has thus a larger impact on these people – although they die earlier.

The lower half of Figure 8.9 shows that the impact is larger for women than for men, although women have lower wages. The main part of the impact of scenario 6 stems from the fact that life expectancy is much higher for women (with an average increase in future discounted income of 4.5%) than for men (with an average increase of 2.5%).

(a) according to level of income

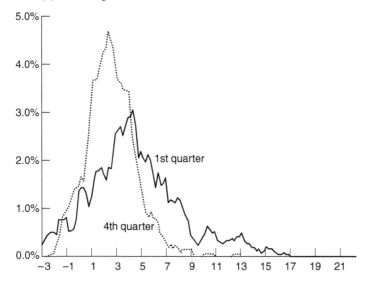

(b) according to sex

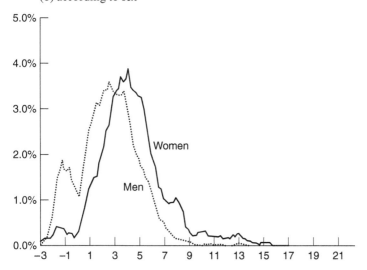

Figure 8.9 Distribution of the impact of scenario 6 on the future discounted income of people born about 1960 (discount rate 3%)
Source: Microsimulation model *Destinie*, INSEE.

8.6 Conclusions

We computed the rate of return of public pensions for the generations born between 1920 and 1974. It is quite high for the first generations and then gradually declines while contribution rates increase. Nonetheless, the rate of return is still quite high for the youngest generations (3.3%), mainly because of the increase in life expectancy (which involves higher life-cycle benefits for the currently young generations).

This long-run decrease should not be viewed as unfair for the most recent generations. It results automatically from the choice of a pay-as-you-go pensions system. It also seems more justified to view things from an *intra*-generational angle and to focus on the redistributive impact of reforms, using microsimulation methods.

Appendix 8.1 The rate of return on a pay-as-you-go system

The impact over the life cycle of transfers may be described by the following model:

We consider here a pay-as-you-go system that manages financial flows that grow at a fixed rate $n+x$, where:

> x is the average growth rate of individual wages,
> n is the demographic growth rate.

The age structure of contributions and benefits is assumed to remain constant: if a is the age, the individual contribution at t may be written as:

$$c(a, t) = \tilde{c}(a).e^{xt}$$

and the individual benefit:

$$\pi(a, t) = \tilde{\pi}(a).e^{xt}$$

Let s be the survival function. The financial balance of the system at t involves:

$$\int_0^\Omega \tilde{c}(a).e^{-na+xt}.s(a).da = \int_0^\Omega \tilde{\pi}(a).e^{-na+xt}.s(a).da$$

i.e.

$$\int_0^\Omega \tilde{c}(a).e^{-na}.s(a).da = \int_0^\Omega \tilde{\pi}(a).e^{-na}.s(a).da \tag{8A.1}$$

But the rate of return $\rho*$ for a generation born at g may be written as:

$$\int_0^\Omega \tilde{c}(a).e^{x(g+a)}.e^{-\rho*a}.s(a).da = \int_0^\Omega \tilde{\pi}(a).e^{x(g+a)}.e^{-\rho*a}.s(a).da$$

i.e.

$$\int_0^\Omega \tilde{c}(a).e^{(x-\rho*)a}.s(a).da = \int_0^\Omega \tilde{\pi}(a).e^{(x-\rho*)a}.s(a).da \qquad (8A.2)$$

The comparison between equations (8A.1) and (8A.2) shows that $\rho* = x + n$ is a solution for the second equation. In a steady-state world, the rate of return of a pay-as-you-go (pensions) system is equal to the growth rate of the economy. As a consequence, the rate of return of a public pension system does not depend on the choice of the pensions index (if we assume that the growth rate of the economy does not depend on the level of contributions).

Notes

1 Results for France are available in Doré and Levy (1998), and Accardo (1998).
2 For a more detailed comparison, see Van Imhoff and Post (1997).
3 Pelé and Ralle (1997) made the same assumption to assess the effects of the 1993 reform (that raised the required number of contributing quarters) on the retirement age. They showed that it was rational behaviour to choose an optimal age of retirement.

9 Validation of longitudinal dynamic microsimulation models: experience with CORSIM and DYNACAN

Steven Caldwell and Richard J. Morrison

9.1 Introduction

In response to the demands associated with prospective social security reforms in the United States and Canada, governments are beginning to use longitudinal dynamic microsimulation models (hereafter, for convenience shortened to 'microsimulation')[1] to supply key policy inputs. Central among these inputs are projected distributions of the winners and losers that result from various policy proposals. Because the microsimulation strategy is relatively new, the use of such models for policy analysis raises several relatively unexplored issues, among which one looms especially large. To what extent are microsimulation-based estimates credible as inputs to policy development? This issue is usually treated under the general term 'model validation'.[2] Since model validation is central to microsimulation's credibility and usefulness, it is important that microsimulation builders and users pool their separate experiences to develop innovative, rigorous validation practices.[3] The empirical eclecticism of microsimulation – by which we mean the extraordinary variety of historical data against which model-generated outcomes can be fruitfully compared – is arguably its most attractive feature. Insofar as that empirical eclecticism is successfully exploited by constructing a gauntlet of heterogeneous validation tests to diagnose and treat flaws in a microsimulation model, the resulting model has the potential to achieve unparalleled scientific credibility and policy usefulness. That credibility and usefulness for microsimulation models have been slow in coming is due to no small extent, we believe, to the widespread failure of microsimulation modellers to validate extensively and effectively. Given the empirical resources for microsimulation validation that are increasingly available in many nations, this failure is a great loss. For microsimulation, validation is not a problem to be avoided, but an asset to be exploited.

This paper describes, at a summary level, selected validation tests carried out on two dynamic microsimulation models now moving into significant policy use in the US (CORSIM) and Canada (DYNACAN).[4] Initial sections provide some background on dynamic microsimulation modelling, and a fuller description of the role of model validation. Subsequent sections of this paper describe validation practices involving (a) administrative data, (b) survey, vital statistics and census data, (c) collateral, or joint, model outcomes, (d) comparisons with results from other models, and (e) Monte Carlo variability. The paper discusses validation results for each of these areas, and ends with a short conclusion on the state of the art.

9.2 Background

It is beyond the focus of this paper to provide a detailed description of microsimulation. Nonetheless, to address the validation of such models in a meaningful way, it is useful to describe their general nature.

The demand for these models arises in part because there is no alternative modelling strategy to address critical policy and research issues. Examples of such issues include: (a) analyses of projected winners and losers on period-specific or lifetime bases; (b) analyses focused on families and individuals simultaneously; (c) exploration at the micro-level of the operation of social security programmes in the context of the broader tax/transfer system; (d) quantification of incentives to work, to save, or to retire at particular life course or period junctures; (e) cross-subsidies across population segments or cohorts; (f) feedback effects of government programmes on population demographics; and (g) longer-term consequences of societal trends in marriage, divorce and fertility.

The CORSIM and DYNACAN models begin with large data files that are representative cross-sections of their respective national populations. Then the models 'grow' the populations through time by simulating the relevant life events for each individual and each family. The model progressively generates synthetic life histories for all individuals and all families (including kinship ties). Such synthetic histories include longitudinal records of earnings, programme contributions, programme benefits and taxes. Though simplified, these synthetic histories capture the processes considered most important for the policy questions at issue, including fertility, mortality, marriage, divorce, education, disability, external and internal migration, labour force entry, employment, retirement and so on. Moreover, the models aim to capture, at the level of the individual and the family, the many interactions among these processes.

The practice of beginning each simulation several decades in the past is deliberate. It permits one to assess, against a considerable quantity of historical data, the realism of the various simulated behaviours and events, and furthermore to ensure that the demographic and earnings histories of the individuals and families are of suitable length as one enters the projection period of the simulation.

Both models are closed; new synthetic individuals come into existence only through births and immigration; existing individuals leave the model only through death and emigration. This means that the models produce, from a population perspective, an exhaustive, representative set of integrated personal, family and programme participation histories.

Powerful data extraction facilities let users distil from this massive amount of information, relatively conveniently and inexpensively, the particular series and tables relevant to particular questions, and for specific policy options.

The models are highly parametric, allowing the user to control the major assumptions about demographics, earnings, and the operation of tax and benefit programmes. Finally, the models are Monte Carlo in nature, thus surmounting the 'curse of dimensionality' that inevitably plagues cell-based models. However, at the same time, carefully crafted variance reduction techniques limit the dispersion of results across alternative runs.

9.3 The role of validation

With all the resource demands faced by those developing and using micro-simulation models, the 'why bother?' question comes quickly to mind, probably right after the question: What does model validation mean? The following points are central to the CORSIM/DYNACAN approach to model validation:

- Validation is a proactive, diagnostic effort to ensure that the model's results are reasonable and credible. The requirement flows from the observation that the models are, at one level, fairly expensive, and are used as key inputs to multi-billion dollar decisions with substantial social implications. At the same time, we note that they are very cheap compared to the monetary and political costs of even a single, small, bad decision that could have been prevented by virtue of their results. Model validation attempts to address the fundamental questions of: 'Is the model working?' 'Is it working well enough?' 'How do we tell?' The proactive thrust is an explicit attempt to move beyond the hunter-gatherer approach to 'debugging' models, of fixing errors only when they 'intrude'. A formal validation exercise – here termed the validation programme – is a central part of the host organisations' culture for building, extending and applying the models.

- The validation programme produces an extensive battery of tests/measures/comparisons.
- Validation is a part of the quality control effort for a model, but it is qualitatively distinct from just making sure the model is doing what one has told it to do; it is more global. Quality control is valuable, desirable, and indeed necessary, in that it indicates, for a variety of processes, whether the model is doing what it is intended to do. Validation seeks, rather, to assess whether the model's outputs are reasonable for their intended purposes.
- Quantitative measures are used for the validation, but the ultimate impact is inherently qualitative. Though the models will never be perfect, users and clients need to know the extent to which the models are 'good enough' in the areas, and for the variables, judged most relevant for the results they seek.

We think there is a great deal more to be learned about validation, and that validation will progressively evolve to become more science and less art. For both CORSIM and DYNACAN, comparisons of the validation results over time show that the results of the models are getting progressively more realistic.

9.4 Special challenges

Validation of dynamic, longitudinal microsimulation models is challenging in a variety of areas not relevant or not critical for cross-sectional models. Key challenges are:

- projections for these models extend well into the future, often several decades beyond the present. There are few sources of 'future data' against which to assess reasonableness
- the models inevitably exhibit statistical variation that flows from their Monte Carlo components. Different runs of the model, with identical parameters but using different random number seeds, give different answers. Decision-makers, however, dislike such variation. Almost without exception, they would prefer to see point estimates
- there can be legitimate questions raised relating to the validity of the comparisons involved in the assessments; even the best available data may be subject to issues of population representation, representativeness or definitional differences
- there is a great mass of information being projected, different portions of which are relevant for various analyses. This poses the unavoidable question of which particular items to validate, given

resource constraints, and of how those validations can most effectively be carried out
- the validation programme must respect the requirement that the models be parametric, even though the reasonableness of models' results depends in part on the parameter values used in its projections
- similarly, there are exogenous requirements to ensure the consistency of the simulation models' results with those of other, less distributionally detailed, cell-based or macro-models
- for longitudinal microsimulation models, one must aim for longitudinal realism for individuals and families, especially for family structures and earnings, for which the appropriate comparison standards may not be obvious, or may be challenging or costly to develop.

9.5 Major principles and objectives

Though it is probably impossible to derive an effective validation programme strictly from *a priori* principles, the following rough principles have informed and inspired our efforts to date:

- the validation process must pay close attention to the union of what the modellers and the clients see as being most important
- though there is certainly value to showing that the model correctly implements the desired assumptions, this is only a part of validation; we also need to gauge the model's performance in areas that depend on the interaction of multiple assumptions, as well as in areas that we do not directly control
- the validation programme should employ presentation formats that are easily understood; we have found that graphics – rather than numbers – are often a superior way to communicate efficiently and to involve less technically skilled persons
- validation outputs should be chosen in part for their diagnostic coverage. Relevant question include: Does the validation programme cover key areas and variables/outputs from the model? Does it provide some basis for fixes or improvements when the inevitable discrepancies appear? Does it address the longitudinal history aspect of the simulations as well as cross-sectional outcomes?
- the validation programme should exhibit flexibility in terms of the kinds of outputs it can produce. It should also permit breakdowns of impacts by cohorts or family types, and produce distributions as well as totals when such detail is needed

- given demands on scarce analytic resources, validation procedures should be economical to implement. Because validation procedures often need to be repeated in the event of significant changes in the model, it should be possible to automate the procedures
- in the absence of demonstrably optimal measures, we rely a good deal on the notion of face validity. If each of several 'central' measures individually looks reasonable compared to an appropriate baseline, then there is some justification for treating the results of the model as a whole as likely to be reasonable, at least relative to the outputs of alternative models, and especially relative to the costs of making major social decisions in ignorance. When possible, comparisons should be made against bases already judged to be reasonable.

The overall validation programmes for CORSIM and DYNACAN have multiple components addressing a variety of areas. Significant aspects include population stocks (by age and gender), demographic flows (birth rates, death rates, marriage rates, immigration totals, etc.), earnings totals and the annual distribution of earnings by age and gender (separately and jointly). Other areas include: social security contributions, programme beneficiaries, programme benefits and taxes, distributions of families by type, including time trends, and the realism of the synthetic earnings histories. We present illustrations for several of these areas in the paper, but we cannot begin to be comprehensive in this short space.

9.6 Comparisons to administrative programme data

The CORSIM and DYNACAN models have been built primarily, or in large part, to simulate the major social security programmes, the US Old Age Security and Disability Insurance (OASDI) for CORSIM, and the Canada Pension Plan (CPP) for DYNACAN. There is a large overlap between typical simulation period ranges, for example, 1971–2030, and the available portion of the historical period for administrative programme data. There is over a third of a century (1960–1997) of overlap for CORSIM, and over a quarter of a century (1971–1997) for DYNACAN. Given this degree of overlap, we can examine how well the models perform for those periods in which we have historical data – often administrative data – that provide good estimates of what actually happened. Administrative data are typically available in considerable detail, especially for those characteristics required for programme administration. Clients for the models' projections will not be reassured if CORSIM and DYNACAN have difficulty tracking historical outcomes. At the same time, a reasonable replication of history by no means guarantees that future projections will prove accurate. Moreover, a capacity to replicate the historical evolution of an existing programme in no way guarantees a capacity to project the impacts of *changes* to the system. This recognition mirrors the standard disclaimer in prospectuses for mutual funds: 'Past performance is no guarantee of future returns.' Nevertheless, as is the case with the historical returns for mutual funds, the past performance is still considered worthy of attention. The capacity to reproduce historical data for the programmes is rather more a necessary condition than a sufficient one, but the information is useful nonetheless.

CORSIM illustration

CORSIM simulates OASDI contributions (taxes) paid by each person during working years, and OASDI benefits paid to each person during retirement. Both contributions and benefits are calculated using actual Social Security rules or close approximations to them. Because CORSIM simulates and retains a full kinship network, the benefit calculations can take account of family links, just as benefit calculations do under Social Security programme rules. For example, a lower paid worker in a two-worker family might be better off with a benefit based on spousal earnings rather than a benefit based on own earnings; CORSIM computes both potential benefits, then assigns the higher benefit, following exactly the same procedure as Social Security. Similar rules based on kinship links in CORSIM are used to calculate family maxima, assign survivors' benefits and so on.

Extensive comparisons of CORSIM-simulated OASDI outcomes with outcomes estimated from administrative data for the 1960–1997 historical period have been presented in Favreault (1998).[5] She examines, for example, mean and median benefits and contributions for specific periods for population subgroups defined by gender, race, education, marital status and birth cohort. Most of these comparisons are reasonably favourable to CORSIM. More importantly, discrepancies uncovered by such comparisons have been treated as diagnostic tools, and doing so has often led to subsequent improvements in the model.

Earlier in this paper we mentioned comparisons of means and medians. However, the distinctive power of microsimulation lies less in its capacity to generate central tendencies, such as subgroup means and medians, than in its capacity to generate full distributions within groups. Administrative data on *distributions of OASDI benefits and contributions within subgroups* therefore provide particularly appropriate, as well as particularly rigorous, validation tests. Figure 9.1, adapted from Figure 5.20 in Favreault (1998), compares the distribution of monthly benefit levels for retired male workers

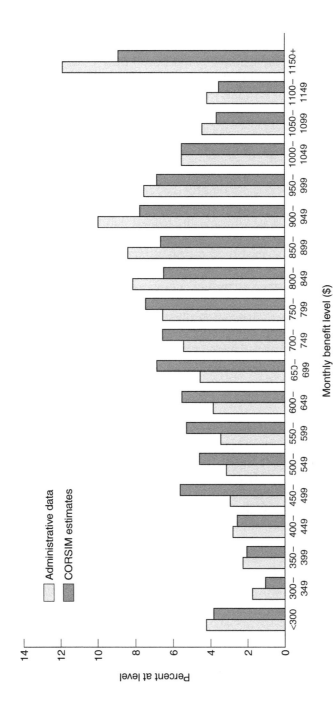

Figure 9.1 CORSIM validation using administrative data: percentage of retired male workers in the US by Social Security benefit level in 1996

in 1996 as generated by CORSIM, with the same distribution as provided by Social Security administrative records. The shapes of the two distributions are fairly similar, though far from identical; the CORSIM distribution is skewed to the left, and CORSIM underpredicts the high-benefit tail. For women (not shown here, but see Figure 5.21 in Favreault, 1998), CORSIM tracks administrative estimates more closely than for men, even though tracking female work and earning outcomes is more difficult. Recall that by 1996, CORSIM has already simulated 36 years in the life of each retired worker. A validation exercise using administrative data hence tests directly the realism of 36 years of simulated work, earnings, retirement, marital and mortality outcomes, and indirectly the realism of other simulated behaviours as well.

A point must be raised about the relationship between validation and alignment (or calibration). Many group-level rates in CORSIM and DYNACAN are aligned to historical estimates of group-level rates. For example, the fertility rate for the group of 20–24-year-old married women in all historical years is aligned to vital statistics estimates of fertility rates for those years. Within the group of 20–24-year-old married women in CORSIM, the micro-dynamic fertility module acts to 'distribute' fertility probabilities according to education, family income, and other individual-level and family-level variables. The alignment mechanism adjusts the individual-level probabilities so that the group-level fertility rates in CORSIM track the group-level fertility rates as estimated by vital statistics. Once this alignment is introduced, one can no longer 'validate' CORSIM's fertility module by comparing group-level CORSIM rates to vital statistics data. The exercise would be meaningless because the vital statistics rates have been used to help determine the CORSIM fertility rates.

This circular trap is analogous to repeated in-sample testing of alternative specifications, in which the testing power of a sample is compromised by the repeated fits. Having used a sample to choose a best-fitting equation, one cannot use the same sample to judge the degree of in-sample fit. To avoid this trap, one uses the fitted equation to predict outcomes for data points not involved in the fitting process. The same logic applies to validating microsimulation models. CORSIM has been aligned in multiple ways using historical group-level data, whose power to validate CORSIM thereby evaporates. One must determine whether those historical data proposed for a validation test have been used to shape the microsimulation in the first place. Has the Social Security administrative data used to validate CORSIM in Favreault (1998) been used previously to construct CORSIM? The answer is a clear negative. Hence, the validation challenge posed by comparing CORSIM estimates with OASDI administrative data estimates has not been compromised; the integrity of the validation exercises is intact, in a way analogous to 'out-of-sample', rather than 'in-sample', comparisons. That the CORSIM estimates exhibit similar patterns to Social Security administrative data therefore can be taken as providing some support for the historical realism of the model.

DYNACAN illustration

Between the periodic published reports and custom extractions from the Canada Pension Plan Master Benefit File and its Record of Earnings file, the CPP administrative data provide many series and distributions relevant to validating DYNACAN. For example, validation data that derive from these sources of administrative data include gross earnings, contributory earnings, contributions and total benefits, plus individual benefits and beneficiaries. The administrative data are available as totals, time series, and in some cases distributions by significant characteristics, for example, gender, age, and levels of earnings, or contributions, or benefits. Much of the benefits data are available in terms of both total benefits and newly payable (emerging) benefits; the distinction is relevant because those benefits already in payment are inherently easier to project than the flows of new beneficiaries and the benefits they receive.

It has generally proved feasible to extract from DYNACAN a set of data comparable to the administrative data. However, some definitional differences can arise, for example, where DYNACAN does not presently model part-year contributions and benefits in sufficient detail. Such differences will affect comparisons that involve counts of persons who have received benefits at any point during the year, as well as certain measures of average benefits. One source of frustration in using administrative data is the absence of many variables of interest to the policy-maker. For example, the CPP Record of Earnings data record the levels of earnings for an individual, but not the individual's level of education, or whether the individual was married or had children during the period. Thus, administrative data do not always provide a good indication with respect to whether the model is performing reasonably as regards any target populations defined in terms of such characteristics.

In practice, the administrative data for the comparison are compiled on a one-time basis, and entered in a spreadsheet. On the DYNACAN side of the comparison, automated scripts extract the relevant data from the output of appropriate DYNACAN runs. These scripts assemble the data into matrices that are then 'pasted into' the spreadsheets. The spreadsheets have been constructed so that they derive appropriate tables and graphics to effect the comparisons. Spreadsheet macros then print out these results. In this way, one can economically update the validation whenever changes

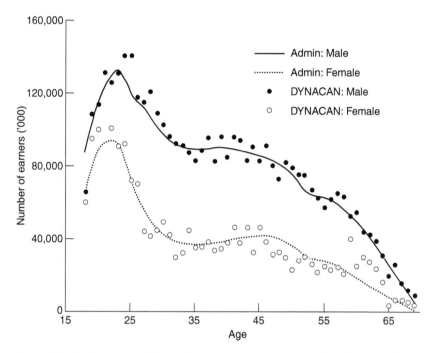

Figure 9.2 RoC persons with earnings over year's basic exemption, by age and sex, administrative data *vs* DYNACAN, 1971

are made to the model; one simply runs the scripts again and inserts the resulting new block of data.

There will also be the potential to carry out further validation against programme data as DYNACAN's development progressively increases the set of variables available for the comparisons. Distributions of tax-related variables (incomes, deductions and credits, and taxes payable) are obvious candidates for comparison against published taxation totals and distributions.

Figure 9.2 shows, for the 1971 calendar year, a comparative graph of average earnings by age and gender for DYNACAN versus administrative Record of Earnings data. Here these apply to the 'Rest of Canada' (RoC), i.e., the population of Canada, exclusive of Quebec (whose workers are members of a parallel Quebec Pension Plan), contributing to the CPP. DYNACAN performs equally well for other years, and for the distribution of the level of earnings by age and gender. Although the fit is not perfect, it is clear that DYNACAN effectively captures these key patterns. Using a larger sample, or averaging several runs would improve the fit further.

Improved alignment procedures already under way should improve this particular set of results considerably in the future, though, by the logic noted above, the alignment will remove this comparison from the realm of validation, and transfer it to that of 'mere' quality control.

9.7 Survey, vital statistics, and census data

As noted above, the CORSIM and DYNACAN models have been built in large part to simulate social security programmes. At the same time, a major focus in analyses by the models is an exploration of the consequences of proposed social security *options* – projections of the impacts of changing those programmes – explicitly evaluated in the context of the broader retirement income system. Unfortunately, many of the variables required for sub-populations of interest are not available, or are not comprehensively and reliably available, in programme administration data. Examples include marital status and family type, family history and marital duration, immigration status, and education, potentially in combination with individual or joint work histories or disability status data. Other variables not available in administrative data, for example, housing and family income or wealth, may also be desired in assessing projected policy impacts.

We previously noted the substantial overlap between the time frames for typical simulations and the historical period. Even when key variables for this overlap period are not available from administrative data, they may be present in survey or census data or in vital statistics data. Once again, it is only natural to examine how well microsimulation outputs compare with survey estimates in their totals, distributions and trends for the overlap period as an input in assessing whether the model is producing reasonable results and, if not, what kinds of changes might be desirable.

Survey data may offer their own challenges to achieving legitimate comparisons. For example, unlike administrative data, where comprehensiveness for a programme is easily attained, comparable 'apples to apples' bases may be more difficult to establish for surveys. One must attempt in the model to replicate the sampling frame for the surveys, for example, excluding those residing in institutions, or reproducing a survey's categorisation of families by type. However, the capacity to assess whether the model is producing reasonable trends and distributions for variables important to analysing policy impacts generally makes the effort worthwhile. Clients for the models' projections will be unimpressed with the credibility of the projections if the models have difficulty tracking credible survey-based estimates.

The same kinds of caveats apply to survey-based validation as they do to administrative data. A capacity to track estimates based on survey data over the historical period is no guarantee that projections into the future will be reasonable. Tracking the performance of an existing system does not prove that one can rely on the model's estimates of the impacts of changes to that system. However, both are useful as indicators.

CORSIM illustration

In August 1998, the US Social Security Administration entered into an arrangement to license CORSIM for one year and bring the model in-house to evaluate its suitability as a permanent in-house modelling tool. As part of the evaluation, analysts in the Office of Research, Evaluation and Statistics in March 1998 requested specific CORSIM output tabulations. The analysts had already created similar tabulations from a data file that matched Survey of Income and Programme Participation (SIPP) data with Social Security administrative data on earnings histories. The latter data are not publicly available, so it was essential that in-house Social Security analysts created the tabulations. The analysts then compared the SIPP–SSA estimates to CORSIM estimates. Figure 9.3 displays one example drawn from that set of comparisons (Bailey, Cohen and Iams, 1998). The comparison is quite detailed, examining males who live in a household that owns its living quarters, and dividing them into three five-year birth cohorts. For each five-year birth cohort of home-owning males, SIPP-based estimates and CORSIM-based estimates are compared. The Average Indexed Monthly Earnings (AIME) of the males at exactly the 10th percentile rank in the SIPP data is compared to the AIME for the males at exactly the 10th percentile rank in the CORSIM data; similar comparisons are made for the males at exactly the 50th percentile rank in both data sets, and at exactly the 90th percentile rank in both data sets. Examining individuals at several specific points in the percentile distribution yields quite fine-grained distributional measures, well beyond the capacity of aggregate models to generate.

The two sets of estimates – untainted by any alignment procedure in CORSIM – exhibit the same overall pattern. The CORSIM estimates are sometimes larger than the SIPP estimates, but just as often they are smaller. There is no apparent pattern to the discrepancies. Once again, the discrepancies cannot be unambiguously attributed to flaws in either CORSIM or the SIPP data, especially in view of the sample variation to which both sets of estimates are subject. With CORSIM, there are of course many possibilities for flaws in the equations and algorithms which represent the behaviours and programme rules leading to individual AIMEs. On the other hand, the SIPP data cannot be said to be a perfectly representative sample of the entire US population. For example, the SIPP

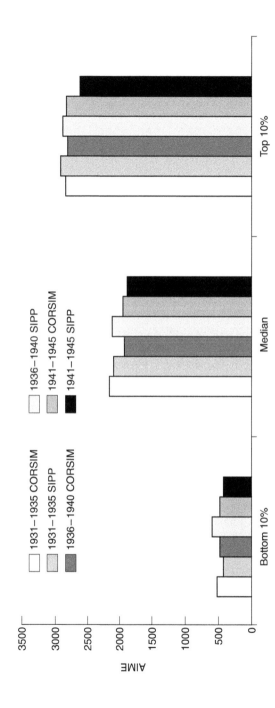

Figure 9.3 CORSIM validation using survey of income and programme participation (SIPP) data: average indexed monthly earnings (AIME) for males with home equity >0 by birth cohort and AIME rank

sample frame is explicitly limited to the non-institutional population, and that might introduce biases in the SIPP estimates. Similarly, surveys such as SIPP will, given the sample size, always be subject to a certain degree of sample variation. The discrepancies are useful in raising questions about both sets of estimates. Perhaps there are advantages to both sets, and the estimates can be combined to create a combined set of estimates superior to either one alone.

DYNACAN illustration

Survey data, particularly the Canadian Survey of Consumer Finances (SCF), and quinquennial census data, provide a variety of variables that also exist in DYNACAN. Particularly important are the population data and their distributions by age, gender and education, all of them 'stock' data. Event/flow data (births, deaths, and several forms of migration) from vital statistics data are also important, and usually contribute to the targets used to align the DYNACAN flows. Recall that DYNACAN, like CORSIM, models only the flows, with the stocks flowing from them as a consequence.

DYNACAN validation against survey/census data over the historical period bears many similarities to the use of administrative data for validation: (a) in the interests of efficiency DYNACAN uses many of the census/survey validation series and distributions developed and used by ACTUCAN in its own validation; (b) historical data are compiled on a one-time basis, while their DYNACAN counterparts are extracted and collated by scripts to facilitate the replication of the validation analyses whenever the model changes; (c) the actual comparisons have been implemented in spreadsheets; they use graphics heavily; and (d) as DYNACAN is extended, additional variables will be added to the validation, for example, housing and health status variables.

Figure 9.4 shows a comparative graph of the population of persons over 65 who reside within Canada, but outside the province of Quebec. This sub-population is particularly important as regards the receipt of CPP benefits. The figure shows the DYNACAN projection relative to a census-based population data series as interpolated in ACTUCAN, for the period from 1972 to the most recent Canadian census. Although the fit is not perfect, DYNACAN tracks this key population category very well, suggesting that the corresponding projections for future years may well prove reasonable. The display shows the results of one particular DYNACAN demographics run, together with the ACTUCAN/Census comparison series. Similar projections by gender perform equally well.

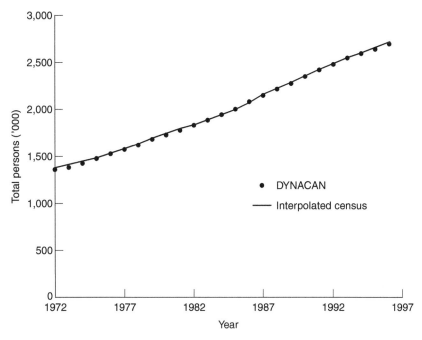

Figure 9.4 RoC population aged 65+: interpolated census *vs* DYNACAN

9.8 Collateral validation

Since the CORSIM/DYNACAN technologies model flows or events, model assumptions and their corresponding parameters directly address those flows, rather than the stocks. Moreover, model alignment can and does affect only those flows. Consequently, in closed models like these, the population stocks themselves cannot be aligned. Thus, the validation of flows such as births and deaths operates largely to ensure that the mechanics of the model are operating correctly; each flow, (e.g. births, deaths or immigration), corresponds to exactly one module in CORSIM or DYNACAN.

But beyond this, there is the opportunity to validate measures that are not directly controlled as flows in the model. We call this collateral validation. Normally, items other than the flows themselves turn out to be the consequences of multiple modules. For example, population stocks are consequences of births, deaths, immigration, emigration and internal migration; numbers of families, their compositions and their distributions are consequences of those same modules, plus the modules for marriage, divorce, remarriage, and leaving home. Thus, collateral validation is 'broader', in the sense of indicating whether whole sets of modules are collectively interacting to produce results that are reasonable.

CORSIM illustration

The CORSIM illustration is drawn from on-going research trying to estimate the magnitudes of the several processes underlying the growth in the number of single-parent families in the US. The overall number of such families is the result of in-flows and out-flows. If the number is growing, it is evident that in-flows exceed out-flows. But which in-flows are most responsible, and how have they changed in magnitude over time? And which outflows have changed as well? Several processes lead to the creation of new female-headed families (with children under 18 present in the family): an unmarried woman has a child; a woman becomes widowed and is left with a child; a woman become divorced and retains custody of a child; a woman with a child moves out from her parental home. Other processes lead to the disappearance of a female-headed family: a single woman with a child marries; a divorced woman with a child remarries; a mother dies; the last child under 18 dies/marries/leaves home to form an independent household; the only child under 18 turns 18. There are virtually no official statistics on in-flows or out-flows to female-headed family status. The existing statistics measure stocks of female-headed families, not flows into or out of that status.

CORSIM simulates the underlying flow processes directly, but the total stock of such families at any time is not directly generated. Rather, it is the outcome of the balance between in-flows and out-flows. Figure 9.5 displays out-flows (exits) by cause as estimated by CORSIM. Because no corresponding flow estimates exist in administrative data, and exist only very poorly in survey data, CORSIM by default might generate the 'best' available flow estimates, though it is difficult to assess the realism of these estimates without corroborative data. What can be done is to compare the *stock* of female-headed families as estimated by census and other cross-sectional data with the stock of female-headed families as estimated by CORSIM. In fact, those stock estimates are quite close. This provides some collateral validation for CORSIM, and it also confers some limited credibility on the CORSIM flow estimates from which the stock estimates are derived. Just as simulations in astronomy are used to 'observe' processes which are difficult or impossible to observe with other methods (e.g., the first seconds of the history of the universe), so microsimulation can be used to 'observe' processes and outcomes for which no respectable data exist from other sources.

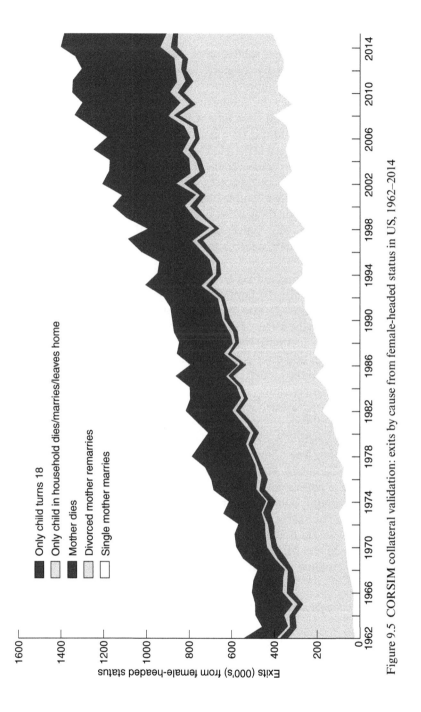

Figure 9.5 CORSIM collateral validation: exits by cause from female-headed status in US, 1962–2014

DYNACAN illustration

Having already noted that validation of stock variables such as population is necessarily at least partly collateral validation, we turn to one collateral validation of particular importance to DYNACAN clients. It involves the distribution of families, by family type, at specific points in time, and trends in the distribution over time. Clients have insisted explicitly that, given the centrality of family type distributions to the desired winner/loser analyses, they want to see DYNACAN producing reasonable distributions and trends for family types over the historical period. At the same time, the standards by which one assesses whether the DYNACAN-generated distributions sufficiently resemble observed distributions are qualitative; it is not necessarily clear 'how close is close enough?' Differences between DYNACAN's effectively 'universal' or 'exhaustive' frame and the sampling frames of the data sources for the comparisons increase the challenges involved.

Family type validation in DYNACAN involves looking at point-in-time distributions of families by family type, and persons by the type of family in which they reside. It also involves examination of the longitudinal trends inherent in the series of distributions. Once again, these are done in a spreadsheet to facilitate the presentation of the information, and to allow convenient updating of this validation analysis when changes are made anywhere in the model.

Figure 9.6 shows how, although the fit is obviously not perfect, DYNACAN does reasonably well in tracking the proportion of the population living in childless couples that contain at least one person aged 65 or older. This proportion is, of course, a key one in projecting a variety of programme benefits. The primary comparison base for this validation component is the Canadian Survey of Consumer Finances. Although it is a relatively large sample, involving about 40,000 families, the measures drawn from it are certainly subject to some sampling variation, so that their values may vary from one survey to the next, especially for subsamples such as this.

Figure 9.7 shows how DYNACAN generally reproduces, over time, the distribution of the fractions of single parent families with respect to the numbers of children in them.

9.9 Other models and projections

Despite our continuing enthusiasm for the capacities of microsimulation, and its promise as the single best technology for addressing many critical issues of interest, we are also quick to recognise that there are other models

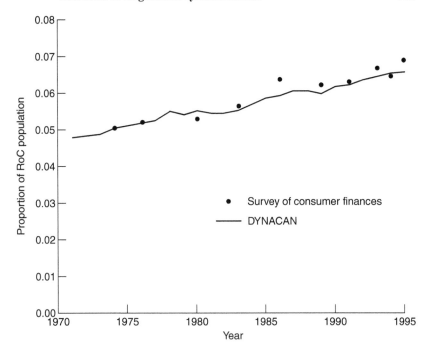

Figure 9.6 Proportion of RoC population living in childless couples with at least one senior

capable of addressing some aspects of those issues. The actuarial valuation models developed by the Social Security Administration and the Office of the Chief Actuary in Canada are key examples. Although they do not permit micro-level winners/losers analyses, or supply the same kinds of detail about individual and family histories, there is significant overlap with CORSIM and DYNACAN in terms of the time series and broad distributions they produce. But, even when CORSIM and DYNACAN adopt the same assumptions, there is, in principle, no guarantee that the two sets of common results will be identical. Validating CORSIM/DYNACAN against these other models piggy-backs indirectly on all the validation efforts that have gone into those actuarial valuation models.

Policy-makers have grown familiar with these other models. Indeed, having had nothing else approaching comprehensive models in the past to help guide their policy deliberations, they are interested in the extent to which CORSIM and DYNACAN produce similar results. Being very reluctant to take on the role of reconciling the results of different models, the policy-makers would prefer to see substantial similarity between the

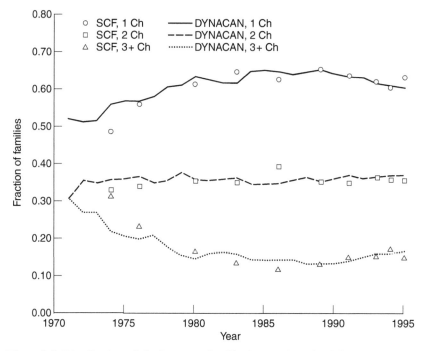

Figure 9.7 Distribution of single-parent families by number of children, DYNACAN and SCF

aggregate results from microsimulation models and the comparable results from the macro-models. There will be a tendency to ask, for those results that both models can produce, how microsimulation models compare with models that have already 'made their bones'. If micro-simulation models' results differ substantially, there will be some pressure for a reconciliation, or for a compelling demonstration that the micro-simulation results are superior.

Another reason for comparing microsimulation results to those of other models is that the projections of those other models will typically be the only source of information about the future. If existing models' projections have met the test of acceptance for policy applications, then microsimula-tion results should be similar, or demonstrably superior. Actuarial valua-tion models as used for social security programmes are particularly important here. We consider it significant that, in Canada, the contribu-tions to model validation go both ways – DYNACAN uses directly a number of the CPP actuarial valuation model (ACTUCAN) results in its own assumptions and operations, but DYNACAN results have, in turn, been used to tune some of ACTUCAN's parameters. In many respects, these two models are symbiotic, functioning as a modelling suite.

DYNACAN illustration

We have noted how the CPP actuarial valuation model, ACTUCAN, plays a special role for DYNACAN. It is a DYNACAN design criterion that it produce results that, when common assumptions are used, are generally consistent with those of ACTUCAN. Beyond the policy-makers' desire to avoid having to reconcile results, this approach is appropriate for valida-tion in that ACTUCAN itself has been heavily validated against pro-gramme and survey/census data. Validation against ACTUCAN is thus a convenient proxy for validation against those same source data.

   As well, ACTUCAN provides a comparison basis for the projected por-tion of DYNACAN runs. In addition, using ACTUCAN as the compari-son base for the historical period, as well as the projection period, avoids discontinuities in the transition from the historical to the projected por-tions of a run's results. ACTUCAN is used as the comparison base for a wide variety of distributional and trend results for the DYNACAN valida-tion. These include population by age and gender, numbers of earners and distributions of earnings and contributions, again by age and gender, and all the types of CPP benefits, once again by age and gender. ACTUCAN also provides a number of more specialised results to which DYNACAN's performance can be compared; examples include emergences for various kinds of benefits, and the age, gender and duration distributions for disabil-ity benefits.

   Figure 9.8 shows how, though once again the fit is certainly not perfect, DYNACAN tracks reasonably well the trend in total projected CPP benefits. Not shown here is that DYNACAN also tracks reasonably well the numbers of beneficiaries, the amounts of benefits, and the average benefits for the various types of CPP benefits, not all of which display the same pattern of growth over time.

9.10 Special considerations relating to Monte Carlo modelling

When one uses a Monte Carlo model, one gets a different slate of results with each distinct stream of pseudo-random deviates; these results cluster around an unknown central tendency. Variance reduction efforts described elsewhere (Neufeld, 1997) help considerably to ensure that the results of individual runs fall fairly close to the central tendency, but a non-trivial variation persists. The extent of such variation is very similar between CORSIM and DYNACAN. For example, the dispersion of the

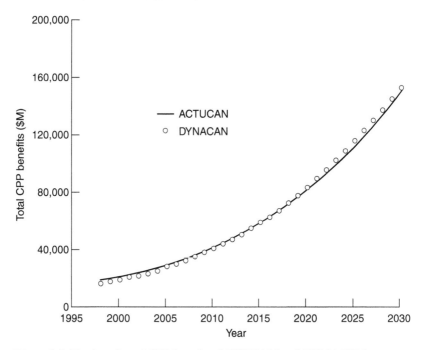

Figure 9.8 Total projected CPP benefits, ACTUCAN and DYNACAN

DYNACAN population of Canada less Quebec after 60 years of simulation exhibits a standard deviation of less than 0.5% of the central tendency. That central tendency is estimated using data from some 300 plus
runs using separate random number streams, all of them conducted using
a 'small sample data base' equal to about 0.2% of the total population.
DYNACAN analyses regularly use such 'small samples' because the pressures of an active policy environment mean that one cannot always afford
the time and processing required to use the largest starting population
sample. Use of that largest sample (a full 1% of the population in the case
of DYNACAN) would reduce, but not eliminate, the size of the variation
relative to the population or policy impact.

A similar challenge occurs for model validation; the results from any
given run are effectively drawn from an unknown distribution. Given the
run times involved, it is not regularly feasible to carry out a large number
of runs in parallel and then average their results. However, one can do this
occasionally, measure the dispersion for a variety of important
series/results, and assume that in the absence of significant changes in the
model, these will not change appreciably. This is the approach taken with

CORSIM/DYNACAN. Dispersions compiled at one point in time are used to provide an approximation of the confidence intervals for results derived later.

CORSIM illustration

Table 9.1 displays some estimates of Monte Carlo variation in recent runs. Means, standard deviations, coefficients of variation, and maximum absolute deviations from the mean are computed across seven CORSIM runs in which only the random number stream is varied. The results are reassuring; the variability is relatively small compared to the mean. This suggests that Monte Carlo variation is not a serious problem for these outcomes, and probably for other similar ones as well. But further continuing experiments are desirable to keep track of this factor.

9.11 Conclusions

This paper has described validation principles and practices, and presented some illustrative results, for the CORSIM and DYNACAN microsimulation models. Validation is important to the models' application. The model teams, and especially their clients, are generally pleased that not only do validation plans exist, and that they have generally been implemented, but particularly that the resulting validation studies have strongly suggested that the models' results are indeed credible as inputs to the policy development process. This result is encouraging, particularly since no other class of models appears capable of generating the kinds of crucial policy inputs, such as the winners/losers analyses, detailed, family-oriented distributions, and realistic longitudinal earnings and kinship histories that these models supply.

At the same time, there is an ongoing challenge to improve validation practices in order to ensure greater credibility for the models' results, and as starting points for improving the models themselves. Existing validation practices make it clear that the field of longitudinal microsimulation model validation is still in its infancy. There is little relevant literature, and little in the way of theory. The relationships between quality control and validation are only beginning to be well understood. Further, it is not necessarily obvious, *a priori*, what aspects of the models' results are the most important to validate, or what are the most appropriate ways of assessing the models' performance in those areas. It is not yet feasible to ascertain what constitutes the optimal balance of resources across the development, extension, application and validation of these models. And it is certainly not always clear how good is good enough. We are nonetheless optimistic,

Table 9.1. *CORSIM Monte Carlo variation, 1965–2035: estimates calculated from seven independent CORSIM simulations*

Year	Per capita FICA tax (mean $)	SD	Coeff. of Variation (SD/ mean as percent)	Max absolute/ percentage deviation from mean (%)	Retired beneficiaries/ total population (mean)	SD	Coeff. of variation (SD/mean as percentage)	Max absolute/ percentage deviation from mean (%)
1965	79	>0	0.62	1/0.9	0.05715	0.0003	0.57	0.0005/0.8
1975	293	2	0.73	3/0.9	0.07549	0.0010	1.36	0.0017/1.8
1985	843	5	0.63	8/0.9	0.09629	0.0009	0.96	0.0016/1.6
1995	1460	9	0.59	14/1.0	0.10562	0.0011	1.04	0.0022/2.1
2005	2376	13	0.57	27/0.6	0.11050	0.0008	0.70	0.0013/1.1
2015	3798	29	0.77	56/1.5	0.13847	0.0008	0.58	0.0014/1.0
2025	5949	34	0.58	43/0.7	0.18472	0.0012	0.66	0.0018/1.0
2035	9330	83	0.90	128/1.4	0.19929	0.0013	0.67	0.0022/1.1

Source: Internal CORSIM results.

on the basis of our experience to date, that increasing practice in using these kinds of models, and in validating them, will see improvements across the board.

Notes

1 We specifically do not treat *static* microsimulation in this paper.
2 Used in this broad sense, the term 'validation' encompasses many distinct model development activities not addressed in any depth in this paper. Examples include: code debugging; alignment; module re-specification; and parameter re-estimation.
3 A substantial literature exists on validation of simulation models generally. However, much of this literature has limited usefulness for our purpose in this paper because it fails to distinguish among different modelling types, or among different modelling goals. This paper treats validation only as it applies to models of a specific type (dynamic microsimulation) and with a specific goal (policy analysis).
4 It is not accidental that we present together results from both the CORSIM and DYNACAN models. When Canada decided to develop its own longitudinal microsimulation capacity, rather than begin construction of DYNACAN *de novo*, it decided to adopt as template an already operational microsimulation model – CORSIM, developed by Caldwell and associates at Cornell University. The source code and subsequent advice provided by the CORSIM team enabled Canada to develop an operational, Canadian model more quickly, more reliably and more cheaply than starting from scratch. And since that initial decision, several major enhancements developed for DYNACAN by the DYNACAN team have subsequently been implemented in CORSIM by the CORSIM team. The co-operation between the two teams has continued, to the considerable mutual benefit of both teams and models. For example, there is a common source tree for the two models' code, and the two teams meet regularly to address joint problems and proposed solutions.
5 We use the word 'estimated' intentionally. All historical data provide *estimates*, not 'true' population value. Even administrative data provide only estimates, though they might be quite reliable ones. Comparing microsimulation outcomes to historical data is not simply a matter of comparing artificial simulated data to true historical values. Both are estimates. Differences in estimates are not necessarily due wholly to microsimulation flaws; differences might arise as well from collection or recording flaws in administrative data or the sampling frame used for the collection of survey data. Comparing microsimulation-based estimates to administrative or survey-based estimates is a matter of comparing alternative estimation strategies.

10 Charging for care in later life: an exercise in dynamic microsimulation

Ruth Hancock

10.1 Introduction

Concern over the way in which social care is paid for and – in the longer term – its total cost is at the forefront of British politics. A Royal Commission report was published in March 1999 (Royal Commission on Long-term Care, 1999) but, at the time of writing, the government has not accepted its recommendations. In the UK, the majority of health care is provided through the National Health Service (NHS) and, for the most part, is free to all at the point of delivery, being financed by general taxation. Social care generally falls outside the NHS and is provided by Local Authorities or providers in the independent sector. People with sufficient resources are expected to meet the costs of social care from their own pockets. Any state help with its cost is subject to a means test. Means-testing has been a long-standing feature of the provision of social care in the UK, although the shifting boundary between health and social care means that some forms of care which would once have been available free under the NHS are now provided on a means-tested basis (Wistow, 1996). Defining the boundary between health and social care remains a contentious, if not futile, endeavour.

This paper arises from the early stages of research which is examining some of the consequences of alternative charging policies for care in later life. The study uses survey micro-data on the incomes and assets of older people living in private households who might need care now or in the next 10 to 15 years. The research is forward-looking so, even though it entails consideration of the financial circumstances of people who may require care in a residential setting, it is the resources of elderly people living in private households, which are the more relevant.

The analysis ultimately aims to derive estimates of the proportions and characteristics of older people who would be required to contribute to care costs, should they need care, and the amounts they would be liable to pay. The financial consequences for older people requiring care, and for any other members of their households, are also being examined.

226

The next section discusses the role of dynamic microsimulation in modelling the effects of long-term care charges. Section 10.3 sets out current rules for charging for residential care and Section 10.4 outlines what is modelled in this paper. Some results are presented in Section 10.5 and Section 10.6 concludes.

10.2 Long-term care and dynamic microsimulation

There are a number of respects in which the subject of long-term care may require dynamic rather than static simulation. From the point of view of total costs, long-term care is a problem for the future, rather than the present, and in particular of the longer-term future. In the next fifteen years the size of the UK population aged 80 years and over is projected to increase by 15% but from a relatively small base of about 4% of the total population. In 40 years, there will be 80% more people in this age group and they will account for nearly 7% of the population. (Government Actuary's 1996-based principal population projections.) It is at these oldest ages that frailty increases fast and with it the need for some form of care on a long-term basis. The 1994 General Household Survey found that the percentage of older people who could not get up and down stairs on their own rose from 8% among those aged 75–79 to 13% in the age group 80–84 and 23% for those aged 85 and over (Bennett et al., 1996, Table 6.22).

Previous long-term care modelling in the UK has been concerned to predict the future need for care – in total and for subgroups defined by age, gender and so forth – and aggregate costs. It has been based on demographic changes, trends in morbidity, assumptions about the availability of informal care and likely changes in unit costs. Key published works include Nuttall et al., (1993), Richards et al., (1996) and Department of Health memoranda to the Joseph Rowntree Foundation inquiry into meeting the costs of continuing care (Joseph Rowntree Foundation, 1996). The Personal Social Services Research Unit have developed a 'cell-based' forecasting model (Wittenberg et al., 1998) using grouped micro-data (see Propper, 1992, for a discussion of a cell-based approach). These models have involved assumptions about the average proportion of costs recovered from the recipients of care and how that might change in the future.

A case could be made for using dynamic microsimulation to make predictions of the total numbers needing care. An even stronger case can be made for using microsimulation to assess the contributions users would be required to pay towards their care, because of the complicated and non-linear way in which liability for charges is related to income and wealth. To the extent that we are interested in the future, this suggests dynamic microsimulation. To the extent that the financial resources of older people are changing, it may be that even if the numbers who need care do not change very much in the near future, their ability to meet the costs may do so. Looking 10 to 15 years ahead, the apportionment of the costs between the state and the individual may change. Leaving aside the question of how many people will need long-term care, an interesting question to ask, is therefore, how the contributions to costs of older people who might need care in the near future may differ from those who might need care in ten to fifteen years' time.

In this paper we concentrate on the ability of older people to meet the costs of residential care. This is simpler than domiciliary care for two reasons. First, there is a nationally-applicable framework for assessing how much individuals should pay for residential care, whereas Local Authorities currently have discretion in charging for services arranged for people living in the community. Second, average weekly fees for residential care homes provide a baseline cost for residential care whereas to derive costs for domiciliary care it is necessary to make assumptions about which and how frequently services are being provided. (For an example of such an approach using hypothetical examples, see Tinker *et al.*, (1999)).

A further dynamic aspect of paying for long-term care concerns how long an individual's resources will last when they have to contribute to the high costs of residential care, since often these costs have to be met by depleting capital.

10.3 Paying for residential care

Since 1 April 1993, people entering a private or voluntary residential or nursing home must first be assessed by a Local Authority as needing such care if they wish to receive any help from the state with the costs of their care, either in the present or in the future. They will be entitled to some Income Support if their capital is no more than £16,000 and their income is less than an amount equal to the level prescribed for someone living in the community plus a residential allowance (£62 a week in London and £56 elsewhere, in 1997–98). Local Authorities are responsible for paying negotiated care home fees but determine contributions from the resident. This contribution is 100% of the fees for those with capital in excess of £16,000. Otherwise it is an amount, up to a maximum of the total fees, which leaves the resident with income at least equal to a 'personal expenses allowance' of £14.10 a week (in 1997–8). In February 1997, average weekly fees for single rooms in private residential homes varied from £229 in Northern Ireland and the North West of England to £332 in London, and for nursing homes, from £315 in the East Midlands to £433 in London

(Laing and Buisson, 1997, Section 5). The UK averages for nursing homes were £343 (£326 for a shared room) and for residential homes £250 (£239 for a shared room) (Laing and Buisson, 1997, Table 8.1).

A particular concern is the treatment of couples when one partner enters residential care and the other remains living in the community. This can have major implications for the finances of the partner remaining at home. The issue has been explored in a preliminary manner without dynamic simulation in Hancock and Wright (1999) and will be the subject of future dynamic simulation. However, it is single older people and in particular those who live alone who are most at risk of entering long-term residential care and it is on these that we concentrate in this paper.

10.4 What is modelled

Our aim is to undertake some preliminary dynamic simulation to explore the contributions to the cost of residential care that older people would be required to make, should they need that care, in fifteen years' time. *Whether* an individual older person is likely to need care is *not* modelled. The universe of interest is defined as people who will be aged 80+ and living alone in 2012–13, the base year from which the simulation is performed being 1997–8. For comparison, we pose the same question of people currently aged 80+ and living alone. The strategy is to put to one side the more researched methodological problems in microsimulation (see, for example, Redmond *et al.*, 1998), concentrating on the aspects of dynamic microsimulation which need to be tackled. Simplifying assumptions are made which need to be varied in future work but, where doing so does not raise particular issues for the practicalities of the simulation, they are not discussed in detail here. The task in hand has also been defined deliberately to be less ambitious than some which require dynamic microsimulation in order to make progress through small steps.

The sample which forms the basis of the simulation is drawn from three years' worth of Family Expenditure Survey (1993–4, 1994–5 and 1995–6) with incomes and capital assets uprated to 1997–8 levels. Within this sample we are interested in two age groups: those currently aged 80+ (in practice it is convenient to exclude those aged 95 or more and work with the closed age interval 80–94 years) and those now aged 65–79 who will be aged 80–94 in 2012–13. For the first group we simulate the effect of an immediate move into residential care.

Before we can pose the same question for the second group in respect of 2012–13, the following steps are involved for each sample member in that age group:

- *Predict whether he or she will be alive in 15 years' time*
  This is done by stochastic simulation using age and gender-specific survival probabilities derived from the Government Actuary's department's 1996-based population projections. Cohort-based survival probabilities have been derived so that the influence of continuing improvements in mortality is captured.
- *Predict whether he or she will have become a widow or widower*
  This is done deterministically once survival of each partner has been simulated.
- *Simulate how the individual's income and wealth will have changed by 2012/13*
  As a starting point the following simple assumptions are made but some are obvious candidates for variation in later work: (1) any earned income has ceased by 2012/13 or at least would cease on entry to residential care (the same assumption is made for those now aged 80–94 in modelling an immediate move into residential care); (2) all sources of state and private pension income maintain their real value, but no more than this, in relation to retail prices (if anything, this is likely to be an over-generous assumption as far as private sector pensions are concerned); (3) all financial assets and income derived from them maintain their real value implying that there is no depletion of existing capital until the age of 80 and no additions to capital, for example from inheritances or the maturation of insurance policies. For those who own their homes, these retain their real value but do not appreciate in value. It is assumed that by the age of 80 any outstanding mortgage on them has been repaid. (Varying assumptions about real increases in house values are obvious candidates for future exploration.)

  Since we are modelling income in the context of a hypothesised need to enter residential care it seems reasonable to assume that the individual would become eligible for an 'underlying' entitlement to Attendance Allowance, if not already receiving that benefit. Whether they would in fact receive this income in residential care depends on whether they had sufficient resources to be required to meet the care home's fees in full. If so, Attendance Allowance is payable in residential care. If not, Attendance Allowance is not payable but an underlying entitlement remains so that the person can be eligible for the Income Support severe disability premium. It is therefore assumed that conditional on the presumption of a need to enter residential care at the age of 80 or more, everyone not already receiving Attendance Allowance receives an actual or underlying entitlement to it at the lower rate of £33.10 in 1997–8. (The assumption of the lower rate is arbitrary and could be varied.)

- *Model any inheritance of income and capital of the surviving partner if there is one*
  Again some simple assumptions are made as a starting point: (1) the survivor inherits all of his/her late partner's financial assets and income from them; (2) he/she inherits all of his/her partner's share in their home if they are owner-occupiers; (3) the survivor inherits half of any private pension income that his/her partner had; (4) the survivor inherits half of the late partner's state earnings-related pension (SERPS) income; and (5) if the survivor is a woman (usually the case) and her own basic state pension is less than that of her late husband's, her own basic state pension is increased by the difference between the two.

The assumptions concerning the state pension are designed to reflect loosely but inevitably imperfectly the rules in this area. One problem in particular is that respondents do not report their basic state pension and SERPS separately. At present, only a rough apportionment of the total state pension into these components has been made. A better approach is described in Hancock and Sutherland (1997).

No other changes in circumstances are modelled. Thus, apart from the possible death of a partner, there is no other change in household composition (although each household member will be 15 years older). This is probably more realistic for older than younger households where children growing up and leaving home are more of a possibility. Residential moves are not modelled, nor is divorce. Again, our focus on the older population who have already retired makes this less of a limitation than it would be for younger people. Nonetheless, it is an obvious oversimplification.

Modelling net income and liability for care charges

To model liability for care charges it is necessary to simulate entitlement to Income Support, which in turn means modelling (pre-Income Support) income net of tax and making an assessment of wealth. For owner-occupiers this must include housing wealth: when someone moves into residential care and no qualifying relative remains living in their home, the value of the home is included in the capital test for Income Support and for assessing liability to meet care charges. Since 1992, home-owners in the FES have been asked the year in which they bought their homes and the original purchase prices of them. This information provides the basis of our estimates of current property values, as explained in more detail in

Table 10.1. *A comparison of some of the characteristics of people currently aged 80–94 and living alone and those of people predicted to be in the same situation in 15 years' time*

	1997/8	2012/3
Average net income (£s per annum, 1997–8 prices)	6,040	6,520
Proportion who own their homes (%)	47	58
Proportion who are women (%)	75	84
Sample size	790	980

Source: Own analysis of 1993/4, 1994/5 and 1995/6 *Family Expenditure Survey.*

Hancock (2000). A static tax–benefit model is used to assess tax liability and entitlement to Income Support and Housing Benefit (an earlier version is outlined in Hancock, 1998).

It is assumed that the care home fees are £280 within Greater London and £235 elsewhere (people are assumed to enter a care home in their current region of residence). These levels would buy fairly modest accommodation in a residential care home. Nursing home fees would be higher, as would better accommodation in a residential home.

10.5 First results

The results presented in this section illustrate the application of the method and highlight some of the areas where it needs to be refined. Some comparisons are shown of the liability to meet charges should they need to enter a residential home, of people now aged 80–94 and currently living alone in a private household, and those currently living in private households who are predicted to be alive, living alone, and aged 80–94 in fifteen years' time. One inconsistency in this comparison is that those currently aged 80 and over exclude people who have already moved into residential care.

Table 10.1 compares some basic characteristics of the two groups of interest. The future generation of 80–94-year-olds living alone is projected to have slightly higher incomes (mainly as a result of higher occupational pensions) and to be more likely to own their homes. There are also predicted to be more women among them. This could be due to the fact that people currently living in residential settings are not in the sample, which probably excludes more women than men from the current generation of 80–94-year-olds.

Table 10.2 shows what proportion of men and women are predicted to have to meet residential care home fees in full or in part. Where someone is

Table 10.2. *Simulated contributions to residential care costs of people currently aged 80–94 and living alone and those of people predicted to be in the same situation in 15 years' time (%)*

	Men		Women		Men and women	
	1997/8	2012/3	1997/8	2012/3	1997/8	2012/3
Pays less than full fees and receives no Income Support	22	26	23	21	23	22
Pays less than full fees, receives Income Support	24	21	33	20	31	20
Pays all of the fees, capital in excess of £16,000	53	52	45	59	47	58
Pays all of the fees, other	0	1	0	*	*	1
Average % contribution to fees						
overall	72	72	65	74	66	73
for those meeting only some of the cost and receiving IS	42	43	42	40	42	41
for those meeting only some of the cost and not receiving IS	37	38	29	31	31	33
Sample size	197	160	593	820	790	980

Notes:
Percentages are shown to the nearest whole per cent. 0 indicates none in sample;
* indicates less than 0.5%.
Source: Own analysis of 1993/4, 1994/5 and 1995/6 Family Expenditure Survey

not required to meet the fees in full, the difference has to be met from the Local Authority's budget. On the stated assumptions, the proportion who would be liable to meet the fees in full is predicted to increase from 47% to 59%, and the average contribution to fees is predicted to rise from 66% to 73%. Most of this change comes from higher contributions from women. The proportion of them predicted to have to meet the full fees because they have capital in excess of £16,000 rises from 45% to 59%. There are decreases for both men and women in the proportion paying some of the cost and receiving Income Support.

Non-take-up of Income Support is modelled on a random basis. Thus, some of those who would be required to pay part of their care costs might be entitled to Income Support. Among those paying only part of the costs, those receiving Income Support contribute more on average than those not receiving Income Support. The incentive for Local Authorities to make sure that those needing care claim this benefit is clear.

Hardly any people are predicted to be liable to pay full charges on the basis of their income alone. For most it is their capital (and most of this is the value of their homes) which precludes them from state help. In general, they must deplete their capital to pay for care. However, the rate at which they are calculated to have to deplete their capital (assuming they first put all their income towards the fees) falls from around £3,300 a year now to £2,400 a year in fifteen years' time.

In view of the important role of housing wealth, and the political debate that surrounds the requirement to use housing wealth to pay for residential care, it is interesting to ask how the results would differ if housing wealth were disregarded in the assessment of liability to meet residential care home fees and in the capital test for Income Support for residents. This is what is shown in Table 10.3. The proportion of current 80–94-year-olds who would now have to meet the full cost of residential care because they have capital other than housing wealth in excess of £16,000, falls to 20%. The corresponding figure in fifteen years' time is higher, at 29%, but still half the figure which applies when housing wealth is taken into account. There are a few cases where housing wealth takes their capital above £16,000 who have sufficient income to make them liable for the full cost of residential care if housing wealth is disregarded. Including these, the total proportions having to meet the full cost of care in 1997–8, at the assumed fee levels, falls from 47% to 21% when housing wealth is disregarded. The comparison for fifteen years' time is a fall from 59% to 31%. Disregarding housing wealth increases the proportions receiving and not receiving Income Support who would have to pay less than full fees but, comparing 1997/8 with 2012/13, there is still a predicted decline over time in the proportions receiving Income Support. The average contribution to fees falls

Table 10.3. *Simulated contributions to residential care costs of people currently aged 80–94 and living alone and those of people predicted to be in the same situation in 15 years' time, housing wealth disregarded in full (%)*

	Men		Women		Men and women	
	1997/8	2012/3	1997/8	2012/3	1997/8	2012/3
Pays less than full fees and receives no Income Support	35	41	48	39	35	39
Pays less than full fees, receives Income Support	35	28	35	30	44	30
Pays all of the fees, capital in excess of £16,000	30	26	17	29	20	29
Pays all of the fees, other	1	3	1	1	1	2
Average % contribution to fees						
overall	59	59	48	57	51	57
for those meeting only some of the cost and receiving IS	42	44	42	40	42	41
for those meeting only some of the cost and not receiving IS	40	41	32	37	34	38
Sample size	197	160	593	820	790	980

Note:
Percentages are shown to the nearest whole per cent.
Source: Own analysis of 1993/4, 1994/5 and 1995/6 Family Expenditure Survey

from 66% to 51% for those currently aged 80–94 and from 73% to 57% for their counterparts in 2012/13.

10.6 Concluding remarks

This paper has presented a first attempt to use dynamic microsimulation to simulate the contributions that older people would have to make towards the cost of care in a residential home should they need it, comparing the results for those in a relatively high risk group now with those likely to be in the same situation in fifteen years' time. We have argued that *micro-simulation* is necessary because of the complex non-linear relationship between an individual's liability for care charges and his or her financial resources; and that *dynamic* simulation is necessary because older people's incomes and wealth are changing so that their ability to meet, and liability for, charges will differ in the future.

A number of simplifying assumptions were made, particularly concerning the simulation of how the income and wealth of those currently aged 65–79 will change during the next 15 years. It is straightforward to make alternative index-linking assumptions about existing pension income. It is less clear how to vary assumptions about changes in capital. The results could be very sensitive to assumptions here and some sensitivity analysis is needed. Likewise, for assumptions about the inheritance of income and capital on the death of a partner. Turning to housing wealth, it is again straightforward to test the sensitivity of the predictions to alternative assumptions about future house price movements. It is harder to allow for the possibility of home-owners releasing some of the capital tied-up in their homes by moving to a smaller home, changing to renting their home or through some form of home equity release financial product.

The strategy here has been to concentrate on the aspects of dynamic simulation which need to be tackled, leaving aside some other methodological issues which will need to be addressed in due course. The scope of the task has also been deliberately restricted to be manageable while remaining of high policy relevance. This has proved valuable in enabling progress to be made and in identifying future priorities.

Note

Financial support from the Nuffield Foundation is gratefully acknowledged. I am also grateful for comments from participants at the workshop on Microsimulation in the New Millennium: Challenges and Innovations held at Cambridge University in August 1998, and in particular to my discussant, Michael Wolfson. Material from the Family Expenditure Survey, made available by the Office for National Statistics and the Data Archive is Crown Copyright and has been used with permission. All responsibility for analysis and interpretation rests with me.

11 Individual alignment and group processing: an application to migration processes in DYNACAN

Denis Chénard

11.1 Introduction

One of the first objectives in dynamic microsimulation models is to generate a synthetic population to which various modules can be added as needed to study phenomena of interest. Credibility of the model depends crucially on its ability to reproduce past history and/or benchmark measures and, since microsimulation models are not yet sufficiently developed to be used for forecasting on their own, we need alignment benchmarks. In the case of DYNACAN our benchmark is the Canada Pension Plan (CPP) actuarial model, a cell-based model named ACTUCAN. DYNACAN has to follow ACTUCAN's results within very close tolerances in order to be of relevance to the policy-makers, and the first step in reaching this goal is to match ACTUCAN's population projections exactly, first in terms of population size and age distribution, then in terms of family structure, as this has an impact on CPP benefit calculations. Reaching this goal entails matching births, deaths, and migration as exactly as possible. This paper describes the process used by DYNACAN in the migration modules to ensure a close fit with ACTUCAN. Other alignment methods used in DYNACAN are covered in Neufeld (1997).

11.2 The migration process

In Canada, migration (especially immigration) constitutes an important component of population change. However, in our modelling exercise we do not have the luxury of access to linked longitudinal population databases (as in Sweden), or detailed migrant information, as is the case in Australia (Walker, 1997). The only data readily available are the yearly distribution of migrants by age and sex, and the Census microdata files. Furthermore, since the Canada Pension Plan does not apply to the province of Quebec (they run a similar but distinct plan), DYNACAN also has to model inter-provincial migration from Quebec to the rest of Canada (ROC), and inter-provincial migration from ROC to Quebec. Finally, each year there is a slight discrepancy between total population movement and the sum of demographic flows, and this discrepancy must also be modelled in order to keep a close population match between DYNACAN and ACTUCAN (we call these 'mole people'). This gives us six distinct processes to model, aligned separately for Quebec and the ROC.

The DYNACAN migration modules 'move' population by using logit equations estimated from the Census Public Use Microdata File. The process works on a family basis, and the characteristics of the family head play a major role in the selection criterion. In the case of immigration, families in the population database are examined, and those selected are 'cloned' by making a duplicate of the selected family. These flows of migration must then be aligned to ACTUCAN's distributions, by age, sex, and region (Quebec and ROC). There lies the difficulty.

11.3 The alignment problem

Other demographic modules, like births and deaths, operate on an individual basis. One implication is that one person's transition probability is generally treated as independent of anybody else's. Migration, on the other hand, works on a family basis, that is, whole families tend to move together. This creates a major problem when it comes to alignment. Standard procedures do not work because the selection probability distribution of migrants is heavily skewed, the average probability of migration is very low (below 0.01 in most cases), and migrants move one family at a time without regard to family size, making the control of the number of migrants (the goal of alignment) impossible.

One approach to solving this problem is to run a search algorithm on the alignment factor. The method goes like this: a series of possible alignment numbers is taken, and in the first pass of the year a tally of the number of migrants is taken using each of these alignment factors. In the second pass, the two factors that give the number of migrants closest to the target are picked and interpolated to give us the alignment number to be used. The finer the grid of numbers, the closer the match. This method works well at matching the total number, but gives no control over the age/sex mix of migrants.

The search method has another related problem. In the case of immigration, the equations that determine the migration probabilities tend to select a distinct subset of the population. This is due in good part to the long tail at the right of the probability distribution that results from passing families through the migration equations, which gives some families probabilities up to 30 times higher than average. As immigrants are 'cloned', that is, the migration module makes a copy of the selected families, this subgroup of cloned families tend to be re-cloned again and again over time, the process feeding on itself. This creates undesirable dips and bumps in the population distribution that get worse over time, which in turn affects all the other demographic modules. One 30-year run of DYNACAN has shown families being cloned up to 18 times, when on average one would expect roughly a 20% probability of being cloned *once* during that period. Consequently, a better alignment strategy is needed.

We need an alignment method that sets targets for the number of migrants (of each type) in the most disaggregated way possible, keeps track of the number of people, controls the flow of migrants in order to reach these targets, minimises the multiple cloning problem, and has a memory to fix any past discrepancies, despite the fact that migrants move by family and get processed in an order unknown to the migration modules. The next section describes one way of reaching these seemingly incompatible goals.

11.4 The 'pageant' method of alignment

This method is based on the pageant principle: many are called but few get chosen. It is set out in some detail in Appendix 11A.1. Instead of declaring a family as migrant, it is declared as a *candidate for migration*. Because the migration modules involve low probabilities, some age/sex/region groups might not have any representatives; to circumvent this problem, and to ensure flexibility in the selection of migrants, the transition probabilities coming out of the migration equations are multiplied by a number large enough to ensure that most age/sex/region groups have representatives in the candidates bank. At present, this number is derived on the basis of experience in running the model; in DYNACAN it stands at 30 for immigration and 60 for the other five modules (emigration and inter-provincial migration to and from Quebec). This pool of candidates represents, on average, people that are more susceptible to become migrants. When a family is selected to be a candidate, each member of the family is tallied according to his/her region/sex/age (in DYNACAN this represents 512 different bins for each migration module). After the first pass, these numbers become the basis for the selection process.

The next step is to determine how many people are wanted for each of the 512 region/sex/age groups. First, the total number of desired migrants is determined by taking the overall proportion of the population that are to become migrants. This resulting number is then distributed by region/sex/age, based on alignment data. At this point we have the number of people we need and the number of people available. Before proceeding to migrate families, we need a few more tools. We need two more arrays of size 512 of the number of people already selected to become migrants and the number of people left in our pool, plus a few more ancillary small control arrays. These control the total number of migrants by region, and keep track of totals by region and sex.

The actual operation goes like this: in the second pass, the migration module checks whether the current family has been declared as a candidate for migration in the first pass. If so, then the module goes through each member of the family and determines the *relative need index* for a person in its region/sex/age, based on the information collected up to then. This number is defined as:

$$\frac{\text{people still needed for this region / sex / age group}}{\text{people still available for this region / sex / age group}}$$

Each member of the family goes through this process, and the highest index across the family is used as the probability used for the selection of the family, the rationale being that the person with the highest need should become the deciding factor for the selection decision. Another possibility would be using the average index for the family; however, experience has shown it to be a less efficient method. Upon reaching a decision whether to 'migrate' this family, the pertinent arrays (people already migrated, people left in the pool, and running totals) are updated. The process goes on until the desired total by region for the year is reached or the pool of candidates is exhausted, whichever comes first.

11.5 Special cases

At a certain point during the second pass, we reach a point where conflicts arise. Our goal being to match the number of selected people with the alignment figures as closely as possible, we want a way to enforce this goal. Conflicts happen when some members of the family belong to region/sex/ age bins that are already full while the other members still have space available, and/or when some members of the family belong to region/sex/age bins that would remain unfilled if this family were not selected. To circumvent this problem, before reaching a decision the number of 'excedent' (excess) cases *versus* the number of 'unfillable' cases is compared for each family. If the excedent exceed the unfillable the probability for this family is set to zero. In the opposite case, the probability is set to one and, if they are equal, the probability is set to 0.5. Also, if the total desired for a region/sex group would be exceeded by selecting the family (even if no single region/ sex/age bin would end up being overfilled) the number of excedent for this family is set to one, unless there are already excedents from the individual bins, in which case the number of excedents remains unchanged. Finally, once the total number of migrants is reached for a region, no one is allowed to migrate, no matter how badly they could be needed to fill a specific region/sex/age bin. The rationale behind all this is to let families move only if they help more than they hurt the migrant distribution, without exceeding our set totals.

11.6 Error correction

Despite all efforts to ensure a perfect match, discrepancies between the desired and the actual number of people migrated will remain. Possible reasons for this include: 'fractional' number of people desired for a group, ordering of the population in the starting database, or exhaustion of the candidates pool before the desired total is reached. 'Fractional' people occur because of the alignment figures and the relatively small size of our model population. The end result is that we might need something like 2.438 people in a given region/sex/age bin; all we can do is select either two or three persons, giving us a fraction of a person to deal with (more on this problem later). The order in which the population gets processed through the module is also important: in DYNACAN, the migration modules have no control over the order of the population and must process the people as they come in. The worst case is when the population is ordered by increasing family size: all other things being equal, large families have more chances of having people whose region/sex/age bins are in excess, keeping all the other members from being selected. Finally, there may be some instances where the desired region total is not reached for a given year because of particularly severe conflicts between excedent and unfillable bins. Whatever the reason(s) for the discrepancies, the alignment method must allow for error correction.

The way this is done is by comparing at the end of the year for each region/sex/age bin the number of people we wanted *versus* the number that actually were migrated by the procedure. The excedent or the surplus is then carried forward to the next year to the corresponding wanted bin *aged one year older*. The arrays for desired totals by region and region/sex are also updated by the overall discrepancies, and carried forward to the next year.

The end result is an alignment methodology that ensures that migration totals fall usually within one family of the alignment numbers, while matching the distribution by age, sex, and region as well as possible, without disturbing the overall population distribution. It also fixes its own mistakes over time, and the computational burden is very low. As for the multiple cloning effect, it is greatly reduced. True, by multiplying the transition probabilities by 30 there are some families that will end up being candidates every year, but because of the selection process in the second pass they are no longer guaranteed selection.

11.7 An important (but subtle) detail

The 'fractional people' problem has a corollary that is not obvious at first sight. In the example mentioned above, we wanted 2.438 people. This raises the question: do we take two or three? It would seem natural to use 0.5 as a cutoff point, and take only two people in our example; however, it does not work that way. One example will illustrate this.

Suppose we have ten bins to fill, and our alignment figures indicate that we want between 0.35 and 0.45 persons in each, with an average of 0.4. The total number of desired people is thus four. If we use 0.5 as a cutoff point we shall not select anybody! Furthermore, we shall carry a deficit of four people for the next year. It is as easy to generate the opposite example, where ten people would be selected. In fact, by taking the first example and carrying forward the deficit into the next year, we should end up with eight people selected in the second year. The average over the two years is four people, as desired, but the year-to-year variation is undesirable. With the size of the bins in DYNACAN (imagine at most 400 people distributed into 512 bins, for a 20% sample) this becomes an issue. In order to solve this problem, the cutoff point is not fixed but is instead determined *via* a search algorithm every year. This algorithm looks for the cutoff point that neutralises these fractions of persons. In practice, the cutoff has ranged from 0.35 to 0.48.

11.8 Results

Figures 11.1 and 11.2 show the cumulative migration up to 2030 from a 60-year DYNACAN run. Figure 11.1 shows immigration, and Figure 11.2 shows emigration. Since the alignment method carries forward any previous discrepancies, one would expect a close match between the actual number of migrants *versus* those required from the alignment numbers. This is indeed what we get. The fit improves with time, which is one of the features of the pageant method. As can be seen in Figure 11.3, the fit after ten years is less tight (emigration is taken as an example here) than after 60 years (as in Figure 11.2), but the pattern nevertheless continues.

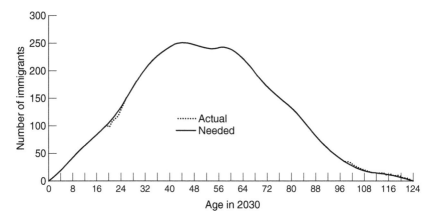

Figure 11.1 Cumulative immigration to the year 2030: actual *vs* needed

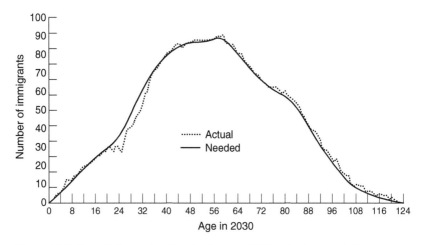

Figure 11.2 Cumulative emigration to the year 2030: actual *vs* needed

11.9 Drawbacks of the method

We have found so far only one drawback with this method of alignment: the method is dependent on the order of the population being processed. More specifically, large families are harder to pass through the migration transition because the probability of one person in the family overfilling his/her specific bin increases with family size. In fact, when the method was first implemented in DYNACAN, the starting popula-

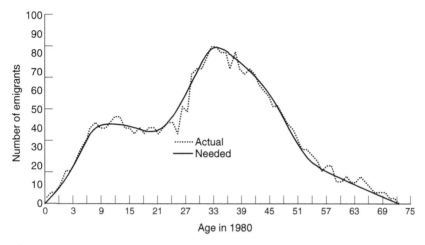

Figure 11.3 Cumulative emigration to the year 1980: actual *vs* needed

tion database was ordered by increasing family size, which represents the worst possible case, and made the method look less efficient than we expected. We reversed the ordering so that the population in the starting database now goes from the largest to the smallest families, which made alignment work as expected. One might argue that the population re-ordering favours the selection of larger families, and we should tend to agree in principle; however, various validation exercises done using DYNACAN runs show no visible distortion in family size or type. Ideally, the starting population should be distributed randomly as to family size, but other considerations in DYNACAN made us decide against doing so.

11.10 Conclusions

This 'pageant' method of alignment solves the migration problem efficiently: with little computing overhead it succeeds in matching the migrant distributions, and gets better over time. The use of the method, however, is not limited to migration or other family-based processes. In fact, the 'pageant' method would succeed even better on individual processes, guaranteeing an *exact* match (plus or minus *one* event) to the alignment numbers. This method has a unique feature in its ability to align very small populations, something other methods have more difficulty accomplishing. It would be interesting to test the method on individual-based modules.

Appendix 11.1 Migration modules

| Before Pass 1 | If not first year of the run, compute leftovers from previous year
leftover[sex][age][year–1]=need[sex][age][year–1]–havesofar[sex][age[year–1] |

| | Determine the total number of migrants
*MIG = POP * % of Migrants* |

| | Distribute total desired migrants, by age and sex
*need[sex][age][year]=MIG * %mig[sex][age][year]* |

| | If not first year of the run, add leftovers from previous year and clear the candidate tags
need[sex][age][year] +=leftover[sex][age–1][year–1]
Sum by sex to obtain need by sex[sex] |

| Pass 1 | Run family through the logistic migration eqations |

| | Multiply the probability by a large enough number (bind probability to 1.0 if needed) |

| | Run through the random selection process |

| | If selected, mark each member of the family as a candidate
have[sex][age][year] +=1 |

| Before pass 2 | Reset counters
total=0
total_by_sex[sex]=0
havesofar[sex][age][year]=0
left[sex][age][year]=have[sex][age][year] |

| | Search for the cutoff point that evens out 'fractions of persons' (see text) |

| Pass 2 | Check if family is marked as a candidate
if so, proceed |

| | Reset unfillable and excedent counters
unfillable=0
excedent=0 |

Figure 11.A1.1 Flowchart of migration models

Pass 2 (*cont.*)   Compute for each family member their 'relative need index'

$$rel\_need = \frac{need[sex][age][year] - havesofar[sex][age][year]}{left[sex][age][year] -}$$

Keep the highest relative need index for the family

Check for overfilled bins
if havesofar[sex][age][year] − need[sex][age][year] the excedent +=1

Check for unfillable bins
if need[sex][age][year] − havesofar[sex][age][year]>=left[sex][age][year]
then unfillable +=1

Check if totals by sex are not already exceeded
if total by sex[sex]>need by sex[sex] and excedent=0 then excedent=1

After family is done, if either excedent or unfillable are not zero, adjust rel_need
if unfillable>excedent then rel_need=1.0
if excedent>unfillable then rel_need=0.0
if excedent=unfillable then rel_need=0.5

Run through the random selection process, using *rel_need* as the propability

If total number of migrants is exceeded do not clone more families

Otherwise

If selected, clone family and update all relevant arrays
clone()
havesofar[sex][age][year]+=1 (done for each family member)
total_by_sex[sex]+=# of people for each sex
total+= family size

Figure 11.A1.1 (*cont.*)

Part Three

Modelling behavioural response

12 Unemployment insurance and labour mobility: analysis using a new Swedish microsimulation model

Neil Swan

12.1 Introduction

Generous unemployment insurance benefits lessen the perceived income gain for any unemployed person who, by migrating, believes that he or she could become employed. Generous benefits may therefore lessen migration. If so, less generous benefits would stimulate migration. Beyond that, if migration of the unemployed could reduce national and regional unemployment rates, less generous unemployment insurance benefits could reduce national and regional unemployment rates.

In this paper we discuss the use of a new, spatial, dynamic microsimulation model to calculate the quantitative importance of these putative effects on unemployment rates. This model, called *Sverige*, is being built at the Spatial Modelling Centre (SMC) in Kiruna, Sweden. The model differs from most microsimulation models in that it includes the location of every person, in Sweden to within 100 square metres. That is what makes it 'spatial'. In other respects, namely its inclusion of demographic transitions, such as births, deaths, marriages and so on, and of economically relevant variables such as labour force participation, earnings, and education, the model is mainstream. In fact, the broad structure of the non-spatial part of *Sverige* was initially developed by adapting for Swedish use a well known and longstanding American model, CORSIM (Caldwell, 1993).

We begin with a discussion of two relevant theoretical issues. The first concerns how changes in the generosity of unemployment benefits might affect the decision to migrate from one labour market to another, in order to find work. The second concerns the theory of labour market functioning embedded in *Sverige*, and its bearing on how to estimate the effect of changed migration on national and regional unemployment rates.

The discussion of the first theoretical issue is supported by a complementary empirical analysis, whose results are presented in the paper. The empirical analysis involves the use of regression analysis to estimate the quantitative importance for migration of changes in the generosity of unemployment benefits. We plan in the future to carry out a second empirical analysis, complementing the second theoretical issue, and thereby arrive at a complete analysis of the importance or unimportance of unemployment insurance generosity in inhibiting migration that might lessen unemployment. This second empirical analysis will require use of the microsimulation model, when building of that is completed. In the last part of the paper we draw some conclusions from the work done so far.

12.2 Two theoretical issues

Migration and the generosity of unemployment benefits

Unemployed people may move to gain work, or to gain income, or both. If work is valued for its own sake, it is possible that unemployment will stimulate the unemployed to migrate, in the belief they could become employed by doing so, irrespective of the financial gain involved. This might happen, for example, if a person's self esteem, or acceptability in society, were linked to working.

Any tests of the effect of unemployment benefits on migration need to take into account the possibility that work is valuable for more than just the income it brings. With this in mind, we define a variable W_{npec} which is the person's annual valuation of the non-pecuniary benefits of work. It is convenient to choose the units of measurement for this as kronor per annum. The variable is not an observable in practice (though it could be in principle), but we shall not need it to be. The person also obtains, if fully employed, W kronor per annum in actual money income.

We suppose that what drives a person to migrate is not the actual gain from a move, financial or of other kinds, but the expected gain. The expected gain from a move may be positive or negative. If negative, there will be no move. If positive, we suppose that the probability of a move is an increasing function of the gain.

The total gain (loss if negative) from moving depends on much more than a person's employment status. For example, stage of the life cycle (young, married, retired, etc.), will matter, attractiveness of big cities *versus* small and country living, housing costs, and status of the person within a household (with secondary earners' incentives differing from those of primary earners) will all play a role. In the regression equation presented below we capture important factors other than unemployment and availability of unemployment benefits with a vector of control variables Z.

The influence of unemployment depends heavily on whether the person expects to be fully employed after a move, in the sense of no longer being subject to any spell or spells of unemployment during years subsequent to the move, even though subject to spells of unemployment before and in the year of the move itself. In fact, full employment is rather unlikely, because the unemployed appear to be a special group. Unemployment is not evenly spread across all labour force members; in Sweden it is disproportionately the burden of a minority, who individually experience long spells of unemployment. Nevertheless, we shall use as our measure of expected gain the gain obtained if full employment were achieved by moving. One implication of this is that persons with long durations of unemployment in the year or years before a move will make greater gains than others if they move, and so they have a greater incentive to move. Another assumption is of a certain degree of optimism among those unemployed and contemplating migration.

The sum of monetary income, and the monetary equivalent of non-pecuniary benefits, would be $W + W_{npec}$, as an annual rate, when fully employed in the contemplated destination region. If the market wage rate is not different in the region of origin and that of potential destination, the annual monetary income in the region of origin is $W(1 - u)$ from earnings, where u is the fraction of each year one expects to be unemployed, plus unemployment benefit. If benefit is at a fraction m of the wage, and can be drawn for a year or longer, it will be at an annual rate of Wmu. Non-pecuniary benefits are not replaced by the unemployment benefit system, so their value in monetary terms, in the region of origin, is $(1 - u) W_{npec}$. If a move is made, a monetary cost is incurred for transportation and moving expenses. If this is C, its annual value is Cr, where r is the interest cost imputed by the person to the capital sum needed to move.

Counting monetary flows and the monetary equivalent of non-pecuniary benefits together we find, defining Y_o as income in the region of origin and Y_d as income net of moving costs in the contemplated destination region:

$$Y_o = W(1 - u) + Wmu + (1 - u)W_{npec}$$

and

$$Y_d = W + W_{npec} - Cr$$

We theorise that the probability of a move is

$$f(\mathbf{Z}, (Y_d - Y_o)/Y_d) \tag{12.1}$$

This formulation can be shown to hold even if we complicate the theory in either or both of two ways. One complication is that it may be the discounted present value of income in all future years, in the original region and in the destination, which should count for a migration decision, rather than just income in the coming year. The other complication is that a person may not be certain that he or she will become, and always stay, fully employed in the destination region and always be unemployed in the region of origin.

In estimating (12.1) we use a logit, with the variables in the Z vector entered linearly. The form of the expression containing Y needs further discussion.

It is convenient to introduce some simplifying notation, and also to begin distinguishing among individuals and time periods when appropriate. Define q as the ratio of the wage W to the sum of the wage and the non-pecuniary benefits $(W + W_{npec})$. The value of q is assumed not to vary among individuals or through time. Define m_{it} as the rate of benefit for unemployment, as a fraction of the money wage. The time subscript is introduced because the rate of benefit may vary with time, and the person subscript because limits on the maximum rate of benefit imply different rates of benefit among individuals above the ceiling income level for benefits. Define c_{it} as the ratio of the flow cost associated with a move to the money wage $(C_{it} r_t / W_{it})$. Costs and wage rates vary with time and among persons, but the interest rate varies only with time. Unemployment varies with time and among persons, so time and person subscripts are added to the unemployment rate and also to the income variables.
Then we have:

$$(Y_{dit} - Y_{oit})/Y_{dit} = (u_{it} - qm_{it}u_{it} - qc_{it})/(1 - qc_{it}) \tag{12.2}$$

Some special cases will help elucidate this expression. If there are zero moving costs $(c_{it} = 0)$, and u and m do not vary among unemployed persons or through time, the relative gain from moving is $(u - qmu)$. If there are no non-pecuniary benefits to the fact of having work, then $W_{npec} = 0$ and $q = 1$, so that the relative gain from a move becomes $u(1 - m)$. The gain in relative income is the unemployment rate, multiplied by the fraction of income not already being recovered in unemployment benefits $(1 - m)$. If $m = 1$, so that benefits equal the wage, the relative gain is zero. If there are no benefits, the relative gain is u. If the non-pecuniary benefits of working are very large in relation to monetary gains from working (people work whatever the wage rate) then q is almost zero. The relative gain, this time with or without moving costs, is now u, whatever the rate of unemployment benefit. In this case, just as one would expect, the rate of benefit makes no difference to the gain from moving.

The expression on the left-hand side of (12.2) is the relative gain to an unemployed person of changing status to employed. The first step in testing whether unemployment benefits affect migration is to test whether $(Y_{dit} - Y_{oit})/Y_{dit}$ does affect the probability of moving. The second step, if the answer is yes and the magnitude of the effect has been estimated, is to find the value of q. If q is zero, the gain from moving makes unemployed persons move, but the monetary aspect of the gain is not what counts. Changing the generosity of benefits will then not change the propensity of the unemployed to move. If q is unity, then the value of $(Y_{dit} - Y_{oit})/Y_{dit}$ is sensitive to the rate of unemployment benefits, being larger the smaller the benefits are. Given $q=1$, an actual estimate of the effect on migration of a change in m could be obtained. If q is positive, but less than unity, mobility is still sensitive to the generosity of benefits, but less so than in the case where $q=1$.

We can find both the effect of $(Y_{dit} - Y_{oit})/Y_{dit}$ on migration and the size of q if we can find data which show enough variation in m_{it}, u_{it}, and c_{it}.

With logit estimation, and defining P_{it}, which is the probability that the ith person will move at time t, a vector of coefficients b, and the discussion so far, we may rewrite equation (12.1) in the more explicit form:

$$\ln (P_{it}/(1-P_{it}) = Z_{it}b + a\,(u_{it} - qm_{it}u_{it} - qc_{it})/(1-qc_{it}) \qquad (12.3)$$

Equation (12.3) represents our theory of the effect of generosity of unemployment benefits on the decision to move. We discuss the data and estimation process in the empirical section later. Meanwhile, we continue with the second theoretical issue – how to estimate the effect of migration on unemployment rates in the spatial microsimulation model *Sverige*.

The labour market in Sverige

Sverige's modelling of the labour market begins with decisions by individuals on whether to participate or not in the labour force sometime during a year, and if they do, for how much of the year, what fraction of it. The equations determining these individual decisions are estimated separately for various age/sex/marital status groups. For the individuals within any one of the groups, the explanatory variables cover factors such as education, presence of children, actual age within the range of ages defining the group, and so on.[1]

The result is a fraction of the year each adult would like to work, from zero to unity. This is not, however, the end of the modelling. *Sverige* draws a distinction between how much people would like to work and how much they actually work. The distinction is enforced by the alignment process.

To implement alignment, the model is solved in two passes. On the first pass, the fraction of the year each person would like to work is calculated. On the second pass, the numbers wanting to work full time, or various part-time fractions of the year, are adjusted by alignment, in order to ensure that the model's estimates for certain *groups* of persons match observed historical values of full-time and part-time working for those groups.

The result is that some expectations are disappointed. Not everyone gets to work as much as they would prefer. They may work less or more, according to discrepancies found for various groups of persons between what the model predicts on average for a group, and the average actually observed for that group. However, differences among persons within each group are preserved, and the time actually worked will vary as much among persons as the time desired to be worked.

An important effect of the alignment process is to introduce exogenous historically-observed constraints on the total employment generated by the model. For example, in recession *Sverige* will constrain total employment to the amount that the market as a whole permits. In expansionary periods, this constraint on total employment will be less severe. The constraint operates not only at the aggregate labour market level, but also in certain sub-labour markets – those for which historical data are available and to which the model aligns. In the case of *Sverige*, this includes historical data for regional labour markets, of which there are 108.

Since most microsimulation models employ alignment, and since many of these also model employment, it will be the case that exogenous historically-observed constraints on total employment will be very common. The phenomenon is not confined to *Sverige*, but is likely to be common in microsimulation modelling.

Once *Sverige* has determined employment, measured for each person as a fraction of a year between zero and unity, the fraction of non-employment is known residually, between unity and zero. The model goes on to predict what portion of any weeks not worked is spent unemployed, and what portion out of the labour force. With unemployment rates modelled for each person (measured in fractions of a year) group unemployment rates, up to and including the national rate, can then be calculated as the ratio of total time spent unemployed, added up for all persons in the group, to the total group time spent employed or unemployed. Under not unreasonable conditions, the unemployment rates thus obtained will be approximately equal to the more conventional measure, which is the average over days when a Labour Force Survey is taken, of the ratios on each day of the numbers out of work in the week of the survey day to the sum of the numbers in work and out of work. The alignment in *Sverige* will be done using Labour Force Survey estimates of unemployment rates in each labour market region, possibly disaggregated into a limited number of age/sex groups.

Consider now a hypothetical simulation experiment in *Sverige*, in which there is greater net migration from region A to region B than in the base case. Regional employment and unemployment rates, and the participation rate which is their sum, cannot change between the base case and the simulation, because they are aligned in both cases to the observed historical rates. The model then says that the effect of greater migration between region A and region B, on the unemployment rates in A and B, is zero. Whether this makes sense or not to the analyst depends on the latter's opinion concerning what theory of labour market equilibrium applies to regions A and B.

For a person who believes that regions A and B have natural rates of unemployment,[2] to which convergence in cases of disturbance is rapid, the result given by the model is reasonable. Neither changes in labour market demand in a region, nor changes in labour market supply, affect the natural rate of unemployment other than temporarily. Increased migration, which is a special case of an increase in the annual rate of increase of supply, will not change the natural rate and so will not affect the unemployment rate, in either region. This is what might be termed a classical view. There will be an effect on the national rate of unemployment, however, if the natural rates in regions A and B differ, due to the re-weighting effect from having more persons in B and less in A.

For a person who believes that regions A and B have rates of unemployment determined strictly by aggregate demand in each region separately, the result given by the model is unreasonable. Shifting labour supply from A to B, in a world where aggregate demand for labour in both A and B separately is at a fixed level, will increase the unemployment rate in B, and lower it in A, contrary to the model result. Unemployment should rise in B by the full amount of the in-migration, and the unemployment rate go up correspondingly. Unemployment should fall in A by the full amount of the out-migration, and the unemployment rate decline correspondingly. This might be termed a Keynesian view. To implement it, standard alignment must be turned off, and replaced by the Keynesian assumptions. Notice that the national unemployment rate is unchanged on this view, and the only change is in the regional distribution of the unemployed.

A third possibility is what we might call the export base view. Suppose there is deficient aggregate demand for labour in A because some key export base industry is in decline, and either excess demand for labour in B, whose export base industries are expanding, or a well-functioning labour market in which unemployment stays at its natural rate. The migration will reduce the unemployment rate in A, while leaving it unchanged in B. In this case the model result is also unreasonable. Notice that the national unemployment rate will fall considerably more in this case than in the classical case, and of course much more than in the Keynesian case.

The regional distribution of unemployment rates will change more than in the classical case, but less than in the Keynesian case. Again, the alignment must be turned off, and replaced by export base assumptions.

The model itself cannot be deemed to embody the results of having tested out which of these views of the labour markets is valid, if any, and to have then made use of the valid theory in developing its equations. Rather, the model has simply duplicated observed historical values, as far as regional and national unemployment rates are concerned. The consequence is that the model will always behave as if the natural rate theory were valid during simulations. However, this does not imply that it is in fact valid. We must decide independently of the model which theory of the labour market applies and carry out the simulation with that in mind.

In our planned further empirical work we shall carry out three simulations. In the first, we shall assume that the model's implicit assumption, that the natural rate theory is valid nationally and regionally, is correct. We can then find the effects on the national rate of unemployment arising from re-weighting. As explained above, in this simulation there will be no effects of migration on regional unemployment rates.

In the second and third simulations, we shall assume Keynesian and export base theories apply respectively, replacing the model's alignment process with procedures consistent with these theories.

We believe that these three kinds of simulation are the most interesting, and also that they are likely to encompass the range of what most people believe is valid in the operation of Sweden's regional labour markets. Of course, other assumptions about labour markets could be implemented.[3] Our main point at this stage is to emphasise that it is not valid simply to accept the results for unemployment that would be given by the *Sverige* model without regard to its implicit labour market assumptions.

By way of general comment, in any dynamic microsimulation model in which unemployment or employment changes, and in which those changes matter for the interpretation of the simulation results, attention needs to be paid to the nature of the labour market assumptions and their realism for the case at hand. As already noted, it matters especially if alignment is used. Cases in point are the CORSIM model, partially ancestral to *Sverige* itself, the Canadian model DYNACAN (Chénard, 1995), and any models in which linkage is made to other macro-models. In Australia, for example, work is proceeding on explicitly linking computable general equilibrium models to microsimulation models (Baekegard and Robinson, 1997). When such linking is done, the labour market assumptions become very clear. In the case cited, they appear to be Keynesian at the national level.

12.3 Regression analysis of migration and unemployment benefits

We now discuss the empirical version of equation (3) used for estimation. It will be recalled that equation (12.3) was:

$$\ln (P_{it}/(1 - P_{it}) = \mathbf{Z}_{it}\mathbf{b} + a\,(u_{it} - qm_{it}u_{it} - qc_{it})/(1 - qc_{it}) \qquad (12.3)$$

In discussing the empirical counterparts of the variables in (12.3) it will be convenient to simplify the notation so that (12.3) is written as:

$$p = Zb + aX \text{ in which } p, Z \text{ and } X \text{ are defined by a} \qquad (12.3')$$
comparison of (12.3) and (12.3').

Data

The database at the Spatial Modelling Centre (SMC) in Kiruna contains administrative data about the Swedish population. Every individual is included, as far as it has been possible to get the data from various national registers, for the 11-year period 1985–1995. Information is available on more than 100 variables, covering: demographic information such as date of birth, date of death if applicable, marital status, family linkages such as number of children, income of spouse, and so on; date of immigration to Sweden if applicable; income information, covering income from earnings in the year, income from various kinds of transfer, including unemployment benefits, taxes paid, etc.; labour force status available either directly, as with participation, or indirectly deducible from other variables with reasonable accuracy, as with fraction of the year unemployed; location in a given year to within 100 square metres, with codes also for county, municipality and parish, which information permits deduction of migration behaviour, whether locally or to a new labour market area, of which there are 108; educational status and highest level of education attained; and much other information not of direct relevance to studying migration.

In addition to the database itself, we have assembled information on levels of unemployment benefits and conditions during the years covered by the database.

The database contains approximately 9 million individuals, observed for 11 years, and so is exceedingly large. The regressions reported on in this paper have been run with a random sample from the database, of some 350,000 persons. The model on which the simulations depend is similarly estimated using random samples from the data. At a later time, checks against the full data set will be run.

Table 12.1. *Rates of unemployment benefit*

Date	Rates of unemployment benefit $(m_{\text{leg } t})$ (%)	Maximum wage for benefit purposes $(W_{\text{ceil } t})$ (kroner per year)
01/01/89–04/07/93	from 91.7 per cent to 90	172,756
05/07/93–31/12/95	80	183,300
01/01/96–28/09/97	75	183,300 (est.)
29/09/97–present	80	188,500

Source: Oral communication to Marianne Öhman from Arbetslösförmedling in Kiruna, Sweden.

Empirical counterparts for the variables in X

Values of m_{it}

Rates of unemployment benefit are set by law. For a person in a given year, the value is constant as a fraction of the wage, if the wage is below some ceiling level. If we call the legislated rate of benefit in year t $m_{\text{leg } t}$, then for persons below the ceiling wage of that year, say $W_{\text{ceil } t}$, the benefit rate is given by $m_{\text{leg } t}$. If a person's wage W_{it} is at or above $W_{\text{ceil } t}$, the benefit rate is given by $W_{\text{ceil } t}*m_{\text{leg } t}/W_{it}$. Thus we obtain:

$$m_{it} = \min (m_{\text{leg } t}, \text{ and } m_{\text{leg } t}* W_{\text{ceil } t}/W_{it})$$

where min (·) denotes minimum.

The values of $m_{\text{leg } t}$ and $W_{\text{ceil } t}$ for regular benefits have been obtained for the period since January 1989, and are shown in Table 12.1.

To calculate m_{it} for persons with wage rates above the ceiling we therefore need values of W_{it}, the person's wage rate when they last worked, which we are able to obtain from our database.

Values of u_{it}

The variable u_{it} in our theory is an expected amount of unemployment. The expectation is formed in the year in which migration is being contemplated. It consists of the average yearly amount of unemployment expected if one does not move.

One plausible measure of this is the completed length of the current spell of unemployment if the person does not move. For a person who does not in fact move, this will be equal to the actual length of the spell by the time it has been completed (for a person who does choose to move, the observed length of spell will be shorter than the expected length, assuming that the move serves its purpose in finding work).

Completed spells average about 30 weeks in Sweden. That means that part of a spell of unemployment being experienced in the current year will often have occurred in a previous year. Thus, we need to use observed unemployment experience in both the current and the previous year for any individuals for whom a spell overlaps two years.

Consider first the persons who do not move, and who also experience only one spell of unemployment (not two or more disconnected spells) which ends in the current year, and which may or may not have begun in the previous year. For such persons, the length of the unemployment spell is simply the sum of observed unemployment in the current and the previous year (note that unemployment spells in our data are measured as fractions, or multiples, of a year, rather than in weeks, as is more traditional). If we denote by $uobs_{it}$ the value of unemployment observed for person i in year t we have for this group,

$$u_{it} = uobs_{it} + uobs_{it-1}$$

In order to exclude from this group anybody who is employed this year (and so not contemplating moving to find work) but who was unemployed last year, we modify this expression to read:

$$u_{it} = uobs_{it} + (uobs_{it}**0.001)*uobs_{it-1}$$

This expression has two properties: first, if observed unemployment in the current year is zero, the variable u_{it} is equal to zero, even if observed unemployment last year was not zero; and second, if observed unemployment in the current year is not zero, u_{it} is equal, to a very close approximation, to the sum of observed unemployment in the two years (assumed to be one continuous spell).

For anyone in the group of persons who do move, the last expression for u_{it} will understate the amount of unemployment expected. I have found no way to correct the specification for this problem, but it can be shown, somewhat surprisingly, that its quantitative importance is likely to be negligible.

Now $uobs_{it}$ and $uobs_{it-1}$ are not directly given in our database. However, they have been calculated from other data for persons who met five conditions: they are in the labour force all year; they qualify for regular benefits, called TKASSA in the database; they do not run out of TKASSA entitlements during the year; they would not run out of benefits if they remained unemployed all next year; and they are full-time workers when employed. The first four conditions are nearly always met for persons aged 26–60, and the fifth very often, though not for all married women in this age group. We therefore confined the analysis to this age group.

Value of c_{it}
This is the cost of a move, multiplied by the interest charge imputed to it, and divided by the current wage rate.

A large part of the cost of moving is paid for under current Swedish regulations. Provided a job is found, the cost of moving is fully covered. Moves that do not result in a job lasting six months or more, and moves purely to explore, are not covered. Nevertheless, it seems reasonable to assume that moves not qualifying for support will be rare, and even if they are not, our assumption earlier that people expect to find work if they move implies also that they expect to have the move paid for. That means that the expected value of c_{it} is zero under current Swedish regulations. Moreover, it has been zero during the whole period covered by our database (1985–1995).

In sum, we can find the values of the components of X for at least an arguably important subset of persons, those who are full-time workers when employed.

Functional form of X
The functional form in (12.3′), for X, is straightforward if c_{it} is zero. We have

$$X = au_{it} - aqm_{it}u_{it}$$

X is linear, with dependent variables u_{it} and $m_{it}u_{it}$.
The notation used for these variables in the later regression is $UREG94_{it}$ and $MUREG94_{it}$ respectively.

We have a simple test of whether q is non-zero, meaning that monetary effects matter. The coefficient on the variable $m_{it}u_{it}$ should be significant and negative. Meanwhile, the coefficient on u_{it} should be positive, and larger in absolute value than the coefficient on $m_{it}u_{it}$, since q is supposed to be between unity and zero and positive. The ratio of the two coefficients gives an estimate of q.

Empirical counterparts for the variables in Z
We need to include variables in the vector Z in (12.3′), other than unemployment and unemployment benefits already allowed for in X, which capture most of the variation in probability of migration, subject to the condition that these variables be available in model runs. We draw here upon the work of Malmberg and Fischer (1997) referred to hereafter as MF. They have used the same database to explore, using probit regressions, the probability of staying which is the complement of the probability of moving.

In their published work, MF denote by z, the ratio of an estimated coefficient to its estimated standard error. A brief exploration of their results suggests that independent variables which have z values less than 7 rarely have large absolute effects on their probit dependent variable. For z values above 7, effects tend to be larger the larger the z value, even though there is no logical necessity that this should be so. And in fact we did find a few very large z values for which the absolute effect of the relevant variable was smaller in magnitude than for most other variables with z values of that size. Nevertheless, by selecting variables with large z values, we seem unlikely to miss any variables which are quantitatively important for migration, even if we risk including a few that are not. We do choose to restrict our initial analysis to variables with large z values, so as to keep the analysis easily manageable. We select only from variables for which MF found z values of 7 or larger.

We choose the one of MF's several specifications which includes duration, socio-economic and life-event variables (their specification (3)). However, this specification includes some variables which we shall be including in our X vector, (e.g., whether or not a person is unemployed), and we therefore omit these from our Z vector. The variables from MF which had z values of 7 or higher are listed below. The MF probit estimation was of the probability to stay in 1994.

Variable in MF	z value
Age	8.2
Duration of stay in months	16.0
Years since immigration	7.4
Ln(income of partner)	9.5
Level of education	−21.0
Number of children	8.7
Metropolitan dummy	7.8
New household built	−8.1
In education	−17.3

Note that we cannot include regional characteristics in our migration equation, if these are not available in the microsimulation model. This is why there is no variable for the regional unemployment rate, at either origin or destination, in the formulation we propose.

At this stage, we have carried out regressions using a subset of the variables, namely: age, entered non-linearly by adding the square of age as well as age alone ($AGE93_{it}$, $AGESQ93_{it}$), years since immigration (maximum 15 for native born or immigrants present for 16 or more years) ($YRSWED93_{it}$), and level of education ($EDUCAT94_{it}$).

The dependent variable

Sweden has 108 labour market areas. To all intents and purposes these areas are 'commuting sheds'. While it is possible for a person to live in one such area and work in another, that is relatively rare. Changing the area where one works normally involves migration to the new area. We therefore treat a person as moving if he or she changes labour market area.

Details of regression

The regression is run as a logit, for persons moving or not moving between the years 1993 and 1994.

As noted, we worked with a random sample of 350,000 persons drawn from the database. Selecting persons aged from 25–60 reduced this to 163,815 cases, and missing data further reduced the number to 158,092.

The version of equation (12.3′) fitted to the data is shown below, as equation (12.4).

$$\ln (P_i/(1-P_i)) = b_0 + b_1 AGE93_i + b_2 AGESQ93_i + b_3 YRSWED93_i + \quad (12.4)$$
$$b_4 EDUCAT94_i + a_1 UREG94_i + a_2 MUREG94_i + \text{error}_i$$

The dependent variable in the logit is unity if a person moved, zero otherwise.

The regression equation as fitted captures cross-sectional variation among individuals in the rate of unemployment benefit and unemployment (as well as the other variables). Although there has also been some temporal variation in the rate of benefit, most variation is between individuals in cross section, since the amount of change in the rate of benefit over time has been very small (from 90% to 80%, with a very short period at 75%).

Results

The results are shown in Table 12.2. All variables have the expected sign and are significant at 5% or better on the appropriate one tailed test. Most importantly, the coefficient on $UREG94$ is positive, and on $MUREG94$ negative, indicating that monetary effects of unemployment insurance benefits matter to the migration decision.

The point estimate of the coefficient on $UREG94$ is greater in absolute value than the coefficient on $MUREG94$, suggesting that the parameter q, defined above as the ratio of the money wage to the sum of money wages and the kronor equivalent of annual non-pecuniary benefits of working, is less than unity, as it should be.

The point estimate of this ratio, q, is approximately 0.8, implying that

Table 12.2. *Logit predictions of moving labour market area*

Independent variable	Expected sign	Fitted coefficient	Standard error	Significance level[a]
Constant	..	2.0067	0.4199	0.0000
AGE94 (years)	−	−0.2530	0.0208	0.0000
AGESQ94	?	+0.0024	0.0003	0.0000
YRSWED93(years)[b]	−	−0.0668	0.0083	0.0000
EDUCAT94[c]	+	+0.2022	0.0142	0.0000
UREG94[d]	+	+1.2345	0.4276	0.0020
MUREG94[e]	−	−1.0068	0.5401	0.0312

Notes:
[a] On a one tailed test, except for AGESQ94.
[b] Set to a maximum of 15 for native born and immigrants resident longer than 15 years.
[c] Seven values, from 1 to 7, indicating progressively higher levels of education.
[d] Length of unemployment spell 1993 and 1994, measured in years, to a maximum of 2.0.
[e] Product of UREG94 and the effective rate of unemployment benefit, which ranges from a maximum of 0.8 downwards, depending on previous wage (see text for further explanation).
Source: estimates by the author (see text).

non-pecuniary benefits of working are only one quarter of the pecuniary benefits. However, we certainly could not reject the hypothesis that q is unity, implying no non-pecuniary benefits.

It is worth adding that the regression results were obtained with virtually no 'data mining'. The only concessions made here were to try slight variations in the age range included (25–55 and 23–55 instead of the 25–60 range used in the above regression), and to try with and without AGESQ94. The results worsen slightly for these alternatives, but, except for the age range 23–55, all variables remain significant at 5% or better, and about the same absolute sizes of coefficients are obtained. With 23–55, MUREG94 becomes significant only at 10%, but the range 23–55 is not preferred on theoretical grounds, as many under 25 are still in the educational process.

The absolute size of the effect of unemployment benefits is of interest. Reverting to m as the notation for the rate of benefit, and u for the unemployment rate, the effect of m in changing the value of the right-hand side of equation (12.4) can be calculated from the effect of m on the expression:

$$1.2345(u - 0.8156mu)$$

If m is reduced dramatically, e.g. from 0.8 (its maximum possible value) to 0.4, the value of this expression will rise by:

$$1.2345*0.8156\,(0.8-0.4)u=0.4027u$$

What this does to the probability of moving of a person depends on the value of the other variables in equation (12.4). If we consider a person aged 30, 15 years in Sweden or native born, with an education level of 5, a six-month spell of unemployment ($u=0.5$) and an effective benefit rate of 0.8 before the change in m, we obtain a value for the right-hand side of (12.4) of -2.827, yielding a probability of moving of 0.056. Changing m to 0.4 makes the right-hand side of (12.4) equal to -2.626, yielding a probability of moving of 0.068. While this is a large percentage increase (21%) in the probability of moving, it yields only a very small increase in the number of moves. This is because the probability of moving is itself very small (0.056 in our illustration).

In sum, the results are perfectly in line with theoretical expectations. It is true that reducing unemployment insurance benefits causes more people to move. On the other hand, while statistically significant, the effect is quantitatively very small.

12.4 Conclusions

It is possible to estimate separately the effects on migration of changes in unemployment and changes in unemployment benefits. The two effects could differ if individuals value work not only for the income it gives, but also for its non-pecuniary benefits, such as the self-respect resulting from having a job. The distinction matters because a change in the generosity of unemployment benefits will affect the pecuniary gains from finding work through migration, but not the non-pecuniary gains.

The effects of migration on regional and national unemployment rates can be obtained from simulations with the Swedish microsimulation model, and others like it, only if additional information is added bearing on how the labour market functions. Simply leaving alignment switched on in the model, for doing the simulation, is equivalent to assuming that the natural rate theory of unemployment applies both nationally and in each region. To find the effects of migration if some other theory is thought to apply, we must replace alignment by procedures which reflect whatever we think to be the proper theory of labour market functioning. We considered two alternatives to natural rate theory, 'pure Keynesianism' in all regions and nationally, and a theory we term 'export base' theory.

Under natural rate theory, the regional distribution of unemployment rates will be unaltered by migration, but the national rate, which is a weighted average of those rates, will change. The size of the change caused by any change in unemployment benefit policy which affects migration can then be calculated using the model. Under Keynesianism, the national rate will not change, but regional rates will, and the sizes of the changes can also be calculated using the model. Under 'export base' theory, both the regional distribution of unemployment rates, and the national average unemployment rate, will alter, and the size of the effects can again be calculated with the model.

Our regression results show that there is a statistically significant effect of unemployment benefit levels on migration. They also show that the benefits from not being unemployed appear to be purely monetary. It is not possible to reject the hypothesis of no non-pecuniary benefits from working.

The regression results also show that the effect of unemployment benefit levels is small absolutely, despite statistical significance. Drastic reductions in benefit levels would alter the amount of migration by very little. It follows that the effect on unemployment rates will surely be very small, whatever theory of unemployment happens to apply in the circumstances underlying the simulation, whether 'natural rate', 'Keynesianism', 'export base', or some other. Nevertheless, it will be possible to estimate the actual size of the effects with the Swedish spatial microsimulation model, nationally and regionally, as soon as its construction is completed.

Notes

1 *Sverige*'s labour market is like CORSIM's, briefly described in Caldwell, 1993. The functioning of CORSIM's labour market is more easily inferred from the actual equations plus the coding of the model plus the logic of the alignment process. Alignment is a technical adjustment, common in microsimulation models, which attempts to solve the problem of poor prediction of average levels, without losing the virtue of accurate prediction of differences between individuals. The CORSIM equations have been gathered together in convenient form in a Canadian publication, which documents an early version of the Canadian model DYNACAN, adapted from CORSIM, and which at that time was using the CORSIM equations unchanged, but aligning their results to Canadian rather than US aggregate totals (see Chénard, 1995).

2 A useful discussion of natural rate theory can be found in Johnson and Layerd (1986)

3 Another possibility is that the national unemployment rate is fixed by aggregate demand, but that the unemployment rate in each region is some constant fraction or multiple of the national rate, or bears a fixed functional relationship to it. Such relationships can be observed empirically, for example, for the major regions of Canada. In such a world, migration from A to B would leave not only the national

rate of unemployment constant, but also the unemployment rates in A and B separately. For example, if the migrants from A to B were unemployed in A but find work in B, there must be a sufficient number of persons displaced in B to keep the unemployment rate unchanged there, and a sufficient number of persons also losing their jobs in A to keep the unemployment rate unchanged there as well. There is a more general question which is relevant here, and which has not yet been resolved by the economics profession, in the writer's opinion. This is the question of whether unemployment rates can exceed their natural rates permanently, on average through time, or not. The former view is that deficient aggregate demand in recessions causes unemployment which cannot be offset later by excess demand in booms, because that causes inflation rather than compensating 'excess employment'. The latter view is that unemployment remains on average through time close to its natural rate. This question is essentially the same as the question of whether the macroeconomy functions in a classical or a Keynesian fashion. That question is unsettled, as can be seen by the treatment of it in popular textbooks of macroeconomics, which typically explain both types of macroeconomic functioning, but fail to assert that either has been clearly refuted by empirical data (see, for example, Begg, Fischer and Dornbusch, 1991, chapter 27).

13   Joint labour supply of married couples: efficiency and distribution effects of tax and labour market reforms

Rolf Aaberge, Ugo Colombino, Steinar Strøm and Tom Wennemo

13.1 Introduction

In this paper we present a microeconometric model which features simultaneous treatment of both spouses' choices; exact representation of income taxes; and quantity constraints on the distribution of hours. Previous structural analyses of labour supply in Italy based on microdata have been carried out for example by Colombino and Zabalza (1982), Colombino (1985), Colombino and Del Boca (1990), Del Boca and Flinn (1984) and Rettore (1990). Most of these studies are based on local samples. None of them develops a truly simultaneous model of partners' decisions. Taxes are either ignored or given a simplified representation.

For the estimation and the simulation we use the data from the 1993 Bank of Italy's Survey of Household Income and Wealth (SHIW93). The analysis is restricted to married couples, with both partners in the age interval 18–54. Self-employed and retired persons are excluded. Household decisions must therefore be interpreted as conditional on not being self-employed or retired.

We run the model to simulate the labour supply responses and welfare effects of replacing the current (1993) tax system (on personal incomes) with hypothetical alternatives, namely a flat tax and two versions of a negative income tax, under the constraint of equal tax revenue.

The paper is organised as follows. Section 13.2 develops the model. Sections 13.3 and 13.4 describe the empirical specification, the data used and the estimates. Section 13.5 presents the results of various policy simulations. Section 13.6 concludes.

13.2 The model

Our study draws upon the framework introduced by Dagsvik (1994) and may be viewed as an extension of the model in Dickens and Lundberg

(1993). Models similar to the one applied here to Italy have also been estimated for Sweden (Aaberge et al., 1990) and Norway (Aaberge et al., 1995). Our approach to modelling labour supply is rather different from the traditional one, originally adopted in a well-specified microeconometric framework by Heckman (1974). A version of the traditional model that also included taxes was later estimated by Hausman and co-authors for the US (Hausman (1980, 1981 and 1985), Burtless and Hausman (1978), Hausman and Ruud (1984)), and also adopted in numerous other studies (e.g. Blomquist (1983) for Sweden, Arrufat and Zabalza (1986) for the UK, Kapteyn et al., (1990) for Holland, Colombino and Del Boca (1990) for Italy).

The traditional approach is essentially based on the standard textbook model. The agent's behaviour is interpreted as the solution to the problem:

$$\max_h U(C,h) \tag{13.1}$$

such that

$$C = wh + I$$
$$h \in [0,T]$$

where h = hours of work, w = wage rate, I = other (exogenous) income, T = total available time and C = disposable income.

In this model the wage rate w is fixed. Given the wage, a job is simply described by a value of h belonging to the interval $[0,T]$. The individual is free to choose any value of h in that interval. The set of 'jobs' in the (h,w) space among which the individual is assumed to choose under this traditional approach is represented in Figure 13.1.

Under standard regularity conditions, if we define $h(w,I)$ as the value of h which solves $\partial U(wh + I,h)/\partial h = 0$, then the solution to problem (13.1) is:

$$h^* = \begin{cases} 0 & \text{if} \quad h(w,I) \leq 0 \\ h(w,I) & \text{if} \quad 0 \leq h(w,I) \leq T \\ T & \text{if} \quad h(w,I) \geq T \end{cases} \tag{13.2}$$

The solution h^* is typically a random variable, due to some unknown preference parameter that is treated as random.

When taxes are introduced, the budget constraint in problem (13.1) becomes $C = f(wh, I)$, where f is the function that transforms gross income into net income. In most countries, f defines a piece-wise linear budget, with each segment k defined by a net wage rate w_k (the slope) and a 'virtual' income I_k (the intercept of the extension of the segment). The solution can be easily characterised in terms of the functions $h(w_k, I_k)$.[1] In principle, this approach can be generalised to any type of tax system that

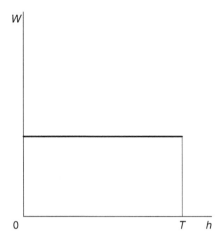

Figure 13.1 The opportunity set in the traditional approach

can be approximated by a piece-wise linear tax rule, and to simultaneous decisions of household members. In practice, the combination of complex rules and household decision-making may become prohibitively burdensome to model. For this reason, the analyses based on this approach tend to rely on some simplified representation of the tax rule and on some recursive structure of household decisions. It seems also very unrealistic to assume that for each individual there is just one market wage and that hours can be freely chosen in the interval $[0,T]$.[2]

The approach that we follow here assumes that agents choose among jobs, each job being defined by a wage rate w, hours of work h and other characteristics j. As an example of j, think of commuting time or specific skills involved in the job. For expository simplicity we consider in what follows a single person household, although the model we estimate considers married couples.[3] The problem solved by the agent looks like the following:

$$\max_{\substack{h \\ h,w,j,}} U(C, h, j) \tag{13.3}$$

such that

$$C = f(wh, I)$$
$$(h, w, j) \in B$$

The set B is the opportunity set, i.e. it contains all the opportunities available to the household. For generality we also include non-market opportunities in B; a non-market opportunity is a 'job' with $w=0$ and $h=0$. Agents can differ not only in their preferences and in their wage (as in the

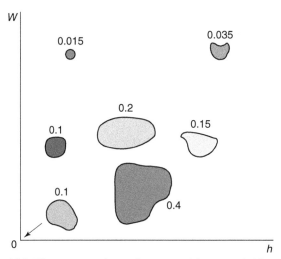

Figure 13.2 The opportunity set in our model approach (the numbers represent hypothetical densities or relative frequencies of alternatives in the corresponding 'spot')

traditional model) but also in the number of available jobs of different types. Note that for the same agent, wage rates (unlike in the traditional model) can differ from job to job. As analysts we do not know exactly what opportunities are contained in B. Therefore we use probability density functions to represent B. Let us denote by $p(h, w)$ the density of jobs of type (h, w). By specifying a probability density function on B we can, for example, allow for the fact that jobs with hours of work in a certain range are more or less likely to be found, possibly depending on agent's characteristics; or for the fact that for different agents the relative number of market opportunity may differ. Figure 13.2 illustrates a possible opportunity set in the (h, w) space as represented in this approach.

From expression (13.3) it is clear that what we adopt is a choice model; choice, however, is constrained by the number and the characteristics of jobs in the opportunity set. Therefore the model is also compatible with the case of involuntary unemployment, i.e. an opportunity set that does not contain any market opportunity; besides this extreme case, the number and the characteristics of market (and non-market) opportunities in general vary from individual to individual. Even if the set of market opportunities is not empty, in some cases it might contain very few elements and/or elements with bad characteristics.

We assume that the utility function can be factorised as

$$U(f(wh, I), h, j) = V(f(wh, I), h)\varepsilon(h, w, j) \tag{13.4}$$

where V and ε are the systematic and the stochastic component respectively, and ε is i.i.d. according to:[4]

$$\Pr(\varepsilon \leq u) = \exp(-u^{-1}) \tag{13.5}$$

The term ε is a random taste-shifter which accounts for the effect on utility of all the characteristics of the household–job match which are observed by the household but not by us. We observe the chosen h and w. Therefore we can specify the probability that the agent chooses a job with observed characteristics (h,w). It can be shown that under the assumptions (13.3), (13.4) and (13.5) we can write the probability density function of a choice (h,w) as follows:[5]

$$\varphi(h,w) = \frac{V(f(wh, I), h)p(h, w)}{\displaystyle\int_x \int_y V(f(yx, I), x)p(x, y)dxdy} \tag{13.6}$$

Expression (13.6) is analogous to the continuous multinomial logit developed in the transportation and location analysis literature (Ben-Akiva and Watanatada, 1981). The intuition behind expression (13.6) is that the probability of a choice (h, w) can be expressed as the relative attractiveness – weighted by a measure of 'availability' $p(h,w)$ – of jobs of type (h, w).

From (13.6) we also see that this approach does not suffer from the complexity of the tax rule f. The tax rule, however complex, enters the expression as it is, and there is no need to simplify it in order to make it differentiable or manageable, as in the traditional approach. The crucial difference is that in the traditional approach the functions representing household behaviour are derived on the basis of a comparison of marginal variations of utility, while in the approach that we follow a direct comparison of levels of utility is involved.

13.3 The empirical specification

In order to estimate the model we choose convenient but still flexible parametric forms for V and p.

$$\ln V(C, h_F, h_M) = [\alpha_2 + a_3 N] \cdot \left(\frac{C^{\alpha_1} - 1}{\alpha_1} \right) + [a_5 + a_6 \ln A_M + a_7 (\ln A_M)^2] \cdot$$

$$\left(\frac{L_M^{a_4} - 1}{a_4} \right) + [a_9 + a_{10} \ln A_F + a_{11} (\ln A_F)^2] \tag{13.7}$$

$$+ a_{12} \, CU6 + a_{13} \, CO6] \cdot \left(\frac{L_F^{a_8} - 1}{a_8} \right)$$

where the subscripts F and M denote female (wife) and male (husband), $C=f(wh, I)$ is household net (disposable) income, N is the size of the household, A_k is the age of gender k, $CU6$ and $CO6$ are number of children below and above 6 years old and L_k is leisure for gender k, defined as

$$L_k = 1 - \frac{h_k}{8760}.$$

For the purpose of estimating the model, we find it convenient to write the density of hours and wages $p(h,w)$ as follows:

$$p(h, w) = \begin{cases} g(h,w)g_0 & \text{if } (h,w) > 0 \\ 1 - g_0 & \text{if } (h,w) = 0 \end{cases} \tag{13.8}$$

where $g(h,w)$ is the conditional density of (h,w) given that $(h,w)>0$, and g_o is the probability density of market opportunities in the opportunity set, i.e. the proportion of market jobs in the opportunity set.

We assume that hours and wages available to the husband and hours and wages available to the wife are independent:[6]

$$g(h, w) = g_{1F}(h_F)g_{1M}(h_M)g_{2F}(w_F)g_{2M}(w_M) \tag{13.9}$$

where g_{1k} and g_{2k} denote the marginal probability functions respectively of hours and wages, for gender k.

Hours in the opportunity set are assumed to be uniformly distributed with a peak in the interval $[1846,2106]$, corresponding to full-time jobs (36–40 weekly hours):

$$g_{1k} = \begin{cases} \gamma_k & \text{if } h_k \in [0,1846] \\ \gamma_k \, \pi_k & \text{if } h_k \in [1846,2106], \quad k=f, M \\ \gamma_k & \text{if } h_k \in [2106,3423] \end{cases} \tag{13.10}$$

where π_k is the full-time peak for gender k, and 3432 is the maximum number of hours observed in the sample.[7] Moreover, since g_{2F} and g_{2M} are defined to be probability densities, we must also have:

$$\gamma_k = \frac{1}{3172 + 260\pi_k}, k=F, M \tag{13.11}$$

The proportions of market opportunities g_{0F} and g_{0M} are assumed to depend on whether individuals are living in northern or southern Italy according to:

$$g_{ok} = \frac{1}{1 + \exp(-\mu_{0k} - \mu_{1k}RE_k)}, k=F, M \tag{13.12}$$

where $RE_k=1$ if the household is living in northern Italy, $RE_k=0$ otherwise. Note that a positive (negative) value of the coefficient of RE means that living in northern Italy increases (decreases) the proportion of market opportunities in the opportunity set.

The density of offered wages is assumed to be lognormal with gender-specific means that depend on length of schooling and on past potential working experience, where experience is defined as equal to age minus length of schooling minus six. Thus, the wage equations are given by

$$\log(w_k) = \beta_{0k} + \beta_{1k}S_k + \beta_{2k}EX_k + \beta_{3k}(EX_k)^2 + \xi_k, \ k = F, \ M \quad (13.13)$$

where S_k = years of education, EX_k = years of potential experience and ξ_k is a random variable i.i.d. normal.

13.4 Data and estimation

The estimation of the model is based on data from the 1993 Survey of Household Income and Wealth (SHIW93). This survey is conducted every two years by the Bank of Italy and, besides household and individual socio-demographic characteristics, contains detailed information on labour, income and wealth of each household component.

The labour incomes measured by the survey are *net* of social security contributions and of taxes on personal income. Therefore, in order to compute gross incomes we have to apply the 'inverse' tax code. In turn, the 'direct' tax code has to be applied to every point in each household's choice set to compute disposable income associated to that point.[8]

Hourly wage rates are obtained by dividing gross annual wage income by observed hours. Only married couples with at least one of the partners working in the wage employment sector are included in the sample used for estimation and simulation. Couples with income from self-employment are excluded from the sample: this is due to the assumption that their decision process may be substantially different from wage-employees' and typically involves a permanent element of uncertainty.[9]

We have restricted the ages of the husband and of the wife to be between 18 and 54 in order to minimise the inclusion in the sample of individuals who in principle are eligible for retirement, since the current version of the model does not take the retirement decision into account.

In view of the above selection rules, the estimates and the simulations should be interpreted as conditional upon the decisions not to be self-employed and not to retire for both partners. The sample covers 2,160 households. Table 13.1 contains the descriptive statistics of the variables used.

The parameters appearing in expressions (13.7) and (13.10)–(13.13) are estimated by maximum likelihood. The likelihood function is the product of the choice densities (13.6) for every household in the sample. The estimates

Table 13.1. *Descriptive statistics: married couples*

	Mean	St.dev.	Min.	Max.
Individual variables				
Annual hours of work (unconditional)				
Husband	1,990	507	0	3,640
Wife	742	893	0	3,640
Annual hours of work (conditional)				
Husband	2,017	453	130	3,640
Wife	1,640	538	108	3,640
Participation rates				
Husband	0.99	0.12	0	1
Wife	0.45	0.49	0	1
Hourly wage rates (1000 ITL)				
Husband	16.7	9.8	0.3	121.1
Wife	16.0	8.8	1.8	111.1
Gross annual earnings (1000 ITL)				
Husband	32,691	1,912	0	185,998
Wife	11,228	14,424	0	69,195
Age				
Husband	41.3	7.5	22	54
Wife	39.4	7.8	18	54
Education (years)				
Husband	9.7	3.9	0	19
Wife	9.4	4.0	0	19
Experience				
Husband	27	9	4	48
Wife	24	9	4	48
Household variables				
Annual net taxes paid (1,000 ITL)	11,026	10,172	−5,042	82,623
Gross annual income (1,000 ITL)	55,090	32,831	1,529	264,907
Disposable annual income (1,000 ITL)	44,064	23,244	3,000	198,932
Region (North)	0.32	0.47	0	1
Number of children below 6	0.34	0.58	0	3
Number of children 6–15	0.58	0.73	0	3

Source: Author's calculations.

Table 13.2. *Estimates of the parameters of the utility function*

Variables	Parameters	Estimates	t-values
Consumption	α_1	0.728	12.8
Constant	α_2	1.470	8.5
Household size	α_3	−0.103	3.7
Husband's leisure	α_4	−12.763	−14.7
Constant	α_5	−1.408	−1.3
log age	α_6	0.760	1.2
log age squared	α_7	−0.097	−1.1
Wife's leisure	α_8	−8.012	−10.3
Constant	α_9	74.509	3.3
log age	α_{10}	−41.708	−3.3
log age squared	α_{11}	5.880	3.3
no of children below 6 years old	α_{12}	0.302	2.4
no of children 6 years old or above	α_{13}	0.277	2.7

Note: Consumption (C) is measured in 10,000,000 ITL.

are reported in Table 13.2 and Table 13.3. Note that the opportunity set of the model is infinite. In order to overcome the computational problems that can arise in estimating models with very large (or even infinite) opportunity sets, McFadden (1978) has suggested a procedure that approximates exact ML estimation and provides consistent estimates. The method essentially consists in representing the true opportunity set with a sample of weighted alternatives, with the weighting depending on the sampling scheme. As a first step, we estimate empirical univariate densities for the variables (w_M, w_F, h_F, h_M). We then draw 199 values from these densities and build 200 alternatives (adding the observed choice). In expression (13.6) every term $V(\ )p(\ )$ is weighted, i.e. divided, by the previously estimated density of the corresponding alternative.[10]

Overall, the parameters are measured quite precisely and their magnitude and sign seem to conform qualitatively to what could be inferred from economic reasoning or previous labour supply estimates. More novel and hard to compare to other research results are the estimates of the market opportunity density and hours density. The market opportunity density estimates imply that market opportunities are relatively more abundant in northern regions. For example, using (13.12) we can compute that the density of market opportunities is 4.3 times larger in northern regions for males, and 1.5 times for females. Also, the full-time peaks of the hours density are very important. The estimates imply that 73% of the

Table 13.3. *Estimates of the market opportunity, hours, and wage densities*

	Parameters	Estimates	t-values
Market opportunities density			
Wife			
constant	μ_{0F}	-0.796	-8.4
region	μ_{1F}	0.631	6.2
Husband			
constant	μ_{0M}	-2.412	-10.9
region	μ_{1M}	1.821	2.9
Hours density			
Wife			
full-time peak	π_F	11.670	27.3
Husband			
full-time peak	π_M	14.454	50.5
Wage density			
Wife			
constant	β_{0F}	0.888	8.7
education	β_{1F}	0.101	24.2
experience	β_{2F}	0.027	3.6
experience squared	β_{3F}	-0.224×10^{-3}	-1.4
Husband			
constant	β_{0M}	1.212	15.1
education	β_{1M}	0.074	25.3
experience	β_{2M}	0.024	4.4
experience squared	β_{3M}	-0.154×10^{-3}	-1.6

jobs available to males and 70% of the jobs available to females require at least 1,846 hours.

13.5 Policy simulations

Once the parameters have been estimated, we can simulate the effects of different policies. A policy can be defined as the introduction of a new opportunity set B^* and /or of a new tax rule f^*. Then we can evaluate the effect of the policy by solving the new problem:

$$\max_{h,w,j} V(f^*(wh, I), (h, j)\varepsilon(h, w, j) \tag{13.14}$$

such that

$$(h, w, j) \in B^*.$$

As a practical matter, the simulation procedure works as follows. First, for each household we simulate the opportunity set, which – as in the estimation procedure – contains 200 points: one is the chosen alternative, the other 199 are built by drawing from the estimated $p(h,w)$ density (or from a different density where the policy is defined also by a change in the opportunity density). Second, for each household and each point in the opportunity set we draw a value ε from the distribution (13.5). And third, for each household we solve problem (13.14). The whole procedure is repeated 10 times, and the results are averaged across repetitions. The results of the policy simulation are uncertain both because they are based on uncertain parameters (estimation uncertainty) and because they also rely on simulated opportunity sets and simulated stochastic components of the utility functions (simulation uncertainty). In the Appendix 13.1 we present a decomposition of total uncertainty into its estimation and simulation component.

Tax reforms

There is an increasing concern in Italy for the efficiency and distribution performance of the tax and benefit system. By and large, we can identify two focal areas of interest. One is centred on the possible merits of a flatter profile of the tax rates, as an instrument to reduce distortions and incentives for tax evasion.[11] The other focuses upon a restructuring of policies in favour of low income groups, possibly switching from a system essentially based on implicit in-kind transfers and categorical benefits to a system based to a larger extent upon means-tested income transfers.[12]

Although interesting, this discussion is lacking support from appropriate measurement of the effects of the policies that are proposed. The models used by default are 'static' microsimulation models, which do not account for behavioural responses.[13] In this matter, however, we think that behavioural responses and incentive effects are crucial.

The first four sections of Table 13.4 report the results of the simulation of different personal income tax regimes, namely, the current (1993) regime, a flat tax and two versions of a negative income tax regime. The hypothetical reforms are connected to the above mentioned discussion since the flat tax is an extreme and simple way of reducing distortion costs and the negative income tax is a general, means-tested way of supporting the poor.

The simulation of the model with the actual tax rules (as of 1993) is used to give us the base-case predictions of participation rates, annual hours of work (given participation), gross earnings, gross family income,

Table 13.4. *Participation rates, annual hours of work, gross income, taxes and disposable income for couples under alternative different tax regimes and labour market reforms by deciles of household disposable income in 1993 (means)*

Tax system	Participation rates(%)		Expected annual hours of work, given participation		Households		
	F	M	F	M	Gross income (1,000 lire)	Taxes (1,000 lire)	Disposable income (1,000 lire)
1993 tax-rules							
I	14.1	95.6	1,030	1,571	15,221	525	14,695
II	20.0	97.6	1,209	1,832	24,372	2,109	22,263
III	43.8	98.9	1,546	1,991	48,187	8,960	39,227
IV	65.5	99.4	1,731	2,117	85,135	19,983	65,152
V	74.4	99.4	1,828	2,237	128,396	34,365	94,032
VI	43.7	98.6	1,590	1,972	54,525	11,074	43,150
FT ($t = 0.184$)							
I	19.6	95.4	1,264	1,706	22,933	4,219	18,714
II	24.4	97.8	1,397	1,924	31,761	5,845	25,917
III	44.7	99.0	1,585	2,048	54,142	9,961	44,181
IV	64.5	99.0	1,741	2,162	89,459	16,460	72,999
V	73.2	99.5	1,834	2,267	132,888	24,452	108,435
VI	45.0	98.6	1,623	2,036	60,189	11,074	49,115
NIT ($a = 0.5$, $t = 0.23$)							
I	16.5	95.3	1,165	1,617	19,348	1,435	17,912
II	21.7	97.5	1,345	1,873	28,979	4,244	24,735
III	43.4	98.8	1,562	2,027	52,147	9,727	42,420
IV	64.1	99.3	1,739	2,155	88,449	18,256	70,193
V	72.9	99.5	1,834	2,261	131,752	28,445	103,307

VI	43.6	98.5	1,608	2,009	58,141	11,074	47,067
NIT($a=0.75, t=0.28$)							
I	14.4	95.3	1,056	1,551	16,404	−1952	18,356
II	19.9	97.1	1,240	1,820	26,199	2,537	23,662
III	41.4	98.6	1,540	1,996	49,801	9,538	40,263
IV	63.3	99.2	1,733	2,138	86,985	20,218	66,767
V	72.6	99.5	1,832	2,252	130,581	32,714	97,867
VI	41.9	98.3	1,589	1,976	55,897	11,074	44,823
Removing hours constraints							
I	28.8	96.3	1,071	1,612	22,776	2,994	19,782
II	35.7	98.2	1,178	1,849	32,080	4,812	27,269
III	44.0	98.6	1,274	1,983	49,647	9,895	39,752
IV	53.8	98.8	1,403	2,095	77,416	18,082	59,334
V	57.9	99.0	1,526	2,189	110,989	28,832	82,157
VI	44.0	98.4	1,307	1,966	54,115	11,409	42,706

Notes:
I = first decile
II = second decile
III = third to eight decile
IV = ninth decile
V = tenth decile
VI = whole sample

taxes and disposable income. The marginal tax rates applied in 1993 are as follows:

Income (1000 Italian lire)	Marginal tax rate (%)
Up to 7,200	10
7,200 – 14,400	22
14,400 – 30,000	27
30,000 – 60,000	34
60,000 – 150,000	41
50,000 – 300,000	46
Over 300,000	51

Besides the application of the basic marginal tax rates, the tax system envisages other tax rates for special categories of income, deductions from taxable income, tax credits and family benefits. All the details of the tax–benefit system are accounted for in the model.[14]

In the second simulation the actual taxes are replaced by a flat tax (FT) on total income. The flat tax rate is determined so as to yield constant total tax revenue.

In the third and fourth simulations we replace the actual taxes by a negative income tax (NIT). For a household with N members, let us define the *guaranteed* household income $G(N)$ as:

$$G(N) = a\sigma(N)m \qquad (13.15)$$

where 0, m is the average per capita disposable income in the total sample and $\sigma(N)$ is given by the equivalence scale proposed by the Commissione di Indagine sulla Povertà (1985):

$$\sigma(N) = \begin{cases} 1.00 \text{ for } N=2 \\ 1.33 \text{ for } N=3 \\ 1.63 \text{ for } N=4 \\ 1.90 \text{ for } N=5 \\ 2.16 \text{ for } N=6 \\ 2.40 \text{ for } N=7 \end{cases} \qquad (13.16)$$

The tax R is then given by

$$R = \begin{cases} Y-G(N) \text{ if } Y \le G(N) \\ t(Y-G(N)) \text{ if } Y > G(N) \end{cases} \qquad (13.17)$$

where t is a marginal (constant) tax rate and Y is total household gross income. The tax is negative if total gross income is less than G. Otherwise the tax is a fixed proportion t of the part of income exceeding G.[15]

In the simulations shown here we set $m = 13473$ (1000 ITL), a is alternatively set equal to 0.5 or to 0.75 and t is determined so that total tax revenue in the sample is constant. According to the definition used in Commissione di Indagine sulla Povertà (1985) the term $\gamma(N)m$ is the poverty threshold for a household with N members. Therefore, we simulate a system where household income is supported up to 1/2 (or alternatively, 3/4) of the poverty threshold, if necessary; otherwise, income exceeding the poverty threshold is taxed at a constant marginal rate equal to t.

In interpreting the following results of reform simulations, it should be kept in mind that what we are using is just a supply model. We assume that the opportunity densities remain unchanged, while of course one might argue that they would change too as a consequence of a new tax regime.[16]

Table 13.4 indicates that the effects on labour supply of the two tax reforms are modest but not irrelevant. Note that the average tax rate paid by the household in 1993 was 0.20. A shift to a FT ($t = 0.184$) increases the labour supply of men and women, in particular poor women who are predicted to participate more in the labour market and to work longer hours, given participation. A shift to a NIT produces an increase of aggregate supply in the ($a = 0.5$, $t = 0.234$) version, and a decrease in the ($a = 0.75$, $t = 0.284$) version, with very modest variations in both versions.

All the reforms would produce a significantly larger disposable income for households. Together with the fact that aggregate hours of work do not increase much, this provides a rough indication that the reforms might be efficient although disequalising when income inequality is measured by the Gini coefficient.[17]

There is one apparently counter-intuitive result in Table 13.4, which provides a good example of the possibly different implications of our model as compared to the traditional approach. Since the flat tax (18.4%) is higher than the first marginal tax under the 1993 system (10%), we might expect a decrease in participation rates. This is even more valid for the negative income tax system, which introduces a guaranteed minimum income coupled with a 23% or alternatively 28% flat tax. Our model predicts instead an increase in aggregate supply as a consequence of the shift to a FT($t = 0.184$) or to a NIT($a = 0.5$, $t = 0.234$) system. A traditional model would assume that every value of h is equally available in the choice set; moreover, given preferences, the utility associated with a particular point in the choice set would be uniquely determined by (h,w). Under these assumptions, a traditional model would indeed predict a decrease in participation rates under either reform. In the model presented in this paper, however, not every value of h is equally likely to be available in the choice set. Job opportunities offering less than 1,846 or more than 2,106 hours are relatively unlikely to be found. The opportunities in the range

Table 13.5. *The Gini coefficient for distributions of households' gross and disposable income, and degree of redistribution under various tax regimes*

Tax regime	Gross income	Disposable income	Degree of redistribution
1993 tax-rules	0.323	0.283	0.875
FT ($t=0.184$)	0.332	0.332	1.000
NIT ($a=0.5$, $t=0.23$)	0.338	0.315	0.935
NIT ($a=0.75$, $t=0.28$)	0.343	0.298	0.869
Removing hours constraints	0.352	0.307	0.872

1,846–2,106 may carry lower tax rates under both reforms than under the 1993 tax code. Thus participation may become more attractive. Moreover, in our model the utility is random; there are unobserved components attached to every market or non-market opportunity which make it more or less desirable. Thus a market opportunity may turn out to be more desirable than a non-market opportunity (non-participation) even though the opposite is true when the comparison is made solely in terms of hours and disposable income.

There is another result that deserves a comment. When NIT ($a=0.75$, $t=0.284$) is applied, aggregate labour supply is slightly reduced. Still, aggregate net income increases, despite the fact that the opportunity densities and tax revenue are invariant by construction. More generally, in all the reforms, average gross income increases far more than labour supply. How does this happen? It must be that the least productive, those with lower wages, reduce (or increase less) their supply, and at the same time the most productive, those with higher wages, increase (or reduce less) their labour supply. So it seems that the reforms interact in a virtuous way with the pattern of elasticities, inducing a sort of favourable selection process.

The Gini coefficients displayed in Table 13.5 suggest that the distribution of income (both gross and net) would be made slightly more unequal as a consequence of the introduction of any of the reforms, more markedly so for the flat tax. Note however that NIT ($a=0.75$, $t=0.28$) is more effective in redistributing than the 1993 tax rule, and its disequalising effect on the distribution of net income is very small.

In Table 13.6 we give the fraction of winners for deciles of the distribution of household disposable income. A household is a winner if the utility level reached under the 1993 system is lower than the utility level reached after the reform. This procedure of course bypasses the problem of inter-household welfare comparison.[18] The results show that the majority of the households would support all the three reforms, with a more robust majority for NIT

Table 13.6. *Decile-specific proportions of winners from two alternative tax reforms, by household disposable income in 1993 (%)*

Tax reform	Deciles of the distribution of household disposable income in 1993					
	1	2	3–8	9	10	All
FT ($t=0.184$)	14.2	19.0	51.3	86.5	90.6	51.8
NIT ($a=0.5, t=0.23$)	45.9	29.9	50.7	76.5	83.3	53.9
NIT ($a=0.75, t=0.28$)	74.1	43.7	44.8	51.1	64.9	50.2

($a=0.5$, $t=0.23$). Behind this almost uniform result, we observe that the effects of the reforms differ dramatically across deciles. No reform receives majority support in all deciles, although NIT ($a=0.75$, $t=0.28$) gets close to it, which suggests that some carefully designed NIT system might be supported by a diffuse majority across the deciles, and possibly even reach a higher degree of equality in view of the results of Table 13.5. It is also interesting to note that NIT ($a=0.75$, $t=0.28$) would be supported in a referendum both by the poorest and by the richest income decile. Of course, a definite judgement upon the reforms would depend on the relative magnitude of gains and losses, and thus ultimately on the comparability issue.[19]

Labour market reforms: removing hours constraints

Constraints limiting the choice of the number of hours worked appear to be very important. Given the estimates of α_{18} and α_{19} reported in Table 13.2, we can compute that the percentage of jobs available in the hours range (1846, 2106) is 49% for females and 54% for males. In this section we report the results of a simulation exercise consisting in removing these constraints: namely, we simulate household behaviour after replacing the hours density specified in expression (13.14) with a uniform density.

In the last section of Table 13.4 we report the results of removing the constraints on the distribution of hours in the opportunity set. For each individual we impose a strictly uniform hours opportunity density, so that, given the wage, any value of hours is equally available in the interval [0, 3432]. The opportunity set of every individual is also adjusted in order to keep fixed the average amount of hours *per* job available in the opportunity set (including non-market opportunities). This can be done by adjusting g_{0k} so that the above condition is met. The tax regime is kept as in 1993. From Table 13.4 we observe that aggregate participation rates are very close to the reference case. This probably reflects the above adjustment that introduces a sort of invariance of the 'average' opportunity available. We note, however, that females belonging to households in the lower deciles of the reference case income distribution increase their participation in the labour market: in the first decile, in particular, the participation rate doubles, from 14.4% to 28.8%. On the other hand, in richer households, females tend to reduce their participation rate. From the next two columns of Table 13.4 we observe that by removing hours constraints, that is, reducing the dominance of full-time jobs relative to other types of jobs, reduces supplied hours among females belonging to the upper deciles of the pre-reform income distribution. This is the result that one would expect. The rigidity of the Italian labour market seems to have forced, in particular women in the 'richest' deciles, to work longer hours than they would prefer. Moreover, it seems that women in the lowest deciles of the income distribution have been prevented by hours constraints from participating. For many of these women, it may be hard to combine the care of children, for example, with working in a full-time job. By making jobs with shorter hours more easily available in the market, the burden of combining market work and other activities at home is reduced. It should be noted that women living in households belonging to the lowest deciles of the income distribution are not necessarily poor in the sense of having a low potential wage rate: they might be poor not because of a poor market potential but because they find it hard to combine market work and other activities.

It is interesting to observe that the tax revenue does not change much after removing hours constraints: in fact it increases slightly. Since this happens together with a reduction in the total amount of hours worked, it must be the case that the post-reform labour force is more productive than before: the average wage rates of those who are working are higher and/or those with higher wages work more and those with lower wages work less with respect to the pre-reform regime. So there appears to be a favourable selection effect similar to the one we already noted in the previous section when considering tax reforms.

From the last row of Table 13.5 we also observe that with uniformly distributed hours, the distribution of gross household income becomes more unequal, despite the fact that household income is increased in poorest deciles. This must be due to changes in the intra-decile distribution.

13.6 Conclusions

We have developed a model of household labour supply that adopts an econometric framework of the continuous multinomial logit type and allows for complex non-convex budget sets, highly nonlinear labour supply curves and imperfect markets with institutional constraints

Policy simulations indicate that less distortionary tax systems such as a flat tax or a negative income tax system would have modest but not irrelevant impacts on aggregate labour supply and on the distribution of disposable income among married couples. The reforms contain incentives to work less for some and to work more for others. The incentive to work more seem to prevail at least for two of the reforms, and the supply elasticity is large enough to induce a significant increase of average household disposable income. There is also some indication that the reforms activate a sort of favourable selection process, by inducing the more productive to work more and the less productive to work less. The results suggest that the reforms might be efficient but slightly disequalising. A majority – although not a large one – of households would support the reforms. The proportion of winners varies widely across the deciles, depending on the reform. There is some indication that a carefully designed NIT-like system might result in an improvement in both efficiency and equality, and possibly also get a majority support in all the deciles. Thus a more systematic search of the reform space looks promising.

We have also simulated a policy consisting of removing the quantity constraints on hours choice, i.e. imputing to every household an opportunity set with uniformly distributed hours. The most noteworthy results are the increase in participation of women in the poorest income deciles and the decrease of hours worked by women in the richest deciles. Thus the results reveal that the low participation rates of women in poor households are due at least in part to the difficulty of combining market work and other activities at home, given that part-time jobs are hard to find. At the other end, women in the richer households can probably substitute 'home production' time with income (market goods). However, if they were given the opportunity, at least some would decide to switch to part-time work.

Appendix 13.1 Estimation and simulation uncertainty

For some of the variables of interest, we have conducted the simulation in a more complex manner than explained in section 13.5. Namely, the procedure of section 13.5 is repeated for 10 different values of the parameter vector, randomly drawn from the estimated joint distribution (multivariate normal). This allows us to account not only for simulation uncertainty but also for estimation (or parameters) uncertainty. Estimation uncertainty stems from the sampling variability of the estimated parameters. Simulation variability is due to the fact that we do not observe all the relevant variables affecting the preferences and the constraints: we do not observe ϵ nor do we observe the exact choice sets, and we are therefore forced to simulate them. This more complex simulation procedure is very time consuming, and the results that we report in what follows are merely suggestive of a more systematic investigation that we plan to complete in a future contribution. For a certain variable X we can define X_{PR} as the value obtained with para-meters P in repetition R, with $P = 1, \ldots, 10$ and $R = 1, \ldots, 10$. We then define:

$$M_P = \sum_R X_{PR}/10 \tag{13A.1}$$

$$M_{.R} = \sum_P X_{PR}/10$$
$$M = \sum_{P,R} X_{PR}/100 \tag{13A.2}$$

$$V_{TOT} = \sum_{P,R} (X_{PR} - M)^2/100$$
$$V_{EST} = \sum_P (M_P - M)^2/10 \tag{13A.3}$$

$$V_{SIM} = V_{TOT} - V_{EST} \tag{13A.4}$$

$$MIN_{EST} = \min_P(M_P)$$
$$MAX_{EST} = \max_P(M_P) \tag{13A.5}$$

$$MIN_{SIM} = \min_R(M_{.R})$$
$$MAX_{SIM} = \max_R(M_{.R}) \tag{13A.6}$$

$$MIN_{TOT} = \min_{P,R}(M_{PR})$$
$$MAX_{TOT} = \max_{P,R}(M_{PR}) \tag{13A.7}$$

The definition of V_{EST}, the variance imputable to estimation uncertainty, and of V_{SIM}, the residual variance imputable to simulation uncertainty, is based on the standard analysis-of-variance decomposition. Table 13.A1.1 illustrates the results of the simulation of the 1993 tax regime.

Table 13.A1.1. *Total, estimation and simulation uncertainty; 1993 tax rules*

	Husband's unconditional hours	Husband's participation rate (%)	Wife's unconditional hours	Wife's participation rate (%)	Household's disposable income (000 ITL)
M	1,960	98.7	704	44.1	43,700
Total uncertainty					
V_{TOT}	357.39	0.04	618.75	0.82	461,824.11
Std. Err. of M	1.9	0.02	2.5	0.09	68.3
MIN_{TOT}	1,927	98.2	672	42.3	41,998
MAX_{TOT}	2,001	98.9	772	45.8	44,603
Estimation uncertainty					
V_{EST}	345.96	0.03	590.49	0.81	450,357.21
MIN_{EST}	1,929	98.3	677	42.6	42,154
MAX_{EST}	1,998	98.9	764	45.4	44,406
Simulation uncertainty					
V_{SIM}	11.43	0.01	28.26	0.01	11,448.90
MIN_{SIM}	1,958	98.6	698	43.8	43,520
MAX_{SIM}	1,962	98.8	712	44.4	43,890

Notes

We should like to thank Chris Flinn for many useful comments to a previous version. We also owe special thanks to Dino Rizzi (University of Venice) for providing us with TBM, a tax–benefit simulation model. S. Strøm and R. Aaberge are thankful to ICER (Turin) for providing financial support and excellent working conditions. U. Colombino gratefully acknowledges financial support from CNR (research grants 96.01648.CT10 and 97.00977.CT10) and from MURST (research grants 1996 and 1997). The main elements of the model together with results of tax reform simulations are also presented in Aaberge, Colombino, Strøm and Wennemo (1998). The present paper contains additional and new simulation results and a more explicit exposition of the model.

1 A very useful and clear exposition of the 'Hausman approach' is given by Moffit (1986).
2 A critical analysis of other aspects of the 'Hausman approach' can be found in MaCurdy et al., (1990).
3 See Aaberge, Colombino and Strøm (1999) for the extension to married couples as decision units.
4 Expression (13.6) amounts to assuming that $\ln(\varepsilon)$ is distributed according to type III extreme value distribution.
5 For the derivation of the choice density, see Aaberge, Colombino and Strøm (1999).
6 The assumption of independence of h and w is standard in microeconometric labour supply studies, where the traditional approach dictates a constant wage rate for any amount of hours of work (an exception is Moffit, 1984). In our model it is essentially a computational simplification.
7 Alternative ways to account for constraints on hours are represented by Ham (1982), Colombino (1985), Ilmakunnas and Pudney (1990), Kaptein et al., (1990), Dickens and Ludberg (1993) and van Soest (1994).
8 Dino Rizzi (University of Venice) provided us with a programme (TBM), written by him, which allows the application of detailed tax–benefit rules to gross incomes and also to recover gross incomes from net incomes by applying the inverse rule.
9 We are currently working on a version of the model that includes the wage-employment / self-employment choice.
10 See various contributions in the *Rivista di Diritto Finanziario e Scienza delle Finanze* 3, 1995.
11 See Commissione per l'analisi delle compatabilità macroeconomiche delle spesa sociale (1997).
12 Interesting applications of non-behavioural microsimulation models to the analysis of recent Italian tax policies or proposals are represented by, for example, Rizzi (1995) and ISPE (1997).
13 Besides labour supply, there are of course many other household choices which are also important to take into account in the evaluation of tax and benefit reforms: fertility, education, occupational choice, savings, housing choices etc.

14 To be more precise, the tax programme that we use accounts for all the details for which the dataset is sufficiently informative.

15 One can think of many different variants of NIT. See Fortin *et al.*, (1993) for a theoretical and empirical analysis of NIT systems.

16 The assumption that the opportunity densities remain unchanged is equivalent to assuming – in a traditional setting – that the aggregate demand for labour is perfectly elastic. This is the case, for example, if the conditions for the so-called *non-substitution theorem* hold.

17 The increase in average household disposable income is of course due to the household behavioural response. No such effect would be there in a non-behavioural simulation. Under the constraint of equal tax revenue, if household behaviour remains unchanged, then average gross income and average net income should also remain unchanged. Note that most of our behavioural effect comes from the (female) participation elasticity, which is probably a robust enough concept even for those who do not particularly trust behavioural and structural modelling.

18 Aaberge, Colombino and Strøm (1998) perform an analysis of policy reforms based on interpersonally comparable welfare measures.

19 We are currently working on the application of appropriate procedures for the social evaluation of reforms.

14　Transitions estimators in discrete choice models

Alan Duncan and Melvyn Weeks

14.1 Introduction

In both the social and physical sciences the use of discrete choice or stimulus and response models is commonplace. This is based upon the recognition that many phenomena involve the choice between or passage through discrete, identifiable states. Survey articles such as Amemiya (1981) provide a large number of references for applications in economics and bioassay. Such models have become popular as empirical tools as much through significant increases in computer power as from the recognition that many processes that are of interest to analysts are inherently discrete.

In many fields of microeconometric study, there has been a movement towards the use of qualitative models to simulate behavioural transitions in response to some exogenous shock. There have been a number of recent studies of labour supply behaviour, for example, where discrete choice models have been used to simulate transitions in labour force status in response to some reform to the tax–benefit system (see Duncan and Giles (1996) and Bingley and Walker (1995) among others). While such applications are undoubtedly of great relevance, the policy impact of transitions studies of this kind tend to be offset to a degree by the notorious, empirically observed tendency for outcome-based measures of fit in such models to be relatively poor in cross-sectional studies. The literature abounds with empirical studies where the authors report a systematic over- or under-prediction of certain state frequencies.[1] Whilst problems of this kind may simply indicate some form of specification error, there is some suggestion that even in functionally well-specified models the predictive performance is poor, particularly where some states are relatively densely or sparsely represented in the data.

The question of whether any discrepancies between observed and predicted choices really matter is, in part, a question of aggregation. For example, Hausman and Wise (1978) note that computation of expected choice at the level of the individual is not necessary if the aggregate expected frequencies are accurate, given the operation of the law of large numbers. Counter to this, Cramer (1991) notes that, when the statistical model is part of a wider microsimulation study, then predicted outcomes for each individual are indeed required. For example, in utilising a discrete choice model of labour supply to examine the impact of tax reform we typically compare predicted labour market states before and after the reform to determine the distribution of 'movers' and 'stayers' and the existence of any systematic patterns in inter-state mobility.

From the point of view of the policy-maker, there is a second reason to be concerned when the accuracy of prediction is poor. One of the most important questions to be answered when a tax reform is to be considered is, how much is it likely to cost the Exchequer, taking account of any behavioural responses to the policy shock? To arrive at a convincing answer to this question, it is important that the econometric model predicts as close to observed behaviour as possible before the behavioural impact of the reform is simulated. By doing so, one will in turn be able to simulate the pre-reform Exchequer costs accurately. If, on the other hand, the model predicts poorly, then one could have little reason to believe the simulated cost of the reform. In continuous behavioural microsimulation studies, one can surmount this potential problem by in some sense *calibrating* the estimated equation to replicate observed behaviour in all cases bar those where observed behaviour is inconsistent with basic economic conditions (see, *inter alia*, Blundell *et al.*, 1988; Duncan and Giles, 1996). Granger and Pesaran (1999) examine this particular issue within the context of distinguishing between point and probability forecasts. In proposing the integration of decision theoretic principles with forecast design and evaluation, the authors consider the general problem of a decision-maker deciding whether or not to act, based upon the probability forecast and the cost of action. Emphasising that the costs of various types of action may be very different, this approach is contrasted with the use of symmetric (quadratic) loss functions as a measure of fit.

In this paper we examine alternative transitions estimators which control for the systematic under- or over-prediction of state frequencies inherent in many discrete choice models. We derive an exact expression for the transitions estimator in a binary choice framework, and suggest how simulation-based transitions estimators may be employed when dealing with higher dimensional problems. A Monte Carlo study compares the properties of our suggested estimator with those more frequently found in the literature under alternative experimental designs. In addition, we compare predicted transitions based upon an analysis of labour market transitions of married women following a tax reform which replaces all in-work and social assistance benefits with a basic income guarantee.

14.2 A statistical framework

Consider as a general framework a statistical model of the choice among J states, where the utility u_j^* to be enjoyed in each state j can be expressed in terms of an observable set of k characteristics $\mathbf{x} = (x_1, x_2, \ldots, x_k)'$ and an unobservable component ε_j with zero mean and covariance Ω.[2] Assume that the utility to be enjoyed in each state depends linearly on characteristics, such that

$$u_j^* = \mathbf{x}'\boldsymbol{\beta}_j + \epsilon_j, \; \forall j = 1, \ldots, J \in \Theta \tag{14.1}$$

where Θ denotes the choice set and $\boldsymbol{\beta}_j = (\beta_{j1}, \beta_{j2} \ldots, \beta_{jk})'$. These latent variables are related to observed quantities via the mapping

$$y = \max_j [u_j^*]$$

Based on the stochastic assumptions on ε_j and for a given vector of parameters $\boldsymbol{\beta}$, we can (in principle, at least) evaluate probabilities $P_j(\mathbf{x}, \boldsymbol{\beta}) = \Pr(y = j \mid, \mathbf{x}, \boldsymbol{\beta})$.

For $i = 1, \ldots, n$ indexing a random sample from the population, and for $P_{ij}(\mathbf{x}_i, \boldsymbol{\beta}) = \Pr(y = j \mid, \mathbf{x}, \boldsymbol{\beta})$ the log-likelihood for (14.1) may be written as

$$L(\boldsymbol{\beta}) = \sum_{i=1}^{n} \sum_{j \in J} y_{ij} \ln P_{ij}(\mathbf{x}_i, \boldsymbol{\beta}) \tag{14.2}$$

with the score

$$S(\boldsymbol{\beta}) = \sum_{i=1}^{n} \sum_{j \in J} (\partial \ln P_{ij}(\mathbf{x}_i, \boldsymbol{\beta}) / \partial \boldsymbol{\beta}) y_{ij} \tag{14.3}$$

Among the range of estimation procedures available for models of this kind, one may apply maximum likelihood techniques to solve the first order condition $1/n \sum_{i=1}^{n} s_i(\beta) = 0$ where $s_i(.)$ is the ith contribution to the score. Alternatively, the method of moments (or simulated moments) may be used.

Examining (14.3) a little more closely, we see that a number of alternate estimation procedures are possible. Maximum likelihood estimation solves the first-order condition $1/n \sum_{i=1}^{n} s_i(\boldsymbol{\beta}) = 0$ where $s_i(.)$ is the ith contribution to the score. The method of moments (or simulated moments) is based upon the difference between the observed random variable y and its conditional expectation, namely, $y_{ij} - P_{ij}(\mathbf{x}_i, \boldsymbol{\beta})$, and proceeds by substituting an unbiased predictor for $P_{ij}(\mathbf{x}_i, \boldsymbol{\beta})$. An alternative method, following the suggestion by Ruud (1986) that the score of the general linear exponential model may be written as a conditional expectation, is to estimate directly the expression $y_{ij} - P_{ij}(\mathbf{x}_i, \boldsymbol{\beta})$. As a result, (14.3) can be written as the conditional expectation of the latent model given the observed data.

14.3 Simulating predicted state transitions

Discrete choice models are frequently used to simulate transitions between states in response to some exogenous shock (see Duncan and Giles, 1996). In a recent study, Keane (1997) utilises panel data on consumer purchases to examine the relative importance of heterogeneity and state dependence in explaining the observed temporal persistence of consumer brand choices. A number of models are specified and one measure of fit is a comparison of observed and predicted transition frequencies across product variants. However, in many cases the analyst has a single cross-section of observed choices and, conditional upon an estimated model, seeks to estimate the impact of one or more counterfactuals. Obviously in this context transitions occur without reference to an observable event, such that there is not a ready-made metric for model comparison.

Consider now the evaluation of model (14.1) based on a sample of data of size n. Let the set $\{y_i, \mathbf{x}_i\}$ for $i = 1, \ldots, n$ denote observations on y and x, and define the $n \times J$ matrix $\mathbf{Y} = (\mathbf{y}_1, \ldots, \mathbf{y}_J)'$ with typical element $\|Y\| = \mathbf{1}(y_i = j)$ for all i, j. For a given parameter vector $\boldsymbol{\beta}$, we may construct a matrix $\mathbf{P}$ of sample probabilities with typical element $P_{ij}(\mathbf{x}_i, \boldsymbol{\beta}) = \Pr(y_i = j | \mathbf{x}_i, \boldsymbol{\beta})$. A common empirical practice is to model discrete outcomes on the basis of probabilities $P_{ij}(\mathbf{x}_i, \boldsymbol{\beta})$ using a maximum probability rule. If we let $\hat{y}_i$ represent the predicted state, then

$$\hat{y}_i = \max_j [P_{ij}(\mathbf{x}_i, \boldsymbol{\beta}), \quad j = 1, \ldots, J]. \tag{14.4}$$

One outcome-based performance measure for a qualitative model of this form would compare within sample frequencies of predicted and observed outcomes over the range of y.[3] Defining the $n \times J$ matrix $\hat{\mathbf{Y}}_{MP}$ with typical element $\|\hat{\mathbf{Y}}_{MP}\| = \mathbf{1}(\hat{y}_i = j)$ for all i, j, where $\mathbf{1}(.)$ represents the indicator function, we can summarise the proximity of predicted to observed states in terms of the $J \times J$ matrix $1/n \mathbf{Y}' \hat{\mathbf{Y}}_{MP}$ the trace of which represents the proportion of observations for which the predicted and observed states coincide. For a model to predict perfectly requires that $tr\,(1/n\, \mathbf{Y}' \hat{\mathbf{Y}}_{MP}) = 1$, an empirical feat which is rare.[4]

It is well known that the current practice of using the maximum probability rule based on (14.4) does not in general lead to correct predictions of transitions frequencies. Here we discuss an alternative estimator which generates more accurate transitions frequencies. For the binary case and under specific distributional assumptions, we derive expressions for transitions frequencies. In higher dimensions, we suggest how one might approximate transitions frequencies using simulation methods.

Simulating transitions: the MP rule

Consider a counterfactual where the vector of characteristics $\mathbf{x}_i$ for each observation in the sample are superceded by some other set $\mathbf{x}_i^R \neq \mathbf{x}_i$. Based upon the same parameter vector $\boldsymbol{\beta}$, we may simulate the counterfactual state $\hat{y}_i^R$ for the ith observation by employing the maximum probability given the counterfactual $\mathbf{x}_i^R$, giving

$$\hat{y}_i^R = \max_j [P_{ij}(\mathbf{x}_i^R, \boldsymbol{\beta}), \quad j = 1, \ldots, J]. \tag{14.5}$$

Standard practice builds a matrix of transitions frequencies as follows: define a matrix $\hat{\mathbf{Y}}_{MP}^R$ with typical element $\|\hat{\mathbf{Y}}_{MP}^R\| = \mathbf{1}(\hat{y}_i^R = j)$ for all i, j. Then, a summary of transitions frequencies based on the maximum probability rules (14.4) and (14.5) can be expressed in terms of the $J \times J$ matrix

$$\mathbf{T}_{MP} = \hat{\mathbf{Y}}_{MP}' \hat{\mathbf{Y}}_{MP}^R, \tag{14.6}$$

the trace of which represents the number of observations for which the predicted states remain the same when one moves from the base to the counterfactual regime. Clearly, $tr(\mathbf{T}_{MP}) = n$ for a counterfactual where no transitions are predicted.

However, since the transitions frequencies are constructed using the maximum probability rule, there is no guarantee that they will converge to their true values even if the behavioural parameters of the discrete choice model are themselves consistent. It is therefore difficult to place any real faith in predicted transitions frequencies of this form unless and until we are able to correct in some way the bias that exists in predictions of frequencies under the maximum probability rule.

Simulating transitions: an alternative estimator

For utilities $u_{ij}^* = \mathbf{x}'_i \boldsymbol{\beta}_j + \epsilon_{ij}$ we may derive probabilities $P_{ij} = \Pr(y_i = j | \mathbf{x}_i, \boldsymbol{\beta})$ for all states j given a specific distribution for ε_{ij}. Our interest centres on the effects on these probabilities following an exogenous shock $\mathbf{x}_i^R \neq \mathbf{x}_i$ which alters utilities from u_{ij}^* to $u_{ij}^R = (\mathbf{x}_i^R)' \boldsymbol{\beta}_j + \varepsilon_{ij}$. That is, we are in general interested in the probability $P_{i(j^* \ jR)}$ of transition from any state j^* to j^R, where in general $P_{i(j^* \ jR)} = \Pr(u_{ijR}^R > u_{ij}^R \ \forall j \neq j^R | u_{ij^*}^R > u_{ij}^* \ \forall j \neq j^*)$. When utilities are expressed in linear form,

$$P_{i(j^* \ jR)} = \Pr(y_i = j^* | \mathbf{x}_i, \boldsymbol{\beta}).$$
$$\Pr(\varepsilon_{ij} - \varepsilon_{ijR} < (\mathbf{x}_i^R)'(\boldsymbol{\beta}_{jR} - \boldsymbol{\beta}_j) \ \forall j \neq j^R | \varepsilon_{ij} - _{ij^*} < \mathbf{x}_i'(\boldsymbol{\beta}_{j^*} - \boldsymbol{\beta}_j) \ \forall j \neq j^*).$$

By culminating transitions probabilities (either unconditional or conditioned on y_i) over the sample, we may derive transitions frequencies $\eta_{(j^* \ jR)}$ where

$$\eta_{(j^* \ jR)} = \sum_{i=1}^{n} P_{i(j^* \ jR)} \ \forall j^*, j^R = 1, \ldots, J. \tag{14.7}$$

$$= \sum_{i=1}^{n} E[y_i | \mathbf{x}_i].$$

The binomial case

Consider the simplest version of the statistical model (14.1) outlined above for which $J = 2$, such that

$$u_{i1}^* = \mathbf{x}'_i \boldsymbol{\beta}_1 + \varepsilon_{i1} \tag{14.8}$$
$$u_{i2}^* = \mathbf{x}'_i \boldsymbol{\beta}_2 + \varepsilon_{i2}$$

Expressing (14.8) in differenced form yields

$$u_{i2}^* - u_{i1}^* = \mathbf{x}'_i (\boldsymbol{\beta}_2 - \boldsymbol{\beta}_1) + (\varepsilon_{i2} - \varepsilon_{i1}) \tag{14.9}$$
$$= \mathbf{x}'_i \boldsymbol{\beta} + \varepsilon_i.$$

Based on the statistical model (14.9) and given some distribution function $F(.)$ for ε_i, we have that

$$P_{i(1 \ 1)} = P_{i1} \left\{ \frac{1 - F_i^R}{1 - F_i} . I_i + I_i^R \right\} \tag{14.10}$$

$$P_{i(1 \ 2)} = P_{i1} \left\{ \frac{F_i^R - F_i^R}{1 - F_i} . I_i \right\} \tag{14.11}$$

$$P_{i(2 \ 1)} = P_{i2} \left\{ \frac{F_i - F_i^R}{F_i} \right\} . I_i^R \tag{14.12}$$

$$P_{i(2 \ 2)} = P_{i2} \left\{ \frac{F_i^R}{F_i} . I_i^R + I_i \right\} \tag{14.13}$$

for all $i = 1, \ldots, n$, where

$$P_{i2} = 1 - P_{i1} = F_i = F(\mathbf{x}'_i \boldsymbol{\beta}), \ F_i^R = F[(\mathbf{x}_i^R)' \boldsymbol{\beta}], \ I_i = 1[\mathbf{x}'_i \boldsymbol{\beta} < (\mathbf{x}_i^R)' \boldsymbol{\beta}]$$

and $I_i^R = 1[\mathbf{x}'_i \boldsymbol{\beta} \geq (\mathbf{x}_i^R)' \boldsymbol{\beta}]$.

A matrix T of transitions frequencies may then be defined as

$$T = \sum_{i=1}^{n} T_i. \tag{14.14}$$

We may condition transitions frequencies on the observed discrete state indicator y_i by replacing P_{i1} and P_{i2} in (14.10) to (14.13) by $1(y_i = 1)$ and $1(y_i = 2)$ respectively.

14.4 Calibration-based transition estimators

Here we consider an alternative strategy which adjusts the maximum probability rule to rectify the problem of misclassification using the naïve criterion (14.5). Our proposed approach brings the method of calibration to bear on the problem of predicting transitions following an exogenous shock $x_i^R \neq x_i$. We first examine two calibration methods.

Calibration methods

Consider the set of J state-specific utilities $u_{ij}^* = x_i'\beta_j + \varepsilon_{ij}$ for the ith observation. To force this model to predict the observed outcome y_i through the maximum probability mapping (14.4), we must place bounds on the values of the unobservable components of utility ε_{ij}. By exploiting any assumptions that are made about the stochastic distribution of the model, we may generate a realisation e_{ij} which can then be factored into latent relationships of the form $u_{ij}^* = x_i\beta_j + e_{ij}$ to recover predictions $\hat{y}_i$ which coincide exactly with y_i.

Suppose that we observe the ith outcome as $y_i = \epsilon(1, \ldots, j)$. For $\hat{y}_i = j^*$ requires that $u_{ij^*}^* > u_{ij}^*$ for all $j \neq j^*$. This implies that

$$(\varepsilon_{ij} - \varepsilon_{ij^*}) < x_i'(\beta_{j^*} - \beta_j) \quad \forall j \neq j^* \tag{14.15}$$

Our two proposed calibration methods derive realisations $e_{ij} - e_{ij^*}$ which respect the bounds (14.15) on the unobserved components of utility such that $\hat{y}_i = y_i$ for all i. We may evaluate $e_{ij} = e_{ij^*}$ as the conditional expectation

$$(\overline{e_{ij} - e_{ij^*}}) = E[\varepsilon_{ij} - \varepsilon_{ij^*} | \varepsilon_{ij} - \varepsilon_{ij^*} < x_i'(\beta_{j^*} - \beta_j)]. \tag{14.16}$$

Gourieroux *et al.* (1987) refer to this expression as the (conditional) prediction error, otherwise known as the *generalised residual*. Alternatively we may realise $e_{ij} - e_{ij^*}$ by drawing at random from the conditional distribution of u_i^* given y_i^*.

$$f(\varepsilon_{ij^*} - \varepsilon_{ij^*} | \varepsilon_{ij} - \varepsilon_{ij^*} < x_i'(\beta_{j^*} - \beta_j)). \tag{14.17}$$

For β unknown we simply replace β by $\hat{\beta}$ in either case.

Simulated conditional transitions frequencies

To calibrate this model using (14.16) for $y_i = j^* \epsilon (1,2)$ we may evaluate the generalised residuals

$$\bar{e}_i = E[\varepsilon_i | y_i = j^*, x_i, \beta] \tag{14.18}$$

given a distribution for ε_i.[5] The calibrated latent predictor then becomes $u_{i2}^* - u_{i1}^* = \mathbf{x}_i' \boldsymbol{\beta} + \bar{e}_i$, to yield a calibrated state predictor

$$\hat{y}_i^{CE} = 1 + \mathbf{1}(\mathbf{x}_i' \boldsymbol{\beta} + \bar{e}_i > 0) \tag{14.19}$$

The alternative calibration technique (14.17) requires that we draw $e_{ij} - e_{ij*}$ at random from the conditional distribution $f(\varepsilon_{ij} - \varepsilon_{ij*} | \varepsilon_{ij} - \varepsilon_{ij*} < \mathbf{x}_i' (\boldsymbol{\beta}_{j*} - \boldsymbol{\beta}_j)) = f(\varepsilon_i | y_i = j^*)$. In the binomial case, we may do so by applying the Inverse Transformation Theorem. In general,

$$e_i = F^{-1}[\mathbf{1}(y_i = 1)\{v_i F_i + (1 - v_i)(1 - F_i)\} + v_i(1 - F_i)] \tag{14.20}$$

gives the conditional draw, where $F_i = F(\mathbf{x}_i' \boldsymbol{\beta})$ for some distribution function $F(.)$ and $v \sim U[0,1]$. This gives an alternative state predictor (calibrated using 4.20) of the form

$$\hat{y}_i^{CD} = 1 + \mathbf{1}(\mathbf{x}_i' \boldsymbol{\beta} + e_i > 0). \tag{14.21}$$

Similarly following an exogenous shock $\mathbf{x}_i^R \neq \mathbf{x}_i$ we define the calibrated state predictors

$$\hat{y}_i^{CD(R)} = 1 + \mathbf{1}((\mathbf{x}_i^R)' \boldsymbol{\beta} + \bar{e}_i > 0) \tag{14.22}$$

and

$$\hat{y}_i^{CE(R)} = 1 + \mathbf{1}((\mathbf{x}_i^R)' \boldsymbol{\beta} + e_i > 0)] \tag{14.23}$$

where $\bar{e}_i$ and e_i are given by (14.19) and (14.21) respectively, and consider two $n \times J$ matrices $\hat{\mathbf{Y}}_{CE}^R$ and $\hat{\mathbf{Y}}_{CD}^R$ with typical $(i, j)th$ elements $\|\hat{\mathbf{Y}}_{CE}^R\| = \mathbf{1}(\hat{y}_i^{CE(R)} = j)$ and $\|\hat{\mathbf{Y}}_{CE}^R\| = \mathbf{1}(\hat{y}_i^{CD(R)} = j)$ for all i, j. By direct analogy with (14.6) we may construct transitions matrices

$$\mathbf{T}_{CE} = \hat{\mathbf{Y}}_{CE}' \hat{\mathbf{Y}}_{CE}^R = \mathbf{Y}' \hat{\mathbf{Y}}_{CE}^R \tag{14.24}$$

and

$$\mathbf{T}_{CD} = \hat{\mathbf{Y}}_{CD}' \hat{\mathbf{Y}}_{CD}^R = \mathbf{Y}' \hat{\mathbf{Y}}_{CD}^R, \tag{14.25}$$

each of which has been calibrated to replicate observed states with 100% accuracy. Of course, given the form of either the generalised residual $\bar{e}_i$ or the simulated residual e_i this is hardly surprising. Indeed, one can guarantee perfect state predictions regardless of whether or not the mean equation is a correct specification of the underlying data-generating process. However, conditional on a correct specification of the mean equation, the marginal effects are consistent also. At least at an intuitive level, this makes it more likely that the transitions frequencies themselves will be more reliable than those in (14.6). Whether they converge to the true transitions frequencies (14.14) is a question we address in the context of a Monte Carlo experiment.

In higher dimensional problems, we require the use of simulation methods to approximate a conditional moment based upon the distribution of the underlying latent variable. This follows since in high dimensional problems the evaluation of the conditional expectation $E(\varepsilon|y)$ encounters the well known case of dimensionality. In discrete choice models where the stochastic terms are normally distributed, the use of generalised residuals as a calibration tool utilises simulation techniques similar to those used in the method of simulated scores. An example of this approach is the simulated EM (SEM) algorithm which approximates the conditional expectation $E(\varepsilon|y)$ by averaging repeated draws from the conditional distribution of u^* given y, and therefore requires draws from the truncated *multivariate* normal distribution.

14.5 Bootstrap confidence intervals

In a number of recent studies (see, for example, Horowitz,1994; Godfrey, 1998), analysts have begun to utilise bootstrap techniques to approximate the empirical distribution function of both estimators and test statistics, thereby facilitating the construction of confidence intervals which are not dependent upon potentially unreliable asymptotic arguments. To date we have demonstrated how estimates of transition frequencies may be generated using a number of alternative methods without recourse to the underlying distribution of the sample transition frequencies. Given that the distribution of these frequencies is unknown and is likely to exhibit considerable asymmetries, we describe below a parametric bootstrap technique to construct confidence intervals. Current extensions of this work include operationalising this technique.

Transition frequencies are generated according to the following process. Consider the aggregate frequency of movers between states j and j'.

$$T_{jj'} = \sum_{i=1}^{n} \mathbf{1}(u^*_{ijk}>0) \cdot \mathbf{1}(u^R_{ij'k}>0) \ \forall_{ij}, \neq k \in \Theta,$$

where $u^*_{ijk} = u^*_{ij} - u^*_{ijk}$. Since u^*_{ijk} are unobserved, estimated aggregate transition frequencies are given by $\hat{T}_{jj'} = \sum_{i=1}^{n} \mathbf{1}(\hat{y}_i=j) \cdot (\hat{y}^R_i=j')$.

Parametric bootstrap confidence intervals are constructed using the following algorithm.

1. Based upon an *estimation* sample of size n, and data pairs $\{y_i, \mathbf{x}_i\}$ we estimate the parameters of the discrete choice model $u^*_j = \mathbf{x}'\boldsymbol{\beta}_j + \varepsilon$, as explained in section 14.2.
2. Generate S samples of size n by resampling from the fitted model

$f(y, \hat{\boldsymbol{\beta}})$. For the sth element construct two $n \cdot J$ matrices, $\mathbf{u}^{*s}$ and $\mathbf{Y}^s$ with typical elements $\|\mathbf{u}^{*s}\| = \{u_{ij}^{s*} = \mathbf{x}_i'\hat{\boldsymbol{\beta}}_j + \varepsilon_{ij}^s\}$ and $\|\mathbf{Y}^s\| = \mathbf{1}(u_{ijk}^{s*} > 0)$ $\forall_{jk} \in \Theta$. The sth *bootstrap* sample comprises the data pairs $\{y_i^s, \mathbf{x}_i\}$ where $y_i^s = \max(u_{ij}^{*s}, \forall_j \in \Theta)$.

3. Given $\{y_i^s, \mathbf{x}_i\}$ estimate the sth bootstrap parameters $\hat{\boldsymbol{\beta}}^s(\hat{\boldsymbol{\beta}})$. Dependent upon the structure of the transition estimator, we then construct $\hat{\mathbf{Y}}^s$.

4. Consider a counterfactual $\mathbf{x}_i^R \neq \mathbf{x}_i$ and construct the counterfactual analogues of $\hat{\mathbf{Y}}^s$, namely $\hat{\mathbf{Y}}^{sr}$.

5. Form the transition estimator $\hat{T}^s = \hat{\mathbf{Y}}^{s\prime}\hat{\mathbf{Y}}^{sR}$.

6. Each $\hat{T}^s$ will have J^2 'separate' transition cells. Let $\hat{T}_l^s(i)$ denote the ith ordered value for the lth cell. An estimate of the pth quantile of T is the $(S+1)p$th ordered value of $\hat{T}_l^s$. For $S = 1000$ the 95% bootstrap confidence interval is $P(T_{l(25)} \leq T_l \leq T_{l(975)}) = 0.95$.

14.6 Computational results

To compare the various transitions estimators covered in this paper, we propose initially to assess performance within the framework of a simulated sample design. By doing so we enjoy an element of control sufficient to highlight the conditions under which predicted transitions deviate from what we know is the true data-generating process. However, we recognise (as do Skeels and Vella, 1995) that Monte Carlo results based on such an approach are clearly design-specific, and may not relate directly to the sorts of economic problems most regularly confronted by applied researchers. We therefore present a second comparison where the simulated sample is replaced by a sample of UK micro-data on the labour market behaviour of married women.

Simulated Design

We simulate a binomial version of the general statistical design (14.1) which gives a (differenced) latent variable of the form $u_i^* = u_{i2}^* - u_{i1}^*$. This latent variable is assumed to depend linearly on a set of three characteristics $\mathbf{x}_i = (1, x_{2i}, x_{3i})'$ through the parameter vector $\boldsymbol{\beta} = [\beta_1, 1, -1]$ to give a latent relationship of the form

$$u_i^* = \mathbf{x}_i'\boldsymbol{\beta} + \varepsilon_i \qquad (14.26)$$

$$= \beta_1 + x_{2i} - x_{3i} + \varepsilon_i,$$

where $x_{2i} \sim N(0,1)$, $x_{3i} \sim U(-1,1)$ and ε_i is distributed logistic with mean 0 and variance $\pi^2/3$. The binomial indicator variable y_i relates to (14.26) through the mapping $y_i = 1 + \mathbf{1}(x_i'\boldsymbol{\beta} + \varepsilon_i > 0)$. By adjusting the value of the constant term (β_1) in (14.26) we are able to control the probability of observing $y_i = 1$ or 2. We consider two cases: a *balanced design* for which $\Pr(y_i = 1) = 0.5$ and an *unbalanced design* for which $\Pr(y_i = 1) = 0.75$.[6]

We examine transitions following an impact on x_{2i}. For the simulated design, we predict transitions once x_{2i} is superceded by x_{2i}^R, where

$$x_{2i}^R = x_{2i} + z.(U[-1,1] + \Delta). \tag{14.27}$$

The parameters z and Δ in (14.27) control, respectively, the scale and the direction of the impact on x_{2i}. The larger is z, the larger is the scale of the impact. If $\Delta = +1(-1)$ the impact is entirely positive (negative), whereas for $\Delta = 0$ the impact is balanced.

Monte Carlo results for this experimental design are reported in Tables 14.1 (for the balanced design) and Table 14.2 (for the unbalanced design). The sample size is set at $n = 1000$. We generate 5,000 replications of ε_i (for fixed $\mathbf{x}_i$) and cumulate transitions matrices following impacts of the form $z = 3$, $\Delta \in (-1,0,1)$. We report in each table the true frequencies P_j for states $j = \{1,2\}$, the true transitions frequencies $P_{(j\ k)}$ from state j to k, for $j,k = \{1,2\}$, and the performance of six transition estimators given below and evaluate $E[T_v - T]/T$ where T is the known transition table and T_v is an estimated transition table with v indexing the set {MP, UT, CT, CE, SCD, MCD}. The six transitions estimators are:

	Transitions Estimators
MP:	averages T_{MP} over repeated estimates of $\hat{\boldsymbol{\beta}}$
UT:	averages T over repeated estimates of $\hat{\boldsymbol{\beta}}$
CT:	averages T over repeated estimates of $\hat{\boldsymbol{\beta}}$ conditioned on y_i
CE:	averages T_{CE} over repeated estimates of $\hat{\boldsymbol{\beta}}$
SCD:	averages T_{CD} over repeated estimates of $\hat{\boldsymbol{\beta}}$
MCD:	averages T_{CD} over repeated estimates of $\hat{\boldsymbol{\beta}}$ and e_i

For the balanced design, the results in Table 14.1 confirm a number of suspicions. Compared with the benchmarks, note first how unreliable is the maximum probability estimator T_{MP} for the majority of experimental designs. Even though the predicted state frequencies are broadly correct, we find a systematic over-prediction of off-diagonal transitions of up to 35% depending on the direction of the transition impact. For the majority of the alternative transitions estimators, Monte Carlo evidence indicates broad convergence to the true values regardless of Δ. The one exception to this general pattern is the transitions estimator T_{CE} calibrated on the

Table 14.1. *Monte Carlo simulations: balanced design*

	$P_{(1)}$	$P_{(2)}$	$P_{(1\ 1)}$	$P_{(2\ 1)}$	$P_{(1\ 2)}$	$P_{(2\ 2)}$
Negative transition impact: $\Delta = -1$						
True frequencies	495.05	504.95	495.05	318.68	0.00	186.27
% deviations (MP)	−1.07	1.05	−1.07	19.56	0.00	−30.61
% deviations (UT)	0.24	−0.23	0.24	−0.39	0.00	0.03
% deviations (CT)	0.24	−0.23	0.24	−0.45	0.00	0.14
% deviations (CE)	0.24	−0.23	0.24	−1.97	0.00	2.73
% deviations (SCD)	0.24	−0.23	0.24	−0.44	0.00	0.12
% deviations (MCD)	0.24	−0.23	0.24	−0.46	0.00	0.15
Balanced transition impact: $\Delta = 0$						
True frequencies	495.05	504.95	399.05	100.52	96.00	404.44
% deviations (MP)	−1.08	1.06	−9.68	31.19	34.64	−6.43
% deviations (UT)	0.23	−0.23	0.30	−0.32	−0.08	−0.20
% deviations (CT)	0.23	−0.23	0.41	−0.45	−0.53	−0.17
% deviations (CE)	0.23	−0.23	6.51	−31.10	−25.89	7.45
% deviations (SCD)	0.23	−0.23	0.43	−0.30	−0.61	−0.21
% deviations (MCD)	0.23	−0.23	0.39	−0.48	−0.44	−0.16
Positive transition impact: $\Delta = +1$						
True frequencies	495.05	504.95	179.89	0.00	315.15	504.95
% deviations (MP)	−0.98	0.97	−35.04	0.00	18.45	0.97
% deviations (UT)	0.30	−0.30	0.85	0.00	−0.01	−0.30
% deviations (CT)	0.30	−0.30	0.90	0.00	−0.03	−0.30
% deviations (CE)	0.30	−0.30	4.02	0.00	−1.82	−0.30
% deviations (SCD)	0.30	−0.30	0.62	0.00	0.12	−0.30
% deviations (MCD)	0.30	−0.30	0.88	0.00	−0.03	−0.30

generalised residual, which under-predicts off-diagonal transitions, particularly for $\Delta = 0$. The intuition for this result is that a calibration using $\bar{e}_i$ tends to place the pre-shock predicted probability well away from the critical level 0.5, and makes the exogenous shock less likely to force the post-shock probability across that boundary.

Table 14.2 reports similar results for the unbalanced design, with more severe biases relative to the true frequencies for estimators T_{MP} and T_{CE}. Notice that, when the design becomes unbalanced, the predicted state frequencies from T_{MP} deviate markedly from the truth. As noted by Windmeijer (1995), the use of the naive maximum probability rule tends to under-predict (over-predict) the sparse (dense) state owing to the wasteful nature of the metric which translates the predicted probability

Table 14.2. *Monte Carlo simulations: unbalanced design*

	$P_{(1)}$	$P_{(2)}$	$P_{(1\ 1)}$	$P_{(2\ 1)}$	$P_{(1\ 2)}$	$P_{(2\ 2)}$
Negative transition impact: $\Delta = -1$						
True frequencies	766.78	233.22	766.78	171.76	0.00	61.46
% deviations (MP)	13.52	−44.44	13.52	−32.53	0.00	−77.69
% deviations (UT)	−0.04	0.12	−0.04	−0.08	0.00	0.68
% deviations (CT)	−0.04	0.12	−0.04	−0.18	0.00	0.96
% deviations (CE)	−0.04	0.12	−0.04	0.84	0.00	−1.91
% deviations (SCD)	−0.04	0.12	−0.04	−0.49	0.00	1.80
% deviations (MCD)	−0.04	0.12	−0.04	−0.19	0.00	0.96
Balanced transition impact: $\Delta = 0$						
True frequencies	766.78	233.22	664.65	55.59	102.13	177.63
% deviations (MP)	13.51	−44.42	10.87	−23.13	30.72	−51.08
% deviations (UT)	−0.04	0.12	−0.02	−0.09	−0.17	0.19
% deviations (CT)	−0.04	0.12	−0.00	−0.14	−0.27	0.20
% deviations (CE)	−0.04	0.12	7.07	−16.72	−46.27	5.39
% deviations (SCD)	−0.04	0.12	0.03	−0.09	−0.45	0.19
% deviations (MCD)	−0.04	0.12	−0.00	0.02	−0.25	0.15
Positive transition impact: $\Delta = +1$						
True frequencies	766.78	233.22	377.21	0.00	389.57	233.22
% deviations (MP)	13.51	−44.42	−5.03	0.00	31.46	−44.42
% deviations (UT)	−0.04	0.13	0.24	0.00	−0.31	0.13
% deviations (CT)	−0.04	0.13	0.25	0.00	−0.32	0.13
% deviations (CE)	−0.04	0.13	5.03	0.00	−4.95	0.13
% deviations (SCD)	−0.04	0.13	0.23	0.00	−0.30	0.13
% deviations (MCD)	−0.04	0.13	0.24	0.00	−0.31	0.13

into a discrete state prediction. The under-prediction of off-diagonal transitions by T_{CE} is also manifestly clear, with errors of up to 46% for some designs. Again, all other measures perform well.

Repeating these simulations over different sample sizes and for transitions impacts of different magnitudes, the same overall patterns are observed.

Sample survey design

As a second experiment we replace the simulated sample with a sample of UK micro-data on the labour market behaviour of married women drawn from the 1993 UK Family Expenditure Survey (FES), a data source which contains detailed information on the labour supply behaviour, consumption choices and socio-demographic make-up of around 8,600 households. For our experiment we estimate a Logit model of labour force participation for a sample of 1,520 women living with employed partners. Non-working women form 21% of this sample, establishing this as an unbalanced experimental design. We condition the behavioural model on wage rates, net incomes, and the following socio-demographic characteristics: age of the woman, age of the youngest child, number of children, level of formal education and marital status (whether married or cohabiting). To generate state-specific net incomes as condition variables for the structural discrete choice model, we simulate tax liabilities and benefit receipts and total net incomes at 0 and 20 hours for each individual in our sample. Since wage rates are not observed in the FES for those not in employment, we base our simulations on wage rate estimates derived from an appropriately corrected reduced form equation.[7] Our estimated model is

$$Y_i^* = 0.87234 - 0.068540.AGE_i - 0.39758.TOTKIDS_i -$$
$$0.95481.DKID02_i - 0.46424.DKID34_i + 0.49823.DKID510_i +$$
$$0.65254.DKID11_i + 0.04746.EDUC_i + 0.59047.WAGE_i -$$
$$0.00236.NETINC0_i + 0.00840.NETINC20_i + u_i \qquad (14.28)$$

where u_i is logistic for $i = 1, \ldots, 1520$, and where AGE is the age of the woman (centred around 35); $TOTKIDS$ is the total number of children; $DKID02$, $DKID34$, $DKID510$ and $DKID11$ are indicator variables taking the value 1 if the youngest child is aged, respectively, between 0 and 2, between 3 and 4, between 5 and 10, and 11 or over (0 otherwise); $EDUC$ takes the value 1 if the woman undertook post-compulsory education (0 otherwise); $WAGE$ is the hourly wage (predicted for non-workers); and $NETINC0$ and $NETINC20$ are weekly net incomes that would be enjoyed if the woman were to work 0 and 20 hours, respectively.[8]

For the purposes of our experiment we take this model as a 'true' definition of the data-generating process which underpins labour market behaviour. Each transition estimator is then applied to an assessment of the likely behavioural responses to a hypothetical reform to the UK tax–benefit system. The reform we choose replaces all in-work and social assistance benefits with a basic income guarantee (set at the level of social assistance for a single person with additions for children). Tax allowances and social insurance contributions are abolished, and the graduated income tax structure is replaced by a single flat rate.[9] A behavioural simulation of the impact of this reform is generated by adjusting the incomes $NETINC0$ and $NETINC20$ for each individual in our sample to take account of the new basic income structure. Adjustments are again calculated using a detailed tax–benefit model. By feeding these post-reform simulated incomes back into our estimated model of labour force status, we can compare predicted

Table 14.3. *Simulated transitions: labour supply design*

	$P_{(1)}$	$P_{(2)}$	$P_{(1\ 1)}$	$P_{(2\ 1)}$	$P_{(1\ 2)}$	$P_{(2\ 2)}$
'True' frequencies	326	1,194	322	77	3	1,117
Absolute deviation						
Deviations (MP)	−245.00	245.00	−241.96	−16.49	−3.04	261.49
Deviations (UT)	0.00	0.00	0.00	0.00	0.00	0.00
Deviations (CT)	−0.54	0.54	−0.53	0.08	−0.00	0.46
Deviations (CE)	−0.54	0.54	2.50	−77.49	−0.304	78.02
Deviations (SCD)	−0.54	0.54	−0.58	−1.31	0.04	1.84
Deviations (MCD)	−0.54	0.54	−0.54	0.17	0.00	0.37
Percentage deviation						
% deviations (MP)	−75.15	20.52	−74.92	−21.28	−100.00	23.42
% deviations (UT)	0.00	0.00	0.00	0.00	0.00	0.00
% deviations (CT)	−0.16	0.04	−0.17	0.10	−0.08	0.04
% deviations (CE)	−0.16	0.04	0.77	−100.00	−100.00	6.99
% deviations (SCD)	−0.16	0.04	−0.18	−1.69	1.29	0.16
% deviations (MCD)	−0.16	0.04	−0.17	0.22	0.10	0.03

transitions with the 'true' transitions in a similar manner to the simulated design experiment.[10]

Table 14.3 reports the results of this simulation. According to the 'true' behavioural model, the reform induces just over 5% of the sample of working married women to withdraw from the labour market. However, the predicted transition from work to non-participation using the maximum probability transition simulator T_{MP} understates this movement by 21%. Note that we were unable to pick up any of the (admittedly small) proportion of women who moved from non-participation to employment. The Monte Carlo evidence on the performance of T_{CE} confirms previous suspicions that it is a relatively poor estimator of transitions from one state to another. In fact, precisely none of the sample is predicted to change labour market state following the basic income reform. The remaining estimators again perform reliably well. Comparing the estimators based on simulated residuals (SCD and MCD in Table 14.3), we slightly favour the estimator which averages over 10 conditional draws.

14.7 Conclusions

We focus in this paper on various estimators of transitions following an exogenous shock to the deterministic component of models of discrete choice. Concentrating on low-dimensional problems, we have been able to confirm the bias of naive discrete state predictors based on the standard maximum probability rule, and show that the problems associated with such predictors extend to the reliability of standard methods by which transitions are simulated. In a two-dimensional framework, explicit forms for transitions frequencies have been proposed. Their reliability has been confirmed using both simulated and sample-survey-based Monte Carlo designs, with particular emphasis on the prediction of labour market transitions. We exploit various methods by which discrete choice models may be calibrated to offer alternative transitions estimators which perform well in Monte Carlo simulations. An extension is suggested which offers a robust and unbiased alternative to transitions estimators in higher-dimensional problems.

This work reveals a considerable agenda for further research. An extension of the methods proposed here to higher-dimensional problems is a line of investigation currently being pursued by the authors. The robustness of transitions estimators to misspecification of either the mean equation or the distribution of the unobserved component of discrete choice will also be instructive. Finally, an analysis of the distributional properties of transitions estimators of various forms is warranted, in order that practical applications in the fields of labour economics, transport and bioassay can offer insight into the significance of predicted transitions.

Notes

We are grateful to Karim Abadir, Richard Blundell and Hashem Pesaran for valuable comments and suggestions. The financial support of the ESRC Centre for the Micro-Economic Analysis of Fiscal Policy at the Institute for Fiscal Studies is gratefully acknowledged. The usual disclaimer applies.
1 See Cramer (1997) for a review of this problem in both the social and natural sciences.
2 For notational simplicity, and without loss of generality, we restrict our attention to observable characteristics which are state invariant.
3 This is not the only measure of fit available; see Windmeijer (1995) for a useful comparison of goodness-of-fit measures in binary choice models.
4 This particular measure is misleading since it has no asymptotic justification. That is to say, $\text{plim} tr(1/n\ \mathbf{Y}'\hat{\mathbf{Y}}_{MP}) \neq 1$ even in the case of well-specified model.
5 If we assume, for example, that the disturbances ε_{ij} are bivariate normal, then the differenced disturbance $\varepsilon_i = \varepsilon_{i2} - \varepsilon_{i1}$ is univariate normal and $e_i = \phi[(y_i - 1) - \Phi_i]/[\Phi_i(1 - \Phi_i)]$, where $\phi_i = \phi(\mathbf{x}_i'\boldsymbol{\beta})$ and $\Phi_i = \Phi(\mathbf{x}_i'\boldsymbol{\beta})$; see Gourieroux and Montfort (1993).
6 For a similar Monte Carlo design, see Windmeijer (1995).

7 The wage equation is identified from the inclusion of demand-side (quarterly unemployment) and regional characteristics (vacancies and redundancies by region) as well as socio-demographic characteristics (quadratics and interactions between age, partner's age and education; age and number of children). Estimates are available from the authors on request. A problem with this approach is that it becomes difficult to correct the standard errors in the structural model for the inclusion of the generated wage rate term, since the simulated net income terms also depend (non-linearly) on the wage rate used. In the structural models, therefore, the standard errors remain uncorrected.

8 The values of *NETINCO* and *NETINC20* are simulated using the detailed tax-microsimulation program EBOR-TAX (details are available from the authors on request).

9 For a similar Monte Carlo design, see Windmeijer (1995). For further details of this particular experiment, see Duncan and Giles (1996).

10 For this experiment, we base the transition estimator for each draw on the 'true' parameters in (14.28).

Bibliography

Aaberge, R., Colombino, U. and Strøm, S., 1998. 'Social Evaluation of Individual Welfare Effects from Income Taxation: Empirical Evidence Based on Italian Data for Married Couples', Discussion Paper No. 230, Research Department, Statistics Norway

1999. 'Labour supply in Italy: an empirical analysis of joint household decisions with taxes and quantity constraints', *Journal of Applied Econometrics* 14, 403–22

Aaberge, R., Colombino U., Strøm, S. and Wennemo, T., 1998. 'Evaluating alternative tax reforms in Italy with a model of joint labour supply of married couples', *Structural Change and Economic Dynamics* 9, 415–33

Aaberge, R., Dagsvik, J. K. and Strøm, S.,1990. 'Labour Supply, Income Distribution and Excess Burden of Personal Income Taxation in Sweden', Report 22, Economic Research Programme on Taxation, Oslo

1995. 'Labour supply responses and welfare effects of tax reforms', *Scandinavian Journal of Economics* 4, 635–59

ABS (Australian Bureau of Statistics), 1987. '1984 Household Expenditure Survey: The Effects of Government Benefits and Taxes on Household Income', Cat. No. 6537.0, ABS, Canberra

1992. '1988–89 Household Expenditure Survey: The Effects of Government Benefits and Taxes on Household Income', Cat. No. 6537.0, ABS, Canberra

1994. 'Projections of the Populations of Australia, States and Territories': 1993–2041, Cat No. 3222.0, ABS, Canberra

1995. '1993–94 Household Expenditure Survey: Users' Guide', Cat No. 6527.0, ABS, Canberra

1996a. '1995 National Health Survey: Users' Guide', Cat No. 4363.0, ABS, Canberra.

1996b. 'Projections of the Populations of Australia, States and Territories: 1995–2051', Cat No. 3222.0, ABS, Canberra

1996c. 'Household Expenditure Survey: Detailed Expenditure Items', Cat No. 6535.0, ABS, Canberra

Accardo, J., 1998. 'Une Etude de Comptabilité Générationnelle pour la France en 1996', Document de travail de la Direction des Etudes et Synthèses Economiques, No. G9802, INSEE, Paris

Adler, H. and Wolfson, M., 1988. 'A prototype micro-macro link for the Canadian household sector', *Review of Income and Wealth* 4, December, 371–91

AIHW (Australian Institute of Health and Welfare), 1996. *Australia's Health 1996*, Canberra: AGPS

1997a. *First Report on National Health Priority Areas: Summary*, Canberra: Australian Institute of Health and Welfare

1997b. *First Report on National Health Priority Areas*, Canberra: Australian Institute of Health and Welfare

1998. *Australia's Health 1998*, Canberra: AGPS

Amemiya, T., 1981. 'Qualitative response models: a survey', *Journal of Economic Literature* 19, 483–536

Antcliff, S., 1993. 'An Introduction to DYNAMOD: A Dynamic Microsimulation Model', DYNAMOD Technical Paper No. 1, National Centre for Social and Economic Modelling, University of Canberra

Antcliff, S., Bracher, M., Gruskin, A., Hardin, A. and Kapuscinski, C., 1996. 'Development of DYNAMOD: 1993 and 1994', Dynamic Modelling Working Paper No. 1, National Centre for Social and Economic Modelling, Canberra

Arrufat, J. L. and Zabalza, A., 1986. 'Female labour supply with taxation, random preferences and optimization errors', *Econometrica* 1, 47–63

Atherton, T., Ben-Akiva, M., McFadden, D. and Train, K. E., 1990. 'Micro-simulation of local residential telephone demand under alternative service options and rate structures', in A. de Fontenay, M. H. Shugard and D. S. Sibley (eds), *Telecommunications Demand Modelling*, Amsterdam: North-Holland

Atkinson, A. B., 1996. 'Income distribution in Europe and the United States', *Oxford Review of Economic Policy* 13, Spring

Atkinson, A. B., Bourguignon, F. and Chiappori, P. A., 1988. 'What do we learn about tax reform from international comparisons? France and Britain', *European Economic Review* 32, 343–52

Atkinson, A. B., Bourguignon, F. and Morrison, C., 1992. *Empirical Studies of Earnings Mobility*, Philadelphia: Harwood Academic Publishers

Atkinson, A. B., Rainwater, L. and Smeeding, T. M., 1995. *Income Distribution in OECD Countries*, Paris: Organisation for Economic Co-operation and Development

Atkinson, A. B. and Sutherland, H., 1983. 'Hypothetical Families in the DHSS Tax–Benefit Model and Families in the Family Expenditure Survey 1980', TIDI Research Note, London School of Economics

Auerbach, A. J., Gokhale, J., and Kotlikoff, L., 1994. 'Generational accounting: a meaningful way to evaluate fiscal policy', *Journal of Economic Perspectives* 8(1), 73–94

Auerbach, A. J. and Slemrod J., 1997. 'The economic effects of the Tax Reform Act of 1986', *Journal of Economic Literature* XXXV (2), 589–632

Baekgaard, H. and Robinson, M., 1997. 'The Distributional Impact of Microeconomic Reform in Australia', paper presented to the 5th Nordic Microsimulation Conference, Stockholm, 9–10 June 1997

Bailey, D., Cohen, L. and Iams, H., 1998. 'Comparison of MIME's Between

CORSIM and SIPP-DPE', paper presented at the annual meeting of the Association for Public Policy and Management, New York City, 29 October 1998

Baker, P., McKay, S. and Symons, E., 1990. 'Simulation of Indirect Tax Reforms: The IFS Simulation Program for Indirect Taxation (SPIT)', IFS Working Paper No. W90/11, Institute for Fiscal Studies, London

Banks, J., Dilnot, A. and Low, H., 1994. *The Distribution of Wealth in the UK*, London: Institute for Fiscal Studies

Batey, P. W. J and Madden, M., 1981. 'Demographic-economic forecasting within and activity-commodity framework: some theoretical considerations and empirical results', *Environment and Planning* 13, 1067–83

Batey, P. W. J. and Weeks, M. J., 1989. 'The effects of household disaggregation in extended input–output models', pp. 119–33 in R. Miller, K. Polenske, and A. Rose (eds), *Frontiers of Input-Output Analysis*, Oxford University Press

Begg, D., Fischer, S. and Dornbusch, R., 1991. *Economics*, third edition, New York: McGraw-Hill Book Company Europe

Ben-Akiva, M. and Watanatada, T., 1981. 'Application of a continuous spatial choice logit model', in C. F. Manski and D. McFadden (eds), *Structural Analysis of Discrete Data with Econometric Applications*, Cambridge MA: MIT Press

Bennett, N., Jarvis, L., Rowlands, O., Singleton, N. and Haselden, L., 1996. *Living in Britain: Results from the 1994 General Household Survey*, London: HMSO

Bernardi, L. (ed.), 1995. 'Studi per un progetto di riforma del sistema tributario italiano: rapporto IRPEF', *Rivista di Diritto Finanziario e Scienza delle Finanze* 3, 435–590

Bingley, P. and Walker, I., 1995. 'Labour Supply, Unemployment and Participation in In-work Transfer Programmes', Discussion Paper, Institute for Fiscal Studies, London

Bishop, J. A., Chow, K. V. and Formby, J. P., 1994. 'Testing for marginal changes in income distributions with differences between Lorenz and concentration curves', *International Economic Review* 35(2), 479–88

Bishop, J. A., Chow, K. V., Formby, J. P. and Ho, C.-C., 1997. 'Did tax reform reduce actual US progressivity? Evidence from the Taxpayer Compliance Measurement Program', *International Tax and Public Finance* 4, 177–97

Blanchard, O. J. and Fischer, S., 1993. *Lectures on Macroeconomics*, Cambridge MA: MIT Press

Blanchet, D. and Chanut, J. M., 1998. 'Situations individuelles des retraités: un essai de projection par microsimulation', *Economie et Statistique* 315, 95–106

Blomquist, S., 1983. 'The effect of income taxation on the labour supply of married men in Sweden', *Journal of Public Economics* 2, 169–97

Blundell, R. W. and Preston, I. P., 1994. 'Income or Consumption in the Measurement of Inequality and Poverty?', IFS Working Paper No. W94/12, Institute for Fiscal Studies, London

1995. 'Income, expenditure and the living standards of UK households', *Fiscal Studies* 16(3), 40–54

Blundell, R., Meghir, C., Symons, E. and Walker, I., 1988. 'Labour supply specification and the empirical evaluation of tax reforms', *Journal of Public Economics,* July, 23–52

Bordt, M., Cameron, G. J., Gribble, S. F., Murphy, B. B., Rowe, G. T. and Wolfson, M. C., 1990. 'The social policy simulation database and model: an integrated tool for tax/transfer analysis', *Canadian Tax Journal* 38, 48–65

Bourguignon F., O'Donoghue C., Sastre-Descals J., Spadaro A. and Utili, F., 1997. 'Eur3: A Prototype European Tax-Benefit Model', DAE Working Paper, MU9703, Microsimulation Unit, Department of Applied Economics, University of Cambridge

    1998. 'A Technical Description of Eur3, a Prototype European Tax–Benefit Model', Microsimulation Unit Research Note MU/RN/25, Department of Applied Economics, University of Cambridge

Bradshaw, J., 1995. 'Simulating policies: an example in comparative method', in B. Palier (ed.), *Comparing Social Welfare Systems in Europe.* Paris: MIRE

Bradshaw, J., Ditch, J., Holmes, H. and Whiteford, P., 1993. *Support for Children: A Comparison of Arrangements in 15 Countries,* London: HMSO

Brungger, H., 1996. 'The Use of Purchasing Power Parities in International Comparisons', paper presented to the Expert Group on Household Income Statistics, Canberra

Brunner, J. K. and Petersen, H. G. (eds), 1990. *Simulation Models in Tax and Transfer Policy,* Frankfurt and New York: Campus Verlag

Budget Papers, 1996a. 'Statement 3 – Outlays', in *Budget Statements,* Budget Paper No. 1, Treasury, Commonwealth of Australia, August

    1996b. *Recognising Older Australians,* various Ministers, Commonwealth of Australia, August

    1997. 'Health and family services', in *Budget Statements,* Budget Paper No. 2, Treasury, Commonwealth of Australia, May

    1998a. 'Health and family services', in *Budget Statements,* Budget Paper No. 2, Treasury, Commonwealth of Australia, May

    1998b. 'Budget strategy and outlook', in *Budget Statements,* Budget Paper No. 1, Treasury, Commonwealth of Australia, May

Buhmann B., Rainwater, L., Schmaus, G. and Smeeding, T. M., 1988. 'Equivalence scales, well-being, inequality and poverty: sensitivity estimates across ten countries using the Luxembourg Income Study (LIS) database', *Review of Income and Wealth* 34, 115–42

Burgess, R. and Stern, N., 1993. 'Taxation and development', *Journal of Economic Literature* 31(2), 762–830

Burtless, G. and Hausman, J. A., 1978. 'The effects of taxation on labour supply', *Journal of Political Economy* 6, 1103–30

Caldwell, S. B., 1993. 'CORSIM 2.0 Model Documentation', unpublished paper, Cornell University, 28 January 1993, Preliminary Draft #5

Caldwell, S. B., 1997, 'Recent Use of Dynamic Microsimulation Models', paper presented at the Symposium on Microsimulation in Government Policy Development, Department of Finance, Ottawa, 25 July 1997

Caldwell, S. B., Favreault, M., Gantman, A., Gokhale, J., Kotlikoff, L. J. and

Johnson, T., 1999. 'Social Security's treatment of post-war Americans', in J. Poterba (ed.), *Tax Policy and the Economy 13*, Cambridge MA: National Bureau of Economic Research/ MIT Press

Caldwell, S. B., Gantman, A., Gokhale, J., Johnson, T. and Kotlikoff, L. J. (forthcoming). 'Projecting Social Security's finances and its treatment of postwar Americans', in A. J. Auerbach and R. D. Lee (eds), *Demographic Change and Fiscal Policy,* Cambridge University Press

Callan, T. and Sutherland, H., 1997. 'The impact of comparable policies in European countries: microsimulation approaches', *European Economic Review* 41(3–5), 627–33

Cameron, G. and Wolfson, M., 1994. 'Missing Transfers: Adjusting Household Incomes for Noncash Benefits', paper prepared for the 23rd General Conference of the International Association of Income and Wealth, August 1994

Chénard, D., 1995. '*DYNACAN 1.0,*' unpublished paper, Microsimulation Unit, Division of the Chief Actuary, Office of the Superintendent of Financial Institutions, Ottawa

Citro, C. F. and Hanushek, E. A. (eds), 1991. *Improving Information for Social Policy Decisions: The Uses of Microsimulation Modeling*, Washington DC: National Academy Press

Clare, R. and Tulpule, A., 1994. *Australia's Ageing Society*, EPAC Background Paper No. 37, Canberra: AGPS

Clasen, J., 1997. 'Social insurance in Germany – dismantling or reconstruction?', in J. Clasen (ed.), *Social Insurance in Europe*, Bristol: Policy Press

Colin, C. and Ralle, P., 1998. 'Evolution des inégalités de salaire : un essai de prospective par microsimulation', 15èmes journées de Microéconomie Appliquée, Pointe-à-Pitre

Colombino, U., 1985: 'A model of married women labour supply with systematic and random disequilibrium components', *Ricerche Economiche* 2, 165–79
    1998. 'Evaluating the effects of new telephone tariffs on residential users' demand and welfare. A model for Italy', *Information Economics and Policy*, 3, 283–303

Colombino, U. and Del Boca, D., 1990. 'The effect of taxes on labor supply in Italy', *Journal of Human Resources* 3, 390–414

Colombino, U. and Zabalza, A., 1982. 'Labour Supply and Quantity Constraints: Results on Female Participation and Hours in Italy', CLE Discussion Paper No. 125, London School of Economics

Commissione di Indagine sulla Povertà, 1985. *La povertà in Italia*, Roma: Presidenza del Consiglio dei Ministri

Commissione per l'analisi delle compatibilità macroeconomiche della spesa sociale, 1997. *Relazione finale*, Roma: Presidenza del Consiglio dei Ministri

Coulter, F. A. E., Cowell, F. A. and Jenkins, S. P., 1992. 'Equivalence scale relativities and the extent of inequality and poverty', *Economic Journal* 102 (414), 1067–82

Cramer, J., 1991. *The Logit Model*, London: Edward Arnold
    1997. 'Predictive Performance in the Binary Logit Model', unpublished paper, Tinbergen Institute, the Netherlands

Dagsvik, J. K., 1994. 'Discrete and continuous choice, max-stable processes and independence from irrelevant attributes', *Econometrica* 4, 1179–1205

Davidson, R. and Duclos, J. Y., 1997. 'Statistical inference for the measurement of the incidence of taxes and transfers', *Econometrica*, 65(6), 1453–65

Davies, E. H., Dilnot, A. W., Stark, G. K. and Webb, S. J., 1987. 'The IFS Tax and Benefit Model', IFS Working Paper No. W87/9, Institute for Fiscal Studies, London

Davies, H. and Joshi, H., 1994. 'Sex, sharing and the distribution of income', *Journal of Social Policy* 23, 301–40

Decoster, A., Delhaye, P. and Van Camp, G., 1996. 'User's Guide for ASTER: A Microsimulation Model for Indirect Taxes', Centrum voor Economische Studien, Catholic University of Louvain

Decoster, A., Schokkaert, E. and Van Camp, G. 1997. 'Horizontal neutrality and vertical redistribution with indirect taxes', pp. 219–39 in S. Zandvakili (ed.), *Inequality and Taxation*, Greenwich CT: JAI Press

Decoster, A., Standaert, I., Valenduc, C. and Van Camp, G., 1998. *Evaluation of Simultaneous Reforms in Personal Income Taxes and Indirect Taxes: Belgium 1988–1993*, Final Report Project PE/VA/07, Brussels: DWTC

   2000. 'What Makes Personal Income Taxes Progressive? The Case of Belgium', Discussion Paper Series DPS 00-08, Center for Economic Studies, Louvain

De Lathouwer, L., 1996. 'Microsimulation in comparative social policy analysis: a case-study of unemployment schemes in Belgium and the Netherlands', in A. Harding (ed.)(1996)

Del Boca, D. and Flinn, C. J., 1984. 'Self-reported reservation wages and the labour market participation decision', *Ricerche Economiche* 3, 363–83

Department of Health and Family Services, 1996a. *Annual Report 1995–96*, Canberra: AGPS

   1996b. *Expenditure and Prescriptions: Twelve Months to 30 June 1996*, Canberra: Pharmaceutical Benefits Analysis Section

   1997. *Expenditure and Prescriptions: Twelve Months to 30 June 1997*, Canberra: Analysis Section, Pharmaceutical Benefits Branch

Department of Human Services and Health, 1994. *Better Health Outcomes for Australians: National Goals, Targets and Strategies for Better Health Outcomes into the Next Century*, Canberra: AGPS

Deville, J. and Särndal, C., 1992. 'Calibration estimators in survey sampling', *Journal of American Statistics* 87, 367–82

Deville, J. and Sautory, O., 1993. 'Generalised raking procedures in survey sampling', *Journal of American Statistics* 88, 1013–20

Dewees, D. N., 1979. 'Estimating the time costs of highway congestion', *Econometrica* 47(6), 1499–1512

Dickens, W. and Lundberg, S., 1993. 'Hours restrictions and labour supply', *International Economic Review* 1, 169–91

Dilnot, A., Kay, J. and Keen, M. J., 1990. 'Allocating taxes to households: a methodology', *Oxford Economic Papers* 42(1), 210–30

Dinh, Q. C., 1994. 'La population de la France à l'horizon 2050', *Economie et Statistique* 274, 7–32

Dore, O. and Levy, J., 1997. 'Generational Accounting for France', IMF Working Paper No. SM/97/250, International Monetary Fund, Washington DC

Drettakis, M. G., 1997. 'Greece has the lowest number of cars and the largest number of car accident casualties', *Kyriakatiki Avgi*, 16 February 1997 (in Greek)

Duncan, A. and Giles, C., 1996. 'Labour supply incentives and recent family credit reforms', *Economic Journal* 106, 142–155

Duncan, A. and Weeks, M., 1997. 'Non Nested Models of Labour Supply with Discrete Choices', unpublished paper, Department of Applied Economics, University of Cambridge

Ertl, H., 1998. 'Towards Sustainable Development: Measuring and Monitoring Sustainable Economic Welfare', Statistics Canada, National Accounts and Analytical Studies, SNA, Input–Output Division

Eurostat, 1996. *Comparison in Real Terms of the Aggregates of ESA: Results for 1994*, Luxembourg: Office for Official Publications of the European Communities

  1997. *Basic Statistics of the European Union, 33rd edition, 1996*, Luxembourg: Office for Official Publications of the European Communities

Evans, M., 1995. 'Out for the Count: The Incomes of the Non-household Population and the Effect of their Exclusion from National Income Profiles', Welfare State Programme Discussion Paper No. WSP/111, London School of Economics

  1996. 'Families on the Dole in Britain, France and Germany', Welfare State Programme Discussion Paper No. 118, London School of Economics

Falkingham, J. and Lessof, C., 1991. 'LIFEMOD – The Formative Years', Welfare State Programme Research Note 24, London School of Economics

  1992. 'Playing God: or LIFEMOD – the construction of a dynamic micro-simulation model', in R. Hancock and H. Sutherland (eds) (1992)

Family Expenditure Survey, various dates. *Family Expenditure Survey*, London: Central Statistical Office

Favreault, M., 1998. 'Whose Safety Net? Social Security, Life-Course Processes, and Inequality in the United States', unpublished PhD dissertation, Cornell University

Flemming, J. S., 1987. 'Debt and taxes in war and peace: the case of a small open economy', in M. J. Boskin, J. S. Flemming and S. Gorini (eds), *Private Saving and Public Debt*, Oxford: Basil Blackwell

Formby, J. P., Seaks, T. G. and Smith, W. J., 1989. 'On the measurement and trend of inequality: a reconsideration', *American Economic Review* 79(1), 256–64

Formby, J. P., Thistle, P. D., and Smith, W. J., 1990. 'The average tax burden and the welfare implications of global tax progressivity', *Public Finance Quarterly* 18, 3–24

Fortin, B., Truchon, M. and Beauséjour, L., 1993. 'On reforming the welfare system: workfare meets the negative income tax', *Journal of Public Economics* 1, 119–51

Friedman, M., 1957. *A Theory of the Consumption Function*, Princeton University Press

Fuchs, V., 1984. 'Though much is taken: reflections on aging, health and medical care', *Millbank Memorial Fund Quarterly* 62(2), 143–55

Gardiner K, Hills, J., Falkingham, J., Lechene, V. and Sutherland, H., 1995. 'The Effects of Differences in Housing and Health Care Systems on International Comparisons of Income Distribution, Welfare State Programme Discussion Paper WSP/110, London School of Economics

Georgakopoulos, T. A., 1991. *Indirect Tax Harmonisation in Greece and the Value Added Tax: Effects on the Greek Economy*, Piraeus: Stamoulis (in Greek)

Godfrey, L. G., 1998. 'Tests of non-nested regression models: small sample adjustments and Monte Carlo evidence', *Journal of Econometrics* 67, 395–411

Goss, J., Eckermann, S., Pinyopusarerk, M. and Wen, X., 1994. 'Economic Perspectives on the Health Impact of the Aging of the Australian Population in the 21st Century', paper presented at the Seventh National Conference of the Australian National University, Canberra, 23 September

Gourieroux, C. and Montfort, A., 1993. 'Simulation-based inference: a survey with special reference to panel data models', *Journal of Econometrics* 59, 5–33

Gourieroux, C., Montfort, A., Renault, E. and Trognon, A., 1987. 'Generalised residuals', *Journal of Econometrics* 34, 5–32

Government Actuary Department, 1994. *Occupational Pension Schemes 1991*, London: HMSO

Granger, C. W. J. and Pesaran, M. H., 1999. 'Economic and Statistical Measures of Forecast Accuracy', DAE Working Paper No. 9910, Department of Applied Economics, University of Cambridge

Gupta, A. and Kaipur, V. (eds), (forthcoming). *Microsimulation in Government Policy and Forecasting*, Amsterdam: North Holland

Hagenaars, A., de Vos, K., and Zaidi, M. A., 1994. *Poverty Statistics in the Late 1980s: Research Based on Micro Data*, Luxembourg: Office for Official Publications of the European Communities

Ham, J. 1982. 'Estimation of a labour supply model with censoring due to unemployment and underemployment', *Review of Economic Studies* 3, 335–54

Hancock, R., 1998. 'Can housing wealth alleviate poverty among Britain's older population?' *Fiscal Studies* 19, August
   2000. 'Estimating property values and housing wealth for older owner-occupiers', *Housing Studies*, forthcoming

Hancock, R., Mallender, J. and Pudney, S., 1992. 'Constructing a computer model for simulating the future distribution of pensioners' incomes for Great Britain', in R. Hancock and H. Sutherland (eds) (1992)

Hancock, R. and Sutherland, H., 1997. *Costs and Distributional Effects of Increasing the Basic State Pension*, London: Age Concern England

Hancock, R. and Sutherland, H. (eds), 1992. *Microsimulation Models for Public Policy Analysis: New Frontiers*, STICERD Occasional Paper 17, London: London School of Economics

Hancock, R. and Wright, F., (1999). 'Older couples and long-term care: the financial implications of one spouse entering private or voluntary residential or nursing home care', *Ageing and Society*, 19(2), 209–37

Harding, A., 1984. 'Who Benefits? The Australian Welfare State and Redistribution', SWRC Reports and Proceedings No. 45, Social Welfare Research Centre, University of New South Wales, Sydney

1990. 'Dynamic Microsimulation Models: Problems and Prospects', Welfare State Programme Discussion Paper WSP/48, STICERD, London School of Economics

1993. 'Lifetime income distribution and redistribution: applications of a micro-simulation model', *Contributions to Economic Analysis 221*, Amsterdam: North-Holland

1996. 'Introduction and overview', chapter 1 in A. Harding (ed.) (1996)

1997. 'The suffering middle: trends in income inequality in Australia, 1982 to 1993–94', *Australian Economic Review* 30(4), 341–58

Harding, A. (ed.), 1996. *Microsimulation and Public Policy*, Amsterdam: North Holland

Harding, A. and Percival, R., 1997. 'Who Smokes Now? Changing Patterns of Expenditure on Tobacco Products in Australia, 1975–76 to 1993–94', Discussion Paper No. 24, National Centre for Social and Economic Modelling, University of Canberra

Harris, G., 1998a. *Assessing the Robustness of Income Distribution Statistics*, Papers and Final Report of the Second Meeting on Household Income Statistics, Voorburg, The Netherlands, 9–11 March, Canberra Group: Expert Group on Household Income Statistics

1998b. *Income Distribution Data for the United Kingdom: Robustness Assessment Report*, Papers and Final Report of the Second Meeting on Household Income Statistics, Voorburg, The Netherlands, 9–11 March, Canberra Group: Expert Group on Household Income Statistics

Harrison, W. J., Pell, C., Jones, P. M. and Ashton, H., 1986. 'Some advances in model design developed for the practical assessment of road pricing in Hong-Kong', *Transportation Research* 20A(2), 135–44

Hausman, J. A., 1980. 'The effects of wages, taxes and fixed costs on women's labour force participation, *Journal of Public Economics* 1, 161–92

1981. 'Labor supply', in H. Aaron and J. Pechman (eds), *How Taxes Affect Behavior*, Washington, D.C.: Brookings Institution

1985. 'The econometrics of non-linear budget sets', *Econometrica* 6, 1255–82

Hausman, J. A. and Ruud, P., 1984. 'Family labor supply with taxes', *American Economic Review* 1, 242–53

Hausman, J. and Wise, D., 1978. 'A conditional probit model for qualitative choice: discrete decisions recognising interdependence and heterogeneous prefer-ences', *Econometrica* 46, 403–26

Haveman, R., 1994. 'Should generational accounts replace public budgets and deficits?', *Journal of Economic Perspectives* 8(1), 95–111

Heckman, J., 1974. 'Shadow prices, market wages and labor supply', *Econometrica* 4, 679–94

1981. 'Heterogeneity and state dependence', pp. 91–139 in S. Rosen (ed), *Studies in Labour Markets*, University of Chicago Press

Heckman, J. and Smith, J., 1995. 'Assessing the case for social experiments', *Journal of Economic Perspectives* 9(2), 85–110

HM Statistical Office, 1993. *Paying for Better Motorways*, CM 2200, London: HMSO

Horowitz, J. L., 1994. 'Bootstrap-based critical values for the information matrix test', *Journal of Econometrics* 61, 149–71

House of Commons, 1995. *Urban Road Pricing*, Third Report of the Transport Committee, Session 1994–95, Cm 104–1, London: HMSO

Ilmakunnas, S. and Pudney, S., 1990. 'A model of female labour supply in the presence of hours restrictions', *Journal of Public Economics* 2, 183–210

Immervoll, H., O'Donoghue, C. and Sutherland, H., 1999. 'An Introduction to EUROMOD', EUROMOD Working Paper EM0/99, Microsimulation Unit, Department of Applied Economics, University of Cambridge

Industry Commission, 1996. *The Pharmaceutical Industry*, Vol. I, Canberra: AGPS

ISPE, 1997. 'La Manovra di Bilancio del Governo per il 1998: Effetti Macro e Microeconomici', Documenti di lavoro No. 68/97

Jenkins, S. P., 1991. 'Poverty measurement and the within-household distribution: agenda for action', *Journal of Social Policy* 20(4), 457–83

1994. 'The Within-Household Distribution and Why it Matters: an Economist's Perspective', Department of Economics Discussion Paper No. 94–05, University of Wales Swansea

Jenkins, S. P. and Cowell, F. A., 1994. 'Parametric equivalence scales and scale relativities', *Economic Journal* 104 (425) 891–900

Johnson, A. and Webb, S., 1993. 'Explaining the growth in UK income inequality: 1979–1988', *Economic Journal* 103, 429–35

Johnson, G. and Layard, R., 1986. 'The natural rate of unemployment: explanation and policy', in O. Ashenfelter and R. Layard (eds), *Handbook of Labour Economics*, Amsterdam: North-Holland

Johnson, P.A. and Rake, K., 1998. 'Comparative social policy research in Europe', *Social Policy Review* 10, 257–78

Joseph Rowntree Foundation, 1996. *Meeting the Costs of Continuing Care: Report and Recommendations*, York: Joseph Rowntree Foundation

Kakwani, N. C., 1977. 'Measurement of tax progressivity: an international comparison', *Economic Journal* 87, 71–80

1980. *Income, Inequality and Poverty: Methods of Estimation and Policy Applications*, Oxford University Press

Kaplanoglou, G., 1999. 'Distributional and Efficiency Aspects of the Greek Indirect Tax System: a Microsimulation Analysis', University of Cambridge, unpublished PhD thesis

Kapteyn, A., Kooreman, P. and van Soest, A., 1990. 'Quantity rationing and concavity in a flexible household labour supply model', *Review of Economics and Statistics* 1, 55–62

Karageorgas, D., 1973. 'The distribution of tax burden by income groups in Greece', *Economic Journal* 83(330), 436–48

Karageorgas, D. and Pakos, T. B., 1988. 'The distribution of the tax burden in Greece: 1982', in Institute for Regional Development PASKE (eds), *In Honour of Saki Karageorga*, Athens (in Greek)

Keane, M. P., 1997. 'Modeling heterogeneity and state dependence in consumer choice behavior', *Journal of Business & Economic Statistics* 15(3), July

Kelmsley W., Redpath, R. and Holmes, M., 1980. *Family Expenditure Survey Handbook*, London: Social Survey Division, OPCS

Laing and Buisson, 1997. *Care of Elderly People: Market Survey*, London: Laing and Buisson Ltd

Lambert, P., 1993. *The Distribution and Redistribution of Income, A Mathematical Analysis*, second edition, Manchester: Manchester University Press

Lambert, S., Percival, R., Schofield, D. and Paul, S., 1994. 'An Introduction to STINMOD: A Static Microsimulation Model', STINMOD Technical Paper No. 1, National Centre for Social and Economic Modelling, University of Canberra

Lee, C. and Pashardes, P., 1988. *Who Pays Indirect Taxes?*, IFS Report Series No. 32, London: Institute for Fiscal Studies

Lenseigne, F. and Ricordeau, P., 1997. 'Assurance maladie un bilan par génération', *Economie et Statistique* 307, 59–76

Lewis, G. H. and Michel, R. C. (eds), 1990. *Microsimulation Techniques for Tax and Transfer Analysis*, Washington DC: Urban Institute Press

Lillard, L. and Willis, R., 1978. 'Dynamic aspects of earnings mobility', *Econometrica* 46, 985–1012

Lockwood, B., 1988. 'Tax Incidence, Market Power and Bargaining Structure', unpublished paper, Birbeck College, London

Lopez, A. and Murray, C. (eds), 1996. *The Global Burden of Disease: A Comprehensive Assessment of Mortality and Disability from Diseases, Injuries, and Risk Factors in 1990 and Projected to 2020*, Boston: Harvard School of Public Health

MaCurdy, T., Green, D. and Paarsch, H., 1990. 'Assessing empirical approaches for analyzing taxes and labor supply', *Journal of Human Resources* 3, 415–90

McFadden, D., 1978. 'Modeling the choice of residential location', in A. Karlquist, L. Lundquist, F. Snickard and J. J. Weilbull (eds), *Spatial Interaction Theory and Planning Models*, Amsterdam, North-Holland

MacKinnon, J. G. and White, H., 1985. 'Some heteroscedasticity-consistent matrix estimators with improved finite sample properties', *Journal of Econometrics* 29 (3), 305–25

McLure, C. E., Jr. and Zodrow, G. R., 1987. 'Treasury I and the Tax Reform Act of 1986: the economics and politics of tax reform', *Journal of Economic Perspectives* 1(1), 37–58

Malmberg, G. and Fischer, P. A., 1997. 'Immobility and Insider Advantages: Empirical Evidence from Sweden', University of the Bundeswehr Hamburg, Europa-Kolleg Hamburg, Workshop on Stay or Go, 5 December

Martin, C., Hobbs, M., Armstrong, B. and de Klerk, N., 1989. 'Trends in the incidence of myocardial infarction in Western Australia between 1971 and 1982', *American Journal of Epidemiology* 139(4), 655–68

Merz, J., 1991. 'Microsimulation – a survey of principles, developments and applications', *International Journal of Forecasting* 7(1), 77–104

Modigliani, F. and Brumberg, R., 1954. 'Utility analysis and the consumption function: an Interpretation of cross-section data', in K. Kurihara (ed.), *Post-Keynesian Economics*, New Brunswick: Rutgers University Press

Moffit, R., 1984. 'The estimation of a joint wage-hours labour supply model', *Journal of Labor Economics* 2, 550–66

　　1986. 'The econometrics of piecewise-linear budget constraints', *Journal of Business and Economic Statistics* 3, 317–28

Morrison, R. J., 1997. 'DYNACAN, The Canada Pension Plan Policy Model: Demographic and Earnings Components', Proceedings of the Micro-simulation Section at the International Conference on Information Theory, Combinatorics, and Statistics, Portland, Maine, July

Musgrave, R. A., 1959. *The Theory of Public Finance*, New York: McGraw-Hill

Musgrave, R. A. and Thin, T., 1948. 'Income tax progression, 1929–48', *Journal of Political Economy* 56, 498–514

National Commission of Audit, 1996. *National Commission of Audit: Report to the Commonwealth Government*, Canberra: AGPS

National Statistical Service of Greece, 1992. *Public Finance Statistics 1988–1989*, T: 62 Public Finance, Athens

　　1994. Data: Family Expenditure Survey 1987/88 [on computer tape], Athens

Neufeld, C., 1997. 'Alignment and Variance Reduction in DYNACAN', Proceedings of the Microsimulation Section at the International Conference on Information Theory, Combinatorics, and Statistics, Portland, Maine, July

Newbery, D. M., 1988. 'Charging for roads', *Research Observer* 3(2), 119–38

　　1995. *Reforming Road Taxation*, Group Public Policy, United Kingdom: Automobile Association

　　1996. 'Pricing and congestion: economic principles relevant to pricing roads', in T. Jenkinson (ed.), *Readings in Microeconomics*, Oxford University Press

Nickell, S., 1982. 'The determinants of occupational success in Britain', *Review of Economic Studies* 49, 43–53

Nuttall, S. R., Blackwood, R. J. L., Bussell, B. M. H., Cliff, J. P., Cornall, M. J., Cowley, A., Glatenby, P. L. and Webber, J. M., 1993. 'Financing long-term care in Great Britain', *Journal of the Institute of Actuaries* 121 (1), 1–68

O'Donoghue, C., 1998. 'Simulating the Irish Tax-Transfer System in Eur6', Microsimulation Unit Research Note MU/RN/26, Department of Applied Economics, University of Cambridge

OECD, 1994. *Main Economic Indicators*, Paris: Organisation for Economic Cooperation and Development (OECD)

　　1996. *Social Expenditure Statistics of OECD Member Countries*, Paris: OECD

　　1997. *National Accounts*, Vol. II, Paris: OECD

OPCS, 1992. *Retirement and Retirement Plans*, London: HMSO

　　1996. *Living in Britain, Results for the 1994 GHS*, London: HMSO

Orcutt, G., Greenberg, M., Korbel, J., and Rivlin, A., 1961. *Microanalysis of Socioeconomic Systems: A Simulation Study*, New York: Harper and Row

Orcutt, G., Merz, J. and Quinke, H. (eds), 1986. *Microanalytic Simulation Models to Support Social and Financial Policy*, Amsterdam: North Holland

Ordover, J. A. and Phelps, E. S., 1979. 'The concept of optimal taxation in the overlapping-generations model of capital and wealth', *Journal of Public Economics* 12(1), 1–26

Pashardes, P., 1988. 'On the Interpretation and Estimation of Equivalence Scales from Household Survey Data', IFS Working Paper No. 88/1, Institute for Fiscal Studies, London

Pelé, L. P. and Ralle, P., 1997. 'Age de la retraite: les aspects incitatifs du régime général', Document de travail de la Direction des Etudes et Synthèses Economiques, No. G9718, INSEE, Paris

Percival, R. and Schofield, D., 1995. 'Modelling Australian Public Health Expenditure', STINMOD Technical Paper No. 8, National Centre for Social and Economic Modelling, University of Canberra

Podger, A., 1998. 'Our Aging Population: Implications for Policy Planning', paper prepared for the seminar 'Where Are We Heading along the Ageing Public/Private Pathway? Social, Health and Economic Challenge', Committee for Economic Development of Australia and National Ageing Research Institute, Melbourne, 21 April

Poole, E., 1993. 'A Guide to Using the Input-Output Model of Statistics Canada', Statistics Canada, National Accounts and Analytical Studies, SNA, Input Output Division, 58–E

Porta, P-L. and Saraceno, P., 1997. *The Mandatory Pension System in Italy*, Country Report of the Phare-ACE Project P95-2139-R, No. 37, Milan: Instituto per la Ricerca Sociale

Propper, C., 1992. 'A cell-based approach to modelling public expenditure', in R. Hancock and H. Sutherland (eds) (1992)

Provopoulos, G. A., 1979. 'The distribution of fiscal burdens and benefits by income groups in Greece', *Greek Economic Review* 1(1), 77–99

Pudney, S., 1991. 'Dynamic Simulation of Pensioners' Incomes: Methodological Issues and a Design for a Computer Model for Great Britain', Microsimulation Unit Working Paper MU9201, Department of Applied Economics, University of Cambridge

Pudney, S. and Sutherland, H., 1992. 'The statistical reliability of microsimulation estimates: results for a UK Tax–benefit model', in R. Hancock and H. Sutherland (eds) (1992)

1994. 'How reliable are microsimulation results? An analysis of the role of sampling error in a UK tax–benefit model', *Journal of Public Economics* 53, 327–65

1996. 'Statistical reliability in microsimulation models with econometrically-estimated behavioural responses', in A. Harding (ed.) (1996)

Rake, K., 1998. 'Ageing and Inequality: Older Women and Men in the British, French and German Welfare States', unpublished doctoral thesis, University of Oxford

Redmond, G., Sutherland, H. and Wilson, M. (1996). 'POLIMOD: an Outline', Microsimulation Unit Research Note MU/RN/19, Department of Applied Economics, University of Cambridge

1998. *The Arithmetic of Tax and Social Security Reform: A User's Guide to Microsimulation Methods and Analysis*, DAE Occasional Paper No. 64, Cambridge: Cambridge University Press

Rettore, E., 1990. 'Institutional Constraints on Working Week Length and Female Labour Supply', FOLA Project, Research Report No. 20, Department of Statistics, University of Padua

Reynolds, M. and Smolensky, E., 1977. *Public Expenditures, Taxes, and the Distribution of Income: The United States, 1950, 1961, 1970*, University of Wisconsin, Institute for Research on Poverty monograph series, New York: Academic Press

Richards, E., Wilsdon, T. and Lyons, S., 1996. *Paying for Long-Term Care*, London: Institute for Public Policy Research

Rizzi, D., 1995. 'Effetti distributivi delle proposte di modifica dell' Irpef contenute nel Libro Bianco', *Rivista di diritto finanziario e scienza delle finanze* 3, 571–88

Rossi, N. (ed.), 1996. *Competizione e giustizia sociale, Terzo Rapporto CNEL sulla distribuzione e redistribuzione del reddito in Italia*, Bologna: Il Mulino

Rothman, G., 1997. *Aggregate Analyses of Policies for Accessing Superannuation Accumulations*, Retirement Income Modelling Task Force, Treasury, Canberra, June

   1998. *Projection of Key Aggregates for Australia's Aged – Government Outlays, Financial Assets and Incomes*, Retirement Income Modelling Task Force, Treasury, Canberra, June

Rowe, G. and Wolfson, M., 1998. *Public Pension Reforms: Canadian Analyses Based on the Life Paths Generational Accounting Framework*, Ottawa: Statistics Canada

Royal Commission on Long-term Care, 1999. *With Respect to Old Age: Long-term Care – Rights and Responsibilities*, Cm4192, London: Stationery Office

Schofield, D., 1998. 'Modelling Health Care Expenditure: A New Microsimulation Approach to Simulating the Distributional Impact of the Pharmaceutical Benefits Scheme', final seminar on doctoral thesis submitted for PhD in Information Sciences and Engineering, University of Canberra

Shoven, J. B. and Whalley, J., 1984. 'Applied general-equilibrium models of taxation and international trade: an introduction and survey', *Journal of Economic Literature* 22(3), 1007–51

Silber, J., 1994. 'Income distribution, tax structure, and the measurement of tax progressivity', *Public Finance Quarterly* 22(1), 86–102

Skeels, C. and Vella, F., 1995. 'Monte Carlo evidence on the robustness of conditional moment tests in tobit and probit models', unpublished discussion paper, Australian National University

Smeeding, T. M., Saunders, P., Coder, J. F., Jenkins, S. P., Fritzell, J., Hagenaars, A. J. M., Hauser, R. and Wolfson, M. C., 1993. 'Poverty, inequality and family living standards impacts across seven nations: the effects of noncash subsidies for health, education and housing', *Review of Income and Wealth* 39(3), 229–78

Smeeding, T. and Weinberg, D., 1998. *Toward a Uniform Household Income Definition*, Papers and Final Report of the Second Meeting on Household Income Statistics, Voorburg, The Netherlands, 9–11 March, Canberra Group: Expert Group

Standaard Belasting-Almanak, 1996. *Standaard Belasting-Almanak*, Antwerp: Standaard Uitgeverij

Statistics Canada, 1987. *The Input–Output Structure of the Canadian Economy 1961–1981*, Catalogue No. 15–510, Ottawa: Statistics Canada

Stern, N., 1987. 'The effects of taxation, price control and government contracts in oligopoly and monopolistic competition', *Journal of Public Economics* 32(2), 133–58

Stone, J. R. N., 1978. 'The Disaggregation of the Household Sector in the National Accounts', paper presented at World Bank Conference on Social Accounting Methods in Development and Planning, Cambridge, England, reprinted in G. Pyatt and J. I. Round, *Social Accounting Matrices: A Basis for Planning*, Washington DC: World Bank (1985)

Sutherland, H., 1991. 'Constructing a tax–benefit model: what advice can one give?', *Review of Income and Wealth* 37(2)

    1995. 'Static Microsimulation Models in Europe: A Survey', Microsimulation Unit Discussion Paper MU9503, Department of Applied Economics, University of Cambridge

    1996a. 'Households, Individuals and the Re-Distribution of Income', Microsimulation Unit Working Paper MU9601, Department of Applied Economics, University of Cambridge

    1996b. 'EUROMOD: A European Benefit-Tax Model', Microsimulation Unit Research Note MURN20. Department of Applied Economics, University of Cambridge

    1997. 'Women, men and the redistribution of income', *Fiscal Studies* 18, 1–22

    1998. 'Les modèles statiques de microsimulation en Europe dans les années 90', *Economie et Statistique* 315 (1998:5), 35–50

Sutherland, H (ed.), 1997. 'The EUROMOD Preparatory Study: A Summary Report', Microsimulation Unit Discussion Paper MU9705, Department of Applied Economics, University of Cambridge

SWRI (Social Welfare Research Institute) 1981. 'MRPIS: A Research Strategy', Boston College, July

    1985. 'Multi-Regional Impact Simulation (MRPIS) Model Level 2.0 Overview', Boston College, November

    1988. 'Multi-Regional Impact Simulation (MRPIS) Model Level 3.0 Analyst's Guide', Boston College

    1992. 'The MRPIS Model', Boston College, January

Tanzi, V., 1987. 'Quantitative characteristics of tax systems of developing countries', in D. M. Newbery and N. Stern (eds), *The Theory of Taxation for Developing Countries*, New York: Oxford University Press

Tinker A., Wright, F., McCreadie, C., Askham, J., Hancock, R. and Holmans, A., 1999. *Alternative Models of Care for Older People: Supporting Evidence to the Report of the Royal Commission on Long-Term Care of the Elderly*, London: TSO

Van der Laan, P., 1998. *Reconciliation of Income Statistics with Aggregated Data*, Papers and Final Report of the Second Meeting on Household Income

Statistics, Voorburg, The Netherlands, 9–11 March, Canberra Group: Expert Group on Household Income Statistics

Van Imhoff, E. and Post, W., 1997. 'Méthodes de micro-simulation pour des projections de population', *Population* 4, 889–932

Van Soest, A., 1994. 'Structural models of family labour supply: a discrete choice approach', *Journal of Human Resources* 30(1), 63–88

Verma, V. and Gabilondo, L. G., 1993. 'Family Budget Surveys in the EC: methodology and recommendations for harmonisation', in *Eurostat, Population and Social Conditions*, 3E, Luxembourg: Office for Official Publications of the European Communities

Wagstaff, A. and Van Doorselaer, E., 1997. 'What Makes the Personal Income Tax Progressive? A Comparative Analysis for Fifteen OECD Countries', unpublished paper, Erasmus University, Rotterdam

Walker, A., 1997. 'Modelling Immigrants to Australia to Enter a Dynamic Microsimulation Model', paper presented at the 'Microsimulation in Government Policy and Forecasting' sessions of the International Conference on Combinatorics, Information Theory and Statistics, Portland, Maine, 18–20 July

    1998. 'Australia's Ageing Population: What Are the Key Issues and the Available Methods of Analysis?', Discussion Paper No. 27, National Centre for Social and Economic Modelling, University of Canberra

Walker, A., Percival, P. and Fischer, S., 1998. 'A Microsimulation Model of Australia's Pharmaceutical Benefits Scheme', Technical Paper No. 15, National Centre for Social and Economic Modelling, University of Canberra

Walker, A., Percival, P. and Harding, A., 1998. 'The Impact of Demographic and Other Changes on Expenditure on Pharmaceutical Benefits in 2020 in Australia', Discussion Paper No. 31, National Centre for Social and Economic Modelling, University of Canberra

Walters, A. A., 1968. *The Economics and Road User Charges*, Baltimore: Johns Hopkins University Press

White, H., 1980. 'A heteroscedasticity-consistent covariance matrix estimator and a direct test for heteroscedasticity', *Econometrica* 48(4), 817–38

Windmeijer, F., 1995. 'Goodness-of-fit measures in binary choice models', *Econometric Reviews* 14, 101–116

Wilson, D., 1993. *Where the Dollars Go: Progress Papers from the Social Outlays Project*, Monograph Series No. 1, Research Advisory Committee, Department of Health, Housing, Local Government and Community Services, Canberra: AGPS

Wistow, G., 1996. 'The changing scene in Britain', in T. Harding, B. Meredith and G. Wistow (eds), *Options for Long Term Care*, London: HMSO

Wittenberg, R., Pickard, L., Comas-Herrera, A., Davis, B. and Darton, R., 1998. *Demand for Long-term Care Finance for Elderly People*, Canterbury: Personal Social Services Research Unit

Yitzhaki, S., 1994. 'On the progressivity of commodity taxation', in W. Eichhorn (ed.), *Models and Measurement of Welfare and Inequality*, Berlin: Springer-Verlag

Index

Aaberge, R. 9, 10, 268–91
Accardo, J. 184, 199
accounting period 126
actuarial models 219–21
Adler, H. 64
administrative data 17, 259
  limited variables 211
  for validation 205–11
ageing techniques 6
alignment 208–9
  'fractional people' 242–3
  pageant method 240–2, 245
  problem 239–40
  process 255–6, 258
  see also calibration
Antcliff, S. 152–3
Arrufat, J. L. 270
Atkinson, A. B. 97, 98, 120, 121, 122, 132–3,
  136, 147
Auerbach, A. J. 25, 175, 184
Australia 28, 258
  health expenditure 149–50
  Pharmaceutical Benefits Scheme (PBS) 6,
    149–71, 149–71
    described 150–1
    earlier studies 152
  see also PBS model

Baekegard, H. 258
Bailey, D. 212
Baker, P. 67
Banks, J. 122
Batey, P. W. J. 55
Begg, D. 268
Belgium 6, 16–39
  Eur6 127–48
  household surveys 16–18
  IPCAL 16–17, 20, 22–33, 26, 31, 33
  SIRe 16, 17
  tax reform 22–4

benefits 206–8
  means-tested 101, 226
  unemployment 8, 251–68
Bennett, N. 227
Bingley, P. 292
Bishop, J. A. 16, 29, 40
Blanchard, O. J. 88
Blanchet, D. 175, 177
Blomquist, S. 270
Blundell, R. W. 69, 293
Bonnet, C. 3, 7, 175–99
bootstrap confidence intervals 300–1
Bordt, M. 65
Bourguignon, F. 148
Bradshaw, J. 97
Brumberg, R. 68, 86
Brungger, H. 137
Brunner, J. K. 11
Buhmann, B. 138
Buisson 229
Burgess, R. 66
Burtless, G. 270

Caldwell, S. B. 4, 7, 10, 200–225, 251, 267
calibration 293
  estimators 9
  transitions 298–300
  see also alignment
Callan, T. 124, 148
CALMAR 156
Cameron, G. 5, 42–65, 65
Canada 5, 7, 28, 42–65
  Census Public Use Microdata File 239
  Chief Actuary 219
  earnings 209–11
  elderly people 214–15
  family type distribution 218
  Health and Social Transfer (CHST) 64
  income security system 57–8
  provincial tax powers 61

life-course alterations 112–19
limitations of 101, 103
simulation 98–103
microsimulation models
behavioural 2–3, 8–9, 251–308
description 43–4, 176–7
dynamic 2–3, 7–8, 175–247
static 2–3, 4–6, 15–171
use of 1–2
migration
alignment 239–42
Canada 238–47
cost of 262
error correction 242–3
family size 244–5
regression 259–66
results 264–6, 267
and unemployment benefits 8, 251–68
Mitton, L. 1–11
model integration 5, 45–6, 52–6
model reconciliation 7
model sensitivity *see* sensitivity
model validation *see* validation
Modigliani, F. 68, 86
Moffit, R. 290
Monte Carlo modelling 9, 101, 202–3,
221–4, 293, 299, 301–4, 306–7
Morrison, R. J. 4, 7, 10, 200–225
Multi-Regional Policy Impact Simulation
Model (MRPIS) 55–6
multinomial logit 286
Musgrave, R. A. 26, 88

national accounts 44, 144, 145–6
household income 131–3
NATSEM 152
Neufeld, C. 221, 238
Newbery, D. M. 75, 77
Nickell, S. 121
Nuttall, S. R. 227

O'Donoghue, C. 6, 10, 124
OECD 16, 66–95, 100
equivalence scales 29, 69, 138–41
old people 4, 14–15, 104–12, 154, 167
projections 155–8, 183–97, 227
Orcutt, G. 11, 176
Ordover, J. A. 88

Pakos, T. B. 68
part-time work 9, 114, 115, 119
Pashardes, P. 69, 83
pay, equal 113
PBS model 153–69
cardiovascular disease 155, 159–60, 168
costs 163–7

distributional outcomes 149
drug prices 154–5, 158–9, 164
numbers of prescriptions 163
population
ageing 154, 167
projections 155–8
and public expenditure 149
Pelé, L. P. 199
PENSIM 100
pension credits 104, 106, 109–13, 115, 119–20
pensions 3, 7, 175–99
baby gap 106, 109–13, 115, 119
basic 180–1
complementary 181–2
cross-country comparisons 96–123
income from 103–72
occupational 100–1, 106, 108–9, 111, 120
pay-as-you-go 198–9
rate of return 183–97
alternative scenarios 186–97
gender effect 186
generation effect 184–5, 194, 196
see also old people
pensions index 189, 194–7
Percival, R. 149–71
personal expenditure, concept and
measurement 47
persons, definition 47
Pesaran, M. H. 293
Petersen, H. G. 11
Phelps, E. S. 88
Podger, A. 150, 158, 167
Poole, E. 44–5
population *see* old people
Porta, P.-L. 86
Post, W. 199
poverty 283
predictive performance 292–3
Preston, I. P. 69
probit regression 262
progressivity, residual 26
Propper, C. 227
Provopoulos, G. A. 67
Pudney, S. 4, 100, 121, 290
purchasing power parity (PPP) 136–7, 142,
144

Quinke, H. 11

Rake, K. 5, 96–123
Ralle, P. 179, 199
Redmond, G. 67, 97, 229
regression 259–66
logit 264
probit 262
retirement age 189, 194

www.ingramcontent.com/pod-product-compliance
Ingram Content Group UK Ltd.
Pitfield, Milton Keynes, MK11 3LW, UK
UKHW012155180425
457623UK00007B/43